FEMINIST INTERPRETATIONS OF JEAN-JACQUES ROUSSEAU

RE-READING THE CANON

Nancy Tuana, General Editor

This series consists of edited collections of essays, some original and some previously published, offering feminist re-interpretations of the writings of major figures in the Western philosophical tradition. Devoted to the work of a single philosopher, each volume contains essays covering the full range of the philosopher's thought and representing the diversity of approaches now being used by feminist critics.

Already published:

FEMINIST INTERPRETATIONS OF JEAN-JACQUES ROUSSEAU

EDITED BY LYNDA LANGE

THE PENNSYLVANIA STATE UNIVERSITY PRESS
UNIVERSITY PARK, PENNSYLVANIA

Library of Congress Cataloguing-in-Publication Data

Feminist interpretations of Jean-Jacques Rousseau / edited by Lynda Lange.
    p.   cm.—(Re-reading the canon)
  Includes bibliographical references and index.
  ISBN 0-271-02200-0 (cloth : alk. paper)
  ISBN 0-271-02201-9 (pbk. : alk. paper)
  1. Rousseau, Jean-Jacques, 1712–1778.
  2. Feminist theory. I. Lange, Lynda, 1943–   .   II. Series.
B2137 .F395   2002
194—dc21   2002001693

The paper used in this publication is both acid-free and totally chlorine-free (TCF). It meets the minimum requirements of American National Standard for Information Sciences—Permanence of Paper for Printed Library Materials, ANSI Z39.48–1992.

Contents

Acknowledgments

My heartfelt thanks to Nancy Tuana for original encouragement, and to her and Sanford Thatcher of Penn State Press for unfailing assistance and courtesy. Warm thanks and respect to all the contributors to this volume. Each reading of their work in the process of thinking about the volume yielded something more. Omissions of excellent feminist interpretations of Rousseau are entirely my responsibility—I am sure they are not all included, and also that there will be more to come. Thanks for the support and patience that seem so necessary for books to come into being, to my husband and best friend, Dan Proudfoot.

LYNDA LANGE, "Rousseau and Modern Feminism" is reprinted by permission from *Social Theory and Practice* 7 (1981): 245–47. The essay also appeared in *Feminist Interpretations and Political Theory*, edited by Mary Lyndon Shanley and Carole Pateman (University Park: Penn State University Press, 1991).

PENNY WEISS and ANNE HARPER, "Rousseau's Political Defence of the Sex-Roled Family" is reprinted by permission of the authors and Indiana University Press from *Hypatia* 5, no. 3 (1990).

SUSAN MOLLER OKIN, "The Fate of Rousseau's Heroines" is chapter 8 of *Women in Western Political Thought* (Princeton: Princeton University Press, 1979), reprinted by permission of the author and Princeton University Press.

MIRA MORGENSTERN, "Women, Power, and the Politics of Everyday Life" is an abridgement of chapter 4 of *Rousseau and the Politics of Ambiguity* (University Park: Penn State University Press, 1996), printed by permission of the author and Penn State University Press.

SARAH KOFMAN, "Rousseau's Phallocratic Ends," translated by Mara Dukats, is reprinted by permission of Indiana University Press from *Hypatia* 3, no. 3 (1988).

LINDA ZERILLI, "Une Maitresse Imperieuse: Women in Rousseau's Semiotic Republic" is slightly abridged from chapter 2 of *Signifying Woman: Culture and Chaos in Rousseau, Burke, and Mill* (Ithaca: Cornell University Press, 1994). Reprinted by permission.

ELIZABETH WINGROVE, "Republican Romance" appeared in *Representations* 63 (1998): 13–38. Reprinted by permission of the University of California Press. Copyright © 1998 by the Regents of the University of California.

REBECCA KUKLA, "The Coupling of Human Souls: Rousseau and the Problem of Gender Relations" is reprinted by permission of the author and Editions Rodopi BU from *Political Dialogue: Theories And Practices*, edited by Stephen L. Esquith, Poznan Studies in the Philosophy of the Sciences and the Humanities, vol. 46 (1996).

MONIQUE WITTIG, "On the Social Contract," from *The Straight Mind and Other Essays* (Boston: Beacon Press, 1992), is reprinted by permission of Beacon Press, Boston. Copyright © 1992 by Monique Wittig.

Preface

Nancy Tuana

Take into your hands any history of philosophy text. You will find compiled therein the "classics" of modern philosophy. Since these texts are often designed for use in undergraduate classes, the editor is likely to offer an introduction in which the reader is informed that these selections represent the perennial questions of philosophy. The student is to assume that she or he is about to explore the timeless wisdom of the greatest minds of Western philosophy. No one calls attention to the fact that the philosophers are all men.

Although women are omitted from the canons of philosophy, these texts inscribe the nature of woman. Sometimes the philosopher speaks directly about woman, delineating her proper role, her abilities and inabilities, her desires. Other times the message is indirect—a passing remark hinting at women's emotionality, irrationality, unreliability.

This process of definition occurs in far more subtle ways when the central concepts of philosophy—reason and justice, those characteristics that are taken to define us as human—are associated with traits historically identified with masculinity. If the "man" of reason must learn to control or overcome traits identified as feminine—the body, the emotions, the passions—then the realm of rationality will be one reserved primarily for men,[1] with grudging entrance to those few women who are capable of transcending their femininity.

Feminist philosophers have begun to look critically at the canonized texts of philosophy and have concluded that the discourses of philosophy are not gender-neutral. Philosophical narratives do not offer a universal perspective, but rather privilege some experiences and beliefs over others. These experiences and beliefs permeate all philosophical theories whether they be aesthetic or epistemological, moral or metaphysical. Yet this fact has often been neglected by those studying the traditions of philosophy. Given the history of canon formation in Western philosophy, the perspective most likely to be privileged is that of upper-class white males. Thus, to be fully aware of the impact of gender biases, it is imperative that we re-read the canon with attention to the ways in which philosophers' assumptions concerning gender are embedded within their theories.

This new series, *Re-Reading the Canon,* is designed to foster this process of reevaluation. Each volume will offer feminist analyses of the theories of a selected philosopher. Since feminist philosophy is not monolithic in method or content, the essays are also selected to illustrate the variety of perspectives within feminist criticism and highlight some of the controversies within feminist scholarship.

In this series, feminist lenses will be focused on the canonical texts of Western philosophy, both those authors who have been part of the traditional canon, as well as those philosophers whose writings have more recently gained attention within the philosophical community. A glance at the list of volumes in the series will reveal an immediate gender bias of the canon: Arendt, Aristotle, de Beauvoir, Derrida, Descartes, Foucault, Hegel, Hume, Kant, Locke, Marx, Mill, Nietzsche, Plato, Rousseau, Wittgenstein, Wollstonecraft. There are all too few women included, and those few who do appear have been added only recently. In creating this series, it is not my intention to rectify the current canon of philosophical thought. What is and is not included within the canon during a particular historical period is a result of many factors. Although no canonization of texts will include all philosophers, no canonization of texts that excludes all but a few women can offer an accurate representation of the history of the discipline, as women have been philosophers since the ancient period.[2]

I share with many feminist philosophers and other philosophers writing from the margins of philosophy the concern that the current canonization of philosophy be transformed. Although I do not accept the position that the current canon has been formed exclusively by power relations, I do believe that this canon represents only a selective history of the tradition. I share the view of Michael Bérubé that "canons are at once the location, the index, and the record of the struggle for cultural representation; like any other hegemonic formation, they must be continually reproduced anew and are continually contested."[3]

The process of canon transformation will require the recovery of "lost" texts and a careful examination of the reasons such voices have been silenced. Along with the process of uncovering women's philosophical history, we must also begin to analyze the impact of gender ideologies upon the process of canonization. This process of recovery and examination must occur in conjunction with careful attention to the concept of a canon of authorized texts. Are we to dispense with the notion of a tradition of excellence embodied in a canon of authorized texts? Or, rather than abandon the whole idea of a canon, do we instead encourage a reconstruction of a canon of those texts that inform a common culture?

This series is designed to contribute to this process of canon transformation by offering a re-reading of the current philosophical canon. Such a re-reading shifts our attention to the ways in which woman and the role of the feminine is constructed within the texts of philosophy. A question we must keep in front of us during this process of re-reading is whether a philosopher's socially inherited prejudices concerning woman's nature and role are independent of her or his larger philosophical framework. In asking this question, attention must be paid to the ways in which the definitions of central philosophical concepts implicitly include or exclude gendered traits.

This type of reading strategy is not limited to the canon, but can be applied to all texts. It is my desire that this series reveal the importance of this type of critical reading. Paying attention to the workings of gender within the texts of philosophy will make visible the complexities of the inscription of gender ideologies.

Notes

1. More properly, it is a realm reserved for a group of privileged males, since the texts also inscribe race and class biases that thereby omit certain males from participation.

2. Mary Ellen Waithe's multivolume series, *A History of Women Philosophers* (Boston: M. Nijoff, 1987), attests to this presence of women.

3. Michael Bérubé, *Marginal Forces/Cultural Centers: Tolson, Pynchon, and the Politics of the Canon* (Ithaca: Cornell University Press, 1992), 4–5.

Introduction

Lynda Lange

It is Jean-Jacques's worst nightmare—scholarly women engaged in critical discussion of his work! Rousseau was a man of high seriousness who feared the power of witty "unfeminine" women to deflate the earnest intellectual projects of men. He exemplifies more than most Linda Zerilli's image of the male political philosopher as "sincere, manly, and quite hysterical" in his preoccupation with women and their proper role.[1] Among much else about women, he predicted no end of moral corruption and social decadence if women were not systematically raised to fulfill a feminine role in a domestic environment, and kept away from the public and intellectual activity that is the proper province of male republican citizens. However, disregarding possible consequences, the women whose work is assembled in this volume have turned their considerable scholarship to the critical scrutiny of Jean-Jacques Rousseau and his philosophy, evidently just as critical and irreverent as he feared.

Nor do feminist scholars agree with one another on the exact nature of the problems with Rousseau's philosophy from a feminist point of view. Some even argue for the potential usefulness for feminist thought of Rousseau's philosophy, but neither do they agree with one another about which aspects could be useful. Although it is easy to find quotations from Rousseau that would now be called sexist or patriarchal, there is great variation in interpretation of his work on gender, both with respect to its influence in his own century and its potential political interpretations in the present. There is, in fact, a great deal of feminist scholarship on Rousseau because of, or despite, his evident sexism, and it is worth considering why that is so.

Although all the major political philosophers, at least until the early twentieth century, had views about the place of women, Rousseau devoted a remarkably high proportion of his work to questions concerning women and the family and insisted that his thought on these matters was crucial to his whole political vision. As with other "canonical" thinkers, however, and despite Rousseau's own declaration of their importance, his views on gender were more or less ignored by scholars for most of the twentieth century. However, once the late twentieth-century "second wave" of feminism and feminist scholarship began, Rousseau attracted a great deal of attention. This happened in the first instance because his views on gender were spelled out so extensively and seemed to cry out for exposure of the great "egalitarian" and intellectual father of republican revolution. Essays by Susan Moller Okin and myself on Rousseau were among early first statements in feminist political philosophy.

The most significant factor in sustaining the feminist philosophical interest in Rousseau, however, was that he had introduced new fields of discussion in modern political philosophy, or opened ancient fields of discussion in a new way, concerning the meaning of gender difference, the relations between family and civil state, and the potential positive contributions of the roles or functions of women, as women, to the development of a liberated polity. In his doing so his work entered the very terrain of current feminist contestation of patriarchal social and political philosophy. Familial, domestic, and sexual practices were brought under the same type of scrutiny as more commonly considered questions in modern political philosophy. This was a basic theoretical move that was necessary for feminist political philosophy to be possible. This was of fundamental importance, even though, with the exception of John Stuart Mill who argued on the other side of the debate, no one of his stature followed his example. Philosophy in this terrain was stifled by the republican revolution at the end of the eighteenth century in France. It flared here and there in Europe in the nineteenth century and then had to fight all over again to be regarded as "real philosophy" in the last thirty years of the twentieth century.

Had Rousseau heard the slogan of early second-wave feminism that "the personal is political," it is conceivable that he would readily have agreed. Of course, he would not have come to anything like the same conclusions regarding liberation in the personal or domestic sphere, yet arguably he intended to theorize what he considered "true" liberation in all spheres, for women and men. For example, in this volume Penny Weiss and Anne Harper argue that Rousseau was at least consistent in presenting his arguments for the distinct roles of women and men in terms of justice, and not just in terms of the functionality for society of women occupying a "feminine" role. However, a greater number of feminist critics take the opposing view, arguing that Rousseau envisioned a feminine role for women that supported and served the purposes of the (male) citizens of democratic republics. This position is most explicit in this volume in Weiss, Else Wiestad, Melissa Butler, Sarah Kofman, and Rebecca Kukla. In her *Women in Western Political Thought,* in work other than that included in this volume, Okin developed the analysis of patriarchal "functionalism" with respect to women. According to Okin, philosophers have not asked "what is woman?" in the spirit in which they might ask "what is man?" but rather "what are women *for?*"[2] Although the view that Rousseau was a functionalist concerning women is predominant, Weiss and Harper make a convincing case that even if his work does not answer the requirements of feminist liberal individualism, it raises appropriate questions for feminist communitarianism regarding the common good.

As Rousseau identified personal, domestic, and familial areas of life— neglected in early modern political philosophy—as ones of crucial importance to civil society, he simultaneously intended to bring closure to debate about them with his own modernist/scientific philosophy. However, once the door was open to contestation in these areas, it seems it could only be effectively barred with patriarchal argumentation for intermittent periods of time. After all, it was not really the political philosopher who opened up these topics. Rousseau may be credited with opening up these fields of discussion because his works came to find a place in the Western canon of political philosophy. However, in making his points against those who might advocate equality of the sexes (who did exist in his time), he sets out points of view (in order to refute them) that are familiar even now as feminist perspectives. It is apparent that these topics were really opened up by "feminists" (before the word was coined) who were his contemporaries. These were mostly the women of talent, wit, and influence in the salons of eighteenth-century Paris—the women he so often makes the target of his considerable polemical skill. Rousseau saw the influence and social dominance of women as an evil gestated by aristocratic decadence, wherein women could be perfectly free, on account of many servants, of any burdensome "women's duties," including early infant care and breast-feeding. However, he was also a severe critic of bourgeois individualist social relations, just emerging in his time, and in general outline still with us today. In his view, the disorder and evil of decadence eventually bore its fruit in the values of this new society, which Rousseau considered to be selfish, competitive, and ultimately destructive of the highest form of morality. He considered the idea that women as individuals, as well as men, could and should pursue primarily their own self-interest to be a logical consequence of these pernicious values. In this Rousseau can be seen to agree in concept with the feminist argument that liberal individualism can in principle apply to women in the same way as to men. However, Rousseau was antiliberal and antibourgeois, and regarded this result negatively as part of the proof of the inadequacy of liberal individualism. He was a collectivist, prepared to recommend sacrifices from both women and men (however unequal in exent) in pursuit of the common good.

Although the criticism of decadent aristocratic women is of no more than historical interest now, the continuing relevance of his criticism of bourgois individualism is one reason why his virulent attacks on "the woman of talent" still seem so vivid and continue to attract both critics and admirers. This, as well as the relief of engaging directly with modern patriarchal perspectives that are to a large extent still with us, but virtually always dropped from text to subtext, help explain the substantial interest in his work now.

An aspect of Rousseau's contemporary relevance is his concept of gender complementarity. "In what they have in common, they are equal. Where they differ, they are not comparable."[3] In the great history of philosophical ideas about gender difference, from the ancient Greeks onward, women were consistently claimed to be inferior to men (especially in rational capacity) with reference to a single standard. Men, or at least *some* men, were claimed to have the potential for the highest forms of human rationality, whereas women were claimed to be lesser beings with reference to the norm of what was held to be distinctively human. The burgeoning egalitarianism and antitraditionalism of modernity, coupled with predominant *methodological* individualism in political philosophy (which Rousseau shared), was in tension with purely descriptive assessments of women (or any other group) as inferior. This tension or contradiction has been mined over and over again in the modern period for liberatory potential, with arguments that if liberal individualism were rid of its contradictions, then it would be truly liberatory for all. Many advances have been made, though arguably still falling short of complete success. The concept of complementarity, however, especially when joined with functionalism, sought to evade this tension and was an important modernization of philosophy of gender difference and patriarchy.

Feminist critics invariably argue that Rousseau's starting position of combined equality and complementarity is starkly contradicted by the very unequal prescriptions he makes for women's and men's roles. Nevertheless, since Rousseau accords women not-insignificant power and has, after all, claimed that their contributions to family life are of crucial importance to a good civil society—potentially a perspective friendly to feminism—curiosity about the extent and nature of the unique power over men accorded to women by Rousseau has fueled quite a bit of feminist investigation. This topic appears in various contexts in virtually all the articles in this volume, but Wiestad makes critical analysis of the exact nature of women's alleged powers in Rousseau the main subject of her essay. It is an important question whether or not there could be such a thing as egalitarian gender complementarity. Feminist affirmation and revaluation of women's ways of thinking and doing, now commonly referred to as women's "difference" from men, is one important school of thought in current feminism and, arguably, may be seen to be in a line of intellectual descent from earlier modern concepts of gender complementarity.[4]

It was suggested above that Rousseau could be credited with opening terrain in political philosophy concerning sexual, domestic, and familial matters, that is, the very terrain in which feminist political philosophy must make its mark. With the raising of the banner that the character and role of women, and the character of the family over all, is crucially important for a good civil state, two questions must be addressed: what is the exact relation of the family to the good civil state according to Rousseau, and what, if anything, in his philosophy on this topic is useful for feminist thought? There is great diversity in feminist interpretation in this area.

My early work sought to establish the neglected point that Rousseau did indeed regard the family, and women's role within it, as crucial to his vision, and that therefore this aspect of his work could not simply be ignored in the study of his political philosophy. I argued that women's role is foundational and that the family is bracketed within the status of the male citizen at its head. Around the same time, Okin identified the theme of functionalism regarding women and argued that Rousseau's views fit this theme, even though she raises questions about whether he really believed it could be made to work. Butler suggests that if one focuses on the political works, especially On the Social Contract, familial functions, and the associated role of women, are wholly repressed and subsumed by an emotionally loaded "caring" state. She suggests that this is much in the spirit of Plato in the Republic (despite Rousseau's disavowal of Plato's scheme of elimination of private property and families).

Most interpreters focus on Rousseau's views that loving child care by a devoted mother produces the capacity in the child for "particular attachments" (a view that is consistent with developmental psychology today) and that it is this capacity that eventually makes devotion to the common good possible. Both Weiss and Harper, and Alice Ormiston, note the plausibility of his basic insight about development, and as a result maintain that feminist communitarianism should not simply denigrate Rousseau's views on women's role in child care, but come up with alternative interpretations of the relation between family and state (or public life in general) that address these psychological requirements. Rousseau's strict injunctions that women must confine themselves to the home and concern themselves solely with the care of husband and children suggests a strong dichotomy between public and private. Mira Morgenstern, however, argues that Rousseau's work actually affirms the porous quality of these categories, wherein the structure and formative influence of one constantly affects the other.

Rousseau's work appears in the context of a long history of ideas concerning the duality of male and female, with many correlated dualities such as reason and emotion, public and private, political and personal. All of these have been normative dualities wherein one term is strongly privileged over the other.[5] Rousseau's achievement from a feminist perspective was not that he actually overturned the privileging of the male or governing side of these dualities, since he remains conspicuously in favor of male dominance. Nevertheless, it was significant for feminist thought, and especially for feminist political philosophy, that he did not simply assume the validity of these oppositions. Although he did not overturn them, he opened them to scrutiny and to some extent revalued them, in an original and modernistic way. Women's contributions to family and society, which in political philosophy since ancient Greece had been deemed to be practical functions, were viewed by Rousseau as directly formative of the character of the body politic. Philosophical engagement with domesticity is ultimately friendly to feminism because it is a necessary precondition for the intelligibility of the feminist critique of personal and domestic life as "political." Arguably, this gives Rousseau too much credit. Yet the amount of feminist work on Rousseau, and the diversity of feminist interpretation of his work, suggest that what is ultimately of importance for the development of feminist political philosophy is not the specific conclusions of a given work, but the topics that are admitted to be relevant.

Rousseau's arguments for gender complementarity and therefore, or so he claims, equality in difference, involves the claim that if the family is rightly established, women will gladly consent to playing their special role in relation to men. They will, he says, be happier than they are trying to be something they are not meant to be, precisely because he has tried to define their role as "natural" and not as "subordination" in the political sense that he, as modernity's first great egalitarian, deplored. In this his claims are very much analogous to those of Sigmund Freud, who maintained in the early twentieth century that feminism merely deflected women from normal feminine development and disturbed the satisfaction that would be theirs if they did not resist the normal exigencies of femininity.

The ideals of consent and affection of the late modern family, which Rousseau was prescient in articulating, are in many ways an advance over previous characterizations of family structure as straightforward rule by the male head. Rousseau's images of what Okin has called "the sentimental family" fed, and were fed by, the romantic movement, which began to develop after his lifetime.[6] Romanticism seemed to accord more importance to women's subjectivity than it had had before and as a result can be seen as an advance for women. However, although consent has become constitutive of the legitimacy of the family, as well as of the state, like "romance" itself, consent can be illusory.

As mentioned above, Wiestad argues in detail that women's use of the emotional and sexual power prescribed for them by Rousseau actually supports male dominance. Morgenstern, however, finds ambiguity in the Rousseauian family, which she believes opens possibilities for greater personal authenticity for all individuals, including women. Rousseau did attract some women admirers in the eighteenth and nineteenth centuries. This appears to be because he acknowledged the great importance of what women do, in a context in which their unique contributions were valued very little. He morally elevated women's capacities for childbearing and breast-feeding far above the mere animalistic, or at best servant-like, functions they had traditionally been. As Morgenstern observes, he asserted that they were actually at the very heart of good civil society, and in a civil society that worked against personal authenticity they could even be revolutionary. His images of romantic (or authentic) heterosexual partnerships based on consent can still be seductive. Perhaps this is because consent in heterosexual relations is still a progressive stance for women, even as we refine our critical philosophy of what really counts as "consent."

The social roles Rousseau prescribes for women are in general outline found throughout the Western tradition of social and political thought. Kofman argues strongly that he reiterates tradition in a manner that converges with his own psychology. However, many feminist interpreters argue that he modernized the philosophical grounds for patriarchy and strengthened them considerably, in a period when they had begun to be openly contested in Europe, and above all in France. As noted above, the concept of gender complementarity/equality was meant to remove the most obvious philosophical charge of inconsistency in his treatment of women and men. But what was the basis of his claim to know that the temperaments of women and men were ideally complementary? His modernization of patriarchy is achieved in a complex manner by a simultaneous politicization of gender and sexuality (the theoretical move that helps open the terrain of feminist political philosophy) and a naturalization of them in ostensibly modernist/scientific grounds. To say that a certain kind of feminine social role can be discovered by secular reason to be natural for women is, on the face of it, an attempt to place it on a firmer modernist foundation, yet still beyond politics. It is to say, at the least, that the feminine role in question is more practical or feasible, or (as noted above with Freud) even preferable to, such unfeminine distortions as, for example, the pursuit of an academic career or a voice in public affairs. Held more strongly, it is to say that there is no use trying to resist the inevitable.

"The politics of the natural" is a long-running play in modernity because even though our main-stage show—modern "natural science"—is the project of acquiring knowledge of an objective "natural" world, the meaning of the term *natural* is extremely unstable, even ultimately undecidable. It slithers from "natural," or empirical, science, to teleology, to moral prescription, and back again, always seeming to carry a degree of normative power that is difficult to counter. For those, such as women, who are oppressed by its force, it is like a choice between defying the law of gravity or defying the will of God. Rousseau deployed the normative power of "the natural" in modernity very effectively. He was a major inventor of "nature" as a standard of value, with his dreamy notions of "getting back to nature" away from urban environments, as well as his poetic visions of sexual and familial love. Feminist critics differ in their understandings of what he really meant to say about the basis of gender difference. It seems clear that he did not mean to claim that gender difference was simply an empirical given. That would be all too easily disproved by the existence of the very women Rousseau criticizes for leading "unnatural" lives. Linda Zerilli takes the strongest position that Rousseau actually acknowledged that gender difference is wholly constructed, hence its fragility, leading to male hysteria. "Ah, nature!" exclaims Keohane, "that most treacherous of female personages, so often invoked to prove the inferiority of other members of her sex."[7]

Rousseau's redrawing of ancient normative dualities between public and private, and reason and nature, comes into play in the grounds he offers for gender difference. "Reason" and "nature" have a complementarity in Rousseau comparable to the complementarity of men and women. While it is possible for nature to defy reason, the reasonable is really also the natural. Rousseau states that if what he maintains is proper feminine behavior is not natural in the sense of "inevitable" (as it clearly is not) then it ought to be inculcated by means of education, and deemed to be natural on the basis of reason, because it is most beneficial to civil society. He seems to be aware that what is deemed to be "natural," and therefore ultimately incontestable, is what would now be called in poststructuralist terms "an effect of discourse," rather than an actual reflection of nonconscious external reality. In other words, the meaning of "natural" is such

as to preclude certain kinds of challenges, most especially political challenges. In this analysis the difference between "socially constructed" and
"given by nature" disappears.

In this, however, Rousseau instantiates a political weakness in posts-
tructural analysis for feminism, namely that the basic insights of posts-
tructuralism can just as well be used instrumentally as they can for social
criticism. This is borne out by Rousseau's belief that meaning can be, and
indeed must be, manipulated for social purposes by means of sentimental
education, civic religion, and emotional spectacle, if there is to be a good
civil society. Lloyd states that "the natural" has become for Rousseau a
means of social criticism.[8] However, to deploy the term "natural" in this
ambiguously normative/scientific manner is to invite the possibility of
correction and opposition in the same terms, which feminist critics have
not hesitated to provide.

Rousseau's work was immensely influential in the shutting down of the
first social movement of women in the West, which occurred in the final
phases of the *ancien régime* in France. After a flowering in the early stages
of the Revolution, the political discussion circles and activism of women
were harshly and thoroughly stopped in their tracks by the revolutionary
leadership.[9] Although there had been activist women in all classes, including rural women and the market women of Paris, the Rousseauean
association of demands for women's advancement with moral corruption
(at the time associated in turn with aristocratic decadence) turned out to
be a highly successful propaganda move, so successful that it has haunted
feminist movements in the West ever since. It was to be a revolution of
manly republican virtue. Yet it is not immediately self-evident that this
would have to be so. We may think now, and many women in France
thought back then, that the basic principles of democratic republicanism
opened the way for radical universalism—the equal citizenship of all individuals, women and men, rich and poor, previously with aristocratic titles
or not.

Throwing tradition aside as a means of legitimation of social order and
authority may be a frightening prospect. What sort of social glue will
replace what had simply been given? Rousseau, in particular, argued that
"reason," which necessarily functions instrumentally as self-interest (enlightened or not), in the absence of any predetermined loyalties, was far
too feeble a motivation to keep together "a people" willing to accommodate themselves to the common good. In his view, in fact, the very appeal
to self-interest will constantly work against the common good. In this,

Rousseau was a critic of what came to be known as Enlightenment belief in reason as the source of progress. For this reason, he has been of interest to many taking a postmodern, communitarian, or poststructuralist approach (not to mention ethnonationalists).

A prospect of radical freedom and accountability for individuals may seem to take on an air of heroism, which in a male-dominated tradition easily becomes a masculine ideal. Be that as it may, it is one of the strongest themes in feminist commentary on Rousseau that his (male) citizen is a very fragile construction. Emotion must come to the aid of reason to make him patriotic, that is, devoted to the state, and willing to fulfill his duty for the common good of the people. Leah Bradshaw, Ingrid Makus, Lori Marso, Zerilli, and Elizabeth Wingrove offer highly diverse interpretations of Rousseau's fragile good citizen and the manner in which his character depends on women's fulfilling their proper role in the home and family, most especially in the nurturance of "particular attachments." True citizenship, for Rousseau, is particular attachment writ large. There is no universal reason that could induce the strong identification needed for the necessary melding of citizens' interests, as Rousseau sees it. Wingrove argues strongly that Rousseau was conscious of his requirement that women must be willing sacrificial lambs on the altar of the new republic. This diverse feminist commentary seeks to figure out how a modern "social contract" such as that of Rousseau, which is premised on universality, can yet result in systematic exclusion of women. Such commentary joins the company of critics of social contract theory and liberal individualist political philosophy in general, including other feminist critique, Marxist, antiracist and postcolonial critique, in addressing this great philosophical and practical/political puzzle—exactly how and why has modern individualist political philosophy that always starts from the presumption of universal equality standardly failed to exclude the possibility of "justified" and systematic subordination of some groups?

The fragility of the "moral heroism" (participation in the famous "reign of virtue") that seems to be required of the citizen has also elicited psychoanalytic analysis of its linking by Rousseau with "manhood." Manhood itself, largely constituted by citizenship, seems the most fragile construction of all. Rousseau's psyche is rather more exposed than that of other political philosophers, on account of his having left us a detailed record of his inner life in his *Confessions*, and many commentators make use of what is found there. However, in other works that are not autobiographical, such as the *Lettre à d'Alembert*, he seems to reveal this same anxiety by the sheer extent of his treatment of the "disorder" and "danger" to men of women if they participate in public intellectual and cultural life. It is a theme of feminist interpretation, therefore, to ask how large a role Rousseau's unique psyche plays in his philosophy, and, more significant, to what extent this is linked to modern masculinity. Kofman accords complete centrality to psychic analysis of Rousseau. Zerilli, employing a semiotic approach, makes a detailed analysis, especially of his sexual predilections, and links his "hysteria" to the exigencies of late modern republican masculinity.

It is a curious problem with Rousseau that in his own work none of his schemes seem to be stable over time or ultimately satisfactory. He delineated an ideal education for a manly individual (Emile) and his womanly wife (Sophie), but also wrote a sad sequel in which they fall prey to all the ills their education was designed to prevent. The death of the "ideal woman in ideal domestic arrangements," Julie in *La nouvelle Héloïse*, has prompted much speculation that it is an indirect expression of his pessimism that his political vision could ever be realized. As noted above, Okin pursues this line of analysis. Why does Rousseau subvert his own philosophy of gender? Or does he? The admonishment that his work is full of inconsistencies has never had the effect of diminishing interest in it. *Paradox, ambivalence, ambiguity*, and *complexity* are the words used to refer to the lasting puzzle of his work. Morgenstern approaches Rousseau with the presumption that he was fully in control of his work, and makes a substantive political interpretation of his "ambiguity." Perhaps his vision can only ever be imperfectly realized and would always be relatively unstable, requiring constant and conscious effort. Morgenstern shares with Wittig an admiration for Rousseau as one whose thought empowers the moral and political agency of all individuals with the feeling that how one chooses to live one's own life can be at least a small part of the revolution.

The relevance of the highly serious Rousseau, who continues to persuade both social conservatives and radicals; the empirical and modernist arguments he uses; and what must be acknowledged to be a barbed insightfulness in his perception of "more equal" gender relations in individualist society has made him a dangerous character indeed, and one of lasting fascination.

In the following remarks I introduce each essay in a manner that tends to further highlight themes or issues that develop as the volume progresses, despite significant diversity of interpretation. I also tend to focus on the central topic of each essay in a manner that emphasizes its relevance to the Western tradition of political philosophy. However, these essays all have other riches as well that will be discovered by the reader. This collection represents primarily contemporary North American feminist philosophy on Rousseau, except for two pieces originally written in French, by Sarah Kofman and Monique Wittig, that have been widely available in English for some time. It seems likely that a whole other volume of feminist pieces on Rousseau by European feminist scholars would find more than enough contributions.

My own essay sets out Rousseau's arguments for the "natural" differences between women and men. I focus particularly on his philosophical anthropology, which is modernist insofar as its method bears some comparison to highly theoretical and speculative contemporary evolutionary biology. He believes that his prescriptions for the social roles of women and men follow from his "scientific" analysis. However, these prescriptions must be understood in the light of his criticisms of the moral decadence of eighteenth-century European civil society. It is argued that the moral flaws of la société civile, as they are identified by Rousseau, can be understood as the flaws of "possessive market society," C. B. Macpherson's model of liberal individualist society, which shows its structural requirements for competition, exploitation, and inequality. Women's presumed seductive power promotes the vanity of comparisons and competition, and exacerbates these social ills, at the same time as it enervates the moral will of (male) citizens to raise their sights from personal interest to the common good, according to Rousseau. Rousseau's methodology is consistent as he traces the transformation, by means of social relations, of female and male human natural qualities. A table illustrates the structural parallels between woman, man, and citizen, as they develop from the state of nature, to the "state of war" (the bogus social contract of possessive market society), to the possibility of "moral liberty" in an as-yet-unattained good civil society. Despite this level of consistency, the natures and roles of women and men in Rousseau are not simply complementary, as he claims, but exemplify significant patriarchal power. I suggest, nevertheless, that he calls us to question the true ethic and motivation of women's demand for equality within unequal, exploitive societies, and to consider what might be required for democratic feminism that aims at the good of all.

Penny Weiss and Anne Harper carefully explore Rousseau's unique defense of differential gender roles and his claim that they are the basis of well-being and justice for both. Finding in Rousseau the acknowledgment that social differentiation of the sexes is not a given, but a social creation, Weiss and Harper point out that it then requires more than the defense of utility and that Rousseau is at least consistent in his claim that it can be defended on grounds of justice. While playing the devil's advocate, Weiss and Harper provide a subtle and perceptive reading of Rousseau's philosophy of gender in his own terms that illuminates its meaning in the context of his anti-individualist, communitarian vision and raises many questions for feminist thought and practice. Since many feminist political philosophers favor communitarianism, Weiss and Harper point out that the task is not to show that his prescriptions for sex roles are unacceptable from the perspective of liberal individualism, but to show that they are also illegitimate as a means to community. If feminists reject gender differentiation as a means of nurturing the moral and emotional growth of persons, what alternatives should be offered to counter exploitation and egoism and develop community?

Leah Bradshaw also provides a careful immanent reading of Rousseau's "monumental effort to wed human desire to the power of will and duty," surveying what he says about the nature of women in the context of his philosophy of human nature and civil society, particularly as it is found in *Emile; or, On Education*. Consistently with Weiss and Harper, Bradshaw notes that the civic virtue that Rousseau would have us love involves "a web of interconnectedness and belonging" that depends on the differentiation of the contributions of women and men. However, unlike their view that these different contributions are "roles" or "functions" that must be accounted for in any feminist political philosophy, Bradshaw's argument is that the functions themselves are profoundly negative for moral consciousness. In her view, women's role prevents them from being free, integrated, or authentic persons (Rousseau's ideal), and men's role leaves them in the vulnerability of illusion. Bradshaw presents a richly detailed analysis of how the "beautiful illusion" of purity and wholeness of the autonomous (male) citizen depends on the careful construction of his environment, first by his primary caregiver and socializer, and then by what could almost be called the ironic performance of femininity by his wife. As Bradshaw makes clear, the Rousseauian woman is destined to be inwardly divided. Her virtue is critical to the whole system, yet she will not participate in the beautiful illusion she herself must sustain. Bradshaw sounds the first note of what will become a theme in these essays—the extent to which all depends in this system on women's proper role (just as Rousseau himself stated!) and the resultant fragility of masculinity and citizenship, as well as the construction of "the natural woman" herself.

Susan Moller Okin analyzes Rousseau's philosophy of the family through the lens of a classical question in political philosophy—the relation between the family united by its particular attachments, and a civil society meant to be based on impartial justice. This question is especially acute in the case of democratic republics that appeal to reason and self-interest rather than to tradition.[10] She interprets the fate of Rousseau's "heroines"—Sophie, from *Emile,* and especially Julie, from *La nouvelle Héloïse*—as evidence of Rousseau's pessimism that his social and political vision could ever work in practice. What causes Julie so much suffering— perpetual self-restraint, a cheerful and serene manner regardless of inner turmoil, the constant requirement for dissembling—is nothing other than what Rousseau maintains is the necessary destiny of a good woman, very much as diagnosed by Bradshaw. What destroys Sophie is her excellent education for femininity. Her passivity and innocence make it unpersuasive that she could provide the moral guidance expected of her in domesticity, and she is unable to function outside that sphere, either morally or practically. It appears that the feminine role, as envisioned by Rousseau, could not be sustained, even were we willing to exact the costs to the happiness of women that Rousseau acknowledges. In addition to the question of the fate of Julie and Sophie, Okin argues that these works call into question Rousseau's fundamental contention that the good family could be the nursery of good citizens. Rousseau's heroines subvert both the family and the community and are destroyed themselves in the process. While Emile must be either an authentically independent man, or a citizen who regards himself as part of a whole (since he cannot be both), Sophie cannot be either. Referring to Rousseau's argument that "partial societies" or subgroups within civil society tend to form a "sub-general" will of their own that may resist the general will, Okin contends that it is unpersuasive that the loyalty of the family, immersed in the teachings of an apolitical mother who lives "only for love" (as she is meant to), would not be in constant tension with the demands of the state. As a result, according to Okin, Rousseau is more than pessimistic, he disassembles his own central political vision.

In contrast, Mira Morgenstern finds in Rousseau an important resource for feminist thought. She faces squarely Rousseau's own depiction of the collapse of the "ideal" marriages he himself has given life—Sophie and Emile, and Julie and Wolmar—proceeding from an assumption that Rousseau is in full control of his philosophical endeavor in the presentation of these seeming self-contradictions, or self-deconstructions. In doing so, she finds that these works are a rich source of information about Rousseau's intentions, which Morgenstern has termed "the politics of ambiguity." Close consideration is given to the potential relations between the family and the state, but Morgenstern notes that Rousseau is contradictory or ambiguous on this score. As the base for the emotional authenticity of the new republican citizen, it seems to threaten social cohesion. This bears on the question for political philosophy of the relation between the particularity of the family and the ideal impartiality of a democratic republic. In addition, however, in Morgenstern's distinctive analysis, the revolutionary family envisioned by Rousseau is at once the catalyst and the outcome of social change, yet theorized to operate ideally as a stabilizing, even reactionary, force in civil society. By mining Rousseau's apparent contradictions, Morgenstern offers a reading of ambiguous possibilities that may allow an authentic self to survive in an inauthentic world. Her essay especially exemplifies the view that Rousseau had moved into the terrains of theory that are now contested by feminist thought. According to Morgenstern, it is apparent in Rousseau that women's lives are the source of critique of the public/private distinction.[11] In addition, Morgenstern suggests that Rousseau offers a very radical view of the political importance, and even potential for revolutionary transformation, that resides in daily domestic life. Besides being of great interest to feminist thought, this view accords hope, and a new kind of political agency, to individuals in all classes of civil society.

According to Alice Ormiston, Rousseau is wrongly accused by many feminist critics of espousing a characteristic dualist conception of reason and feeling, wherein reason is identified with (male) culture, and feeling with the (female) natural world. Ormiston outlines what she argues is a more accurate picture of Rousseau's ideas, going beyond the interpretation of Genevieve Lloyd.[12] According to Ormiston, Rousseau "founds an altogether new conception of the subject in modernity," one that is very compatible with much contemporary feminist thought. In light of this, Ormiston considers what model of self and citizen may be needed for feminist purposes. She agrees with those who think Rousseau did not claim an essential difference between women and men. The difference that women contribute is the result of their role as wives and mothers. In this role, women are less subject to the structural pressures of competition and struggle for recognition that create the consciousness of *amour-propre* in public life. Since the ostensible rationality of *amour-propre* is a reflection of the structure of public life, women cannot simply import a different subjectivity into that sphere by moving into it. A new, feminist conception of self and citizen points to a need for significant social renegotiation of child care and affective education, which, as women move into public life, can no longer simply be presupposed. Rousseau points to the ineliminable need for a developmental process in which reason and feeling are kept in harmony in relationships of deep attachment. Although Rousseau wrongly assigned that task exclusively to women, it still must be accomplished somehow if there are to be citizens of conscience with the capacity to care for the good of the community.

Ormiston also points out that Rousseau's requirements for censorship and civic religion to maintain adequate affective relations between citizens, and between them and a just state, follows from his new conception of a more unified self. She argues that these requirements are therefore theoretically parallel to feminist concerns to incorporate the "knowledges" of intuition and emotion in developing more just political structures. To the extent that Rousseau's requirements may be objectionable, feminists need to confront the disturbing elements of these parallel tendencies. Ormiston attempts to track the source in Rousseau of troublingly illiberal recommendations, to suggest the possibility of a more hopeful and liberationist feminist solution.

As will be seen in the essays in this volume, a key controversy for analysis of Rousseau's gender philosophy is whether or not the gender roles he idealizes show balance and complementarity. This is, of course, what Rousseau himself claimed, and this claim has been defended by some of his interpreters. Else Wiestad isolates four different kinds of feminine power prescribed by Rousseau as appropriate. According to Wiestad, feminine and masculine forms of power do indeed represent complementary standards, which supplement and maintain each other. She argues, however, that female strategies recommended by Rousseau never contradict or threaten male power, but actually support it.

Wiestad's analysis of how this functions substantiates her observation of two significant ideological shifts in modern patriarchy. One is a shift from women's external patriarchal constraint to their internalized constraint, the result of education in the widest sense, or what would now be called "socialization." This is consistent with the new modern requirement that consent be constitutive of ideal heterosexual relations, and hence she must *desire* her own subordination to him. The other ideological shift adds to women's practical functions as bearers and caretakers of small children. It is an expanded requirement for the care of men as well, now pertaining to emotional and moral nurture as well as physical and sexual needs, wherein she continually subordinates her own needs. The emphasis on affection and voluntariness regarding marriage, both at its prospect and subsequently within it, represented some advancement for women, Weistad affirms. However, her work reinforces that of Susan Moller Okin on "the sentimental family" in maintaining that the claims of women for equality ultimately suffered from this new ideology of marriage and family. According to Wiestad, it could be called a "romantic" pattern of oppression, designed to get women to combine being oppressed with a pleasing and happy tone.

According to Ingrid Makus, what Rousseau feared the most, and most felt the need to contain, was women's capacity for concealment and deception. This is especially so in matters of sexual arousal and desire, and the paternity of children, but this tendency becomes an analogue of women's tendencies in general. Modesty is the virtue within civil society that keeps the desire of husbands alive with careful rationing of her sexual favors and with acceptance of a secluded domestic life that assures him of his paternity. Yet, paradoxically, she must also be "seen to be modest," for, quite the opposite of a man's, a woman's reputation in the opinion of others is key to her virtue. She must be educated to deceive her husband, and only her husband, only for beneficial ends. Indeed, as several essays have shown, her ability to manipulate him for good is literally fundamental to the common good.

At the same time, as Makus points out, the "effeminate" inclination of those driven by *amour-propre* to affect qualities they do not possess is the poison at the core of morally corrupt, unequal, civil society. Rousseau is preoccupied with the need for openness and authenticity. As Morgenstern argues, and Wingrove will argue as well, this can assume authoritarian proportions. If women's ascendancy is equated with "deception, pretense, and the hidden exercise of power," this helps to account for Rousseau's near hysterical demand that they be kept away from civic power. However, Rousseau's men cannot escape the power of women. What they must do is domesticate it.

Yet at the same time, Makus argues, the feminine principles of deception and covert influence reappear in Rousseau's philosophy of the tutor and of the Legislator. The Legislator is charged with transforming the hearts of citizens by means of what seem to be distinctly feminine forms of indirect influence. Makus also examines the curious figure of Emile's tutor, the "male mother," who only relinquishes his relentless stage management of Emile when he is given to the influence of Sophie, who will set a new stage. Makus concludes by distinguishing several senses of the "natural" in Rousseau and by reflecting briefly on perceptions of fearful, female power in contemporary politics.

Women and domestic life are completely absent from Rousseau's most well known political philosophy, most notably *On the Social Contract*. Most of the essays in this volume focus largely on the works where Rousseau deals explicitly with women and family. Melissa Butler considers the implications for women of Rousseau's utopian vision of the state, in his familiar political works, in the light of the work of Carol Gilligan.[13] Noting that the effect of Gilligan's work has been equivalent to a paradigm shift that has affected work in many disciplines, Butler invites us to look at Rousseau's political philosophy from the standpoint of care as a political issue. For Rousseau, after all, care was "something central, not something marginal," in his life experience and in his philosophy. Butler traces the roots of this in Rousseau's *Confessions*. Butler highlights the extraordinary central fantasy of *Emile; or, On Education*—a male tutor who takes over the care of a child from birth, raising him as a virtual work of science and art, and doing it as a high calling, much better than any woman could! She then delineates the range of familial tasks and functions Rousseau assigned to the perfected state, as well as the role he expected the state to play in the emotional lives of its citizens, maintaining that Rousseau has created "a maternal state," in which women seem virtually to "wither away." Yet the possibility that men can perform *all* social roles, even appropriating care and nurturance for a maternal state, deepens the argument that Rousseau did not believe that the social roles of women and men are due to any inherent, or biological, properties.

Although Rousseau always calls on Mother Nature to justify his claims about women's destiny as wives and mothers, Sarah Kofman proposes that "good Mother Nature" is a mere pretext for pursuing the ends of "phallocracy." Unlike some other feminist critics, Kofman does not find new, modernist arguments in Rousseau on women, but only the "most traditional" phallocratic discourse, such as may be found in Aristotle or even the Bible. She exposes the tattered logic of Rousseau's arguments from nature that women's best virtue in civil society is shame, and applies a psychoanalytic analysis to show that the point of it all is to spare the sexually enervated male "some loss or narcissistic wound." Kofman furthers this (psycho)analysis with the argument that Rousseau is driven by his simultaneous desire and fear of becoming woman. (This issue will reappear in different terms in the essay by Linda Zerilli.) His strictures on women are rendered a severe deconstruction as evidence of various neuroses.

According to Lori Marso, Rousseau may have been the first to philosophize that the identities of women, men, and citizens are all fragile constructions, never complete, never wholly stable. In several essays, we have seen various interpretations of Rousseau's requirement that women play a feminine role that supports, even makes possible, the role of the "manly citizen" of a republic. If their power is misused, women have the capacity to enervate and feminize men and fatally subvert civic virtue. But Marso asks, Why are women so dangerous to men? She argues that the instability of male identity "points the way toward recognition of an alternative democratic principle at the heart of Rousseau's work."

Marso shows that Rousseau's (male) citizen always seeks what is common to all citizens. What he knows of himself as a man and citizen, he extends to other men and citizens, always tending toward what he believes will unify them for the common good. He projects what he knows of himself onto others. Feminine women, however, are trained to be observant of those unlike themselves (men) and to develop a general capacity to respond to difference between people. Marso depicts the exact nature of Rousseau's distaste for urbanity, which he found most exemplified in the woman-dominated diversity of the Parisian salons. Rousseau vilifies city life, dominated by the feminine, as inauthentic and lacking in seriousness. However, Marso argues that the fates Rousseau assigns to Sophie and Julie invite questions about the legitimacy and value of that from which they are excluded. She suggests that Rousseau himself was ambivalent about the human price of his ideal community, which would be unilateral, univocal, and provincial (noncosmopolitan).

Linda Zerilli offers a rather different account of Rousseau's apparent fear of the power of women. In her view, Rousseau's horror of "the disorder of women" and the inversion of sexual relationships was given its note of hysteria by his own vivid personal awareness of its pleasurable attraction. What can suppress women's desire for mastery, when the "prison" of subservience to a dominating woman may arouse in men, not spontaneous aversion, but unguarded erotic desire? In Zerilli's view, gender roles are recognized by Rousseau as having no foundation in nature whatsoever. The detailed artifice of education is what creates the arbitrary system of signs that announces "woman" or "man." Strict adherence to these signs becomes essential to maintaining a masculine social contract that depends on man's ability to project onto excluded woman "that uncanny other woman in himself," the potential source of perversion and chaos.

The signs of republican (male) citizenship can only be linguistic and sartorial, thus requiring a male renunciation of the finery associated with aristocratic diversity and decadence (sexual and otherwise). Zerilli provides a detailed analysis, first, of Rousseau's condemnation of the theater and, second, of the education of Emile, showing the relation of both to his fear of the seductive dissimulations of unconstrained woman, with many references to the ancient models that provided so much inspiration to Rousseau for his creation of "the semiotic republic."

Elizabeth Wingrove focuses on one source of the power of Rousseau's constructions of woman, man, and citizen, which is that consent is a necessary part of the constitution of gender relations and is as important in the case of women as it is in the case of men. In modernity, social and political relations in general, and not just gender roles, are characterized ideally by consent. So it is not surprising that Rousseau has striven to show that women who are properly educated, and not corrupted by a corrupt society, will gladly consent to the feminine roles he has assigned them. Wingrove analyzes a text of Rousseau not addressed by any of the other essays—his prose poem *Le Lévite D'Ephraïm*—putting it in conjunction with his more familiar political texts, to illustrate how far Rousseau seems prepared to go in the harshness to which women may be thought to give their consent. Arguing for the convergence of political and sexual practices—"to be a citizen *is* to be a man"—Wingrove produces a disturbing radicalization of the claim that women's proper feminine role is constitutive of republican politics. Rousseau's *Lévite* is a retelling of the bloodthirsty scriptural story in Judges 19–21, in which (in Rousseau's version) young women virtuously and voluntarily decide to accept and marry their violent abductors, because it will reconstitute a community fractured by war. Employing a nuanced theory of social identities as "performativity," Wingrove's analysis shows that for Rousseau women hold in place a political community whose foundation is consent to the terms of one's own domination. As Wingrove comments, it remains necessary to retheorize sexuality as a critical location of consent.

Rebecca Kukla centers her investigation of gender in Rousseau in his central philosophical project: how can free beings be brought together in an association that protects each one with the common force, yet leaves each one obeying only him- or herself, as free as before? What if the same question were posed about marriage? Was this Rousseau's intention? Kukla points out that members of a couple, like citizens, ideally are transformed by their relationship, giving up their original nature and taking on a new one. Similarly to Marso, Kukla notes that men unite with others (as citizens) by eliminating differences between them, while women are expected to unite with men as *other*. Since according to Rousseau women and men have (or should have) drastically different temperaments, it is a "non-trivial problem" for his vision how they can be brought to identify with each other. Contrary to the assumption of many interpreters that there is a single Rousseauian story about gender relations, Kukla unravels three distinct models. She suggests further that the masculine dilemmas of Rousseau's (male) citizens, of identity, dependence, and freedom, would have been less acute without his failure to problematize the patriarchal family. Kukla delineates most clearly the final outcome of all of Rousseau's writings on gender relations: that there are diverse possibilities for heterosexual couplings that Rousseau explores, but in his own terms none of them are stable over time or ultimately satisfactory. The reader is left uncertain about what standard of gender relations, if any, has been professed as both possible and desirable.

Monique Wittig's "On the Social Contract" brings the discussion in this volume to a close on a different footing from that of critique. Appropriating the very title of Rousseau's most famous political work, Wittig asks, Is the philosophical device of a social contract superceded because of its presumptions of individual choice and voluntary association, which are locatable in early modernity? She points out that we live, inevitably, in social contracts as pacts, agreements, compacts, that we all assume in everyday life. Yet we need not assume that the nature of the pact is unchangeable, especially with respect to the extent to which heterosexuality and patriarchy overlap the very notion of a social contract. Rousseau, as Wittig reminds us, was the first philosopher who did not take it for granted that ultimately in the social contract "might is right." She maintains that the general philosophical question of a truly inclusive social contract, encompassing all human activity, thought, and relations, remains relevant as long as, quoting Rousseau, "humankind [that] was born free . . . is everywhere in chains." But what can we do? Perhaps, like precapitalist serfs, women have to "run away one by one." Or like Socrates (and perhaps Rousseau himself), if we are denied a new social order, we still may "find it in ourselves." In this essay, Wittig goes beyond the oppositional stance of feminism as critique and locates feminist thought within a tradition that both constitutes, and is constituted by, historical gender differences.

Notes

1. Linda Zerilli, *Signifying Woman: Culture and Chaos in Rousseau, Burke, and Mill* (Ithaca: Cornell University Press, 1994).

2. Susan Moller Okin, *Women in Western Political Thought* (Princeton: Princeton University Press, 1979).

3. Jean-Jacques Rousseau, *Emile; or, On Education*, trans. and with introduction and notes by Allan Bloom (New York: Basic Books, 1979).

4. "The idea that women have their own distinctive kind of intellectual or moral character has itself been partly formed within the philosophical tradition to which it may now appear to be a reaction" (Genevieve Lloyd, *The Man of Reason: "Male" and "Female" in Western Philosophy*, 2d ed. [Minneapolis: University of Minnesota Press, 1993]), 105.

5. See Lloyd, *The Man of Reason;* also Alison Jaggar, *Feminist Politics and Human Nature* (Totawa, N.J.: Rowman and Allanheld, 1983), esp. chap. 3.

6. Susan Moller Okin, "Women and the Making of the Sentimental Family," *Philosophy and Public Affairs* 11, no. 1 (1982).

7. Nan Keohane, "'But for Her Sex'": The Domestication of Sophie," *University of Ottawa Review* 49 (1979): 390–400.

8. Lloyd, *The Man of Reason*, 61.

9. Christine Fauré, *Democracy Without Women: Feminism and the Rise of Liberal Individualism in France*, trans. Claudia Gorbman and John Berks (Bloomington: Indiana University Press, 1991).

10. See Carole Pateman, "The Disorder of Women," *Ethics* 91 (1980): 20–34; and Lynda Lange, "A Feminist Reads Rousseau: Thoughts on Justice, Love, and the Patriarchal Family," APA *Newsletter on Feminism and Philosophy*, June 1989.

11. This dichotomy is "central to almost two centuries of feminist writing and political struggle; it is, ultimately, what the feminist movement is about" (Carole Pateman, "Feminist Critiques of the Public/Private Dichotomy," in "The Disorder of Women," 118).

12. Lloyd, *The Man of Reason.*

13. Carol Gilligan, *In a Different Voice: Psychological Theory and Women's Development* (Cambridge: Harvard University Press, 1982).

1

Rousseau and Modern Feminism

Lynda Lange

Jean-Jacques Rousseau has often been charged with inconsistency, despite his own assertion that all his writing is informed by the same principles.[1] Recently, however, there has been a different sort of charge of inconsistency. It is claimed that his spirited opposition to sexual equality is grossly inconsistent with his defence of equality for all citizens.[2] On the other hand, the conservative Allan Bloom, who claims to detect consistency in his approach to women and men, finds him a stay of contemporary antifeminism.[3] I propose an interpretation of Rousseau which is different from both of these perspectives. In my view, Rousseau is basically consistent in his treatment of men and women, despite a few discrepancies. However, writing as a feminist, I believe his views can be studied to advantage by feminists. Rousseau addresses almost every social issue that contemporary feminism is concerned with, and he does this in a manner which proves on examination to be surprisingly relevant to present problems, whether one agrees with his precise conclusions or not. With regard to sexual equality, it is possible to "turn Rousseau on his head," in a manner of speaking.

The theory of womens' nature and their role in society which I shall present has been developed on the basis of ideas and insights found in many works of Rousseau. The years 1756 to 1759, immediately following the writing of the First and Second Discourses, saw Rousseau's production of a large body of work devoted to a great extent to the relations of the sexes and the nature and role of women. His major work on the subject is found in *Julie ou la nouvelle Héloïse*, the *Lettre à M. D'Alembert sur les spectacles*, and *Emile ou de l'éducation*, all written during this period. Book V of *Emile*, on the education of women, was written before the other books of that work, immediately after the *Lettre à M. d'Alembert*. Prior to this period, some footnotes in the Second Discourse, as well as the philosophical anthropology concerning the origin of the family in that work, show that this subject had earlier been of interest to Rousseau as well. In other words, it is not peripheral to his central work as a political philosopher, even from his own point of view.

Rousseau was a severe critic of what he regularly referred to as *la société civile*. It is my view that *la société civile*, as Rousseau pictures it, has the main features of capitalism, or "possessive market society," as it is modelled by C. B. Macpherson.[4] Just as Macpherson demonstrated that the work of Hobbes, Locke, and others had the effect of justifying the crucial features of "possessive market society" by showing that their assumptions and conclusions conformed to that model of society, and not by showing that they had a concept of "possessive market society," I believe that Rousseau's criticism applies to that model, but not that he actually perceived the emergence of capitalism out of feudalism. The view that Rousseau's criticisms are applicable to a certain form of civil society, and not to civil society *per se*, bridges the gap between the vitriolic criticism of "civil society" in the early discourses, and the ideal of a good and legitimate society present later in *Du Contrat Social*.

All the evils of modern civil society, according to Rousseau, are derived ultimately from the fact that personal or particular interest (*l'intérêt personnel, l'intérêt particulier*) is the dominant rationale for action. What is worse, according to Rousseau, is that society is structured in such a way as to make this type of behavior rational in the circumstances. For Rousseau, the incompatibility of this with our authentic interests, and its deeply corrupting effect on our moral character, only appear after a thorough study of nature and history.

Feminist ideas were widely discussed in prerevolutionary France, but Rousseau thought that the idea that the sexes might *both* operate on these modern principles and that women should not be denied the right to advance their particular interests as men do was one of the most absurd and lamentable consequences of this modern philosophy. It is in this area that I find his views insightful and potentially instructive. It has been a theme of feminist criticism that the opposition of interests, exploitation, competition, and so on, endemic to our social and economic system, are, in some sense, male values. Yet because these values *are* endemic, they tend to shape feminism in their mold, and may be perfectly compatible with a lack of social discrimination between the sexes. It is another question, however, whether these individualist principles are ultimately useful to *democratic* feminism. This essay addresses these concerns through an examination of Rousseau's works.

Origins and Foundations of Sexual Inequality

According to Rousseau, and contrary to contractarian theory, the innate drive for self-preservation (*amour de soi*) does not, in itself, suggest any necessary opposition of interests. The gradual development of interdependence and entrenched inequality of power and wealth transform the expression of the drive for self-preservation into rational egoism, or *amour propre*. Since all develop these same concerns, their interests are necessarily in constant opposition. It is frequently apparent that Rousseau's views on women are a response to feminist arguments, and he was a severe critic of these arguments, in a manner which was consistent with his general criticism of individualist thought.[5]

In Book V of *Emile*, Rousseau states the following essential difference between the moral potential of men and women:

> The Supreme Being wanted to do honour to the human species in everything. While giving man inclinations without limit, He gives him at the same time the law which regulates them, in order that he may be free and in command of himself. While abandon-

ing man to immoderate passions, He joins reason [*la raison*] to these passions in order to govern them. While abandoning woman to unlimited desires, He joins modesty [*la pudeur*] to these desires in order to constrain them.[6]

The functions of these virtues, it may be noted, have a difference that corresponds to the difference in their character. The man "controls" or "governs" (*gouverner*) his own behavior with the use of reason; the woman merely "restrains" hers (*contenir*).[7]

While the man under the sway of *amour propre* may be thought to display his human potential for rationality in a corrupted form, the woman so swayed is sharply deflected from her unique human virtue of modesty. How has Rousseau concluded that there are such great differences between the sexes? It is done, surprisingly enough, in a manner which appears on analysis to be determinedly empiricist. Contrary to expectation, Rousseau does not rely on custom, prejudice, or God's will in the course of this attempt to justify a unique and inferior feminine role for women. It is probably because he uses these modern methods that Rousseau's theories of feminine and masculine social roles have remained influential even to the present.

In the *Discours sur l'origine et les fondements de l'inégalité* (Second Discourse), and in *Emile,* Rousseau's method is that of philosophical anthropology, and he even uses a type of argument found in contemporary evolutionary biology. This putatively scientific approach seems to him to justify the quick inference of a principle with vast consequences. It is one which is only too familiar to the contemporary reader, but by no means evidently true: "the man should be strong and active; the women should be weak and passive."[8] The different biological contributions of the sexes to their common aim (*l'objet commun*) of reproduction dictates this principle, according to Rousseau. Equal strength and self-assertion are inconsistent with the reproductive biology of each sex. This argument concerns *homo sapiens* in the pure state of nature, prior to the development of any specifically human culture or society. From a biological point of view, for procreation to occur, Rousseau writes, "One must necessarily will and be able; it suffices that the other put up little resistance."[9]

In another direct response to feminist debate, he argues that it is scarcely natural that men and women should enter with equal boldness on a course of action that has such very different consequences for each of them.[10] This response, however, presumes that the woman in the state of nature knows the consequences of sexual interaction for herself, which is at least debatable given what Rousseau says about the total inability of *homo sapiens* to formulate ideas or project expectations in the pure state of nature.[11]

Is sheer physical domination of women by men then natural? No. In the pure state of nature men are not very aggressive about anything, including sex, and natural compassion (*pitié*) is undiminished. We may suppose that a rebuff, or flight, or even a display of fear on the part of a woman would probably be sufficient to discourage an unwanted partner in the pure state of nature. Most importantly, honor is not at stake for men. According to Rousseau, the violence and incessant competition commonly attributed to male sexuality are a result of the knowledge and pride of *amour propre* developed in social relations. They are not "natural."

The timidity and weakness of the woman, according to Rousseau, inspire her to be pleasing to a man out of the basic impulse of self-preservation, that is, if she is pleasing he is less likely to be violent. Rousseau thinks this behavior simultaneously makes the man more inclined to remain with her (an important consideration if one has given up one's autonomy). These are the means she is given to supplement her weakness, and therefore, to act to please men is a quality of women directly derivable from nature. Rousseau writes: "If woman is made to please and to be subjugated, she ought to make herself agreeable to man instead of arousing him. Her own violence is in her charms. . . . From this there arises attack and defence, the audacity of one sex and the timidity of the other, and finally the modesty and the shame with which nature armed the weak in order to enslave the strong."[12]

However, as we have seen, these responses, based on natural compassion (*pitié*), are corrupted by the individualistic society of *amour propre*. If within civil society the man is stronger and dependent on the women only through desire, as Rousseau claims, whereas she depends on him through desire and need,[13] why should he bother to please her, and refrain from simply exercising his will? Rousseau has provided two answers to this question in *Emile*, concerning women and men in what Rousseau considers a good society.

The first argument is that real violence in sexual relations is contrary to its own ends since it is a declaration of war which may result in death, whereas the goal of sexual relations is the perpetuation of the species. This is clearly a restraint which is based on sophisticated rationality.

Rousseau believes that it is reason that restrains masculine sexuality, and it is noteworthy that it is not the mode of rational egoism which is said to be the restraint in question. The goal of sexual relations is here defined as a collective goal of the species, rather than in terms of individual self-interest.

The other argument is related to the ultimately conventional character of paternity. It is that "a child would have no father if any man might usurp a father's rights."[14] This is meant to be a consideration that a *man* might use to govern his own behavior, and is once again a collective, rather than a purely individual, motive. However, from a feminist perspective, this is a surprisingly explicit admission of male solidarity opposed to women, rather than of fully social motivation.[15] Here Rousseau tips on his head quite easily!

As we have seen, the male-dominated family is not a purely natural phenomenon for Rousseau, inasmuch as he does not suppose it to be present in the pure state of nature. In the speculative history of the Second Discourse, women are depicted in the state of nature as able to provide for themselves and their dependent children. It is a momentous development for humanity when increasing population drives some to less balmy climates where they are motivated to learn to build permanent shelters. Rousseau writes:

> The habit of living together gave rise to the sweetest sentiments known to men: conjugal love and paternal love. Each family became a little society all the better united because reciprocal affection and freedom were its only bonds; and it was then that the first difference was established in the way of life of the two sexes, which until this time had had but one. Women became more sedentary, and grew accustomed to tend the hut and the children, while the men went to seek their common subsistence.[16]

Though able to meet her own needs when solitary, the woman is assumed to be weaker than the man, so that living together is assumed to result in a division of labor.[17] It also results in more frequent pregnancy, which is thought to entrench the dependence of the woman on the man. The man, though quite insensible to love in the state of nature and utterly ignorant of his connection to children, is thought to become attached to both woman and children through constant association. This response is similar to that of the woman in the state of nature, who is thought to care for her offspring because she grows fond of them "through habit."[18] However, there is a crucial philosophic difference, which is a good example of the way in which thought may be shaped by male bias. The woman's attachment to her dependent offspring is "natural" in the fullest sense of the word: it could be said to be merely instinctive, since it is presumed to occur when human beings live exactly like animals. Paternal affection, however, is said to be a significant development, the result of socialization, and based on a rather abstract knowledge.

As such, paternity is a product of human artifice, based on knowledge and custom, and therefore, according to this philosophy, specifically human in a way that maternal love is not thought to be. Because of this, paternity will not be treated as a disqualification for the highest forms of human artifice, namely, political life and rational discourse. Allegedly natural maternity, on the other hand, is typically treated as such by political theorists, including Rousseau. This difference has important implications for the structure of Rousseau's political philosophy. For the moment, however, we will confine our discussion of this issue to the terms of Rousseau's own theory.

The sexual division of labor which appears as a result of the association of the sexes is not simply the result of practical cooperation for Rousseau, but a reflection of the essential difference between the sexes. The woman is so constituted that passivity and timidity are assets to her "proper purpose" (*leur destination propre*) once social relations have developed. This purpose is to reproduce within a family whose unity depends entirely on her behavior. Natural passivity and timidity in sexual relations, according to Rousseau, form the natural base for modesty (*la pudeur*) which is the specifically feminine virtue in civil society.

Modesty is the virtue which may ensure biological paternity of the children to the man she lives with, and the necessity Rousseau sees for this dictates the retiring and wholly domestic life of good women. "She serves as the link between them and their father; she alone makes him love them and gives him the confidence to call them his own."[19] On account of the artificiality and apparent fragility of the bond of the father to his children, the woman is required to live a life dictated by the necessity to appear respectable, that is, to convince her husband and everyone else that she is sexually monogamous. Nothing less than this degree of certitude, bolstered by public opinion, is thought to be sufficient to induce him to remain attached to that particular family and provide for its support.

By the very law of nature women are at the mercy of men's judgments, as much for their own sake as for that of their children. It
is not enough that they be estimable; they must be esteemed. It is
not enough for them to be pretty; they must please. It is not
enough for them to be temperate; they must be recognized as
such. Their honor is not only in their conduct but in their reputation; and it is not possible that a woman who consents to be
regarded as disreputable can ever be decent.[20]

The wholly incompatible bases of masculine and feminine virtue are
summed up in the following sentence from *Emile:* "Opinion is the grave
of virtue among men and its throne among women."[21]

This abandonment of moral autonomy for women is particularly
damning from Rousseau, who considers such autonomy essential not only
for citizenship, but even for true humanity.[22] That the male-headed family requires women to abandon moral autonomy functions without alter-
ation as a severe criticism of that institution.

Rousseau does not leave himself completely exposed to empirical refu-
tation concerning the nature of women. In the *Lettre à M. d'Alembert sur
les spectacles*, he writes: "Even if it could be denied that a special sentiment of chasteness was natural to women, would it be any the less true
that in society their lot ought to be a domestic and retired life, and that
they ought to be raised in principles appropriate to it? If the timidity,
chasteness, and modesty which are proper to them are social inventions,
it is in society's interest that women acquire these qualities."[23]

Thus although Rousseau does not argue that the male-headed biological family is natural and unaffected by history, he does argue that it is
nevertheless a social institution that may be grounded on nature by reason. He writes: "When woman complains on this score about unjust man-
made inequality, she is wrong. This inequality is not a human institution—or at least, it is the work not of prejudice but of reason."[24] This
type of willingness to come to grips with a "tough necessity" still seems
to be bracing to conservative antifeminists!

It is of philosophical significance that virtuous women in civil society
are characterized as closer to "nature" than virtuous men. The men must
be transformed and denatured in a good society, according to Rousseau.[25]
The modest woman appears still as little more than uncorrupted. As such
she will form a necessary link between the supreme artifice of the good
society on the one hand, and nature, on the other.

The Problem of Female Power

According to Rousseau, the social equality of the sexes poses a serious danger to civic virtue. His view of this danger is based on the critical analysis of modern "civil society," especially the concept of *amour propre*. It is Rousseau's belief that if women attempt to act in society according to the norms of *amour propre*, engaging in constant competition to further their "particular interest," they will inevitably be bested by the men. But this does not signify his admiration for the success of the male within that mode of social interaction.

The basic inequality of Rousseau's approach appears, however, in his belief that the woman who enters public life on the terms of *amour propre* does even more violence to her nature than the man caught up in that mode of interraction.

In the *Lettre à* M. *d'Alembert*, Rousseau argues at great length that one of the major reasons why there ought not to be a theatre established at Geneva is that this will result in women going out in public in company with men. Because of the very nature of sexual relations, according to Rousseau, the presence of women in public life undermines masculine excellence and exacerbates *amour propre*. The frequent attendance of men and women at public entertainments will focus attention on the natural impulses of the sexes to be pleasing to one another. While this is an expansion of the domain of women, since love is their "empire," it diminishes men. This occurs because the standards of behavior appropriate to love and courtship are inevitably feminine standards, given Rousseau's view of female power. According to Rousseau, men who lead a life of constant association with women become enervated and weak.[26] Such men will be far more prone to turn their learning or talent to the pleasing performance arising from *amour propre*, rather than to the rigorous, or morally challenging, pursuit of truth, since they will inevitably compete with one another for feminine approbation. He writes: "By themselves, the men, exempted from having to lower their ideas to the range of women and to clothe reason in gallantry, can devote themselves to grave and serious discourse without fear of ridicule."[27] Why these "grave and serious" intellectuals should be such an easy prey to ridicule is probably a question best answered by feminists over a few drinks at the faculty club. It does not seem to occur to Rousseau that the importance of the feminine role for the good society is rather dicey if there is this degree of tension between the masculine and feminine spheres. From the perspective he presents, a presumed seductive power of women to impose their standards, on account of the nature of sexual relations, enables women to dominate even in areas which are thought to be ultimately beyond their competence. It appears in the Second Discourse, and in *Emile*, that "love" may have been the original stimulus to the appearance of *amour propre*, even though it quickly lost sight of its origin. At the beginning of the "state of savagery," when people first settled in shelters of their own making, they were soon seduced by the pleasures of social life:

> People grew accustomed to assembling in front of the huts or around a large tree; song and dance, true children of love and leisure, became the amusement or rather the occupation of idle and assembled men and women. Each one began to look at the others and to want to be looked at himself, and public esteem had a value . . . that was the first step toward inequality and, at the same time, toward vice. From these first preferences were born on one hand vanity (*la vanité*)[28] and contempt, on the other shame and envy; and the fermentation caused by these new leavens eventually produced compounds fatal to happiness and innocence.[29]

In civil society, according to Rousseau, the consequences of the combination of *amour propre* and "love" as a value in itself (that is, unconnected to duty) are morally disastrous. According to him, this is an important reason why women should be confined to the sphere of their true competence: childcare, household tasks, and "rest and recreation" for men. Regarding the actual mental capacity of women, Rousseau does what is rare for him—he confuses a social artifact with a natural quality, a lack of education and opportunity for development, with an inherent deficiency.

Much of what Rousseau writes concerning the desirability of a separate feminine sphere centers around the evils to be thus avoided, and the harshness of his strictures are no doubt partly constructed out of his fear of female power. There is, however, a substantive contribution which can be made to the good of society by women, according to Rousseau, one which is an essential feature of a truly legitimate society governed by the general will.

The Foundation of the Good Society
Is Built Out of Women

The contribution women make to a good society by playing a feminine role has ramifications for virtually every issue in moral and political life, according to Rousseau. The scheme he presents also includes a fully developed romantic ideal of the relations of the sexes, presented in a very complete form in *Julie ou la nouvelle Héloïse*, and to a lesser extent in *Emile* in Book V dealing with the education of women. Nevertheless, the place of the feminine role in Rousseau's political philosophy may be focused around two basic themes. These are:

1. The need for the family and its particular attachments as a natural base for patriotism (*amour de la patrie*), and hence as a nursery for good citizens; and,
2. The need for certainty of paternity in connection with the requirements of the institution of private property.

Regarding the first of these themes, it is apparent that it concerns education in the widest sense of the term, which is to say, the whole socialization of citizens. It is not surprising, therefore, that Rousseau addresses this issue most directly in his work on education, *Emile*. Like Plato, he puts correct education at the very foundation of the good society. The contractarian solution to the conflict between individual self-interest and the existence of the civil state, which is to attempt a logical identification of the two in the terms of enlightened self-interest, was rejected by Rousseau as an inadequate foundation of political right.[30]

Rousseau fields a third alternative in which he attempts to sustain the materialist epistemology which was a philosophically progressive element in early contractarian theory. It is the injunction not to obey the law because it is rational (though it ought to be in fact rational), but to love it, and thus bring into harmony particular and public interest. This emotional leap is what makes possible the transcendence of *amour propre* required for the determination of the general will.

It is Rousseau's belief that those who are incapable of loving those near to them and who have no particular attachments will be even less capable of the love of their country and its laws or of any sacrifice for the common good. Particular affective relationships are an essential part of the personal development of the citizen for Rousseau, and play a foundational role in civil society. Although the virtue of citizens consists in a conformity of the individual will to the general will, which may in principle be justified by reason, Rousseau places a great deal of emphasis on the necessity for appropriate feeling to make such a civil state possible in fact. Mere abstract principles, he argues, even if backed by force, will never be enough to prevent individual self-interest from undermining the state. He recommends patriotism (*amour de la patrie*) as the most efficacious means of raising the sights of individuals from self-interest to the good of the state, for "we willingly want what is wanted by the people we love."[31] Patriotism, therefore, is not an abstract principle for Rousseau, but an active sentiment which promotes the type of personal development needed to create citizens.

Even supposing the average citizen were a philosopher, according to Rousseau, this would not solve the problem of sustaining the general will in a good state. Reason, because of what it is, is cosmopolitan in its outlook. Patriotism is therefore ultimately based on a lie, though a "noble lie," if you will. The shared customs and religion that give a nation cohesion, when regarded dispassionately and objectively, cannot be shown to be any better in reality than those of any other nation. But each nation, according to Rousseau, needs emotional loyalty from its citizens, rather than mere approval of its authority on the basis of reason.

It is the same with the family. As Allan Bloom puts it, we would think it monstrous if a man neglected his own children in favor of some others he thought superior.[32] The strong claim is that these loyalties are arbitrary—accidents of history. This is why, according to Rousseau, philosophers make poor kinsmen and citizens.

Particular affective relations in the family are therefore a foundation for particular affective relations to a given state. The relation of mother and child is the prototype of particular attachment, whether considered in relation to the philosophic history Rousseau provides in the Second Discourse, or in relation to the development of the individual within the civil state. It is the human relationship that precedes all others, for the species and for the individual. As we have seen, it provides the link between children and artificial paternity. Without a feminine role grounded on motherhood, the family, viewed from within this model, loses its unique quality of being a human artificial institution which incorporates natural relations. Losing that, it can no longer function as a "natural base" for the development of *amour de la patrie* and hence civic virtue.

In addition to the need for a family as a natural base for the development of *amour de la patrie*, Rousseau needs a mechanism to ensure certainty of paternity for the inheritance of property. In spite of Rousseau's criticism of bourgeois individualism, there is no doubt that from Rousseau's point of view private property is an inviolable requirement of civil life. In *Emile* he writes: "The unfaithful woman . . . dissolves the family and breaks all the bonds of nature. In giving the man children which are not his, she betrays both. She joins perfidy (*perfidie*) to infidelity. I have difficulty seeing what disorders and what crimes do not flow from this one." To the husband, a child not his own represents "the plunderer of his own children's property."[33]

Much of the force of this may be traced to the theme already presented—that the family is not a family unless united in the manner described by the woman's playing a correct feminine role. It is only necessary to establish a link between this and property.

In spite of Rousseau's criticism of economic inequality, as well as other forms of inequality, he never moves toward the view that private property ought to be done away with. Whatever other reasons there may be for Rousseau's repeated insistence that private property is a basic, even a "sacred" right, the male-headed private family has a basic inexorable economic requirement: it requires to have its subsistence in the form of private property in control of the male head of the family. This is necessary because the family is not "private" if the mode of acquisition, use, and disposal of its subsistence and surplus do not meet the basic requirements of the institution of private property; and it is not male-headed unless these rights and duties are centered on the husband and father.

It is clear that Rousseau's ideal family is made up of a male provider and a dependent wife and children, so that the basic requirement of privacy is met. Family privacy, because of the way it particularizes the individual's relations to certain others, is necessary, as we have seen, for the particular attachments so important to the early development of citizens and for the provision of a link between nature and social life. On the other hand, an equal distribution of private property among men is seen as necessary for the autonomy of the male head of the family in relation to other males. The particularity of his relation to his family would collapse if he did not have unique responsibilities and rights in relation to them.

The Transformation of Natural Qualities by Social Relations

The Pure State of Nature	The State of War (There may or may not be a bogus social contract)	Legitimate Civil State
Emotional autonomy	*Amour propre*	Moral liberty
Practical autonomy	Master/slave relations	Equality
Self-preservation	Particular or personal interest	Virtue (conformity of the particular will to the general will)
Female weakness and sexual timidity	Sexual manipulation or pseudo-masculinity	Modesty
Male sexual spontaneity	Compulsive and violent sexuality, domination of unsuccessful female manipulators	Male sexual spontaneity, governed by reason and knowledge
Spontaneous compassion (*pitié*)	(All but destroyed)	Patriotism Friendship Romantic love

From Nature to Virtue

In his treatment of the nature of the sexes, Rousseau's principles and method are precisely the same as what he exhibits in connection with all his important claims concerning human nature. The structure of his views can be shown to be parallel to that of his views of the natural man and citizen (see table). A natural quality is transformed by social relations. It may be corrupted by bad social relations, a process which occurs as the "golden age" of savagery degenerates into civilized social relations dominated by particular interests and *amour propre*. This process results in the development of a state of war like that of Hobbes, that is, one in which the interests of each individual are opposed to the interests of every other individual. This state, according to Rousseau, may or may not be characterized by a bogus social contract which primarily serves the interests of the rich.[34] Alternatively, a good civil society ruled by the general will would make possible the development of the uniquely human potential of these natural qualities.

Democratic Feminism

Reading Rousseau helps to provoke thoughts as to what sort of social arrangements would be most conducive to sexual equality. In particular, it challenges the liberal individualist view that women's liberation can be furthered primarily by means of the removal of legal and social obstacles to the advancement of individual women.

In a period when political philosophy was still preoccupied with the new ideal of equality before the law, Rousseau leapt ahead to the insight that where there is objective inequality, virtually any law helps the powerful and harms the less powerful.[35] Therefore, no legal system can morally reform the relations of men and women so long as there is social and economic inequality of the sexes, or general social and economic inequality. So long as women are socially and economically unequal to *each other*, and occupy the society of individualism and *amour propre*, relations between the sexes will be either patriarchal, or competitive and manipulative. In view of the differences in physical strength, this would also undoubtedly include continued male violence against women.

Rousseau's analysis of the particular interest and *amour propre* of social inequality reveals the pitfalls of attempting the integration of women, on the same footing as men, into an unequal, competitive, society. Particular interest and the consciousness of *amour propre* militate against the abandonment of male attempts to dominate women, and also against the abandonment of sexual manipulation of men by women. Reading Rousseau makes it clear that in possessive individualist society, it is imprudent to abandon any potential source of power over others. It is therefore very unlikely that moral improvement can occur without basic social change.

Rousseau contended that women who demand equality with men usually do not abandon the feminine wiles that presuppose inequality. They attempt to play two incompatible roles, and as a result succeed at neither.[36] He wrongly thought that the continued inequality of women despite substantial sentiment in favor of their equality was the result of inferior capacity, but the hampering effects of contradictory role-playing remain as Rousseau perceived them.

Despite some substantial sentiment in favour of the equality of women in the present age, and in spite of some legal and economic reforms, for most women, particularly if they want children, dependence on a particular man remains their best option for a livelihood. Sexual monogamy and other adherence to his wishes remains part of the price they pay. If we were to extend Rousseau's philosophy of moral autonomy to women, it appears that these cannot be truly *moral* choices unless and until women have personal autonomy. The male-dominated family is therefore an immoral institution which corrupts its members and is inimical to the development of a good society. It is clear, for example, that men resist reform of the abuses of sexism to a large extent because they do not want to lose their personal privileges based on power over women. At the same time, women are often afraid to resist sexism because of their dependence on men. It also should not be forgotten that the sexual division of labor between public and private spheres is undemocratic even in the relatively narrow, liberal individualist, sense of "democracy," never mind Rousseau's more thoroughgoing sense of egalitarianism. It prevents women from participating in public discourse as autonomous citizens with the freedom to speak out about social reforms.

Reading Rousseau serves two functions. First, because he was a modern thinker, he was and still remains useful to antifeminism. For this reason reading him is an exercise in "knowing the enemy." However, he understands very clearly many aspects of the structure of male dominance, which from the critical perspective of feminism function as effective criticisms of that system, often virtually without revision. The second, and larger, message for feminist thinkers in this study is that they cannot afford to do less than examine the whole of the social structure, for any attempt to examine the relations of men and women in isolation from other questions may be very misleading.

Since the early 1980s, grassroots and socialist feminism in North America have suffered marginalization, while liberal individualist feminism has institutionalized itself, and presented itself as if it *is* feminism. Some individual women have made stellar careers for themselves within institutionalized feminism, but women's condition in general has benefited little from it. Considering Rousseau's epigraph to the First Discourse, from Horace, it may also happen to feminists that: "We are deceived by the appearance of right."

Notes

1. "J'ai écrit sur divers sujets, mais toujours dans les même principes." "Lettre à Beaumont" (1762), in Jean-Jacques Rousseau, *Oeuvres Complètes,* ed. B. Gagnebin and M. Raymond (Paris: Editions de la Pleiade, 1959–), vol. 4, 928.

2. Work on this subject includes: Susan Moller Okin, *Women in Western Political Thought* (Princeton: Princeton University Press, 1979); Nannerl O. Keohane, "But For Her Sex . . . the Domestication of Sophie" and Lynda Lange, "Women and the General Will," both in *Trent Rousseau Papers*, ed. MacAdam, Neumann, Lafrance (Ottawa: University of Ottawa Press, 1980); and Eva Figes, *Patriarchal Attitudes* (London: Panther, 1972), 105.

3. Allan Bloom, introduction to Jean-Jacques Rousseau, *Emile: Or, On Education*, trans. and annotated Allan Bloom (New York: Basic Books, 1979).

4. C. B. MacPherson, *The Political Theory of Possessive Individualism* (London: Oxford University Press, 1962), 53.

5. My interpretation of Rousseau substantiates the claim of C. E. Vaughan that Rousseau attacked individualism "in its theoretical stronghold." Vaughan, introduction, *Political Writings of Rousseau* (Cambridge: Cambridge University Press, 1915).

6. *Emile*, trans. Bloom, 359.

7. Rousseau, *Oeuvres Complètes*, vol. 4, 695.

8. *Emile*, trans. Bloom, 358.

9. Ibid., 358. Compare Sigmund Freud, "Femininity," in his *New Introductory Lectures on Psychoanalysis*, trans. and ed. James Strachey (New York: W. W. Norton, 1965): "it is our impression that more constraint has been applied to the libido when it is pressed into the service of the feminine function . . . And the reasons for this may lie—thinking once again teleologically—in the fact that the accomplishment of the aim of biology has been entrusted to the aggressiveness of men and has been made to some extent independent of women's consent" (179–80).

10. *Emile*, trans. Bloom, 359.

11. Jean-Jacques Rousseau, *Discourse on the Origin and Foundations of Inequality* (Second Discourse), ed. Roger D. Masters, trans. Roger D. and Judith R. Masters (New York: St Martin's Press, 1964), 117.

12. *Emile*, trans. Bloom, 358.

13. Ibid., 364.

14. Ibid., 359.

15. These observations of Rousseau appear to be a remarkable substantiation of the theory of reproduction in Mary O'Brien, *The Politics of Reproduction* (Boston and London: Routledge and Kegan Paul, 1981).

16. Second Discourse, trans. Masters, 146–47.

17. The "naturalness" of a sexual division of labor is widely assumed. Even Marx, who infers no "natural" inequality of the sexes as a result, *assumes* this, rather than concluding it after reflection or investigation. See, for example, *Capital*, vol. 1, part 4, ch 14, section 4; and *The German Ideology*, part A.

18. Second Discourse, trans. Masters, 121.

19. *Emile*, trans. Bloom, 361.

20. Ibid., 364.

21. Ibid., 365.

22. Jean-Jacques Rousseau, *On the Social Contract*, Book I, ch. 8.

23. Jean-Jacques Rousseau, *Politics and the Arts: Letter to M. d'Alembert on the Theatre*, trans. Allan Bloom (Ithaca: Cornell University Press, 1977), 87.

24. *Emile*, trans. Bloom, 361.

25. "Forced to combat nature or the social institutions, one must choose between making a man or a citizen, for one cannot make both at the same time." Ibid. On the Legislator, essential to the founding of a good society, he writes: "One who dares to undertake the founding of a people should feel that he is capable of changing human nature, so to speak; of transforming each individual . . ." *On the Social Contract*, Book II, ch. 7.

26. *Letter to M. d'Alembert*, trans. Bloom, 103.

27. Ibid., 105.

28. It is *la vanité*, and not, as yet, *amour propre*. Rousseau, *Oeuvres Complètes*, vol. 3, 170.

29. Second Discourse, trans. Masters, 149.

30. See, for example, the first version of *Du Contrat Social* (Geneva manuscript), in *On the Social Contract*, ed. Roger D. Masters, trans. Judith R. Masters (New York: St Martins Press, 1978), 158.

31. *Political Economy*, in *On the Social Contract*, ed. Masters, 218.

32. Interpretative essay, in Plato, *Republic* (New York: Basic Books, 1968), 385.

33. *Emile*, trans. Bloom, 361.

34. Second Discourse, ed. Masters, 159–60.

35. "Under bad governments, this equality is only apparent and illusory. It serves merely to maintain the poor man in his misery and the rich in his usurpation. In fact, laws are always useful to those who have possession and harmful to those who have nothing." *On the Social Contract*, trans. Masters, 58.

36. *Emile*, trans. Bloom, 364.

2

Rousseau's Political Defense of the Sex-Roled Family

Penny Weiss and Anne Harper

The task of returning to the major historical figures of philosophy in order to document the sexual inegalitarianism in their thought seems of limited usefulness for projects on the agenda of feminist theory and practice. It would appear that there are endless tasks for feminist scholars more pressing, constructive, and relevant to the attainment of sexual equality than reconstructing the arguments of someone such as Rousseau—an eighteenth-century, white, male, European writing in defense of enforced sexual differentiation.

It is necessary, however, for the cogency of feminist theory and the success of feminist politics to hear and answer the concerns and questions of the opposition, concerns and questions too often ignored or oversimplified. Rousseau, for example, was not simply a misogynist determined to interpret nature, history, or culture in such a way as to bless male supremacy with the stamp of inevitability or justifiability. In fact, the concerns that led him to support sexual differentiation, especially the concern with moving beyond self-interest to real community, are often laudable and shared by many feminists. We will argue that Rousseau's resistance to feminism, as expressed in his endorsement of the sex-roled family, is not based on the same morally offensive principles and logically flawed reasoning as are many other anti-feminisms. But because Rousseau's anti-feminism is as troubling in its implications as are the others, it is one that deserves to be heard and responded to.

Recent feminist critiques of Rousseau's sexual politics have generally been severe (Okin 1979, Lange 1979, Eisenstein 1981). Perhaps more was reasonably expected of someone with such high praise for liberty and equality, one actually familiar with feminist ideas, an individual with painful personal experience of second-class treatment, and a thinker utterly convinced of how fatal oppressive power is to the existence of true community. When, in spite of these experiences and principles, Rousseau sends women to the home and men to the assembly, there is some cause for thinking he was in a position to know better and want more.

There is, however, much disagreement in the secondary literature regarding both what Rousseau prescribes for the sexes, and why. We are left with often incompatible descriptions and explanations of his sexual politics that sometimes mirror more general disagreements about his politics and philosophy. It has been claimed, for example, that Rousseau limits women's activity because he is fearful of women's power (Wexler 1976), that he thinks women's inferior nature requires a circumscribed role (Christenson 1972, Okin 1979), that he endorses women's subservience as a necessary condition of men's freedom (Eisenstein 1981), and that he empowers the sexes differently from real concern with establishing sexual equality (Schwartz 1984, Bloom 1985). Consequently, Rousseau's treatment of the sexes has been held to be both a major breech of his principles and an integral part of his politics.

We hope to offer an interpretation of Rousseau's sex-roled family that can incorporate and surpass some of these incompatible interpretations of his work, and that can demonstrate what he might have been trying to accomplish in endorsing sexual differentiation. We argue that at least on the theoretical level he is internally consistent. Rousseau's advocacy of sexual roles is based on his understanding of their ability to bring individuals outside of themselves into interdependent communities, and thus to combat egoism, selfishness, indolence and narcissism—goals that consistently inform much of his politics. In order to demonstrate this, we show that Rousseau's rejections of both aristocratic and bourgeois families are founded upon their inability to accomplish politically what the sex-roled, affectionate family can accomplish.

Defenses of the "traditional" family are often thought to arise either from ignorance of its oppressiveness, disdain for women, or belief that its differentiated roles fulfill the distinct natures of women and men. While each of these explanations does capture a part of the reality, the picture they paint of defenses of the sex-roled family is seriously incomplete.

Rousseau's rationale for sexual differentiation in general, and within the family in particular, is not to be found in an appeal to the different natures of the sexes. By his own account no natural differences in strength, intellect, reproductive capacities or interests mandate a strict sexual division of roles and traits in society (Weiss 1987). But if Rousseau does not resort to claims about the different natures of the sexes, and if his scheme reflects more than the misogyny or blindness of its author, as we believe it does, then how is it possible to explain his system of sexual differentiation?

While frequently making rhetorical reference to the different natures of men and women in defending his proposals, Rousseau ultimately appeals to claims quite unrelated to sexual natures. For instance, in discussing female chastity he speaks of how the "Supreme Being . . . while abandoning woman to unlimited desires . . . joins modesty to these desires in order to constrain them" (Rousseau 1979, 359). However, despite the apparent reliance here on the (divine) given of woman's nature, his more consistent and convincing position emerges when he writes that "Even if it could be denied that a special sentiment of chasteness was natural to women . . . it is in society's interest that women acquire these qualities" (Rousseau 1960, 87). By referring to what traits women should *acquire* "in society's interest," Rousseau introduces a completely independent, and more internally consistent justification for his rigidly sexually differentiated society. Instead of focusing on the supposed *causes* of sexual differentiation, as found in nature, we must turn instead to an examination of the *effects* of sexual differentiation on various social relations. Then we can discover why it is that Rousseau considers sexual differentiation to be "in society's interest."

Rousseau's strategy of evaluating and justifying sexual differentiation by its consequences, especially after comparing them to the effects of the alternatives, is not so surprising. It is not the question, "Is X good in itself?" that preoccupies the citizen of Geneva but, instead, "Is X beneficial and useful?" For example, the *Letter to d'Alembert* inquires into the effects on different peoples of establishing a theater. He writes in that letter that "To ask if the theater is good or bad in itself is to pose too vague a question. . . . The theater is made for the people, and it is only by its effects on the people that one can determine its absolute qualities" (Rousseau 1960, 17). Similarly, Rousseau's famous opposition to the Enlightenment stems not from a belief that the arts and sciences are unequivocally bad in themselves, but from reflection on the consequences of imperfect learning by the masses. Thus, the suggestion that Rousseau's sexual scheme is devised for its social consequences is not as idiosyncratic as it might at first appear.

Figuring out why Rousseau sees sexual differentiation as socially beneficial requires considering Rousseau's preferred family in two related contexts. The first context is his general thought, where sexual differentiation can be understood as a response to certain aspects of what he perceives as "the human condition." For example, according to Rousseau, the bonds created in the sex-roled family, and the interdependence fostered by sex roles in general, motivate and teach us how to be part of a political community, which he holds to be necessary for survival and morality. The second context is the historical forms of the family with which Rousseau was familiar. Rousseau witnessed the decline of the traditional, aristocratic family, and the emergence of the bourgeois family (both of which may be considered patriarchal), and found both politically unacceptable. A look at the families Rousseau rejects gives a sense of both what goods he is trying to attain by creating sexual differences, and what evils he is trying to skirt.

Rousseau'a views on the sexes are thus strongly political, in at least two senses. First, Rousseau is certain that the private and public affect each other in numerous and central ways—that women, children, sexuality, families, etc. matter to politics as much as do the actions of men in the assembly. Because the private has political consequences, Rousseau to a great extent constructs the private with an eye to its political repercussions. The private becomes the parent and servant of the public: sex roles serve political ends and teach us lessons that give birth to certain desirable social possibilities. Rousseau's views on the sexes are also political in a second sense, in that they reflect assumptions and choices about what kinds of communities are possible, necessary, and desirable, and involve practical strategies for attaining them.

Rousseau might be considered anti-feminist at the outset because he evaluates the role of women in a light other than simply what women want to or can do. However, it is at least true that Rousseau does the same for men (Martin 1981, Weiss 1990), and that what women want to or can do is not irrelevant. Indeed, some opposition to feminism, including Rousseau's, may arise from viewing feminists as evaluating the role of women abstracted from political considerations. Rousseau's argument is that certain necessary social benefits result from the establishment of sexual differentiation, far-reaching benefits that serve as a large part of its justification. Such a defense of the traditional family presents a different set of questions to feminists than do more familiar ones based on appeals to biological determinism, and needs more thorough understanding and critique by feminists.

The first two sections of this paper develop the two contexts in which the ends of Rousseau's sexual politics can be discerned. The succeeding two sections explore the negative personal and social consequences of the aristocratic and bourgeois families he rejects. These "case studies" offer a picture of what Rousseau thinks a family ought to provide for its members and to society and why he finds the sex-roled, affectionate family to be the most personally and politically beneficial. The conclusion will point out some of the questions Rousseau's defense of the sex-roled family raises for feminist theory and some of the questions feminist theory raises for Rousseau.

Rousseau and the Human Condition

Rousseau portrays people in the state of nature as free, happy, independent, amoral, innocent, and isolated. They are without need for the services or esteem of others and can generally satisfy their minimal desires independently. While self-absorbed, they do not desire to harm others. These asocial individuals possess numerous faculties in potentiality, but neither internal nor external forces naturally operate to motivate them to do any more than is necessary to survive. Rousseau's primitives are lazy, content, independent, and generally harmless.

All relations in the state of nature are temporary and amoral, and provide no precedent or model for the sorts of relations needed between social beings. There may be some infrequent instances of cooperation in the search for food, but such liaisons are temporary and based entirely on self-interest. Sexual encounters are random and fleeting, motivated by the coincidence of desire and opportunity, and cause no lasting attachment between the partners.

Even the mother-child relation in the state of nature provides a poor model for the interdependent, moral, sustained relations modern social people need. As Rousseau portrays it, mother-child relations in the state of nature do not differ significantly from those of other animals. He sees the demands of children in the state of nature as simple, of short duration, and compatible with the satisfaction of the mother's meager needs and desires. A father's assistance is unnecessary, even were he able to grasp his relation to a child, which Rousseau thinks he is not. A mother cares for a child to relieve her own swollen breasts of milk, out of compassion for a crying creature, and finally out of affection born of habit. But Rousseau imagines that in the state of nature children venture off on their own permanently at a very young age—as soon as they have learned to feed and defend themselves—and that this rather uneventfully marks the end of all relations between mother and child.[1]

However, accidental events and developments alter the easy balance between desires and powers in the state of nature, until interdependence finally becomes necessary for survival. The question now becomes how to teach and motivate asocial, lazy, independent individuals to work with and for each other as well as for themselves. Rousseau considers this change radical and difficult. The fact that people need each other does not automatically mean that they will cooperate for mutual advantage rather than attempt to exploit each other for personal gain. Self-love, once complicated by social relations, easily leads to selfishness and concern with advantage over others, bringing about the long train of personal and social evils so magnificently described in the first *Discourse*.

Rousseau does not take egoism, competitiveness or conflict to be endemic to the human condition. Nor does he assume, however, that by nature people are as concerned with others, including children, as with ourselves. Rousseau's quest is to establish a social framework that can provide us with the skills and desire both to end the isolation, self-absorption, and independence of natural people, and combat the egoism, competitiveness, and conflict among "civilized" people who have become interdependent.

The contrast between childhood in the state of nature and modern social childhood helps clarify Rousseau's "political problem." As society "advances," the period of childhood is extended, and being a parent becomes more demanding. In civil society children are dependent for much longer than in the state of nature, for they must learn to speak, to read, to earn a living, to behave properly—the list is virtually endless, and the specific skills needed can change rapidly.[2] Further, parents are now subject to judgments by others regarding the quality of the care they bestow upon their children, making their task even more burdensome.

It is the case that the range of solutions considered by Rousseau is narrow. Or, perhaps more accurately, his very framing of the problems itself colors the solutions. Looking at Rousseau's thoughts on sexual differentiation and the family in the context of his general thought, the problems he addresses might include the following: "How can we help ensure that women, once sufficiently motivated by pity, full breasts, and modest requests to pay some minimal attention to a child for a relatively short period of time, will now invest so much more for so much longer? And what will turn a naturally lazy and asocial male, whose participation in child rearing was once largely unnecessary, into a father? What will turn both into citizens?"

What such questions indicate is that the possible range of child-rearing arrangements considered all generally appeal to some form of the nuclear, heterosexual family. The attempt to motivate parental, especially maternal, "sacrifice" presupposes both a particular model of public-private relations and a distinct conception of community that can fairly be said to beg as many questions as they answer. Nonetheless, such are the questions Rousseau considers and, as we will argue below, his position on sexual relations provides a large part of his answer to them. Rousseau's rejection of certain families arises from their inability to respond to fundamental crises of the human social condition, and their tendency to support corrupt political and social relations. His defense of the sex-roled, affectionate family is likewise based on its beneficial social consequences.

The Changing Family

In the traditional noble family of sixteenth, seventeenth, and early eighteenth century France, the male exerted powerful rule over both his children and wife. Arranged marriages were standard, with economic and family advantage the criteria in mate selection. "Within these marriages, relations between husband and wife and between parents and children were cold, distant, and unloving. . . . Noble wives were poorly treated by their husbands," and remote from their children (Fairchilds 1984b, 97, 98). "The marriage contract seemed to have little meaning in Paris, except in separating a man and woman effectively, so that they were ashamed to seem to care for each other, and in most cases lived apart, slept in separate apartments, and had each other announced when they called" (Josephson 1931, 123–124).

Needless to say, this family was not a reliable source of emotional satisfaction for any of its members, and illicit relationships regularly filled the vacuum. Even here, it has been said that "The ceremony of taking a lover was momentous; position, family, social attainments, were all weighed" (Josephson 1931, 126). Children were cared for by wet nurses, nursemaids, and tutors, successively. This aristocratic family was thus seldom more than a reproductive and economic entity, with birthing legitimate heirs a primary function. Rousseau, we shall see, rejects this family on a number of grounds. It is to this family that his remarks about "unfaithful" wives, "brilliant" wives, and women turning to "entertainments of the city" (Rousseau 1979, 44, 409) are directed, as are comments about tyrannical and neglectful fathers (Rousseau 1979, 38n).

In addition to analyzing the defects of the family of the Ancien Regime, Rousseau focuses his attention on its likely successor: the bourgeois family. Actually, in Rousseau's view the self-absorbed bourgeois individual is incapable of really being a member of a family. This is because

> he is the man who, when dealing with others, thinks only of himself, and on the other hand, in his understanding of himself, thinks only of others. . . . The bourgeois distinguishes his own good from the common good. His good requires society, and hence he exploits others while depending on them. . . . The bourgeois comes into being when men no longer believe that there is a common good . . .[3]

These self-interested bourgeois "role-players" are not part of a greater whole, be it the family or community, in any sense but the limited and inadequate one based on self-interest. "I observe," writes Rousseau, "that in the modern age men no longer have a hold on one another except by force or by self-interest" (Rousseau 1979, 321). People are self-centered and view others as means to their ends. The bourgeois family, accordingly, is without a common interest or firm bond. Members of the family pursue their own interests, considering the others and fulfilling their obligations when it is useful or convenient, or when they are forced to do so. Such relations are superficial and unreliable, and do nothing to teach us the important lessons Rousseau thinks we need to learn about interdependence, loyalty, and community. It is to this emerging family that Rousseau's remarks about families of strangers are directed, as are many of his comments about women seeking entry into previously male arenas—comments, that is, about liberal feminism.

The general framework of Rousseau's thought and his particular understanding of the propensities inherent in aristocratic and bourgeois families provide a basis for interpreting his views on sexual differentiation. Examining specific features of the families he condemns offers a picture of what Rousseau held to be their negative effects on parent-child and male-female relations and, consequently, on general social and political arrangements. These families are cast aside on political grounds—because of their inability to mitigate, or their propensity to encourage, undesirable human relations—and the sex-roled affectionate family is offered as a better alternative.

Parent-Child Relations

As discussed above, parent-child relations in the state of nature are of limited usefulness in helping establish the kinds of human bonds Rousseau asserts we now need. He also considers the families of his own time inadequate. The status quo to which Rousseau was responding was parental neglect of children, and the lowly status of the child as uninteresting, useless, or sinful (Charlton 1984). Until almost the very end of the Ancien Regime, child care in most noble and bourgeois households was handled primarily by servants. Even in the 1760s, '70s, and '80s, when a few notable women began to breast-feed and supervise their own children, household servants played a major role in childrearing (Fairchilds 1984a).

The role of servants in the lives of children began at birth when the infant was immediately sent to a wet-nurse (*nourrice*). This custom was deeply rooted by Rousseau's time, having begun as early as the thirteenth century, when Paris had a bureau of *recommanderesses* that arranged hired nurses. In the eighteenth century the hiring of wet-nurses was prevalent among the bourgeoisie and the artisanate as well as the aristocracy. In artisanal families the motives for wet-nursing were primarily economic: the mother's labor was essential to the family economy, and she could not afford the interruption that nursing would entail (Fox-Genovese 1984). There were social reasons for wet-nursing as well: nursing was considered a degrading and vulgar activity which supposedly ruined one's figure and strained one's health. Another reason was sexual: there were folk taboos against resuming sexual intercourse during lactation. Thus wet-nursing was an economic necessity for some women and their families and a response to social pressures and taboos for others. Rousseau's opposition to wet-nursing in particular, and to parental neglect of children in general, is unwavering, and he is given much credit for persuading mothers to breast-feed their babies and for contributing to "what was almost a cult of the mother figure" (Jirmack 1979, 161).

Sounding like some twentieth century anti-feminists, Rousseau states that in certain childcare arrangements, greater risk of poor care exists because the caretakers generally have no long-term stake in the child's upbringing. Their primary concern is simply minimizing the amount of trouble a child causes them while under their charge, and no more. (It is interesting to note how often today infants are called "good" who are, more precisely, easy to care for, i.e., who sleep a lot and cry but a little.) Rousseau refers to wet nurses as "mercenaries" (Rousseau 1979, 44), evoking the imagery of professional soldiers who serve any country *merely* for wages. Rousseau's inference is that the nurse really takes no interest in the child him or herself, but is basically concerned with earning an income and saving herself trouble. This assumption explains the practice of swaddling infants, which Rousseau abhors, and which he uses as representative of the poor treatment of children under such arrangements. However, while there is no reason to doubt Rousseau's sincere concern with the physical health and welfare of children, and while the stories of neglect and abuse of children by nurses in his time were numerous (Fairchilds 1984b, 100; Sussman 1982, 73–97), such concern accounts for but the smallest part of his reconstruction of the family.

That Rousseau's concern is not primarily the quality of care given children outside the nuclear family is supported by his awareness of the need to strengthen family ties beyond what may "naturally" exist; he never takes their strength, safety, or reliability for granted. Rousseau does not believe that nature goes too far in ensuring that children will be cared for because, as discussed earlier, outside of pity, which motivates one to help a suffering child, and full breasts, which encourage women to nurse for their own comfort, nature is essentially silent. The point is that even if Rousseau could be shown that children are as well-tended by nurses or childcare workers as by parents, he would hesitate to endorse the former. By spelling out some of the numerous negative consequences of such arrangements, it is possible to understand that the basis of Rousseau's objection to them is essentially political.

Rousseau first notes the simple fact that with a child under the charge of one other than her or his parents, the family spends less time together. He finds the consequences of this worrisome, for habit is not then allowed the opportunity to strengthen the ties of blood (Rousseau 1979, 46). Given his assumption that such blood ties are fragile and require reinforcement, extra-familial childcare will not enhance the potential care and love between family members that Rousseau would want to develop. Spending so much time apart, and in different pursuits, family members do not even know each other well. Rousseau's concern is that in the end they will be like residents of a corrupt city, polite strangers (Rousseau 1979, 49) who really think first of themselves.

The habit of caring for another is vital to the strengthening of blood ties, which alone are easily broken. Rousseau's definition of nature is important here: he would like the word to be "limited to habits conformable to nature" (Rousseau 1979, 39). Such habits would never be lost once learned, because they would conform to our dispositions as strengthened by our senses, but not yet corrupted by our opinions. Thus habit can strengthen nature, even though it can also stifle it. In this case, the habit of caring for one's own infant can strengthen the rather meager biological bond just as the habit of not caring can destroy it. In the family that does not spend ample time together, members may not be drawn to one another from affection born of habit, an arrangement that threatens to maintain original human separateness and fails to combat egoism.

From the child's point of view, as well, extra-familial childcare has drawbacks. A child spending long hours away from the family can easily come to love the care-giver rather than the parents (Rousseau 1979, 49) or become prone to making "secret comparisons which always tend to diminish his esteem for those who govern him and consequently have authority over him" (Rousseau 1979, 57). The "losing" party in such comparisons—whether parents, wet-nurses, or tutors—may consequently find it difficult to elicit affection and obedience from the child, making their already unnatural duties more distaseful and possibly leading to lack of concern for child-rearing responsibilities. Or they may attempt to win back the child's affection by educational practices which are of dubious merit. Even if parents are preferred, their children may resent them for having entrusted them to those whose care is inferior, rather than providing it themselves.

Rousseau also fears that a child cared for by "mercenaries" may "bring back the habit of having no attachments" (Rousseau 1979, 49). It is especially this politically dangerous possibility that arouses his concern. While not uninterested in nutrition and the high rate of infant mortality, the alienation of affection between mother and child was what most bothered Rousseau about a practice like wet-nursing. Once wet-nursing was finished, at about two years of age, the child was usually brought back into its family of origin and taught to regard its former nurse as a servant. Sometimes children were no longer allowed to see their nurses. Weaning is often traumatic for a child, no matter how well or poorly cared for, and some infants shed tears upon being separated from their nurses. Rousseau thinks this attempt to make children forget or disdain their first caretakers instills in them a general contempt and ingratitude (Rousseau 1979, 45). He fears the child will in the end despise both the biological parents, who do not offer much care during infancy, and the substitute parents, whose class or status now makes them an unacceptable object of affection. In addition, the failure of the mother to nurse her child robs her of an opportunity to learn to care for someone other than the self.

Thus, Rousseau's argument for breast-feeding is not a materialist one. His main concern is not infant health and the quality of milk—its vitamins, antibodies, or other nutritional aspects emphasized by some twentieth-century advocates—but the quality of human relationships formed from the beginning of life. If one allows a young child to be completely cared for by a servant for whom one then teaches the child contempt, one creates a monstrous person who does not know how to treat anyone else properly.[4]

Rousseau's arguments are not directed only to "neglectful mothers." His injunction to fathers to take responsibility for their children is less well-known than his pleas to mothers, but it is no less important and is based on similar considerations.

Rousseau first tries to counter the notions that fathers are either inept parents or rightly consumed with more "important" tasks than caring for their children. "He will be better raised by a judicious and limited father than the cleverest master in the world; for zeal will make up for talent better than talent for zeal. . . . But business, offices, duties. . . . Ah, duties! Doubtless the least is that of father?" (Rousseau 1979, 48–49). It is possible and important that men be fathers, for Rousseau regards "surrogate fathers," or tutors, in the same light as wet-nurses—as mercenaries who corrupt the family just as mercenary soldiers do the state. Rich men who claim that they do not have time to care for their children purchase the time of others to perform their parental duties.[5] As Rousseau well knew, preceptors were often picked from among the male domestics in the household and were treated as family servants. He chastises fathers for subjecting their children to a master-servant relationship that ultimately produces a servile mentality. "Venal soul! Do you believe that you are with money giving your son another father? Make no mistake about it; what you are giving him is not even a master but a valet. This first valet will soon make a second one out of your son (Rousseau 1979, 49).

Hiring tutors may leave children and fathers unattached, and thereby also fail to develop a common interest between parents. Use of "mercenaries" teaches children that money buys servants and that people only "care" out of self-interest; further, it fails to allow any true attachment even between child and tutor to develop, for theirs is in fact a relationship based on money.

The family in the Ancien Regime was an institution primarily organized for the transmission of property and rank from one generation to the next. Rousseau's new definition of fatherhood is rooted in the anti-patriarchalism of Locke's political theory. He expands Locke's view of the father as friend of his children to include the notion of father as educator or governor of his sons (Locke 1968). Like Locke, Rousseau emphasizes that the legacy or "portion" that a father bestows on his children should be a personal involvement in their education. While Locke still places high value on the transmission of property along with the "good breeding" of a gentleman, Rousseau is occupied with the transmission of a set of values that will enable children to be *independent* of wealth and rank.

Rousseau wants fathers to give their children something of themselves, rather than only their money. He wants them to provide an example of citizenship that rests on love and benevolence for others rather than on wealth. At the outset of *Emile*, he complains about "Fathers' ambition, avarice, tyranny, and false foresight, their negligence, their harsh insensitivity" (Rousseau 1979, 38n). Fathers are rather like the laws, which Rousseau finds "always so occupied with property and so little with persons, because their object is peace, not virtue" (Rousseau 1979, 37n).

Another negative political consequence Rousseau cites of having two sets of care-givers is the risk of presenting conflicting guidelines to children. Rousseau writes,

> A child ought to know no other superiors than his father and his mother or, in default of them, his nurse and his governor; even one of the two is already too many. But this division is inevitable, and all that one can do to remedy it is to make sure that the persons of the two sexes who govern him are in such perfect agreement concerning him that the two are only one as far as he is concerned. (Rousseau 1979, 57)

Certainly, if Rousseau expresses doubts about two people sharing care of a child, he will be extremely hesitant to involve more parties, who might introduce additional principles into education. But why is this so problematic?

Rousseau's concern about the conflicting guidelines of multiple care-givers seems to involve the way children will come to regard the guidelines themselves as well as their source. If different authorities espouse conflicting rules, children may conclude that the guidelines are merely reflections of individual wills, and/or may see authority as merely an obstacle, a set of arbitrary rules that one may be able to evade with sufficient study of them. Such perspectives, according to a Rousseauean framework, encourage rebellion and disrespect for rules, and maintain a picture of human relations that is essentially based on subjectivity and self-interest. Thus, multiple care-givers potentially undermine the rule of law, considered by Rousseau to be the basis of all legitimate states, and complicate the already difficult project of moving self-absorbed individuals into a greater whole.

According to Rousseau, then, aristocratic and bourgeois families pose grave problems both for the bonds between parents and children and for general social relations. First, these families fail to reinforce natural ties with habitual ones, leaving people separate and self-absorbed. Second, these arrangements present children with torn loyalties, leading to any of three negative consequences: childcare, already "unnatural" and a sacrifice, is made more onerous by the weak bonds; education, essential for making us responsible social creatures, may be compromised for the sake of children's affection; or, most important, children cared for by "mercenaries" may learn that people only tend to others when it is in their interest or convenient for them to do so. The ultimate danger is that respect for persons and for law is not learned. Rousseau's firm belief in the insufficiency of self-interest as a basis for community, and in the necessity and difficulty of combatting natural human isolation and egoism, leads him to reject aristocratic and bourgeois families as personally and politically useless or dangerous. Similar problems are presented by the relationships between spouses in these families.

Male-Female Marital Relations

Rousseau advocates not only that women and men be good parents, but good spouses, as well. We next explore Rousseau's sense of the negative repercussions of an aristocratic or bourgeois family structure on relations between spouses, and the consequences of these "inadequate" male-female relations on general social arrangements.

Rousseau's words on sex education are often remarkable for the sense of danger they portray. "How many precautions must be taken!" (Rousseau 1979, 335), he exclaims. The relations one will have with other people in general will, Rousseau believes, be affected by how one deals with the need for a partner. Human sexuality has political implications.

In the contemporary discussions of marriage there was a debate about ill-matched marriages (*mesalliances*), which meant marriages between members of the aristocracy and the bourgeoisie. Rousseau changes the meaning of the term: for him an ill-matched marriage is one where the characters of the partners, rather than their ranks, are not compatible. Rousseau draws a further inference: "the farther we are removed from equality, the more our natural sentiments are corrupted; the more the gap between noble and commoner widens, the more the conjugal bond is relaxed; and the more there are rich and poor, the less there are fathers and husbands. Neither master nor slave any longer has a family; each of the two sees only his status" (Rousseau 1979, 405). The message here is striking: Rousseau is saying that the greater the social and political inequality, the less husbands and wives are bound to each other. Apparently this is because people marry for reasons of social rank and not for compatibility of character, thus making it less likely that they will love each other and be sexually faithful. The "family" is destroyed, or is never truly established in the first place, by the inequality of the social structure. The quality of married life affects the morality of the citizens. Rousseau witnesses individuals who by and large seem incapable of establishing meaningful relationships as family members or as fellow citizens.

In contrast to eighteenth-century French law and practice, Rousseau emphasizes that a woman should have a voice in determining whom she will marry, and that marriage is a social institution requiring mutual respect and fidelity from both partners. He opposes the authoritarian relations of parent and child whereby parents choose the husband for the daughter based on wealth and rank. Aristocratic families with arranged marriages based on economics did not establish an arena of love and affection between the spouses. Rousseau seems to see this as encouraging adultery. In fact, it can be said that adultery was institutionalized at the highest level of French society, for the married Louis XV had a publicly-acknowledged relationship with Madame de Pompadour, herself a married bourgeoise who played a powerful role in France as advisor to the King and as patron of the arts.

Rousseau has the greatest wrath for the adulterer, who inevitably "destroys the family" (Rousseau 1979, 324). His argument here is quite different from many offered today, for Rousseau does not consider that only one model of male-female relations is somehow ordained and that any straying from it is sinful. One need only consider relations in his state of nature, where sexual encounters occurred when and with whom the desire arose, and established no moral bond.

Infidelity is condemned because of its undesirable personal and political effects, which may be several. First, there is the possibility of a woman bearing children which biologically are not her husband's. A man unsure of his biological relation to his wife's children may see less of himself in them, identify with them less strongly, and be less motivated to work and sacrifice for them; this injures both his relation with his children and his partnership with his wife. Given Rousseau's assumption that such motivation to sacrifice for others is already in short supply, the loss could be a significant one for the family unit. Second, an unfaithful partner, male or female, causes one to distrust others outside the family, who become potential competitors. This creates strained social relations in general, precisely what Rousseau wants to avoid. Third, with suspicions of infidelity in the air, spouses do not trust one another, and only feign love. "Under such circumstances the family is little more than a group of secret enemies" (Rousseau 1979, 325).

The worrisome political consequence here is that without love of one's nearest, it is difficult to develop love for the larger community. There appear to be two connections between familial love and patriotism for Rousseau. First, the "unnatural" lessons of cooperation and obligation are more easily learned on the "micro" level of the family—where habit breeds affection, and others are known well—and then extended to larger groups. Second, one is motivated to sacrifice for the state in large part by the protection and other benefits the state offers one's family. In either case, Rousseau's opposition to aristocratic spousal relations is rooted in their failure to move people beyond the self, while responsible, reliable bonds within the family help establish the habits and motives for true political community.

Rousseau also rails against the aristocratic wife "seeking entertainment" in the city, and the bourgeois wife demanding entry into previously male educational and social institutions. In both cases, according to Rousseau, women are not fulfilling their domestic duties. This seems to be both symptom and cause of political problems for him.

Women engaged in activities outside the household may come to see motherhood as a burden. They are apt to try to avoid pregnancy through birth control (Rousseau 1979, 44), to which Rousseau objects vehemently. The basis of his objection is at least in part related to population increase, a familiar concern in eighteenth-century France, where one-quarter of the babies born died before their first birthday. But Rousseau also sees reproduction as a barometer of attitudes toward parental sacrifice and the level of self-interestedness;[6] in this sense, neglect of domestic duties is a symptom of political problems.

Rousseau in several places focuses on the negative consequences of women's refusal to dedicate themselves to their mates. He responds to women's demand for education in short shrift: "They have no colleges. What a great misfortune! Would God that there were none for boys; they would be more sensibly and decently raised!" (Rousseau 1979, 363). This may be taken as an example of Rousseau's general response to the desire of some women to engage in heretofore male activities, rather than devoting themselves to their families. That is, his response is to question the worth of the (male) enterprise.

All the evils of modern civil society, according to Rousseau, are derived ultimately from the fact that personal or particular interest is the dominant rationale for action. . . . Rousseau thought that the idea that the sexes might *both* operate on these principles and that women should not be denied the right to advance their particular interests as men do was one of the most absurd and lamentable consequences of this modern philosophy. (Lange 1981, 246–47)

To the extent that women's participation in certain arenas expands the mentality of self-interested individualism, it is a cause of continued political decline. In this light, Rousseau's opposition to liberal feminism, with which he was familiar, can be understood as rooted more in an opposition to liberalism than to women's equality. And, it must be noted, Rousseau does not desire men to be self-interested individuals either.

Rousseau also says that if women do not dedicate themselves to the home it will not be a refuge for men, who will then be less devoted to the family (Rousseau 1979, 46), will seek their pleasure elsewhere, and will not fulfill duties owed to their wives and children. Her concentration on her husband, however, causes him to respect and support her—to be a good husband. Once again Rousseau's assumption is that these domestic relationships are not "natural" and that without certain "enticements" to draw people to them, isolation and egoism are likely to prevail. The arrangement he envisions is at least intended to "entice" both sexes and to involve a sharing of the burdens and benefits of social life.

In the bourgeois and aristocratic families Rousseau portrays, the family is of little importance to any of its members. The children are burdensome strangers to the parents, who find their principal pleasures separately outside of the family. None is firmly attached to the others, and each remains self-interested and essentially alone.

Rousseau's vision of the family, however sentimental, is an attempt to control the "civilized" Hobbesian individual. In a world in which the individual is posited as a self-interested actor whose only legitimate obligations are those she or he contracts, Rousseau proposes that the marriage contract should be akin to the social contract—an irrevocable commitment freely undertaken, a set of legitimate chains that makes true community possible.

Conclusion

Rousseau's endorsement of a sex-roled, nuclear, sentimental family has been contrasted with the aristocratic and bourgeois families he rejects. His advocacy of sexual differentiation has been shown to be rooted in his understanding of the human condition. He is concerned with establishing a family that can lead people to be better social creatures, capable of attachments to others that go beyond limited and destructive self-interested liaisons. His argument is that natural independence, self-absorption, and asociality, as well as social competitiveness and egoism, must be countered and that a politically effective means is found in the relations of the sexes.

Rousseau's political advocacy of the sex-roled family differs from much anti-feminist argument today. For example, contemporary opponents of extra-familial childcare tend to emphasize the "enormous care" demanded by children, "the nurture and support" only a mother can offer, or how "vitally important" to women mothering is.[7] Rousseau, as we have seen, does not think a natural nurturing ability or desire exists in either sex and does not assume that only parents can possibly tend to the health and welfare of a child. Rousseau's general defense of sexual differentiation thus also differs from more familiar ones, which frequently appeal to different sexual natures finding fulfillment in different social roles. In fact, Rousseau provides a potent critique of biological determinism that feminists can make use of.

Rousseau at least deserves some credit for not assuming, as do so many figures in the history of political thought, that a certain (usually patriarchal) form of the family is dictated by nature, for not assuming that sex roles are biological givens, for realizing the political centrality of the private, and for calling upon both sexes to transcend narrow individual interests and establish true community. He should also be distinguished from anti-feminists who make harmful or derogatory assumptions about women's potential or character; for example, he does not portray women as inherently more evil, sinful, ignorant, immoral, selfish, or selfless than men. While simply condemning Rousseau for advocating sexual differentiation at all, for whatever reasons, is tempting, it is worth at least pausing to consider his reasons, and the questions they raise for feminists.

Rousseau assumes that humans are originally asocial and self-interested, but survival requires the overcoming of both of these conditions, and that human malleability allows them to be overcome, though such a task is as difficult as it is important. It is these assumptions that lead Rousseau to endorse sexual differentiation. Its consequences are a major part of the solution to what he sees as the fundamental human dilemma. It is a solution that purports to bring parents together in a common enterprise and to bring each together with children in a situation in which they are bound by love and duty, not just self-interest. That each sex is made "incomplete" by sexual differentiation is usually held against such arrangements by feminists—yet this result is precisely what Rousseau wants, for it creates a reliable need for others, for interdependence, which nature did not take care of and which is essential to survival and non-exploitative relations. Rousseau is concerned that in the quest for equality, for each having the right to live as he or she chooses as an individual, liberals, including liberal feminists, fail to address the instrumental and inherent goods of interdependence and community. While women in his scheme are in a sense treated as means to greater ends, so are men, and the ends are held to be legitimate and advantageous to both. Each must play a part in the whole on which Rousseau's eyes are turned, a part which directs her or him toward certain things and away from others, developing some potentialities in each and leaving others dormant. And it is important to remember here that Rousseau often challenges the supposed superiority of such things as the public over the private realm, abstract over practical reason, and reason over affection. Thus, that both sexes are excluded from certain activities may not result in inequality according to his standards.

Rousseau sees the sentiment of attachment and the lessons of legitimate obligation as best learned in a loving family and as necessary developmental predecessors of unselfish dedication to the common good in the state.[8] He comes to endorse what feminism will not by his attention to questions that feminists need to show can be answered differently. What devices can we suggest to overcome exploitation and egoism, and develop community? Do the diverse forms of the family feminism supports nourish community? Can any supersede Rousseau's by both alleviating the tension between self-development and care for others, and constructively contributing to politics? It is not enough to say that competitiveness and conflict are not "natural"—indeed, Rousseau would agree! Instead, we need to work out educational, political, and familial institutional arrangements that combat the egoistic, privatistic status quo without the sexual differentiation Rousseau's remedy relies upon. Rousseau's sense of the dangers of forsaking the affectionate, sex-roled family needs to be addressed thoroughly, and showing that his means are unnecessary to and/or destructive of his own ends are avenues to pursue.

Feminist theory raises questions for Rousseau, as well. The motive behind Rousseau's advocacy of the sex-roled, affectionate family is its ability to develop communal bonds, an ability he finds other families lacking; thus, his family is a means to other ends, ends which are both necessary and desirable. Rousseau is not so crude, however, as to argue that the ends justify any means—a family which oppresses any of its members would be both unjustifiable and ineffective. That is, it would not teach us to treat others decently and to sacrifice for them. Thus, like the larger political community, in order to be legitimate the family must involve the members fairly sharing the benefits and burdens of social life, and must in fact establish the equality he deems essential to community.

Since Rousseau's family and society are based on sexual differentiation, the tasks of each sex are different. For feminists, Rousseau must show that these differences, in the family and in politics, really are compatible with equality, and thus with community. Too often anti-feminists simply claim the sexes are different but equal. In the first book devoted to the question of Rousseau's sexual politics, Joel Schwartz seems to follow this trend, for he tends to assume that the fact that women have *some* power is an argument that the sexes are *equally* empowered (Schwartz 1984). While he is right to assert that Rousseau's women are not powerless, the burden is on Rousseau to show that different kinds of empowerment really can be compatible with equality, with equal voice and respect for all. For example, is indirect authority, which is what women have most access to, as effectively heard and dignifying as the direct authority to which men have most access? Does Rousseau (or Schwartz) show that the personal and social costs, as well as the positive potential, of the sexually differentiated forms of empowerment in fact balance out?

While anti-feminists are too quick to assert that sexual differentiation poses no problem for equality, feminists should not be too quick to point to any difference as proof of inequality. The differences have to be evaluated in terms of their personal and political consequences. A closer analysis of Rousseau's "balance sheet" would not only help in resolving questions of consistency in his thought, but, in answering the question of when different can be equal, could be part of a truly feminist political theory.

Notes

1. Rousseau's discussion of mother-child relations in the state of nature is noteworthy for a number of reasons, including that it takes the fact that we are born dependent as relevant, and that it assumes female independence from males in childrearing. It is certainly intriguing that mothers tending to children is not thought by him to necessarily entail lasting emotional attachment on either side, or to lead to any further desire for communal relations. Perhaps he understands the bond between mother and child to be superficial, like bonds between corrupt social people, which also entail little attachment and fail to lead to community. It's debatable, however, whether this understanding does full justice to the reality of a nursing, teaching, protective mother, even in his state of nature.

2. The period called "childhood" is not stable. Even among lower-class families of late eighteenth-century France childhood was remarkably short by our standards. "Children in poor families had to work instead of play. From the age of four, they were considered able to work; and they were set to gathering wood, feeding chickens, or helping to card wool. . . . Children left the family at very young ages—nine to twelve—to work as apprentices and servants" (Fairchilds 1984b, 106). Further, "Work constituted the very fabric of the lives of most French women during the eighteenth century. At least ninety percent of them, from the age of fourteen on, spent most of their waking hours engaged in one or another form of work . . ." (Fox-Genovese 1984, 111).

3. Allan Bloom, Introduction to *Emile*: 4–5. The sexist pronouns are Bloom's—Rousseau thought it was equally possible for both sexes to be bourgeois in this sense, and equally undesirable, as will be explained later.

4. See the play *Master Harold and the Boys*, where a white South African is disturbed by his relationship with the black servants who have cared for him as a child. Adrienne Rich has also written of this problem for whites in the South, brought up by black mammies whom they were later taught to despise as black people. Even without the aspect of racism, Rousseau sees the danger of allowing people for whom one has no respect to be the primary caretakers of one's children.

5. Likewise, in the *Social Contract*, Book III, Chapter XV, Rousseau considers it a sign of social decay when we pay others to do our jobs, or pay taxes instead of doing the work ourselves.

6. This would explain why, in the *Social Contract*, Book III, Chapter IX, Rousseau considers the fertility rate a sign of the health of the state.

7. These quotes are taken from a roundtable discussion among contemporary conservatives in "Sex and God in American Politics," *Policy Review* (Summer 1984): 15–17. The first quote is from Phyllis Schlafly, the second from Rabbi Seymour Siegel, and the last from Midge Decter.

8. We thank one of *Hypatia*'s anonymous readers for this wording of the issue.

References

Bloom, Allan. 1985. "Rousseau on the Equality of the Sexes." *Justice and Equality Here and Now*. Frank Lucash, ed. Ithaca, New York: Cornell University Press.

Charlton, D. G. 1984. *New Images of the Natural in France: A Study in European Cultural History 1750–1800*. Cambridge: Cambridge University Press.

Christenson, Ron. 1972. "The Political Theory of Male Chauvinism: J.-J. Rousseau's Paradigm." *Midwest Quarterly* 13:291–99.

Eisenstein, Zillah. 1981. *The Radical Future of Liberal Feminism*. New York: Longman.

Fairchilds, Cissie. 1984a. *Domestic Enemies: Servants and Their Masters in Old Regime France*. Baltimore: Johns Hopkins University Press.

———. 1984b. "Women and Family." *French Women and the Age of Enlightenment*. Samia Spencer, ed. Bloomington: Indiana University Press.

Fox-Genovese, Elizabeth. 1984. "Women and Work." *French Women and the Age of Enlightenment*. Samia Spencer, ed. Bloomington: Indiana University Press.

Jirmack, P. D. 1979. "The Paradox of Sophie and Julie: Contemporary Response to Rousseau's Ideal Wife and Ideal Mother." *Women and Society in Eighteenth-Century France*. Eva Jacobs, et al., eds. London: Athlone Press.

Josephson, Matthew. 1931. *Jean-Jacques Rousseau*. New York: Harcourt, Brace & Co.

Lange, Lynda. 1981. "Rousseau and Modern Feminism." *Social Theory and Practice* 7:245–277.

———. 1979. "Rousseau: Women and the General Will." *The Sexism of Social and Political Theory*. Lorenne Clark and Lynda Lange, eds. Toronto: University of Toronto Press.

Locke, John. 1968. *The Educational Writings of John Locke*. James L. Axtell, ed. Cambridge: Cambridge University Press.

Martin, Jane Roland. 1981. "Sophie and Emile: A Case Study of Sex Bias in the History of Educational Thought." *Harvard Educational Review* 51:357–72.

Okin, Susan Moller. 1979. *Women in Western Political Thought*. Princeton, N.J.: Princeton University Press.

Rousseau, Jean-Jacques. 1979. *Emile, or on Education*. New York: Basic Books.

———. 1978. *On the Social Contract*. Roger Masters, ed. New York: St. Martin's Press.

———. 1960. *Politics and the Arts*. Ithaca: Cornell University Press.

Schwartz, Joel. 1984. *The Sexual Politics of Jean-Jacques Rousseau*. Chicago: University of Chicago Press.

Sussman, George. 1982. *Selling Mother's Milk: The Wet-Nursing Business in France: 1715–1914*. Urbana: University of Illinois Press.

Weiss, Penny. 1987. "Rousseau, Anti-Feminism, and Woman's Nature." *Political Theory* 15:81–98.

Wexler, Victor. 1976. "Made for Man's Delight: Rousseau as Anti-Feminist." *American Historical Review* 81:266–91.

3

Rousseau on Civic Virtue, Male Autonomy, and the Construction of the Divided Female

Leah Bradshaw

Rousseau is a puzzling figure. He is part of the early modern contractarian tradition that includes Hobbes and Locke, and there is a deep commitment in his writings to the notion that the only legitimate political community is one grounded in the freely given consent of equal individuals. However, Rousseau's political writings do not justify political covenant on the grounds that it assures the freedom that propels it. Freely constituted contract appears to be justified by him on the grounds that it contributes to a greater good than the guarantee of individual freedom and potential. The greater good is a form of civic virtue, a virtue that is supposed to elevate natural freedom to "moral liberty."[1]

The civic virtue that Rousseau exalts has an ambiguous basis in human nature, by his own account,[2] and does not necessarily accord with happiness.[3] Human nature, insofar as such a thing can be identified, has its roots in a prehistorical state of mutual indifference and a kind of blessed independence.[4] The civic virtue that Rousseau would have us agree to is, by contrast, a web of interconnectedness and belonging. It requires, for its realization, a monumental effort to wed human desire to the power of will and duty.[5] Three questions that compose the core of this discussion are, Why does Rousseau uphold a vision of civic virtue that struggles so tautly against natural human inclination? Who benefits from this civic virtue and how? Is Rousseau's civic virtue a plausible model of pursuit?

Civic virtue is a higher good for Rousseau, because it serves as a focus for the will, and free will is regarded by Rousseau as the highest human agency. Rousseau believes that free will can manifest itself in its higher forms only inside political covenant because political community provides the safety, the sustenance, and the education that makes it possible for men to achieve their highest potential. Man by nature may be free, but he can hardly be said to have a free will. Free will comes into play only when there is a tension between natural desire and the will to achieve (either creatively or morally). The ideal situation for Rousseau is one in which natural desire for pleasure (satiated appetites) and the cultivated will to achievement are brought into the closest possible alliance with each other. His aim is for an integrated self that can combine natural inclinations of sentience and independence with the achievement of self-directed morality.

Rousseau's vision of civic virtue has been embraced as one of the most powerful democratic projects of the modern world, but his political covenant excludes women. Political exclusion is not Rousseau's deepest offence against women, though; more serious is his artificial construction of women as tragically divided selves who must sublimate natural desire in order to sustain a civic life that bolsters male independence. It is not merely women's capacity for public participation that is thwarted; women's 'nature' has to be suppressed. Men are the ones inside Rousseau's political covenant who live out an illusion of wholeness and purity of being that at least replicates the wholeness and simplicity of their existence in the state of nature. Women clearly in Rousseau's account do not live out this beautiful illusion. It is only the male sex that potentially can be satisfied in the artificial construction of political community, because it is men who live out the illusory synthesis of their natural desire and their free will. Women, in Rousseau's account, are the foundations of this artifice, the ones who sustain politics, and indeed civilization, through the self-conscious sublimation of desire to will. Rousseau writes exten-sively about the supporting role of women, and about their permanently and tragically divided selves: they are to perpetuate a vision of freedom that is at odds with their experience. They do not get to play any public role in the drama that they have created. What women get is protection of themselves and their children. They are divided selves, responsible for perpetuating a vision of freedom that necessarily excludes them.

If political community is not natural, but willed, and if it sits on top of a natural human disposition of apolitical and solipsistic self-absorption, and if women are not accorded a share of public honor or virtue that is the reward of political engagement, and if women are not sufficiently motivated by the promise of protection for themselves and their children, then clearly this elaborate edifice of Rousseau's collapses. When and if women cease to participate in the illusory world of civic virtue, the politi-cal realm crumbles into the disarray of atomism. Freedom is destroyed. Men revert to their natural self-enveloped independence, a sort of mute version of the independence they enjoyed inside the bonds of commu-nity, and women remain as they are: divided selves, trapped between desire and will.

It seems that atomism is the necessary consequence of women's refusal to participate in the role that Rousseau has assigned them. Since civic virtue is an artificial construct, it requires the full cooperation of men and women to make it work; once that cooperation is withdrawn, there is no reason why the community should sustain itself. Rousseau is not Aristotle, and does not hold to the view that politics is the natural dis-pensation of the human condition. We can, with Rousseau, lament the waning of political connectedness and strive to bolster republican virtue, but if we do so on the grounds that this virtue is freely chosen, we are on precarious ground. For Rousseau, people commit freely to associations only when those associations benefit them, and only when those associa-tions do not conflict with natural inclination.

Civic Virtue

The development of civic virtue in Rousseau owes its origin to a masterful combination of reflections on nature, history, and imagination. Rousseau can never be accused of being a reductionist, in that unlike many political theorists, he does not anchor his prescriptions for political community in any singular or monolithic conception of what human beings are fitted for.

By nature, Rousseau conceives that human beings, particularly men, are singular and alone. They are mostly preoccupied with staying alive pleasantly: having enough to eat, enjoying shelter from the harsh elements, and satiating sexual desire whenever it hits them. They revel in the appetites.[6] As is well known, the only nonappetitive quality that Rousseau ascribes to people in the state of nature in sentience. They are moved by the suffering of others, though in a self-interested way. They are capable of identifying with the suffering of others, in much the same way that they would identify suffering in themselves.[7] Their compassion and pity is therefore diffuse: they almost see another as they see themselves. There is no altruism or other-directedness in this natural pity and compassion. People are not acquisitive and they are certainly not ambitious. Any thinking that they do appears to be nonintrospective, which is to say that they do not reflect on their own motives. They are "whole" in that they are not split (in the Hegelian mode) between consciousness and self-consciousness. Rousseau idealizes this wholeness, though not necessarily its stupidity.

Initially, Rousseau characterizes men and women as equally sentient and indifferent in the natural state. Both live in the present, without regard for future sustenance or safety. Nature, however, places an extraordinary burden on women, and that is pregnancy and birth. Rousseau is cagey on whether women and men share the same levels of sexual desire. At times, he depicts women's natural sexuality as timid, and this seems to fit with physiological differences. The man penetrates, and the woman receives. The natural dispensation of women as receptors of male sexuality does not speak automatically to levels of desire, though. Elsewhere, Rousseau seems to suggest that the sexual desire of women is constant and insatiable, whereas male sexual desire is intermittent.[8] In any case, coupling between men and women in the state of nature, Rousseau makes clear, is random, nonmonogamous, and appetitive (any partner will do).[9] Sexual desire is not connected to the consciousness of reproduction, so in fact, there is not really any convincing argument in Rousseau for why coupling by nature should be primarily or exclusively between men and women.

Coupling between men and women does occur, and women conceive children and give birth. On this natural difference, much rests. Women become attached to their children. Rousseau thinks that this natural attachment grows initially from a mutual interdependence of mother and child. The mother's body swells with milk, and the natural relief is in the nursing of the child.[10] Through this natural, physiological interdependence, a mutual attachment grows. This is the *only* binding natural attachment of one human being to another that is discernible in Rousseau's state of nature. The ramifications of this natural bond are fuzzy in Rousseau's account. On the one hand, he suggests that women with small children are, as a dyad, as independent and self-sufficient as they were without infants.[11] On the other hand, Rousseau leaps from these reflections to his postulation that some version of the family develops. Women are rendered less mobile and dexterous when they have children to care for, and a pattern developed whereby women stayed close to the hearth with their children, and men became attached to women and children as providers and protectors.[12]

Little is said by Rousseau about whether this tale about the development of the 'natural' family owes its persuasiveness to the fact that women corralled men into a role as providers and protectors, or whether men developed an affection for their own children. In a state where there is little acquisition (and so no property to protect and hand down), and where children can hardly be thought to contribute to wealth and happiness, it is difficult to see how Rousseau could argue that men develop an easy affection for children. It makes more sense to imagine that women have a vested interest in soliciting men to care for themselves and their loved dependents. It is women, after all, whose bodies demand of them that they care for others. It is women who by nature become fragmented from the natural solipsism of the wandering nomad. Women and their children, by Rousseau's own admission, are the first and only natural human society.[13]

Rousseau says that the origin of inequality can be traced to he who first enclosed a piece of land and called it his.[14] His arguments about property and the way in which possession of it has distorted human relations are well known. Rousseau must mean here the origin of inequality among men, or families, because we have already identified a natural inequality that is rooted in the bodily differences between men and women. Moreover, before the introduction of private property, Rousseau had talked extensively about the emergence of pride in human relations. The first instance of competition and rivalry must have occurred, he tells us, when men dancing around a fire struggled to see who could outjump another, so as to establish his superiority.[15] Rousseau implies that wherever two or more are gathered, there is immediately a basis for comparison. One begins to see himself not mirrored in the other, but as rival to the other. This is the beginning of self-consciousness. But perhaps it is the beginning of self-consciousness only for men. Women are already self-conscious, because their very beings have been split into two by the natural occurrence of birth. By nature, women's sense of self is both self-same and other (although not necessarily competitive and acrimonious); men's sense of self is by nature self-same, and becomes other only through the introduction of competitive social relations. If this is correct, then the introduction of social relations, and community, only expands what is natural to women who have children; the same set of relations corrupts, or at least transforms, what is natural to men.

The combination of pride and property leads to the morass of history, Rousseau tells us, in which arts, letters, and wealth preponderate. Language becomes sophisticated; deception becomes rife; people use one another in all sorts of ways to advance their own self-interest. The more people become interconnected and interdependent, the greater their unhappiness.[16] As usual though, for Rousseau, the root of this unhappiness is ambiguous. People have lost their natural compassion and pity for one another, precisely because every man is perceived as a rival and a threat; at the same time, they (men in particular) have lost their sense of wholeness and self-sufficiency, which was complexly intertwined with natural compassion and pity. They are encumbered with duties that they resent and ambitions that rail against their desires. Men become split consciousnesses, divided against themselves. The problem for Rousseau is, How do we become whole again?

There are two routes to redemption that Rousseau seeks: one in *The Social Contract*, and one in the *Emile*. There is considerable debate about whether these two works compliment each other, or whether they are two distinct paths: one political, in the reform of institutions; and one personal, in the creative construct of the romantic family.[17] In *The Social Contract*, the task is to build a society governed by a general will, in which each individual, while giving himself to the whole community, gives himself to no one. The echoes of Rousseau's natural man are strong here: one is both self and other without tension between the two. The political community of *The Social Contract* is Rousseau's crowning feat of nature, history, and imagination. We are dealing now with a hyper-self-conscious modern man, who longs to fuse his historically educated self with natural sentience. Through an act of political will, man becomes self-governing in such a way that his rational self is in concord with his passions and desires.

The *Social Contract* requires myth-making on a grand scale. A legislator is required who can give a community laws without being bound to them. The participants in the General Will must understand their commitment as one that is simultaneously willed by them, yet ordained by mystical forces that are beyond human caprice. In order for the social contract to work, men must obey laws that they desire. The goal is an undivided self. Civic virtue requires a civil religion that will penetrate the core of every soul, so that no man will feel conflict between what society demands of him and what he wills for himself,[18] an act of political will that shall undo historical forces that have made man into the competitive and contentious creature that he is. The historical degeneration of natural man is replaced by the art of politics. From the historical genesis of prideful and possessive man, fused with natural sentience, and bound by will, emerges the civic community.

Emile

The *Emile* is the story of the education of one man and one woman so that they will be able to form a harmonious nuclear family within a political community. Throughout the *Emile* are Rousseau's castigations of his contemporaries. He criticizes men for their wanton and cavalier attitudes, and he judges French women harshly for their coquettishness, their seduction, and their manipulations. What the *Emile* aims for is the education of Emile as a self-sufficient and self-satisfied man, combined with his role as the husband and father that is required of him in civil society.[19] One can argue about whether the *Emile* is a practical guide to conjugal relations, or whether it is meant to be fit as a microcosm into the larger picture of the *Social Contract*, but in either case what is interesting about this book is the artifice with which Rousseau works in order to produce Emile.

Emile is tutored carefully throughout his early life, principally so that he will cultivate an undivided soul. A dominant theme in all Rousseau's works is the damage that he thinks is wrought to human contentment by the anxieties of divided motives. Unlike what would have occurred in the natural state, in which an infant is raised by its mother, Emile is treated as an orphan, responsive to only one male figure. His governor is not by nature interdependent with this child, in the way that natural mothers are with their infants, and his objective is to make Emile into as self-sufficient a human being as possible.

From an early age, Emile is steered through his developmental phases so that he will be able to conquer himself. The tutor makes sure that when the child is hungry, he is fed; when he is tired, he sleeps. No order is imposed upon him, so that he will not become habituated to, or dependent upon, externally imposed routines. The child is made to think that the world is at one with his will as far as possible.[20] This means that Emile should not get into the pattern of having to accept authority against his inclinations. He should never experience the thrill of asserting his will against the will of others bigger and more powerful than he. Emile is to be without resentment, and without anger. He must also learn to conquer fear, so that he will not have a slavish disposition (87–89).

The child ought to get everything he needs, but "the words *obey* and *command* will be proscribed from his lexicon, and even more so, *duty* and *obligation* . . . arrange it so that as long as he is struck only by objects of sense, all his ideas stop at sensations; arrange it so that on all sides he perceive around him only the physical world. Without that, you may be sure that he will not listen to you at all, or that he will get fantastic notions of the moral world of which you speak to him, notions that you will never in your life be able to blot out" (89).

The child should be guided by his own sense of pleasure. Rousseau is disdainful of employing reason with Emile (which could only make him feel stupid) and of using force to govern him (this will only make him rebellious, devious, and cowering).[21] The conventional means of social and political restraint are not to enter Emile's childhood, precisely because they will set up in his young soul the conflict between what he desires and what he cannot do. Rousseau wants Emile to experience a wholeness of pursuit that is not possible once one experiences the constraint of pleasure by duty and obligation.[22]

Emile's education is not a learned one, at least not initially. He is to be given no books, save one, the tale *Robinson Crusoe*, a story about a man who survives and flourishes unto himself in the midst of nature. The tutor exposes Emile to nature, and natural processes, but preaches no science to him. Emile is to know nothing in early childhood about morality, poetry, science, or any other cultivated art. He is, in short, to be raised as much as possible as a natural man. "Everyone wants to be happy," Rousseau writes, "but to succeed in being so, one would have to begin by knowing what happiness is. The happiness of the natural man is as simple as his life. It consists in not suffering; health, freedom, and the necessities of life constitute it. The happiness of the moral man is something else. But that kind of happiness is not the question here" (177). Emile's education to be a moral man waits for the onset of puberty, when sexual passion overtakes him, and he moves beyond his self-containment to the raging desire for another.[23] Critical for Rousseau, however, is the early childhood from birth to age twelve. If the tutor is successful in educating Emile up to this point, he will have established a core that is resistant to all vice. "The most dangerous period of life is that from birth to age twelve. This is the time when errors and vice germinate without one's yet having any instrument for destroying them; and by the time the instrument comes [i.e., reason], the roots are so deep that it is too late to rip them out" (93).

If the most dangerous period of life, according to Rousseau, is the period from birth to age twelve, the most critical juncture is the onset of puberty, when sexual passion dominates. The task is to channel this passion toward a fruitful end. On the nature of sexual passion, and its natural object, in the *Emile*, Rousseau is obscure. Rousseau writes: "The source of our passions, the origin and principle of all the others, the only one born with man and which never leaves him so long as he lives is self-love—a primitive, innate passion which is anterior to every other, and of which all others are in a sense only modifications" (213). A child naturally loves himself, and secondarily loves those near to him because they are of use to him. Because the child will not be able always to live alone (214), it will be difficult for him to direct his passions toward that which is good for him. He has to live among others, and this means necessarily that he will have to take into account the needs and desires of others. Upon puberty in particular, Emile will have to change course so as to accommodate himself to the world of *amour-propre*. Rousseau explains that a great exercise of "art and care" is required to prevent sexual passion within the arena of *amour-propre* from contaminating Emile's cultivated sense of self-sufficiency.

Love, apart from self-love, is for Rousseau entirely a product of imagination and will. There is nothing natural about it. "Love has been presented as blind because it has better eyes than we do and sees relations we are not able to perceive. For a man who had no idea of merit or beauty, every woman would be equally good, and the first comer would always be the most lovable. Far from arising from nature, love is the rule and the bridle of nature's inclinations. It is due to love that, except for the beloved object, one sex ceases to be anything for the other" (214). Love for Rousseau is really the civilized and preferred way of transforming neediness and interdependency into an idealized condition. It is a fact that in political community, human beings are interdependent and interconnected. It is weakness that makes them so. It is our "common miseries" that make us aware of our common humanity. "Every attachment," according to Rousseau, "is a sign of insufficiency" (221). A truly happy being is a godlike being, but since men are not gods, they cannot be alone. (In the state of nature, they came closest to it; in civil society they cannot even try to approximate this aloneness).

Again, we might question whether Rousseau's ruminations on "human miseries," and the need for attachment that grows from them, really applies equally to men and women. A case can be made that women, insofar as they are mothers, develop a natural attachment that predates the kind of interdependency that Rousseau argues is brought about by neediness in social relations. There is nothing artificial about the interdependency of mother and child; Rousseau suggests that love is the "bridle of nature's inclinations," but by his own account, love of mothers toward their children may be the expansion, rather than the bridle, of nature's inclinations. It may be simply natural sexuality, and not weakness, that makes women connected to their children. For men, however, Rousseau makes it clear that interdependence with others, especially specific women, is a sign of weakness and of deviation from the natural state. Rousseau's model for "love" as the second best thing to being alone applies much more easily to his characterization of men than women.[24]

Emile's neediness for others can be tempered by being channeled first into friendship. It is important to acquaint the pupil first with his attachment to the species as a whole, and only secondarily to the female sex. This attachment is made by identifying with the sufferings of others as one's own. The adolescent boy who is made aware of his common humanity with others will be affectionate and gentle; the adolescent who is acquainted too early with women will become debauched and cruel. This is because identifying with others whose needs and sufferings are similar to one's own breeds compassion. But the experience of sexual passion directed at women breeds a sense of difference, rather than commonality. Emile's independence is seriously threatened by his sexual urges. Rousseau writes, at Emile's sexual awakening: "He was free, and now I see him enslaved. So long as he loved nothing, he depended only on himself and his needs. As soon as he loves, he depends on his attachments. Thus are formed the first bonds linking him to his species" (233).

Rousseau's project, at this critical juncture of puberty, is to direct Emile's passions in such a way that Emile does not feel enslaved; that he will be able to love in such a way as to sustain a moral order, yet be able to retain his independence.[25] If love is an artifice, why does Rousseau value it? Because love, properly imagined and willed, produces a moral order, and properly conceived moral order is in the end preferable to the unconsciousness of the state of nature. If "the first voices of conscience arise out of the first movements of the human heart in the state of nature . . . the first notions of good and bad are born of the *sentiments* of love and hate." Justice and goodness, which Rousseau values above the amorality of the state of nature, require the cultivation of the sentiment of love. "Love of men derived from love of self is the principle of human justice" (235).

Emile needs a companion, and Rousseau says that she "ought to be a woman as Emile is a man—that is to say, she ought to have everything which suits the constitution of her species and her sex in order to fill her place in the physical and moral order" (*Emile*, 357). The only thing we know with certainty about men and women, says Rousseau, is that what they have in common belongs to the species, and in that which they differ, they belong to their respective sexes. The differences, Rousseau conjectures, must have a moral influence, and this conclusion can be drawn from our senses and our experience. What sorts of differences does Rousseau identify as having a critical moral importance? The woman is made to please man (358). She "ought to make herself agreeable to man instead of arousing him"; she ought to exude modesty and shame (the tools with which nature has armed the weak to enslave the strong).

However, it is doubtful whether Rousseau believes uncategorically that these are natural laws of sexual difference. On the dictum that woman is made to please man, Rousseau comments that this is necessary, but he does not say that it is natural. What he does say is that power is the male's by nature in sexual relations: male strength is not the law of love, but the law of nature. The female's subjugation to the male, by contrast, is a way of constraining desire and making use of it, and Rousseau says clearly that this subjugation is a product of the union of *amour-propre* and desire (358). Shame and modesty is required of women in order to sustain amicable relations between the sexes, because, Rousseau suggests, female sexuality is all encompassing and insatiable.[26] Women do not even have the natural instinctive brake on sexuality that most animals do. What would be the alternative, if women were deprived of modesty? Rousseau answers: "To wait until they no longer care for men is equivalent to waiting until they are no longer good for anything" (Emile, 359). Whether the female share the males desires or not, she repulses the male, and uses the violence of her charms to control sexual relations.

The strength of males is then actually a chimera in some sense, for Rousseau says that it is an invariable law of nature that women have more facility to excite desire than men have the capacity to satisfy them.[27] Men may have immoderate passions that overwhelm them intermittently, but they learn to govern these passions by reason, according to Rousseau. That reason would appear to be born of self-interest: by inflicting himself on unwilling partners, a man risks his life.[28] Women have unlimited desires, and they are to constrain these desires by modesty. Modesty does not accord with natural desire for women, but neither does it necessarily accord with self-interest. The only reason that Rousseau gives for why women should willingly take on the mantle of shame and modesty, is the concern for their children. She needs care during pregnancy, rest during childbirth, and "a soft and sedentary life to suckle her children," and she can best provide for these by cultivating gallantry and strength, and the pride of these things, in men. The woman alone makes a man love his children, and he must have the confidence that they are his (Emile, 361).

The "moral differences" between men and women, then, are not rooted unequivocally in nature. The pattern of behavior that Rousseau has identified as moral in sexual relations between men and women seems to support a natural basis for male sexuality (it is intermittent, much as in the state of nature, although it is to be fixed on a monogamous object), and a conventional basis for female sexuality (unlimited desire is to be constrained by modesty and shame). Of course, in supporting morality in sexual relations, women are engaged in the protection of their children, a responsibility that is natural to them, but in assuming the modesty that belongs properly to them, they are willfully subordinating desire and independence. Men forfeit their independence, but not their natural desire. Everything that Rousseau says about Sophie can in some senses be traced to her divided self. Sophie must be educated to separate her obligations from her desires; or perhaps a better way of putting it is to say that Sophie must learn to separate one natural desire (the preservation of her children) from another (her independence). Rousseau says that women have to do this, because they have desires and needs that demand of them that they enlist the help of men. Men have sexual desire for, but no need of, women. "By the very law of nature, women are at the mercy of men's judgments, as much for their own sake as for that of their children" (*Emile*, 364). In sum, Sophie has to sublimate part of her natural self in order to persuade Emile to care for her and her children. Emile has no natural disposition to do this, and he will not do it willingly if he experiences his responsibilities as coming into conflict with his natural desires. Sophie must then make it her life's project to support the illusion of Emile's independence, and to sustain moral and political order at the same time.[29]

In *The Letter to M. D'Alembert on the Theatre*, Rousseau says: "Even if it could be denied that a special sentiment of chasteness was natural to women, would it be any the less true that in society their lot ought to be a domestic and retired life, and that they ought to be raised in principles appropriate to it? If the timidity, chasteness, and modesty which are proper to them are social inventions, it is in society's interest that women acquire these qualities; they must be cultivated in women, and any women who disdains them offends good manners [morals]."[30]

The principles appropriate to a domestic and retired life are outlined in detail in *Emile*. Just as Emile's education must begin early, so that he will be raised properly to be the independent, self-sufficient, and moral being that Rousseau regards as the civilized maturity for men, Sophie's education must begin early too, so that she will be the submissive, dependent, and moral being that Rousseau regards as the civilized maturity for women. Girls have to be constrained very early; if this is a misfortune, Rousseau remarks, then it is one that women must accept as necessary. "All their lives they will be enslaved to the most continual and the most severe of constraints—that of the proprieties. They must first be exercised in constraint, so that it never costs them anything to tame all their caprices in order to submit them to the will of others" (*Emile*, 369).

Since young girls tend toward excess in the exercise of freedom, they must be habituated from an early age to the repression of this tendency. "Do not allow for a single instant in their lives that they no longer know any restraint" (370). From this habituated docility, Rousseau remarks that they will be well served, for women have to be prepared for a life subjected to a man, or more broadly, to the judgments of men. "As she is made to obey a being who is so imperfect, often so full of vices, and always so full of defects as man, she ought to learn early to endure even injustice and to bear a husband's wrongs without complaining" (370).

Sophie's education is to be primarily at the feet of her mother, who is already habituated into the role that Rousseau has designated as appropriate for women. This is far different from Emile's education, which is an "unnatural one" insofar as it takes place not in the care of his mother, or even his mother and father, but in the hands of a tutor. Sophie is to be trained both to please men and to be proficient at domestic tasks. She must learn the art of adornment, but only so as to make herself pleasing, not dazzling. A beautiful women is a plague to her husband. She must learn to be pleasing, but not truthful, in speech; to be polite; to cultivate taste rather than knowledge; to accept the authority of religion without questioning its principles. Industriousness and cleanliness are high in the order of useful qualities that she must acquire in order to run a successful household.

Unlike Emile, who is educated toward the aspiration of combining independence with political and moral obligation, Sophie is educated to sublimate independence into her subordination to others.[31] Sophie defines herself by what others, and particularly men, think of her. "Sophie has a mind that is agreeable without being brilliant, and solid without being profound—a mind about which people do not say anything, because they never find in it either more or less than what they find in their own minds" (*Emile*, 395, 396).[32] Whereas Emile is to be indifferent to the opinions of others—indeed, this is his great strength—Sophie is to be governed by opinion.[33]

The separate and distinct educations of Emile and Sophie are intended to make them complement each other so that they can form a union that will sustain a family within moral and political order. The partnership, according to Rousseau, "produces a moral person," of which woman is the eye and man the arm. In their dependence upon each other, the woman learns from the man what must be seen, and the man from the woman what must be done. Emile is the "theoretical" one, and Sophie the "practical" one (*Emile*, 377). How much of this union owes its craft to nature, and how much to artifice, is not stated clearly by Rousseau, except, as usual, by his pointing to the disasters of any other configuration. "If woman could ascend to general principles as well as man can, and if man had as good a mind for details as woman does, they would always be independent of one another, they would live in eternal discord, and their partnership could not exist" (377).

Rousseau may be right about the alternative, but he is disingenuous when he says that "in the harmony that reigns between them [man and woman], everything tends to the common end; they do not know who contributes more. Each follows the prompting of the other; each obeys and both are masters" (*Emile*, 377). It is Sophie who obeys Emile, and it is Emile who is master. Sophie may exert some control in the manipulations of emotions, in the seductiveness of her sexuality, and in her flattery of Emile's pride, but these are the designs of the oppressed. In order for the partnership to work, Sophie has to maintain a split consciousness, in which she consciously manipulates her sexuality in order to sustain the illusion of harmony. She is supposed to run the household in an authoritative way, while at the same time upholding the public status of her husband as the real authority. She has to carefully orchestrate sexual relations so that she remains an object of sexual desire for her husband, constraining his passions within this monogamous relationship.

What are the convincing reasons, in the end, for why both men and women would comply with this elaborate artifice of deception and illusion? For women, there is only one explanation for why they would want to govern men, while perpetuating the illusion of obeying them: "Woman has everything against her—our defects, her timidity, and her weakness" (*Emile*, 371). Women thus participate in this illusion for conscious and calculated reasons: to protect themselves and their children, by enlisting the support of men inside civil society. Men, by contrast, participate in this illusion because they are unaware of it. Emile is attracted to Sophie because everything has been arranged so that he will focus his desire on her particular being.[34] Emile will love Sophie and her children, but only if this elaborate artifice is maintained, one in which Emile is led to believe that it is within this artifice that his passions and his purpose can best be served. It is incumbent upon Sophie to sustain this illusion.

The success of Rousseau's project really depends, in the end, on how badly women want, or need, the support of men to protect part of what is important to them: the sustenance of their children, to whom they are attached by nature. It also depends on whether women are willing to forego the other part of what is important to them—their independence. Rousseau has made it plain that by nature, women are neither weak nor timid. The fact that they bear children has enormous consequences for them, primarily in the fact that women become attached by nature to others, whereas men do not. Rousseau, however, has nowhere made the argument that the fact that women become mothers threatens or challenges their fundamental autonomy from any human beings other than their own children.

The construction of moral and political community, and the sustaining of the family as the foundation of that community, depends above all upon the *willful* sublimation in women of part of what is natural to them. Men, however, must be convinced that moral and political order makes them whole, rather than divided. They must be able to function within the family and within the social and political order in a way that appears to bolster, rather than threaten, their natural independence.[35] They must then, be the masters of women, arbiters of their sexuality, and owners of their children. Rousseau cautions: "Never has a people perished from an excess of wine; all perish from the disorder of women."[36]

Conclusion

Rousseau fascinates us, I think, because he articulates so powerfully the centrality of the individual, and the nascent conflict between desire and will that seems so much at the heart of contemporary anxiety. *Emile*, in particular, is a remarkable analysis of the kind of self-consciousness that informs an individual's development. Rousseau begins with the premise that man is alone. He may be connected to others in a hazy way, through sentience and pity, but the strongest assertion of nature, according to Rousseau, is toward independence.

Starting with this assumption, Rousseau attempts to build human connectedness, either politically or domestically, on an intricate grid of self-interest, passion, and moral reflection. Human beings are supposed to work toward an integration that will provide for the continuation of the species and the possibility of moral virtue and sociability. For this to work well, the inclination toward solitude and independence that is man's by nature has to be molded into this artifice. Rousseau is adamant that suppression of what is natural will lead only to rebellion and resistance.

Rousseau's assumptions about what is natural to man, however, fit uneasily on women, even by his own account. Women, he suggests, by nature, enjoy the same independence as do men until women become mothers. Then, by nature, they cease to be solitary, although there is no necessary reason in Rousseau's account why women and their offspring should expand their attachments to include men. Rousseau is silent on whether he thinks that the natural attachment of mothers to children alters their sense of themselves (they become less independent), although it seems pretty clear that the first human attachments between mother and child are born of mutual interdependence, then affection.

Everything that Rousseau says about the origins of civil society—that mutual need and dependency occasioned community, that pride and comparison established possessiveness in human relations, that the same pride made of easy sexual relations a battleground of competition—accords with his analysis of men in the state of nature. It does not necessarily accord with the analysis of women in the same state, at least women in their relationships with their children. It is as though the birth of children, the natural consequence of female sexuality, were a mutation of what is natural to both sexes.

Everything that Rousseau says about the ideal of family, and civil society, also accords with his analysis of men in the state of nature. The objective is to form domestic, or political and moral, union, in such a way that natural independence appears not to have been thwarted. The male is to become attached to the female and her children in an obligatory way that will leave him with the self-understanding that he is free. This is accomplished only through a web of deception, in which the woman self-consciously supports this illusion.

One might want to argue that this artifice serves the interests of women more than it does men. If women do indeed have a "natural" attachment to their children, and if their primary concern is the maintaining and sustenance of that attachment, then this might make sense. But it does not make sense on Rousseau's terms. For one thing, he has said nothing about how the birth of children transforms female consciousness in such a way that they abandon the desire for autonomy and independence that Rousseau has ascribed to all people by nature. He has spoken of the affection that grows between mother and child as a consequence of habit, but he has not expounded upon whether this attachment fundamentally alters the female's autonomy. He seems to suggest that mothers, by nature, accept their responsibility of motherhood with nary a blink. They pick up the infants and make their ways in the world much in the way that they did when they were alone. The only way that this construction of Rousseau's could work, is if women who have children have a *completely* different kind of self-interest than do men, occasioned by the fact that they are mothers. There is nothing in Rousseau to suggest that this is the case.

The most severe reading of Rousseau, following upon his own views about natural autonomy and self-love, is that women and their children constitute one kind of independence peculiar to their sex; and men constitute another, more solipsistic, independence peculiar to their sex. Sexual desire is not naturally identified in any way with procreation for men, either before or after they conceive children. They have no natural responsibility for children, no natural affection for them, and no claim on them. The artifice of civil society establishes all three. This may be thought to benefit both sexes, but only at the cost of a self-induced fractured state in women, and a fragile and ultimately deluded notion of autonomy in men. Surely such a scheme is destined to fail.

Rousseau's artifice may illuminate the dominant self-understandings of our age. Looking at the moral controversies of contemporary liberal democracies, we see a standoff between those who argue for the bolstering of the traditional family, and all the necessary institutional supports that seem to be required to sustain it; and those who argue for the autonomy of individuals, male and female, in choosing their sexuality; and for the rights of women in particular, to choose whether they will be mothers or not, with or without men to assist them. Both scenarios are present in Rousseau. If Rousseau's characterization of the natural proclivities of people is right, the scenario attached to the autonomy of individuals is the more likely to win out because it would have its grounding in natural inclination. The artifice of the family is less inclined to prevail, because it requires monumental acts of will that have to conquer natural impulses. Certainly, it does not make sense for women, who would have to consciously relinquish any independent desire and would remain forever divided against themselves.

The really big question, of course, is whether Rousseau is right about nature, history and virtue. However one construes the relations among these things, the most powerful voice in Rousseau is the one of nature: the voice that claims that human beings are basically solitary, sentient, and compassionate, but asocial. Rousseau proscribes this nature for both sexes, but female 'nature' is somewhat complicated by the fact that it is women who give birth to, and develop natural affection for, children. The manner in which Rousseau constructs social relations sets up a tragic dilemma in women: independence versus 'care'. But this dilemma may be more a product of artifice than of true tragedy, especially since Rousseau has identified a unitary self as definitive for both sexes in nature, even that sex that bears children. In the final analysis, for Rousseau, the divided female self is constructed as a necessary support for political and moral community, and for sustaining the illusion of independence and autonomy for men. Women may be Rousseau's most artful construction of all.

Notes

1. In *The Social Contract* (trans. G. D. H. Cole [London: Everyman, 1973]), Rousseau writes: "What man loses by the social contract is his natural liberty and an unlimited right to everything he tries to get and succeeds in getting; what he gains is civil liberty and the proprietorship of all he possesses. . . . What man acquires in the civil state is 'moral liberty'" (178).

2. Rousseau writes that "the mere impulse of nature is slavery, while obedience to a law which we prescribe to ourselves is liberty" (*The Social Contract*, 178). This suggests that "moral liberty" is a work of artifice that transcends, rather than rests upon, natural inclination.

3. Speaking to Emile, in his book about the education of one man, Rousseau says that the virtue Emile has acquired surpasses the happiness that he would have experienced as a natural man. Of Emile's cultivated virtue, Rousseau writes: "Oh, Emile, where is the good man who owes nothing to his country. Whatever country it is, he owes it what is most precious to man—the morality of his actions and the love of virtue. If he had been born in the heart of the woods, he would have lived happier and freer. But he would have had nothing to combat in order to follow his inclinations and thus he would have been good without merit; he would not have been virtuous" (*Emile*, trans. Allan Bloom [New York: Basic Books, 1979], 473).

4. Natural man is "solitary, indolent and perpetually accompanied by danger." Rousseau, *Discourse on the Origin of Inequality* (trans. G. D. H. Cole, in *The Social Contract and Discourses* [London: Everyman, 1973], 53). Men in a state of nature have "no moral relations or determinate obligations—they are neither good nor bad, virtuous nor vicious" (64). What men do have is natural compassion, which originates in self-love and extends to the preservation of the species. Rousseau's maxim for the state of nature is: "do good to yourself and as little evil as possible to others" (69).

5. In *Emile*, Rousseau praises Emile for having learned to be virtuous in spite of his passions. After the conclusion of his education, Emile is prepared to embrace willingly his duties as a man and citizen. Rousseau characterizes this as a "conquering" of himself. Emile's embracing of political and moral order have made him free, but only in the sense that "they have taught [Emile] to reign over himself" (*Emile*, 473).

6. For savage man, "his desires never go beyond his physical wants. The only goods he recognizes in the universe are food, a female and sleep: the only evils he fears are pain and hunger" (*Discourse on the Origin of Inequality*, 55).

7. Pity is central to Rousseau's understanding of natural compassion. The fact that pity originates in a kind of self-interest strengthens the argument for natural compassion, according to Rousseau, because it means that the concern for others is coincidental with the concern for oneself. Rousseau writes: "Were it true that pity is no more than a feeling, which puts us in the place of the sufferer, a feeling obscure yet lively in a savage, developed yet feeble in civilized man; the truth would have no consequence than to confirm my argument. Compassion must, in fact, be the stronger, the more the animal beholding any kind of distress identifies himself with the animal that suffers" (*Discourse on the Origin of Inequality*, 68).

8. In *Emile*, Rousseau describes the "audacity" of the male sex and the "timidity" of the female sex. He suggests that the differing sexual responses are part of the merging of *amour-propre* and

desire, that is to say, that they are cultivated responses. There is also some suggestion, however, that these responses are natural to the sexes. In defense of the natural argument, Rousseau argues that it is unlikely that nature would have bestowed an equal audacity and abandon on both sexes when the consequences (namely, pregnancy) are so radical for the females. But this means that it is the *knowledge* of pregnancy, and not necessarily desire, that makes the critical difference. Since Rousseau has made the case elsewhere that coupling in the state of nature is random, without forethought or knowledge of consequences, his argument for natural difference in desire is somewhat weakened.

In fact, Rousseau goes on to say that *if* reserve did not impose on one sex the moderation that nature imposes on the other, the result would be the ruination of both. In this case, Rousseau implies that moderation belongs to the male by nature (his desire is intermittent), whereas reserve belongs to the female by design. Sexual reserve in females is an acquired and rational response to the potentiality for motherhood. If women actually acted on their desires, without reserve, "men would be tyrannized by women" and men "would see themselves dragged to their death without ever being able to defend themselves" (*Emile*, 358–59).

9. "The sexes united without design, as accident, opportunity or inclination brought them together, nor had they any great need of words to communicate their designs to each other; and they parted with the same indifference" (*Discourse on the Origin of Inequality*, 59).

10. "The mother at first gave suck to her children for her own sake; and afterwards, when habit had made them dear, for them" (*Discourse on the Origin of Inequality*, 59).

11. Primitive people are without permanent dwellings, according to Rousseau. This is no obstacle to their survival, because they have two legs to run and two arms to defend themselves with. In the case of women with infants, "their mothers are able to carry them with ease" (*Discourse on the Origin of Inequality*, 52).

12. The first expansion of the human heart, Rousseau tells us, arose from a "novel situation," which united husbands and wives, fathers and children, under one roof. The *habit* of being together, he says, "gave rise to the first feelings known to humanity, conjugal love and paternal affection." The women, consequentially, became more sedentary and stayed close to the hearth, and the men took on the role of hunter-protector (*Discourse on the Origin of Inequality*, 79–80). By Rousseau's own account, this novel situation, born of habit, is not really the first expansion of the human heart. The truly first expansion, occasioned by the habit of lactation, is the affection between mother and child in nature.

13. In this I concur with Allan Bloom, in his discussion in *The Closing of the American Mind*.

14. This is the opening sentence of part II of the *Discourse on the Origin of Inequality*. "The first man who, having enclosed a piece of ground, bethought himself of saying 'This is mine,' and found people simple enough to believe him, was the real founder of civil society" (76).

15. Rousseau says that "the first step towards inequality, and at the same time, towards vice" was occasioned by comparison. "Whoever sang or danced best, whoever was the handsomest, the strongest, the most dexterous, or the most eloquent, came to be of most consideration" (*Discourse on the Origin of Inequality*, 81). Importantly, these comparisons are associated by Rousseau with the tension between the sexes, exacerbated by their confinement to proximate spaces. Men and women "assembled together with nothing else to do" seems to be the catalyst for competition and display.

16. "From the moment that one man began to stand in need of the help of another; from the moment it appeared advantageous to any one man to have enough possessions for two, equality disappeared, property was introduced, work became indispensable, and vast forests became smiling fields, which man had to water with the sweat of his brow, and where slavery and misery were soon seen to germinate and grow up with the crops" (*Discourse on the Origin of Inequality*, 83).

17. I agree with Tracy Strong, who says that although the pursuits of *Emile* and *The Social Contract* are similar—the task is to discover how one can experience the common in oneself—*Emile* is a route to this end in which public education and public space are not possible. We are left with domestic education (Tracy Strong, *The Politics of the Ordinary* [Thousand Oaks, Calif.: Sage, 1994], 105).

18. In *The Social Contract*, civil religion is critical in performing this synthesis. The civil religion is to be a profession of faith without which a man cannot be a good citizen or a faithful subject. It must perform the function of making him "love his duty" (274).

19. Rousseau says that it is the good son, the good father, and the good husband who makes the good citizen (*Emile*, 363). This means that Emile has to be deeply embedded in various levels of belonging and obligation that will bind him to civil society. At the same time, however, Emile is to understand himself as being completely free. Emile tells his tutor that he has learned that freedom is not the opposite of necessity, but is the embrace of it. "It is you, my master, who have made me free in teaching me to yield to necessity" (472). Emile's only chain is his sexual passion, and he embraces this chain willingly and its exclusive attachment to Sophie (473).

20. Rousseau's view is that children do not experience any thwarting of the will when they run up against natural obstacles, any more than natural man experiences a collision with his natural world. What intensifies their will is the resistance of other wills. Consequently Rousseau's advice is "As long as children find resistance in things and never in wills, they will become neither rebellious nor irascible, and will preserve their health better" (*Emile*, 66).

21. There is no object more deserving of pity, Rousseau says, than a fearful child (*Emile*, 89). And reason applied to a child, who cannot possible grasp it, only makes him "stupid" (*Emile*, 89).

22. Emile's education is constrained by artifice, but only so that he will come to know his constraints as given. The important thing for Rousseau is that the child not know that his education is contrived; else he may resist its imposition. Emile must never see his early education as a set of commands imposed by the will of another, but rather as the bonds of necessity. An absolute maxim of Rousseau's in Emile's early education is that he see the necessity in things, "never in the caprice of man" (*Emile*, 91). In this way, Emile will be habituated to the coincidence of freedom and necessity, and later, open to the fusion of freedom and duty.

23. Rousseau remarks in the *Discourse on the Origin of Inequality* that of all the passions that stir the hearts of men, "there is one that makes the sexes necessary to one another, and is extremely ardent and impetuous; a terrible passion that braves danger, surmounts all obstacles and in its transports seems calculated to bring destruction on the human race which it is really destined to preserve." Rousseau says this in the context of a discussion about *natural* passions, although it seems that the "boundless rage" of sexual passion, as Rousseau characterizes it, owes its character to what he elsewhere calls "moral love": the kind of passion that values exclusive attachments over the diffuse and indiscriminate sexuality of the state of nature (69).

In any case, sexuality is problematic, and disturbs natural equilibrium once it becomes attached to exclusive objects. Tracy Strong says that while Rousseau sees sex as a necessary thing, he does not regard it as a "human" quality. "The terms of the sexual relations are precisely those of inequality and dissimulation" (*The Politics of the Ordinary*, 132). Joel Schwartz argues, convincingly, that there are two teachings in Rousseau concerning sexuality. In the first, Rousseau praises sexuality because it is through it that we can live morally in social relations of mutual dependence; the second teaching condemns sexuality precisely because it occasions interdependence, and so leads to a loss of autonomy for men. "The second teaching is based upon a vision of a radically individualist autonomy and independence of others, to which Rousseau believes (a few) men but no women could reasonably aspire" (*The Sexual Politics of Jean-Jacques Rousseau* [Chicago: University of Chicago Press, 1985], 6). Since the second teaching is the one that supports the most freedom, one may conclude that it is the more 'human' for Rousseau.

24. Diana Coole has an interesting analysis of this difference between the motivation for male attachment and that for female attachment. She argues that as we move out of the state of nature in Rousseau, the androgynous character of the sexes splits into a gendered dyad. Women develop their compassionate side (because they have children) and men develop their self-interested side. "Beings who were in fact androgynous in their sentiments now evolve gendered personalities as the dyadic disposition which was originally so well-balanced, splits. Its two halves can no longer bind

one another and so one part flourishes in a distorted manner, varying according to sex" (Diana Coole, *Women in Political Theory* [Sussex, Eng.: Wheatsheaf Books, 1988], 115). My reading of Rousseau is slightly different, in that I see Rousseau as not accounting adequately for the genesis of the "civilized woman," or not as adequately as he does for the "civilized man." If men and women are both possessed of *amour de soi* in the state of nature, and women bear children in the state of nature, is women's *amour de soi* different from men's? I do not see compelling evidence in Rousseau that the birth of children makes women abandon their natural passion for self, although it may be that they see their children as an extension of that self-love, and not a threat to it; there is plenty of accounting in Rousseau of how it is that social relations cause men (and women) to become self-interested in a negative way.

Penny Weiss makes the argument that sexual difference is wholly constructed in Rousseau. "Rousseau can be most clearly understood as saying that the sexes are not relevantly differentiated by nature, but that sex differences can and should be created, encouraged and enforced because of what he considers to be the necessary and beneficial consequences" ("Rousseau, Anti-Feminism, and Women's Nature," *Political Theory* 15, no. 1 [1987]: 83). This seems to me to be closer to the aims of Rousseau's project, although it seems pretty clear that Rousseau is aware of natural sexual differences. The question is really: what do we make of these differences politically, when nature is at best ambiguous about their value?

25. According to Allan Bloom, this requires that Emile's first sexual experience takes place in the glow of idealized love. Emile's desires have to be sublimated prior to his capacity for distinguishing between sex and love, so that by the time he knows the distinction between the two, he will have no interest in it (*Love and Friendship* [New York: Simon and Schuster, 1993], 61).

26. See note 8. Rousseau does speak about modesty and shame being "natural" to women, but Rousseau points out that this does not necessarily mean that it has its roots in the state of nature. "One must not confound what is natural in the savage state with what is natural in the civil state" (*Emile*, 406).

27. Lynda Lange argues that male strength is not really an issue in the state of nature, and becomes so only under the rule of *amour-propre*. Male strength, and particularly the issue of sexual violence of men toward women, becomes significant outside the bounds of the state of nature because women abandon their natural sexual timidity outside the bounds of the state of nature. According to Lange, it is because of the threat of sexual violence that women are compelled to adopt the mantle of modesty ("Rousseau and Modern Feminism," *Social Theory and Practice* 7, no. 3 [1981]). This is plausible. Certainly, Rousseau does not regard male sexuality as predatory in the state of nature, although from what Rousseau says about rape, one may see this as less the consequence of female timidity as that of male interest in self-preservation. Rousseau discounts rape as an untenable proposition. Nature opposes rape, he says, because women have as much strength as is required to repel sexual advances when it so pleases them. Rape does not make sense for men, since man puts his life in jeopardy by violating a woman without her consent. Reason also opposes rape, he says, because if rape were permitted or condoned within civil society, no man would have assurance of the fatherhood of his own children, and so no man could claim rights over his children (*Emile*, 359).

What Rousseau is really saying here is that there are no natural grounds for regarding rape as an offence against women. They are capable by nature of resisting rape if they want to, and so any man who attempts it must accept his punishment (death). Rape is an offence only inside civil society, and that is because it is a violation of paternity rights.

28. See note 27.

29. As Peter Emberley says: "The basis of community is found in domestic partnership. The problem Rousseau seeks to solve is how to induce men to devote their energies to an interest which can produce commitment to something other than the satisfaction of their selfish desire. The family is the solution because private intimacies bind together desire and duty without causing turbulent resistance in men" ("Rousseau and the Domestication of Virtue," *Canadian Journal of Political Science*, 17, no. 4 [1984]).

Rousseau states baldly that Emile is unchanged by his love for, or attachment to, Sophie. Emile loves Sophie because she appears to love those qualities that he possesses. Emile is attracted to Sophie because of her "sensitivity, virtue and love of decent things," which is to say that he loves her because she recognizes the admirable things about him. Sophie is attracted to Emile because of his "esteem of true goods, frugality, simplicity, general disinterestedness, contempt for show and riches." Emile had all these virtues, Rousseau remarks, before love imposed them on him, so how is he changed by love? "He has new reasons to be himself. This is the single point where he differs from what he was" (Emile, 433).

Sophie, however, has to believe that her whole life aims toward love: love will complete her. Rousseau advises: "Depict for them [women] the good man, the man of merit; teach them to recognize him, to love him, and to love him for themselves; prove to them that the man alone can make the woman to whom he is attached—wives or beloved—happy" (Emile, 392). Allan Bloom notes that in an earlier draft of Emile, Rousseau had added the sentence "Lead them to virtue by means of amour propre" (Emile, 493 n. 27).

30. Rousseau, The Letter to M. D'Alembert on the Theatre, trans. Allan Bloom (Ithaca: Cornell University Press, 1960), 87.

31. Rousseau says that "woman is made to yield to man and to endure even his injustice. You will never reduce young boys to the same point. The inner sentiment in them rises and revolts against injustice. Nature did not constitute them to tolerate it" (Emile, 396). There is a serious, and unanswered, issue in Rousseau here, about the origin and meaning of justice. Is justice natural to only men? If so, does justice accord with radical independence and autonomy, which is by definition exclusive to men because they are the only ones by nature who are autonomous? Do women accept injustice because they are mothers, and so by nature excluded from radical autonomy?

32. Rousseau writes that it is desirable for a man to take a wife who has sufficient education so as to inculcate in her children a love of virtue, and of the estimable qualities that are exemplified in her husband. But still, he says: "I would like a simple and coarsely raised girl a hundred times better than a learned and brilliant one who would come to establish in my house a tribunal of literature over which she would preside. A brilliant wife is a plague to her husband, her children, her valets, everyone. From the sublime elevation of her fair genius she disdains all her woman's duties and always begins by making herself into a man after the fashion of Mademoiselle de l'Enclos. . . . Her [woman's] dignity consists in her being ignored. Her glory is in her husband's esteem. Her pleasures are in the happiness of her family" (Emile, 409).

33. In his final speech to his governor, Emile announces: "All the chains of opinion are broken for me; I know only those of necessity" (Emile, 472).

34. Emile is far more affected by the idea of Sophie than by her real presence. In his courtship of her, Rousseau says that he spends far more time hoping to see her, or congratulating himself on having seen her, than actually being with her. When he is away from her, "he is Emile again. He has not been transformed at all" (Emile, 435). In the words of Susan Okin: "Emile is his own man, and Sophie is his own woman" (Susan Okin, Women in Western Political Thought [Princeton: Princeton University Press, 1979], 119).

35. The tenability of this synthesis between male independence and the preservation of political order, can be questioned. Mary Nichols writes that "Rousseau ends the Emile allowing us to believe that Emile has achieved a reconciliation between independence and love or between nature and society, and that he himself has educated a man 'uniquely for himself' who is also 'for others'. He veils the tensions or contradictions between the independence and freedom that Emile is supposed to possess and his actual independence" ("Rousseau's Natural Education in the Emile," Political Theory 13, no. 4 [1985]: 553). Nonetheless, Rousseau presented the goal of self-contentment as desirable, Nichols says. This is true, but only for men. Lynda Lange makes a similar point about Rousseau's attempt at synthesis, although she broaches the question in terms of the contrast between politics and philosophy. If Rousseau's ultimate goal in supporting the family is the foundation of

civic virtue, there remains the tension between the cosmopolitan self-contained philosopher and the good patriot. "Patriotism is therefore ultimately based on a lie, although a 'noble lie' if you will" ("Rousseau and Modern Feminism," 262).

As for women, there is no attempted synthesis, only mastery of desire. This makes the project even less likely to be successful. Rousseau's own commentary on this may be read into *La nouvelle Héloïse: Julie; or, The New Heloise, Letters of Two Lovers, Inhabitants of a Small Town at the Foot of the Alps*, trans. Judith McDowell (University Park: Pennsylvania State University Press, 1968), his novelistic account of the loves and duties of one woman. *La nouvelle Héloïse* is the story of a woman who gives up her real desire for a life of domestic duty and order. She willingly adopts her dutiful role, and tries to convince herself that it fulfils her, but in the end she breaks under the duality of her divided self. Allessandro Ferrara writes that Julie lived her life in accordance with ideas of 'rightness', "but this forcible act of self-mastery has failed to enhance her inner life. Virtue, after all, was not on the side of virtue, and true morality was not on the side of autonomous principle" (*Modernity and Authenticity* [New York: State University of New York Press, 1993], 101).

36. Rousseau, *Letter to M. D'Alembert on the Theatre*, 109.

4

The Fate of Rousseau's Heroines

Susan Moller Okin

Rousseau was acutely aware, perhaps more than any other political philosopher, of the conflicts of loyalties in people's lives, and the incompatible demands made by the various personal and group relationships in which people participate. A moderate degree of self-love, love of another individual, love of one's family, of one's fellow countrymen, of humanity as a whole—all these he perceived as by no means easily reconcilable. All, however, he valued as important in their own way, and it was his ultimate conviction of their incompatibility that made his philosophical conclusions so deeply pessimistic. After outlining the denouements of *Emile* and *Les Solitaires* (its unfinished sequel), and *La Nouvelle Héloise*, I will draw on the fates of Rousseau's characters to explore the repercussions of his ideas about women on the already conflicting demands of the human condition as he perceived it.

In accord with his tutor's plan, Emile on attaining adulthood rejects all existing governments and chooses to be an independent man.[1] All he wants, he says, is a wife and a piece of land of his own, and the one chain he will always be proud to wear is his attachment to Sophie. However, Rousseau points out that it is not so easy to be an independent man, since although his need for a mate and companion is perceived as natural, in becoming the head of a family, he becomes necessarily the citizen of a state.[2] "As soon as a man needs a mate, he is no longer an isolated being; his heart is no longer alone. All his relations with his species, all the affections of his soul are born with this one. His first passion soon makes the others develop."[3] Moreover, citizenship of a state is not treated, even in the case of Emile, as a necessary evil. Rousseau convinces Emile that he owes much to the laws of the country in which he resides, however far they may fall short of that genuine law that originates in the social contract and popular sovereignty. He is indebted to them not only for protection, but also for "that which is most precious to man, the morality of his actions and the love of virtue."[4] While a man in the depths of the forest might have lived more happily and more freely, "having nothing to struggle against in order to follow his inclinations . . . , he would not have been virtuous. . . ." In civil society, on the other hand, a man can become motivated for the common good: "He learns to struggle with himself and to win, to sacrifice his interest to the general interest."[5] The laws do not prevent man from being free; rather they teach him to govern himself.

With this introduction of virtue and civic duty as ideals, not just necessities, for Emile, one wonders just what has happened to the natural man whom Rousseau had set out to educate. In the last part of Book 5, he seems to be trying to do what he had said was impossible—to make Emile into a natural man and a citizen at the same time. It is decided that Emile should live where he can serve his fellow men best, which is not, in this corrupt world, by immersing himself in town life, but by presenting an example of rural simplicity.[6] The important point is that the rural life is not decided on simply because it is best for Emile and Sophie themselves, but because of the example it will provide others. Moreover, while it is unlikely that he will be called upon to serve the state, since a corrupt world has little use for such a man, if he *is* called upon, like Cincinnatus he must leave his plow and go.[7] Thus Rousseau clearly attempts to make of Emile a citizen, as well as a natural and independent man.

The impossibility of these demands—that the naturally educated man should also fill the roles of husband, father, and citizen—is clearly asserted by Rousseau in the two letters that were all he completed of *Les Solitaires*. It very soon becomes apparent that it was only through the covert authority of the tutor and his continual manipulation of the environment that the illusion of Emile's success as a natural man in society was maintained. The adult Emile is in fact still hopelessly dependent on his tutor, and when left by him to lead his own life he fails as a husband, a father, and a citizen, and feels unequivocally free only when he has divested himself of all these attachments and responsibilities and become an emotional isolate. The conclusion that he eventually draws from his experience is a complete confirmation of the irreconcilability of the man/ citizen dichotomy. "By breaking the ties that attached me to my country," he says, "I extended them over all the earth, and I became so much more a man in ceasing to be a citizen."[8] And, as Judith Shklar has noted, "What is impossible for the perfectly reared Emile, who possesses every virtue except the quality that controls men and events, is certainly not possible for lesser men."[9] Rousseau's conclusions about the man and the citizen could not be more clear.

Emile's education, however, is both a failure and a success. It has failed to make him into both a natural man and a citizen, but Rousseau had already told us at the outset of the work that this was impossible.[10] As Emile himself acknowledges, he cannot fulfill his duties as a husband and father without the constant help of his tutor. He is fitted neither for emotional closeness and dependence nor for the loyalty of a patriot, as his desertion of his family and his country makes clear. On the other hand, however, the end of his story shows that, in the sense of forming an autonomous, internally free man, his education has been a success. When he becomes literally enslaved, it is vitally important to him that, although his work and his hands can be sold from one master to another, his will, understanding, and real essence are inviolable.[11] He rejoices that, because of his unique education, he has, as Rousseau intended, internal freedom, of which no one can deprive him. His personal, moral autonomy renders him essentially free even when his body is enslaved. His education has failed to do the impossible; but it has, Rousseau concludes, succeeding in making Emile into a universal man, adaptable to any situation and free of all restricting attachments.

What, though, of Sophie? Her ideal female education, as we have seen, was designed to endow her with that combination of alluring charm and chaste modesty that befits the wife of the patriarch. Like Emile, she "has only a natural goodness in an ordinary soul; every way in which she is better than other women is the result of her education."[12] The outcome described in *Les Solitaires* is therefore undeniable testimony to the failure of the ideal female education, just as it is to the failure of the attempt to make a natural man fit for social life.

First, Sophie, who has not been taught like Emile how to accept necessary evils, is so upset by her daughter's death that Emile has to take her to Paris in order to distract her from her grief. Inevitably Paris, the cesspit of civilization, proves their downfall. Emile, corrupted by the city, breaks his marital vows by faltering in his love and devotion for Sophie. She, whose whole life has been made to revolve around love, whose entire self-esteem depends upon whether she is pleasing to men, cannot cope with her feelings of rejection, commits adultery, and finds herself with child by another man. Even though Emile is convinced by her honesty and remorse that Sophie's heart has remained pure throughout, and he is aware that the temptations she faced were greater than any he could ever be expected to resist, he is unable to see any alternative to leaving her and their surviving child. Neither is it conceivable that she could accept his pardon, were he to offer it; she sees herself after her adultery as irredeemable. Instantaneously, in her own eyes, and in those of Emile and Rousseau, she has fallen from the pedestal of the madonna to the gutter of the prostitute. Having fallen once, there can be no possible guarantee that she will not do so again, since when a woman has lost her chaste reputation, she has no viture left to preserve: "the first step toward vice is the only painful one." Emile does, in fact, consider whether, being such an independent man, he should ignore that social prejudice which holds a wife's crime against her husband's honor. He concludes, however, that it is indeed a reasonable prejudice that deserves to be heeded. For any such crime *is* her husband's fault, either for choosing badly or for governing her badly. Though thus acknowledging that he is largely to blame, Emile decides that it is impossible for him to take Sophie back as his wife. The final decision is made when he reflects on the horror of her being the mother of another man's child, for in sharing her affection between her two children, his son and this usurper, she must likewise share her feelings between their two fathers. His feelings of revulsion against this are such that he exclaims: "I would sooner see my son dead than Sophie the mother of another man's child."[13]

Here we are presented with a very clear case in which the feelings of the natural man and the interests of his family and country are in direct conflict. His feelings prevailing, Emile is of course far better able to cope with the consequences of the break-up of his family than is Sophie, with the responsibility of two dependent children. Though saddened by what he sees as the irreparable loss of the woman he loves, he leaves his family and country and goes off, independent and self-sufficient, to be a real "solitaire." Soon reveling in his new-found independence, he owes no one anything, and finds himself at home and self-supporting wherever he goes. "I told myself," he relates to his tutor, "that wherever I lived, in whatever situation I found myself, I would always find my task as a man to do, and that no one needed others if each lived agreeably for himself." "I drank the waters of forgetfulness, the past was erased in my memory."[14] Sophie, however, is in no position to forget the past; she has two children, of whom one soon dies, no status in society, and no respectable means of support unless she relies on Emile. Surely neither her self-respect and shame nor his obvious lack of responsibility make this a viable solution. She has no alternative but to die, which she obligingly does, charming to the end.[15]

The importance of this fictional denouement arises, of course, from the fact that *Emile* and its sequel are not just novels, but the account of the fates of a man and a woman educated to be paragons of their respective sexes. Sophie's adultery, which together with what is regarded as Emile's inevitable reaction to it destroys this ideal family, is of supreme importance because, after all, *not* to commit adultery was the aim of her entire education. As Emile acknowledges, "If Sophie soiled her virtue, what woman can dare rely on hers?"[16] Sophie's failure is indicative of the failure in the society of Rousseau's time, of the best possible education he thought a woman could have. She is designed to be very conscious of her charms, "consumed with the single need for love,"[17] and ruled by the judgment of public opinion. As Burgelin has pointed out, it is Eucharis, the seductive nymph, with whom Sophie identifies when she fantasizes about Telemachus, not the chaste wife, Antiope.[18] It is hardly surprising, then, that, neglected by her husband in a licentious city, she acts according to its lax moral code. The narrowness of what is considered to be her proper sphere, and the contradictory expectations placed on her—not least that she behave like a concubine with her husband and like a nun with all other men—make it inevitable that she will "fall" as she does. The corrupt city certainly compounded the problems that resulted from Sophie's education, but an examination of the fate of Julie, who never leaves the idyllic countryside, reveals that the issue is more complex than this.

Julie is Rousseau's ideal woman—the kind of woman he himself would love.[19] She is extremely sensitive and emotional; she abounds in those qualities—modesty, romanticism, and sexual attractiveness—without which Rousseau considered a woman to be worthless. The central theme of La Nouvelle Héloïse is the conflict between her feelings and her duty which Rousseau believed a sensitive woman must confront. Julie is torn between her passionate feelings for her tutor, Saint-Preux, and her strong sense of duty to her mother, and to her impossible father, who will have nothing to do with the commoner and wants to marry his daughter to a noble friend.[20] When Julie's violent love for Saint-Preux overpowers her devotion to her duty to preserve her virginity, as one would expect of such a passionate character, she feels that she is utterly destroyed. In a desperate letter to her cousin and confidante, she writes: "Without knowing what I was doing I chose my own ruin. I forgot everything and remembered only love. Thus in a wild moment I was ruined forever. I have fallen into the depths of shame from which a girl cannot recover herself; and if I live, it will be only to be more wretched."[21] Having lost her virginity, she feels that she has no further worth as a person, and, overwhelmed with guilt, cries out to Saint-Preux, "Be my whole being, now that I am nothing."[22]

Through Julie, who in spite of her exaggerated piety is a far more real and intelligent character than Sophie, Rousseau acknowledges to the reader that her plight is a terrible one, and one that no man could ever suffer from. As Julie writes to her lover:

> Consider the position of my sex and yours in our common misfortunes, and judge which of us is more to be pitied? To feign insensitivity in the turmoil of passion; to seem joyful and content while prey to a thousand sorrows; to appear serene while one's soul is distressed; always to say other than what one thinks; to disguise what one feels; to be obliged to be false and to lie through modesty; this is the customary position of all girls of my age. Thus we spend our finest years under the tyranny of propriety, which is at

length added to by the tyranny of our parents' forcing us into an unsuitable marriage. But it is in vain that they repress our inclinations; the heart accepts only its own laws; it escapes from slavery; it bestows itself according to its own will.[23]

Apart from forced marriages, all of these misfortunes are regarded by Rousseau as inevitable consequences of being born female. While Saint-Preux is affected as much emotionally by their enforced separation, he is not, like Julie, degraded by shame or obliged to hide his feelings. Neither is he forced to marry someone whom he does not love, but instead can go off on journeys and exploits, and enjoy an autonomous existence insofar as he can without the woman he loves. Since Julie was not married when she committed her terrible crime, and the child she conceives miscarries, there is still hope for her moral redemption. Whatever course of action she chooses, however, she cannot herself be happy, and the choice is never put in terms of what *she* wants to do, but always as a contest between the wills of the three men who surround her—her lover, her father, and later her husband. "Whom shall I give preference to, out of a lover and a father?" she asks, when deciding whether to elope or to marry the man of her father's choice; ". . . whichever course I take, I must die both wretched and guilty."[24] Again, while she cannot marry Saint-Preux without her father's consent, she promises her lover that she will not marry anyone else without *his* consent.[25] On the occasion of her reluctant marriage, Julie describes her fate in this male-ruled world in which she lives: "Bound by an indissoluble chain to the fate of a husband, or rather to the will of a father, I am entering into a new way of life which must end only with death."[26]

By placing her duty to her parents before her love for Saint-Preux and marrying the man her father forces on her, in Rousseau's eyes Julie has redeemed herself. The whole of the rest of the novel, however, consists in her never-ending struggle against her feelings, and her repeated attempts to convince herself that she has conquered her passion. Slowly, she recovers her honor and virtue, in the role of wife and mother which, she says, "elevates my soul and sustains me against the remorse resulting from my other condition."[27] Nevertheless, by her own account she is not happy, despite the worthy Wolmar, her husband, who treats her like a delightful child, despite her healthy children, her religion, and her reunion (on a strictly non-physical level) with Saint-Preux. Though the rural domestic situation in which she lives is described as the happiest possible life on earth,[28] and Julie herself as the perfect mother and most tasteful mistress of the house, she confesses to Saint-Preux, toward the end of her life, her inexplicable unhappiness. Though she sees only reasons for happiness around her, she says, "I am not content," and then "I am too happy; happiness bores me." Tormented by a "secret regret," she laments "my empty soul reaches out for something to fill it."[29] The final denouement, Julie's pseudo-accidental death, and her posthumous confession of her still unconquered passion for Saint-Preux, can only be seen as tragic commentary on her deluded sense of victory over her feelings. As she at last realizes, "Great passions can be stifled; rarely can they be purged."[30]

Julie has behaved as she ought to have done, ever since her first great sin. She has preserved her virtue intact throughout her marriage, although she was deluded in believing that she was cured of her love. When, therefore, she realizes that she has always been and still is in danger of succumbing to temptation, her death is the only way out of the dilemma. Any reunion between her and Saint-Preux from that point on would be so dangerous that God takes the matter out of their hands. Indisposed after saving her son from drowning, Julie loses the will to live. Thus her passion has escaped destroying the ideal Wolmar family, but only by destroying her instead.

As Judith Shklar has asserted, Julie, as the human sacrifice, is a Christ figure.[31] Since, however, she is the ideal woman, loving and lovable, honorable, kind, and struggling always to be virtuous, the fact that she is sacrificed has profound implications for Rousseau's whole theory of women. Julie is his heroine, it must be recognized, *because* in spite of her rigid and repressive upbringing and her love of virtue, she is passionate and, like the original Héloise, "made for love." However, given this personality, she is doomed to spend her entire adult life fighting her natural feelings, for the sake of her all-important chastity, her duty to her class-conscious parents, and her obedience to the prejudices of an inegalitarian world. Rousseau asserts in *Emile* that "in our senseless conditions, the life of a good woman is a constant struggle against herself,"[32] but his own ideas about women's education and proper position in society, taken together with his convictions about love and marriage, make it clear that in any conditions he was prepared to envisage, the kind of woman he idolized would not only be condemned to perpetual struggle, but might very well be required (not only in the corrupt city, but even in the pure countryside) to sacrifice her life for the sake of virtue. The ancient two-

fold demands made of woman—that she be both the inspiration of romantic, sexual love, and the guardian of marital fidelity—are seen at their
most tragic in Rousseau.

There are three important sets of conflicting claims on the human
individual which are discussed in Rousseau's works, and which must be
reviewed in the light of his theories about women and the examples of
ideal womanhood that he created. The first is the conflict between the
impulses of the individual and the requirements of the republican state.
Rousseau says that men must be educated as either individuals or citizens,
but his education of women does not fit them to be either. The second
is the conflict between the consuming commitment to a dyadic love-
relationship and the needs of the wider world—whether family, state, or
mankind as a whole. The third set of claims, which Rousseau considers
but ultimately does not acknowledge to be in conflict, consists of the
demands made by the family and those made by the ideal republic. It is
my contention that, however problematic these second and third conflicts of loyalty are for man, it is woman, educated and defined as Rousseau
would have her, who will opt for what he considers to be the less valuable
of each pair of alternative commitments, and whose inevitable tendency
will be to subvert both of his ideal institutions—the patriarchal family
and the patriotic democratic republic.

The central theme of Rousseau's social theory is the conflict between
the ideal of the independent, natural man, and that of the man who is
part of a large whole, his country—between the man and the citizen. At
the beginning of Emile, he frankly states the dilemma which to him is
the necessary starting point of any honest social theory: no person can
be both man and citizen: "The natural man is altogether for himself; he
is the unit, the absolute whole, who has no relation to anyone but himself
or those like him."[33] In educating the natural man, the essential thing is
to let nature take its course: "The whole [education] consists in not spoil-
ing the natural man by making him conform to society."[34]

The education prescribed for the citizen, however, is very different.
Rousseau considered that he had proved through his construction of an
hypothetical state of nature that man's natural tendency is to be good, in
the sense that he finds it pleasant to be kind to his fellows, so long as
they do not thwart his needs or desires. The citizen, however, is required
to have far more moral fiber than this. Living in close proximity to and
mutual dependence on others, he will be required to perform duties that
may well be disagreeable to him and involve considerable sacrifice. Thus

it is not sufficient for him to rely on his natural tendency to be kind because it makes him feel good; he must, in short, learn to be virtuous.

> The citizen is but the numerator of a fraction which belongs to the denominator, and whose value is in his relationship with the whole—the social body. Good social institutions are those which best know how to denature man, to take away his absolute existence and to give him a relative one, and to move the individual self into the community; so that each does not think of himself as one, but as part of the whole, and has feelings only as a member of that whole.[35]

The education of a real citizen, such as Rousseau considered the Spartans and the Romans to have been, thus involves no less than the destruction of most of man's natural tendencies, and the transformation of his personality. As examples, he cites Brutus, who condemned his sons to death for their betrayal of the Republic; Pedaretes, who was rejected for membership of the Spartan Council and rejoiced that there were three hundred citizens better qualified than himself; and the Spartan mother, who ran to thank the gods for her country's victory though her five sons had all been killed in the process of attaining it.[36] The citizen socialized as Rousseau advocates would live for his country; he would think neither of his individual self nor of humanity as a whole, but solely of his fellow-citizens. He would be a patriot "by inclination, with passion, by necessity."[37]

Rousseau held up Plato's *Republic* as the outstanding account of true public education. In the *Discourse on Political Economy* and in *Considerations on the Government of Poland,* we have his own treatments of the subject, and in the *Letter to d'Alembert* he asserts that the only way of proving that education has improved is by showing that it makes better citizens. In *Emile*, however, stating that there are neither fatherlands nor citizens in his time, he argues that there can therefore be no public education, and that he will discuss the other alternative—private and domestic education.[38] His essential point is that the choice must be made; the socialization process must combat either society, in order to make a natural man, or nature, in order to make a real citizen. "He who wishes to preserve the supremacy of natural feeling in civil life does not know what he is asking. Always in contradiction with himself, always fluctuating between his inclinations and his duties, he will never be either a man or a citizen; he will be no good to himself or to others."[39] At this point in his argument, Rousseau poses the problem of how a man educated for himself, as he intends to educate Emile, could live with others. He says that "*if* perhaps the double aim proposed could be reunited into a single one, by getting rid of man's contradictions one would remove a major obstacle to his happiness."[40]

Rousseau's denial of the possibility of such a reunion of the two aims is expressed by what becomes of Emile. For Emile is not intended to be by any means an isolate, but rather to be "a natural man living in society, . . . a savage made to live in town."[41] He must know how to live, if not *like* its other inhabitants, at least *with* them. His choice to be a husband and father entails the obligations of the citizen.[42] Emile's failure in all these three roles is the proof of the irreconcilable conflict between manhood and citizenship. His education has fitted him to be his own man, but not to tolerate any attachments, personal or patriotic. The denouement of Emile's story is simply a confirmation of what was stated at the beginning of Book 1—one must choose to educate a man or a citizen, but not both.

There is, however, for Rousseau, only one possible method of educating a woman. She is not, like Emile, educated to be her own person, with independent judgment, economic self-sufficiency, and an acquired ability to accept necessity and adapt to any situation in which she finds herself. Neither is she, like the Polish children, to be first and foremost her country's citizen, socialized so as to think of the fatherland in every waking moment and to subordinate her wishes always to the public welfare. There is no mention of such alternatives with respect to Sophie's and Julie's educations. They are educated, instead, to be the appendages—the obedient and submissive daughters, wives, and mothers—of the men on whom they will depend for livelihood and for self-respect. The relationships they are prepared for are entirely personal ones; because their only proper means of influence or power are through the men who are closest to them, they are taught to manipulate them for their own ends.

It seems extraordinary, therefore, that Rousseau should have expected the Genevan women to utilize their single means of power in the world to expedite civic virtue and the public interest. For them or any other women educated in the mode he regarded as proper—having had no public socialization and sharing no part of the duties or rights of the citizen—to place the public welfare before their own or that of the persons closest to them, would certainly be remarkable, according to Rousseau's own reasoning. At the beginning of *The Social Contract*, he attributes his conviction that it is his duty to study governments and public affairs to the fact that he was born a citizen of a free state and voting member of the sovereign.[43] No woman he could envisage would ever be so motivated. Nothing in his prescribed education for girls leads to the expectation that patriotic loyalties will take precedence over personal or selfish ones.

The second conflict of loyalties that Rousseau's social theory confronts is that between the exclusiveness of intimate love and the welfare of the outside world—whether family, fatherland, or humanity. Although he admired romantic love and pined for it, he depicts it as founded on mere illusion.[44] It creates its own love objects, by covering those in the real world with a veil of fantasy. "We are," as Julie says, "far more in love with the image we conjure up than with the object to which we attach it. If we saw the object of our love exactly as it is, there would be no more love in the world."[45] The one time Rousseau himself fell in love, with Mme. d'Houdetot, was the result of his investing her with the qualities of Julie, whom he was currently creating. Similarly, Emile is carefully prepared in advance for his meeting with his future wife by having an idealized Sophie presented in detail to his imagination, and it is not, we notice, on their first meeting that he falls in love with her, but on hearing her name and realizing that this girl is indeed the embodiment of his fantasies.[46] Based as it is on illusion, love is necessarily evanescent. As Julie writes to Saint-Preux, though one may feel it so violently that it seems indestructible, love will inevitably fade, and boredom and oversatiation follow. Love "wears out with youth, it fades with beauty, it dies under the iciness of age, and since the beginning of the world two lovers with white hair have never been seen sighing for each other."[47] (The love of Julie and Saint-Preux, of course, is no exception, since they were parted at such an early stage that there could be no question of oversatiation. The tone of their letters, indeed, suggests strongly that their passion was kept alive by being thwarted.)

While love lasts, however, Rousseau does not question its intensity. How exclusive and all-consuming he considered a dyadic love-relationship to be is clearly expressed in *The Confessions* as well as in his other writings.[48] Plato is referred to as the true philosopher of lovers because of his conviction that "throughout the passion, they never have another."[49] The exclusive nature of love is clearly illustrated in the melodramatic outbursts of Saint-Preux, who lives for his passion alone. After he and

Julie finally contrive to spend the night together, he writes to her: "Oh, let us die, my sweet friend! Let us die, beloved of my heart! What is there to do, henceforth, with an insipid youth, now that we have exhausted all its delights."[50] He gives up himself and his will totally to Julie's disposal, discounting any connection except with her. When separated from his love, he cries out to her cousin, Claire, "Ah, what is a mother's life, what is my own, yours, even hers, what is the existence of the whole world next to the delightful feeling which united us?"[51] The anarchistic tendencies of exclusive love are pointed out by Lord Bomston, Saint-Preux's confidant, as he talks of the bond between two lovers. "All laws which impede it are unjust," he says, "all fathers who dare to form or break it are tyrants. This chaste or natural bond is subject neither to sovereign power nor to paternal authority, but only to the authority of our common Father, who can govern hearts. . . ."[52] The rights of the family and of the state are seen by Bomston as having no precedence over those of love.

It was the absolute demands made by love, as Rousseau conceived of it, and as described by Bomston and exemplified by the complete self-abandonment of Saint-Preux, that led him to see it as such a threat to the other loyalties required of us. The worth of a man who speaks in the way Saint-Preux is quoted above, as a member of a family, a country, or even of the human race, is surely questionable. All he can think of is his passion for Julie. However, although Rousseau conceives of romantic-sexual love as so all-consuming and intense, his conclusion seems to be that, like all passions, love is good if we are the masters of it and do not let it master us. A man is not guilty, he tells Emile, if he loves his neighbor's wife, so long as he controls his passion and does his duty; but he is guilty if he loves his own wife so much that he sacrifices everything else to that love.[53] In a letter, his thoughts on the subject are summarized, thus: "We are justly punished for those exclusive attachments which make us blind and unjust, and limit our universe to the persons we love. All the preferences of friendship are thefts committed against the human race and the fatherland. Men are all our brothers, they should all be our friends."[54]

If even friendship is a theft, then *love* and wider loyalties are far more liable to clash. Where there is opportunity to devote oneself to groups and causes outside the narrow circle of intimacy—to fatherland or humanity—then exclusive dyadic love is to be eschewed as a threat to civic or humane loyalties. This is why Rousseau was so opposed to introducing the romantic love of the theater into Geneva, since he believed that city to have a level of morality and civic feeling that could only be lowered by the fostering of personal and sexual intimacy.[55] For although "it is much better to love a mistress than to love oneself alone in all the world . . . the best is he who shares his affections equally with all his kind."[56]

Because he perceived romantic love to be so exclusive and marriage to be an essential and functional *social* institution, Rousseau was by no means sure that the continuation of intense passion was compatible with marriage. Certainly at times he expresses the wish that they were. He laments the fact that, although if the happiness of love could be pro-longed within marriage we would have a paradise on earth, this has never been seen to happen. Unfortunately, "in spite of all precautions, posses-sion wears out pleasures, and love before all others."[57] He advises Sophie to forestall the fading of Emile's amorous interest in her as long as possi-ble, both by continuing to be alluring and by granting her sexual favors sparingly. In spite of this, however, the time will inevitably come, as in any marriage, when the husband's ardor will cool. Thus, the feelings on which marriage is based must ultimately be tenderness and trust, mutual esteem, virtue, and the compatibility of the partners, strengthened by the extremely important bond that children form between their parents—"a bond which is often stronger than love itself."[58]

In *La Nouvelle Héloise*, however, Rousseau has Julie argue not just that romantic love cannot last in marriage, but that it has no place in a good marriage. As she writes,

> Love is accompanied by a continual anxiety over jealousy or priva-tion, little suited to marriage, which is a state of joy and peace. People do not marry in order to think exclusively of one another, but to fulfill together the duties of civic life, to govern their houses prudently, and to bring up their children well. Lovers never see anyone but themselves, are concerned only with each other, and the only thing they can do is love each other. This is not enough for married people who have so many other cares to attend to.[59]

Marriage, then, is a serious social institution, which by no means suc-ceeds easily; it *should* be based on honor, virtue, and compatibility, and is indeed better off without the disturbances of passion. While Saint-Preux has been an ideal lover, Julie (and her creator) doubt that he could be a good husband, for Rousseau believes that the combination is ex-tremely rare.[60] Between Julie and her husband, Wolmar, a man totally without passion, there is none of that illusion which maintains such a state of heightened tension between her and Saint-Preux. It is Wolmar, moreover, who is billed as the ideal husband, father, and head of household. The marriage of the Wolmars is depicted as admirable and orderly, and the family they form as a model for others. However, the achievement of this model is founded on the overriding of passionate love, which entails the sacrifice of Julie's feelings, and eventually of her life.

Thus, while in one respect Julie's impossible position might have been alleviated if the laws and customs which gave fathers so much power over their daughters were different, the important conflict between love and marriage would not thereby be resolved. Without the despotism of fathers and the requirements of the property system, Julie would have married her lover, but we are not given the impression that such a solution would have been either a happy or a socially useful one. After all, at the height of their passion, what they had thought of as the climax of their relationship was to die together, more than to live together, and Rousseau was very skeptical about the fate of their kind of love if it was subjected to the trials and disillusionments of many years of day-to-day life. It is made very clear to us that although it was Saint-Preux whom Julie always loved so passionately, Womar was undoubtedly the best man to be her husband and her children's father. In fact, then, for the sake of virtue and her social duties, the only alternative for Rousseau's ideal woman is to do exactly as she does, even without the coercion of her father. She must marry, without love, a worthy and dispassionate man, and make an orderly and happy home for him and his children, even though she is all the while in torment herself, and finally her only means of victory over love is to die.

Julie, however, is an exceptional paragon of virtue—a Christ figure. This is why, though she must be destroyed, she is able to place her duties to her family and to society above the feelings of love which possess her. Sophie, on the other hand, though she has received the ideal education for her sex, succumbs to the temptation of illicit love after marriage, thereby dooming both herself and her family. The attempt to create a woman in the image of a seductive nymph, Eucharis, and then have her behave like the virtuous wife, Antiope, is as much a failure as the attempt to make a natural man into a citizen. The ideal woman's need to please and to be loved continually, and her dependence on men's approval for her self-esteem and on public opinion for her moral code, make it virtually certain that in conditions of stress, sexual love will prevail over the demands of monogamy, which is the basis of all social order. Since "love is the realm of women,"[61] and virtually their sole means of power, they can only be expected to exaggerate its importance, whether at the expense of the calmer affections on which marriage should be based, or to the detriment of their families, fellow countrymen, or fellow humans.

Rousseau's conviction that intimate dyadic relationships are threatening to the larger community has been asserted by many other leaders or theorists of groups which demand their members' undivided loyalty. As a recent sociological study by Lewis Coser documents, libidinal withdrawal has been perceived as a threat by close-knit communities and sects as diverse as the Church and its religious orders, the early Bolsheviks, and many of the early American utopias. In order to prevent the drawing off of energies and affections from the common purpose, such groups have tended to require of their members either celibacy or promiscuity, which, as Coser points out, "though opposed sexual practices, fulfill identical sociological functions."[62] Citing much evidence of this type of reasoning from the writings of theorists of the three groups named above, Coser also points to a finding that all except one of the successful nineteenth-century American utopias practiced either free love or celibacy at some time in their history. Of the twenty-one unsuccessful communities, however, only five did so, and of these, four permitted couples to form if they wished.[63] Thus, for the type of community in which total allegiance of the members is perceived as essential, it would seem that there is good reason to place controls on dyadic relationships.

Rousseau gives a small scale example of such practice, in the sexual segregation in the Wolmar's household at Clarens. Masters who are at all concerned with being well served by their servants should realize that "too intimate relations between the sexes never produces anything but evil," and that therefore, "in a well-regulated household the men and women should have little to do with each other."[64] The ruin of the richest families, he warns, has been brought about by the intrigues of the men and women in their service. Thus segregation, in addition to preserving the chastity of the female servants, will also ensure that servants of both sexes perform their duties to the household faithfully and without distraction. On the republican level, arrangements such as the Genevan clubs perform the same function of preventing the distractions of sexual intimacy from harming the greater cause of civic life.

It is important to note, at this point, that those "greedy" communities which Coser analyzes are not only antagonistic to intimate sexual love relationships but also decidedly hostile to the family. The Catholic priesthood, the early Bolshevik militants, and the successful utopias in America either bluntly prohibited, or at least strongly discouraged, their members from committing themselves to the demands of family life. A number of philosophical creators of utopian communities made similar recommendations. Plato in the *Republic*, Campanella in his *City of the Sun*, and Fourier in his projected *Phalansteries*, all extended their wariness of intimate relationships to the family.[65] In the light of this fact, Rousseau's treatment of the possible conflicts between the family and the republic and his conclusion that the family must indeed be preserved as the basis of society, are extremely interesting. Almost alone among creators of close-knit utopian communities, Rousseau was so far from hostile to the family that he idealized it.

In spite of his distinction between the natural basis of the family and the conventional basis of political society, Rousseau envisaged his ideal, small, democratic republic as, in many respects, like a big family. In the *Letter to d'Alembert*, for example, he refers to the public balls which he regards as so salutary for the peace and preservation of the republic as "not so much a public entertainment as . . . the gathering of a big family."[66] Again, he recommended to the Poles that republics should be small enough so that the citizens' behavior can be supervised by their rulers and their peers alike, which is far closer to his description of a family than to that of a political society.[67] Finally, in a single noteworthy sentence in the *Discourse on Political Economy*, he refers to the state as a loving and nourishing mother, and its citizens when children as each other's "mutually cherishing" brothers, and when adult as the fathers and defenders of their country.[68] While the metaphor is somewhat strained, its implication is unmistakable. The highly community-oriented method of socialization administered to the citizens of the ideal republic was intended to produce a family, a brotherhood, rather than a collection of individuals.

While discussing the dilemma that one cannot be both a man and a citizen, Rousseau had made a sociological observation, very like the arguments put forward by other utopians, about the functioning of groups and their tendency to demand all of their members' loyalties and emotions. "Every partial society," he writes, "when it is close-knit and well united, alienates itself from the larger society. Every patriot is harsh toward foreigners; they are only men, they are nothing in his sight. . . . The essential thing is to be good to the people with whom he lives."[69] Moreover, just as patriotic loyalty detracts from one's love for humanity as a whole, one's membership of and loyalty to subgroups within one's country was recognized by Rousseau as being likely to detract from the patriotic loyalty required of the true citizen. Thus, since "the same decision can be advantageous to the small community and very harmful to the large one," it follows that "a person could be a devout priest, a brave soldier, or a zealous professional, and a bad citizen."[70] In *The Social Contract*, therefore, since the aim is to develop real citizens joined in one "moral and collective body"[71] with a general will, and the ascendancy of particular interests over the common interest is perceived as an ever present danger, the existence of partial societies is distinctly frowned upon. For "when particular interests begin to make themselves felt and the smaller societies to have an influence over the greater, the common interest changes and finds opponents, unanimity of opinion no longer reigns, the general will is no longer the will of all. . . ." With the growth of particular and group interests, each will come to focus on his own particular benefit, and will neglect the decline of the public welfare.[72]

It would seem that one of the most obvious applications of this theory of conflicting interests would be to the family. This is a group, surely, which requires its members to have a very strong loyalty to its needs and wishes, which may well conflict with the good of the greater society. Since the family's "principal object," as Rousseau says, is "to preserve and increase the patrimony of the father, in order that he may one day share it amongst his children without impoverishing them," and since private property and inheritance are regarded by him as the most sacred rights of citizenship,[73] there must obviously be many occasions on which the interests of individual families will be opposed to the needs of the country as a whole. Any circumstances requiring taxation, the absence of the breadwinner for public duties, or the regulation of private property for the general good, for example, are more than likely to cause conflict between family and patriotic loyalties. However, in spite of the fact that Rousseau's conflict of interest theory is applied to the level of patriotic feelings versus humanitarian ones, and to *some* partial groups within the republic, he refused explicitly to recognize that it can be applied also to the tension between the demands of the greater society and those of the family.

It is important to point out, at this point, two occasions in his writings when Rousseau does come very close to recognizing the potential conflicts of interest between his two ideal institutions—the democratic republic and the property-owning patriarchal family. First, the most striking examples he cites of Spartan and Roman patriotic devotion are those of citizens who subordinated their family feelings and attachments to the requirements of their fatherlands. Even though Brutus and the Spartan mother must have privately grieved over their children's deaths, they were undoubtedly citizens before they were parents. These two real citizens were sufficiently able to abstract themselves from their family feelings to hold the state always dearer, but the conflict of interest and loyalties was undeniably present in both cases.

Second, and even more significantly, Rousseau did not consider the family to be a trustworthy dispenser of the education required by the citizens of a republic. He regarded public socialization of children from the earliest possible age as "one of the most fundamental principles of popular and legitimate government."[74] It is by this means that the young citizens will develop in such a way as to transcend that individualism which is so threatening to the general will. In the rough draft of the *Discourse on Political Economy*, moreover, Rousseau was more explicit than in the final version as to *why* this type of socialization could not be entrusted to families. In the final draft, the reasons given are that, just as his civic duties are not left up to the individual to decide upon, so the education of children should not be left up to the individual father's ideas and prejudices, since its outcome is of even more importance to the republic than to the father. He, after all, will die, and often does not experience the fruits of his work, but the state endures forever, and the effects of its citizens' education are its lifeblood.[75] However, the significant reason that is not included in the final version, but was written and subsequently crossed out in the earlier one, is that fathers cannot be entrusted with the task of education in a republic because "they could make [their children] into very good sons and very bad citizens."[76]

In these two examples, then, Rousseau was to some extent in agreement with those other utopia builders who recognized the threat of the family to the cohesion of the larger community. In general, however, his theory of the relations between the family and the state is in direct opposition to this tendency. He refers to marriage as "certainly the first and holiest of all the bonds of society," an institution which "has civil effects without which society cannot even subsist."[77] Thus in a republic it is inconceivable that it be left to the clergy alone to regulate.[78] His belief in the central place of the family in society was what made Rousseau so disgusted by the plots of Greek drama. *Oedipus* and other such plays depicting incest and parricide were likely to corrupt the spectator's imagination with "crimes at which nature trembles." Molière's comedies were equally deplorable, because so satirical about the very most sacred of relationships. By ridiculing the respectable rights of fathers over their children and husbands over their wives, he "shakes the whole order of society."[79]

In Book 1 of *Emile*, Rousseau makes it clear that he regards the family as the principal socializing unit for the preservation of social order. It is with mothers that one must begin, in order to "restore all men to their original duties." When mothers resume nursing their children, "morals will be reformed; natural feelings will revive in every heart; the state will be repopulated; this first step alone will reunite everybody." The best counterpart to bad morals, he asserts several times, are the attractions of domestic life.[80] When mothers become devoted to their children again, men will become just as good in their roles of husband and father, which is crucial. For a "father, in begetting and providing nourishment for his children accomplishes only a third of his task. He owes men to the species, sociable men to society, and citizens to the state."[81] In agreement with this, Saint-Preux affirms that the principal duty of man in society is to rear his children well and provide them with a good example. The Wolmar family is certainly a model in this respect, laying great stress on the education of its young.

This whole trend of thought, which seems so inconsistent with Rousseau's insistence that one must choose to educate a child to be either man or citizen, and with his acknowledgment that educating him to be a loyal family member by no means coincides with making him into a loyal citizen, is brought to a climax in the attack, in Book 5 of *Emile*, against Plato's proposal that the family be abolished. This objectionable suggestion, Rousseau claims, constitutes the

> subversion of the tenderest natural feelings, sacrificed to an artificial feeling that cannot exist without them; as if one had no need of a natural attachment in order to form the bonds of convention; as if the love that one has for those nearest to one were not the basis for that which one owes to the state; as if it were not through the little fatherland that is the family that one's heart becomes attached to the great one; as if it were not the good son, the good husband, the good father who makes the good citizen.[82]

Here, no tension is seen to exist between family interest and republican interest, and the arguments for public education seem to be completely undermined. Given Rousseau's belief that human nature had to be deformed in order to make men into citizens, his calling upon natural feelings to aid in the development of the artificial ones of patriotism is highly puzzling. An individual reared in a very private atmosphere, with affections for and loyalty to just a few people, is scarcely likely to grow up feeling that all his compatriots are equally his siblings, the state his mother, and all the members of its ruling generation his fathers.

If the men who are members of nuclear families will have difficulties in becoming the sort of citizens Rousseau requires for his republic, the conflict for women, as he would have them, must inevitably be worse. Since the family is regarded as their only proper sphere of influence, and they receive no preparation for civic participation, it is not reasonable to expect them to use the powers that they have over their husbands for the promotion of any but the most narrow interests—those of their immediate households. Since their children are explicitly seen as their vital link with a husband whose affections may be otherwise declined, they are hardly likely to sacrifice the interests of these children, let alone their lives, for the sake of a republic which can have very little reality in their own purely domestic lives. No woman educated and confined as Julie and Sophie are would ever be able to behave like the Spartan mother whose patriotism Rousseau so much admired.

Thus, Rousseau's women are even more vulnerable than men to the conflicts of loyalties that he was so much aware of in the human condition. They were, moreover, almost bound to lend their support to the side he considered the less desirable. For in spite of his yearnings for isolation and independence, he believed that the wider one extended one's affections, the better one was as a person. "The most vicious of men," he asserts, "is he who isolates himself the most, who most concentrates himself in himself; the best is he who shares his affections equally with all his kind."[83] Women, however, socialized in the restricted way he considers suitable for them, and placed in the only position he believes proper, have no reason to choose their country before their families, and have few defenses that would make them able to prefer any wider sphere of loyalty than that of sexual love, which provides them with their only means of power. Thus, in addition to the fact that Rousseau's prescriptions for women are in flagrant contradiction with those values, equality and freedom, which he regards as so crucial to humanity, the women he envisages are not only likely to be destructive of themselves, but are also likely to be subversive of his two most idealized institutions, the patriarchal family and the small democratic republic.

Rousseau's philosophy as a whole is by no means optimistic. What he asserts is the ultimate insolubility of the dilemma of being a man in society. However, he did construct a republic of denatured men, transformed into devoted patriots, and his intentions that this should not be considered simply an intellectual game are manifest in his works on Corsica and Poland. On the other hand, the end of the story of Emile is not totally pessimistic either. Emile survives the abortive attempt to make him into a husband, father, and citizen, and becomes what he was always intended to be—a natural and autonomous man. The fates of Rousseau's women, however, could not be more tragic. Though ideals of their sex, they cannot be allowed to live in the patriarchal world, since there is no way they can fulfill the totally contradictory expectations it places on them. At least Rousseau allows that a man can be either an individual or a citizen. He does not allow a woman to be either.

Notes

1. *Emile*, O.C. 4, pp. 835, 855–57.
2. *Emile*, p. 823.
3. *Emile*, p. 493.
4. *Emile*, p. 858.
5. *Emile*, p. 858; see also p. 818.
6. *Emile*, pp. 858–59.
7. *Emile*, p. 860.
8. *Emile et Sophie*, O.C. 4, p. 914.
9. *Men and Citizens*, p. 150.
10. *Emile*, pp. 249–50.
11. *Emile et Sophie*, p. 918.
12. *Emile*, p. 763.
13. *Emile et Sophie*, p. 904.
14. *Emile*, pp. 911–12.
15. *Emile*, p. 884. Emile reports that "the last day of her life showed me (charms) that I had not known of."
16. *Emile*, p. 887.
17. *Emile*, p. 751.
18. "L'Education de Sophie," pp. 126–27. See *Emile*, p. 762.
19. *Confessions*, O.C. 1, p. 430.
20. It is significant that only the women in Rousseau's novels appear to have any parents, and

therefore, to be faced with the potential conflict of family duty with their own feelings and consciences.

21. *La Nouvelle Héloise*, O.C. 2, p. 96.

22. *La Nouvelle Héloise*, p. 103.

23. *La Nouvelle Héloise*, p. 212.

24. *La Nouvelle Héloise*, p. 201.

25. *La Nouvelle Héloise*, pp. 226–27.

26. *La Nouvelle Héloise*, p. 340.

27. *La Nouvelle Héloise*, p. 401.

28. *La Nouvelle Héloise*, p. 528.

29. *La Nouvelle Héloise*, p. 694.

30. *La Nouvelle Héloise*, p. 664.

31. *Men and Citizens*, p. 120. René Schaerer, too, says that Julie plays the part of the redeemer, "Jean-Jacques Rousseau et la Grande Famille," in *Jean-Jacques Rousseau*, Baud-Bovy, et al. p. 199.

32. *Emile*, p. 709.

33. *Emile*, p. 249.

34. *La Nouvelle Héloise*, p. 612; *Emile*, p. 251.

35. *Emile*, p. 249.

36. *Emile*, p. 249; *Réponse à M. Bordes*, p. 60.

37. *Considerations on the Government of Poland*, O.C. 3, p. 966, and see chap. 4; also *Letter to d'Alembert*, pp. 125–26.

38. *Letter to d'Alembert*, p. 111; *Emile*, pp. 250–51.

39. *Emile*, pp. 249–50.

40. *Emile*, p. 251 (emphasis added).

41. *Emile*, pp. 483–84, and see p. 654: "as a member of society he must fulfill its duties."

42. *Emile*, p. 823.

43. *The Social Contract*, O.C. 3, p. 351.

44. *Emile*, pp. 493–94; *Confessions*, p. 414. For two recent and interesting discussions of Rousseau's philosophy of love, see John Charvet, *The Social Problem in the Philosophy of Rousseau*, pp. 114–17, and Elizabeth Rapaport, "On the Future of Love: Rousseau and the Radical Feminists," pp. 185–205.

45. See Second Preface to *La Nouvelle Héloise*, pp. 15–16, and text pp. 372–73.

45. *Emile*, pp. 775–76.

46. *La Nouvelle Héloise*, p. 372.

48. See, e.g., *Confessions*, p. 424.

49. *La Nouvelle Héloise*, p. 223.

50. *La Nouvelle Héloise*, p. 147.

51. *La Nouvelle Héloise*, pp. 56 and 312.

52. *La Nouvelle Héloise*, p. 194.

53. *Emile*, p. 819.

54. *Correspondence générale*, vol. 4, p. 827.

55. *Letter to d'Alembert*, p. 118.

56. *Letter to d'Alembert*, p. 117.

57. *Emile*, p. 866.

58. *Emile*, p. 866.

59. *La Nouvelle Héloise*, p. 372.

60. *La Nouvelle Héloise*, p. 373.

61. *Letter to d'Alembert*, p. 47.

62. *Greedy Institutions*, p. 139.

63. *Greedy Institutions*, p. 140, from Rosabeth Kanter, *Commitment and Community*, Cambridge, Mass., 1972, p. 87.

64. *La Nouvelle Héloise*, pp. 449–50.

65. See Coser, chaps. 7, 8, 9, and 10; Plato, *Republic* v; Campanella, *The City of the Sun*, pp. 282–93; Fourier, *The Utopian Vision of Charles Fourier*, parts 5, 6, and 7.

66. *Letter to d'Alembert*, p. 131.

67. Compare *Considerations on the Government of Poland*, pp. 970–71 with *Discourse on Political Economy*, O.C. 3, p. 241.

68. *Discourse on Political Economy*, p. 261.

69. *Emile*, pp. 248–49.

70. *Discourse on Political Economy*, p. 246.

71. *The Social Contract*, p. 361.

72. *The Social Contract*, p. 438.

73. *Discourse on Political Economy*, pp. 286, 263–64.

74. O.C. 3, p. 1400 (note to *Discourse on Political Economy*, p. 261).

75. *Discourse on Political Economy*, pp. 260–61.

76. *Discourse on Political Economy*, p. 1400.

77. *Letter to d'Alembert*, p. 128; *The Social Contract*, p. 469 (Rousseau's note).

78. *Social Contract*, p. 469, note.

79. *Letter to d'Alembert*, pp. 34–35.

80. *Emile*, p. 258; *La Nouvelle Héloise*, Second Preface, p. 24.

81. *Emile*, p. 262.

82. *Emile*, p. 700.

83. *Letter to d'Alembert*, p. 117.

5

Women, Power, and the Politics of Everyday Life

Mira Morgenstern

Throughout his writings, Rousseau remains aware that a fully transformational politics might not be within man's grasp. He recognizes that a political solution to the challenges posed by modern life might be partial or tentative. In those circumstances, it would be logical for Rousseau to attempt to find within the confines of everyday life a structure that would guard and even nurture whatever embers of authenticity might exist within an inauthentic world. At worst, this would allow man to retain a measure of honesty and self-realization within his private life. At best, it would provide a platform for man to establish a fully authentic life on both the personal and political levels. Rousseau believes that he has found such a structure in his conception of the family.

It is important to emphasize that it is the family, as Rousseau understands it, that would provide the haven and launching pad for authenticity in an inauthentic world. Certainly the reality of eighteenth-century family life, especially as manifest in both the noble and bourgeois classes and as reflected in Rousseau's own experience, offered little hope for such a rejuvenation. As a young apprentice, Rousseau's suffering at the hands of unsympathetic, avaricious families had led him to run away from Geneva. His observations of family life among the nobility of eighteenth-century France did little to raise his opinion of the quality of family life as it actually existed.[1] In fact, Rousseau's musings at the end of the fourth book of *Émile* reveal his ideal family unit to be actually the gathering of a few carefully selected friends at a secluded chateau.[2] Nevertheless, in his theoretical writings, Rousseau does look to the family as the "keeper of the flame" of authenticity and even as the harbinger of the revolution that would restore authenticity to its rightful place as the cornerstone of the human condition. This is evident particularly in Rousseau's emphasis on breast-feeding at the beginning of *Émile*, which is actually his attempt to reestablish the family on an emotionally honest basis. In the same spirit, *Émile* closes with the founding by Émile and Sophie of a New Family that is supposed to serve as the exemplar of the authentic personal life and might also herald the advent of an authentic political system.

Rousseau supports this positive notion of the family by tracing its genesis to the State of Nature. It is not Rousseau's intention here to deduce the teleological end of the family from its origins.[3] Rather, Rousseau wants to emphasize the natural status of the family in order to establish its character and orientation as basically good, in the manner of all things emanating from the State of Nature. On the other hand, Rousseau also notes that the family is the outcome of the first "great revolution," resulting in the socialization of Savage Man, with all the attendant good and evil that this implies.[4] The mixture of socialized evil along with natural goodness in Rousseau's description of the family underlines the extent to which the family sits astride a great historical divide. This is seen both in terms of the affective content and the structural makeup of the family. Emotionally, the family combines within itself the immediacy of man's intimate relationships in the State of Nature and the rifts that obtain from social concourse. Structurally, the family is characterized as both revolutionary and reactionary. On the one hand, the family is both the outcome of and the catalyst for major changes in the operation of daily life and social norms. On the other hand, the family as a social unit works to counter change and solidify the status quo. The family that started out as a revolutionary entity operates in actuality as a reactionary force within society.

These conflicting aspects of the family's nature and method of operation—emotional authenticity versus social destructiveness, revolutionary origin versus reactionary operation—structure Rousseau's discussion of the family. The family is important to Rousseau with regard to two major issues. First, the family as depicted by Rousseau plays a major role in defining one's notion of one's Self. This is particularly true with reference to the learning of sex roles and acceptable conduct within the context of everyday, intimate relationships. Second, the family serves to educate man to live in society in general and in political society in particular.[5] It is clear that conflicting aspects exist within and between these categories. The contradictory elements present within the family's emotional notion of the Self, as well as the structural opposition between the two conceptions of what the family's social role should be, can combine to stultify the individual and paralyze the family unit in their respective developments. Similarly, the clash between the role of the family as the vehicle for the nurturing of the individual and as the vehicle for communicating the ethic of the surrounding society can mean that the needs and desires of the individual may not mesh with the socially and politically accepted norms that the family is trying to transmit. As a result, the education of the individual to social and political life may fail. One may conjecture that this failure may be unavoidable. It can be understood as the inevitable result of forcing one structure—the family—to serve as both the cradle of society's existence and the catalyst of social upheaval.

However, despite the contradictory forces within the family that can conspire in its failure to achieve its goals, Rousseau persists in trying to fashion a coherent understanding of the role of the family within his social and political system. The stakes for Rousseau in accomplishing this are high. If Rousseau is successful, he will have achieved a goal that has thus far proven elusive. The family can then serve to establish an affective basis of cohesion for Rousseau's political system. On the other hand, failure to achieve even a theoretical understanding of the nature of the family casts doubt upon any realization of Rousseau's political vision. Of course, the successful construction of a theory of the authentic family does not guarantee its automatic implementation. However, even if this theoretical understanding does not yield immediate practical solutions, a coherent theoretical grasp of the family's structure and function can be of great help in understanding why certain approaches may not prove as fruitful as others, and wherein lie their weaknesses as solutions. In this context, Rousseau's critique of how families have failed their own constituent members in furthering their true personal and communal interests is particularly important, for it points to the moral bankruptcy in the categorization of existence that has been spawned by the emergence of the family as a social structure. In effect, Rousseau argues that the family as it has developed throughout history is responsible for the cognitive misperception of life. The negative repercussions arising from these ill-founded notions explain what Rousseau claims is modern man's inability to ask the proper questions and thus to elucidate effective solutions for the ills plaguing him. One cognitive misperception that Rousseau concentrates on is the mutually exclusive division of the private and public dimensions of life. He demonstrates how adhering to these categories dooms any realization of authenticity on either the personal or political level.

Rousseau's analysis of the family as it has developed throughout history and in its present-day incarnation pays special attention to the position of women. This is because, in Rousseau's view, women are the linchpin of the family, influencing both its nature and mode of operation. Therefore, Rousseau considers the role of women crucial to the fate of the transformational revolution that would promote the development of private and political authenticity. Since asking the proper questions is indispensable, in Rousseau's view, to the possibility of achieving this authenticity, he argues that the fate of the family and of the correct perception of cognitive categories are linked. In other words, Rousseau will use the family not only to demonstrate the misbegotten content of man's existence in an inauthentic world, but also to highlight the skewed understanding of the realities of man's life and surroundings that effectively prevents any solution from ever being recognized. In the process, Rousseau demonstrates how his analysis of women and the family serves as a universal metaphor for the personal and political concerns that affect us all.

Rousseau writes of the family in both of his novelistic works, *Émile* and *La Nouvelle Héloïse*. Relatively little concrete detail about family life per se is given in *Émile*: the book ends with Sophie's pregnancy, and its sequel, *Les Solitaires*, opens with the account of the death of Émile and Sophie's daughter. Aside from general remarks that Rousseau (or the Tutor/Narrator) makes on the ills of family life in the eighteenth century and the proposed remedies for them, the failure of Émile and Sophie's marriage and of their attempt to build a family together can most fruitfully be analyzed as the result of a flaw in their relationship and the deficiencies of Sophie's own education, rather than the outcome of the actualization of a specific concept of the family as such.

Rousseau's most extended descriptions of family life and various concrete models thereof occur in *La Nouvelle Héloïse*. First, there is the traditional patriarchal model, as exemplified by the d'Etanges family. Second, there is the Wolmar household, run on the enlightened principles set forth by M. de Wolmar. This model emphasizes partnership and communal effort. Finally, there is the estate at Clarens, which functions as a setting for and an extension of the Wolmar household that lies at its center. Although the estate at Clarens is clearly not a political entity, its relationship and proximity to the Wolmars make it an interesting case study for the analysis of the relationship between the family, as an intimate grouping based on love, and the outside society with which it must interact. It should be added that there is a ghost of yet a fourth model of family in *La Nouvelle Héloïse*: a family founded completely on romantic love against the conscious dictates of society's norms. This is the family that is conceived by Saint-Preux and Julie before her marriage to Wolmar. Like Julie's projected union with Saint-Preux, this family is spontaneously aborted.

Analysis of these three models of the family shows that contrary to what Rousseau's pronouncements in *Émile* regarding the contemporary dissolution of the family suggest, all of these models of the family contain morally virtuous members. Moreover, all of them function behind a veil of peacefulness and orderliness that masks the deep unhappiness that lies at their core. In addition, all of these models make use of the minutiae of everyday life to conceal the power plays that maintain the oppressive status quo. The fact that these three families in effect do disintegrate even though they share none of what Rousseau labels as the "bad" characteristics of the contemporary family forces us to reevaluate the family not only regarding its moral character, but also in terms of its ability cognitively to structure the way in which we view the world at large vis-à-vis our own private lives.

The Patriarchal Model: The d'Etanges Family

La Nouvelle Héloïse first presents us with a picture of the d'Etanges family, a typical patriarchal family that appears happy and peaceful from the outside. Into this well-defined landscape comes Saint-Preux, whose love for Julie, the cherished, only daughter of the d'Etanges household, threatens the order of this world.[6] Saint-Preux's love for Julie is seen as a menace not just on the social level but on the moral plane as well. Socially, the fact that Saint-Preux, a man of no specific class, dares to love a daughter of the nobility defies the notion of the hierarchy that underlies the foundations of the eighteenth-century social universe.[7] Saint-Preux's lack of birth is emphasized by the circumstance that he, unlike Julie, has no family. Furthermore, his lack of name—Saint-Preux is just a pseudonym—indicates that he does not belong to the aristocratic milieu into which he has entered. Thus, Saint-Preux is in a prime position to serve as both critic and victim of this world—both of which functions he fulfills, to a greater or lesser extent, by the end of the novel.

The moral dimension of the critique of the patriarchal family is manifest first on the level of personal narrative. (Lord Eduard Bomston delivers an additional moral critique, from a more rational, removed standpoint; but this is analyzed later.) Julie and Saint-Preux, who are both victims of a social system that refuses to countenance their marriage, struggle with the moral implications of the patriarchal family system. Strictly speaking, it would be more accurate to say that it is Julie who attempts morally to justify the demands of the patriarchal family while still reckoning with the requirements of her heart. Saint-Preux, bereft of family, feels little need to take to heart the wishes of the family or to find an ethical justification for them. On the other hand, it is understandable that Julie, as a product of the patriarchal structure, feels compelled to do just that.

The crux of Julie's internal struggle revolves around the use of the word "Nature." Since, in Rousseau's lexicon, the "natural" is identified with what is morally good (or at least without evil), it seems logical that if Julie can find which of her loyalties is the "natural" one, she will have discovered the moral solution to her dilemma. Unfortunately, Julie's confusion is mirrored, rather than resolved, by her use of language. Both her feelings for her family and her love for Saint-Preux are described by her, at different junctures, as "natural."[8] Interestingly, however, Julie's use of Nature to explain her devotion to her family reveals a portrait of her family that increasingly takes on the coloring of an authoritarian power structure. When Julie speaks of the "natural" character of the family and thus the rectitude of its demands upon her, she uses the term *droit du sang*.[9] She does not understand this term in the sense her father uses it: that is, to indicate that possession of the same blood makes for the self-identification of a group of individuals as part of the same clan.[10] Rather,

Julie understands the *droit du sang* to evoke the right of command over another individual, a right that accompanies that individual's creation. Because her parents are the authors of her being, they rightfully exercise authority over her entire life.[11] In the end, Julie rejects the attempt to find a solution by determining which position is morally "natural." Instead, she reverts to an analysis of what is emotionally possible. She refuses Bomston's suggestion to go to England with Saint-Preux, because she claims that she cannot be happy if the cost is her parents' misery.[12] Still, it is clear that the images provoked by the criterion of "Nature" have a very strong effect on Julie. It is one to which she ultimately succumbs, even while criticizing its process and its results. This is seen in Julie's reaction to what she perceives as her sale in marriage to Wolmar, which she describes as both the exercise of her father's "natural" proprietary rights and evidence of his "unnatural" and unfeeling character. Reacting to the news of her forthcoming marriage to Wolmar, she writes to Clare, "Has my father then sold me? He pays for his life with my own . . . barbaric and denatured father!"[13]

Eventually, Julie does yield to being so used. We subsequently see that Julie's marriage to Wolmar and subsequent life at Clarens can be understood at one level as a reworking of the patriarchal family model under a more benevolent guise. The fact that Julie actively works to perpetuate a patriarchal system is already subtly evident in her argument rejecting Bomston's offer of asylum. One reason she refuses the offer is her fear of undermining her future authority as a parent. How, she asks, will she receive any respect from her children if she flouts the wishes of her own parents?[14] Clearly, at some level, Julie feels that she has a stake in the endurance of the patriarchal system, even if that system continues to oppress her.[15]

Although Julie has a very confused notion of where her interests lie, Lord Eduard Bomston is keenly aware of the moral and psychological forces that are at play. Bomston's commentary serves as the second level of moral critique of the patriarchal family. Because he is a foreigner in Switzerland and a stranger to the family of Julie, Bomston stands above the narrative and does not get sucked into its vortex. He exemplifies the ethical and rational approach to this vexed situation. In his conversation with Julie's father and in his letter to Julie, Bomston shows a clear understanding of where the rights of Nature lie. Unlike the Baron d'Etanges, whose concept of family is exclusively allied to blood, Bomston recognizes that deeds, not lineage, are what really count.[16] In this view, family is a moral concept to be lived up to by its members, rather than an institution that ruthlessly controls their lives. Nobility—that is, excellence of family—is a function of what the individual does, not of what group he belongs to.[17] Bomston cites "glory of country" and general "human happiness" as yardsticks by which to measure the nobility of individual acts.[18] It seems clear that Rousseau is using these ideas as expressed by Bomston to criticize the corrupt nobility of France at the time. In that, Rousseau—via Bomston—is echoing the general Enlightenment critique of what was viewed as a degenerate and parasitic feudal class. But Bomston is also making another point. Nature, as a moral category, cannot take the part of institutions over people. For a structure to be morally acceptable, it must value the happiness of its constituent members even above its collective honor. Thus, Bomston has no qualms about identifying Julie's and Saint-Preux's happiness with Nature and implying that a society that does not recognize happiness as a morally good end is, in fact, a society of unjust laws.[19] Bomston is also shrewd enough to realize that Julie is confused in her moral judgment. Thus, he advises her that listening to her father would not be obeying the higher dictates of Nature as embodied in duty, but rather would be merely caving in to the demands of public behavior (bienséance).[20] He tries to make Julie appreciate this ethical contradiction, but ultimately does not succeed in this goal.[21]

The acuity of Bomston's judgment, especially regarding the tyranny of Julie's father, is borne out almost immediately in an incident that, while small in itself, can be seen as a metaphor for the development of the rest of the novel. Enraged to hear of Julie and Saint-Preux's attachment for each other, the Baron d'Etanges hits Julie, causing her to fall and bleed. The family is subsequently reconciled, but Julie miscarries Saint-Preux's child as a result of this incident. The outward scene of restored family harmony, peace, and understanding following the physical reestablishment of the baron's authority over his own family serves as an ironic counterpoint to the horror of bloodshed and violence that it succeeds. The establishment of family peace upon a moment of violence calls into question the moral underpinnings of the patriarchal family structure. In this context, Claire's remark—"[Q]ue fait la voix publique à ton inflexible pere"[22]—proves remarkably prescient. Elsewhere, Rousseau defines the public voice as possessed of a divine nature.[23] Julie's father, motivated only by his own idiosyncratic and selfishly conceived desires, stands in total opposition to the moral will of the people. If this kind of patriarchal family structure—that is, one that is depraved and immoral by nature—is shown to be generalized throughout the various models of the family presented by Rousseau, it will cast into doubt Rousseau's entire enterprise of trying to keep alive the personal and political goals of authenticity through the institution of the family.

The Benevolent Patriarchy: The Wolmar Family at Clarens

The family structure that Wolmar sets up at Clarens appears to be very different from the patriarchal model of the d'Etanges house. For one thing, the Wolmar family is much more closely linked to the surrounding society. In fact, it is one of the central tenets of their family life that the entire purpose of marriage is for the couple to devote themselves to the betterment of humankind.[24] In this scheme, the family serves primarily as an exemplar of good living and as a socializing agent for the lower classes. In addition, the family as a reproductive agent also serves physically to keep the society itself in existence. The Wolmar household defines itself by and expands itself over the people living on their estate at Clarens. The Wolmar household itself cannot be fully understood unless it is viewed in its capacity as the center of the society that it has molded and continues to control.

The second way in which the Wolmar household appears to differ from that of the d'Etanges is in its emphasis on collegiality and inclusiveness rather than strict hierarchy and exclusivity. In underlining his bloodlines and commandeering his family by virtue of his absolute authority as patriarch, the Baron d'Etanges runs his family in a manner typical of the nobility, who supported a political system that was itself structured along authoritarian lines. By contrast, Wolmar sets up his family so that each person's tasks are made to complement the generalized goal of the entire unit. By making each individual aware that he is working for a purpose higher than personal satisfaction or gain, Wolmar imbues each individual with a feeling for the larger structure of which each individual is a part. This method is used both within the Wolmar family proper and throughout the estate at Clarens, thus strengthening the collective identity of each structure and deepening the bonds between them.

The inclusiveness that is typical of Wolmar's familial and social structures at Clarens is a result of the collegiality with which he runs his various enterprises. Since participants understand their tasks as part of the goal of the greater whole that they aim for in unison, they come to see themselves and to be defined by the job they do. Consequently, it is function, rather than blood, that carries with it a sense of belonging. Such a familial structure, or society, is more open to accept new members than are ones in which the right of membership is defined exclusively by one's blood. Thus, at Clarens, Wolmar's immediate family expands to include Claire, her daughter, and even Julie's former lover, Saint-Preux. As long as they play their assigned roles, they are members of the family. Similarly, for the workers on the estate, the right to remain at Clarens is acquired not by birth but by adhering to the social system and work rules set up by Wolmar. Disobedience is punished by dismissal.

Wolmar's family structure and the entire estate of Clarens appear to be collegial and relatively open. However, the affable inclusivity of these structures is a mirage. In reality, the family and society at Clarens operate much like a ruthless patriarchy disguised as benevolent paternalism. The strains that are created by the dissonance between appearance and reality open up the possibility for a critique of the family structure in general that can reveal new avenues for the attainment of personal and political authenticity.

The Tyranny of Intimacy

Underlying Wolmar's patriarchal management style and his perpetration of favorable belief systems on both servants and family is the structure of substitution that contradicts the atmosphere of transparency that Wolmar claims to establish as the moral and emotional climate at Clarens. This substitution takes the form of disguise. Wolmar controls the servants by making the unnatural state of servitude appear pleasurable to the servants and by making them believe that they are working for their own best interests.[25] Wolmar's genius is that he makes the natural emotions of servitude work to his own best interests, with the servants remaining totally unaware of this manipulation. Consequently, instead of complaining about their masters, the servants feel upset if they are not singled out for special favors; instead of banding together against their masters, they unite to serve them better.[26] Wolmar is chiefly concerned with controlling the servants' belief system in order to assure himself of unquestioning obedience and good service. Once this goal is attained, the assumption is that the belief system and the consciousness of the servants have been sufficiently governed. The smooth running of Clarens is the proof of the servants' successful indoctrination.

The achievement of complete control of the family is a little trickier because there Wolmar's priorities are reversed. His interest is not, as with the servants, to dominate their belief systems in order to control their actions. Rather, he wants to command the hearts and minds of his family as such. The actions of his family are of no particular concern to Wolmar because Wolmar has never entertained any real doubts on that score. This is evident in Wolmar's statement to Julie that even before their marriage he had already satisfied himself that she would never be unfaithful to her marriage vows.[27] The desire to direct his family's emotional responses and philosophical beliefs causes Wolmar to surround his family with an entire network of appearances that masquerades as the real thing. Thus, for example, the environment of Clarens appears to be one of liberty, gaiety, and abundance, but it is actually one of restraint, order, and frugality.[28] The servants and masters seem to live in a spirit of equality, but there are unspoken rules and limitations that, if violated, earn the servants instant dismissal.[29] While nobody appears either to command or to obey, Clarens is too well regulated to have emerged from spontaneity and happenstance. In fact, Wolmar's master stroke at Clarens is to create a deliberate inversion of spontaneity and order. This is exemplified by Julie's garden, whose riotous, seemingly abandoned vegetation conceals the carefully controlling hand and labor of Julie and Wolmar.[30] Still, at first glance, it is difficult to find any concrete evidence of deliberate subterfuge or manipulation done for selfish purposes. Such small indications as appear can be easily justified as completely benign. Thus, for example, the fact that the local wines of Clarens are disguised to resemble more expensive foreign wines can be readily understood as a function of Clarens's autarkic system.[31] Since the rationale for Clarens's self-sufficiency is Wolmar's desire to remain uncorrupted by the luxuries and false needs of the outside world, there seems to be nothing wrong with varying the tastes of the local produce to avoid boredom.

Where, then, can evidence be found of selfish manipulation on the part of Wolmar, who acts ostensibly to maximize the happiness and transparency of his family at Clarens? The first hint of dissonance is to be found in Julie's reaction to Clarens: she finds her happiness tiresome and ultimately unfulfilling.[32] This is not yet the philosophical condemnation of the system at Clarens that appears in Julie's deathbed confession. Rather, it is a perplexing indication that something is not quite right. In a society of transparency, nobody should be bored. On the contrary, the unmediated authenticity should be a source of mutual stimulus and discovery. That life is, instead, monotonous points to a rigidity that exists when life is lived according to an empty formula.[33] Viewed from this vantage point, other heretofore unremarkable incidents at Clarens begin to take on a new significance. A certain amount of cynicism and hypocrisy is evident in the descriptions of the everyday routine at Clarens. For example, if the relationship between masters and servants is so open and frank, why does Saint-Preux find it necessary to comment that the only time the family can be truly open and at ease with one another is when no servants are permitted to be present?[34] The acknowledgment that the master-servant association is not in actuality what it is proclaimed to be strengthens the suspicion that the disjunction between appearance and reality at Clarens is more sinister than benign. This is confirmed when Wolmar admits that there is nothing that cannot be obtained from "beautiful spirits"—his way of referring to Julie and Saint-Preux—by the use of confidence and frankness.[35] While this apparently is no more than a factual statement, closer analysis reveals it to be a description of technique. As already noted, Wolmar is concerned not so much with Julie's and Saint-Preux's overt actions as with their emotional responses to each other. To "cure" them of their "malady," he treats them with overt frankness and trust. But Wolmar has his plans for both of them: he notes that Saint-Preux is "easy to subdue."[36] The language of submission and domination in Wolmar's letter to Claire outlining his strategy for his wife and her former lover reveals that Wolmar's major concern is not really everyone's happiness and self-development, but rather centers on Wolmar's own preoccupation with power and his desire to achieve total control of the society at Clarens.[37] The appearance of openness and transparency is merely a means that Wolmar cynically uses to attain his ultimate goal of a society fashioned entirely in his own image.

The strength of Wolmar's technique is that he uses people's goals of honesty and authenticity against them. By convincing people that they have achieved transparency, he can guarantee himself that they will physically act and emotionally react in ways beneficial to Wolmar while still believing that they are living lives of philosophical authenticity. That is why Wolmar cautions Saint-Preux to disregard his presence and to speak to Julie exactly as if he were in private conversation with her.[38] This exemplifies what Richard Sennett has called the tyranny of intimacy: the use of emotional closeness to justify the moral content of public actions.[39] In this case, Wolmar uses the intimacy of the inner circle at Clarens to "prove" the moral content of his own organizational management of Clarens. As we have already seen, however, the celebration of intimacy and transparancy does not mean that they actually exist. Furthermore, intimacy itself is no guarantee of moral goodness. Sharing a moment of spontaneous, simultaneous emotion in the family sanctuary, the Salon d'Apollon, is no proof that one is living an authentic life.[40] On the contrary, by internalizing Wolmar's standards and assessments, the inhabitants of Clarens happily delude themselves that they are living in an idyllic world—which perfectly suits Wolmar's plans.[41]

The success of Wolmar's scheme depends on his ability to control the emotional reactions of his extended family, the intimate circle of Clarens. It is interesting to note, however, that Wolmar does not control and manipulate the reactions of everyone in the intimate society of Clarens in the same manner. The characters of La Nouvelle Héloïse can be divided into two categories according to their different reactions to the system of appearances and masks at Clarens: those who need to believe in the moral existence of transparency, and those who cynically use that nomenclature quietly to pursue their own private goals. The first group includes Julie and Saint-Preux; the second encompasses Wolmar and Claire.

Reactions to the Tyranny of Intimacy

Of all the characters in La Nouvelle Héloïse, Claire has received the least scrutiny. Most often, she is seen as merely a foil for Julie, the fourth player needed to round out the quartet of intimate friends.[42] However it is Claire who, while remaining within the traditional confines set for women, manages to carve out an area of independent action for herself. Unlike Julie, Claire as a youth never harbored romantic ideals for herself and consequently does not seek them in marriage. She feels herself incapable of loving[43] and openly admits that she married primarily to escape an intolerable family situation at home.[44] Although the structure of Julie's situation is somewhat similar to Claire's—with the illness and subsequent death of her mother and the tearful pleas of her father, the atmosphere

in Julie's girlhood home is not exactly conducive to a tranquil existence—Julie's belief in and need for authenticity make the responses of
these two cousins to their respective lives vastly different. Claire views
marriage as a state of slavery, to be gotten through in order to attain a
certain measure of autonomy that is otherwise denied to women.[45] That
is why widowhood is not a period of sorrow for Claire. No longer subject
to the constraints of marriage,[46] she is now free to be herself: she travels
and indulges her wide-ranging interests in culture and foreign political
systems.[47] Claire sees her life as a series of opportunities to play various
roles. She herself mentions the "coquette" and the "merry widow" as two
parts that she has played. By playing a role, Claire manages to create a
distance between her public persona and her private Self. By accepting
that the constraints of society will never allow these two to be one and
the same, she makes a virtue of necessity. The space between her public
and private lives provides for her an area of autonomy in which she can
examine her options and her actions. It is true that achieving this measure of control is dependent on a willingness to put on a mask and to
experiment with one's life. For Claire, however, there is no other option
if she is to enjoy any autonomy at all. She advises Julie to do the same,
for Claire believes that this emotional distance between private thoughts
and public actions can be achieved even in marriage and within the
traditional feminine roles of wife and mother.[48] The result, according to
Claire, would be that Julie would achieve greater mastery and power over
her own life.

The creative play that Claire recommends is a game plan that Julie
cannot follow. Julie is committed to searching for authenticity and to
creating a common thread of honesty and fulfillment linking the private
and public aspects of her life. This is first evident in her desire to marry
Saint-Preux—that is, to introduce personal love into an institution that,
in her day at least, carried considerable social significance. It is only when
Julie is convinced of the correctness of an alternative moral criterion—
that is, convinced that the existence of happiness is a reliable judge of
ethical value and that the presence of love in marriage destroys such
happiness—that she consents to a loveless marriage.

In her life at Clarens, Julie still strives to unite the personal and public
aspects of her life through the medium of transparency: being the same
at all times regardless of context. The one exception to this rule is prayer.
Julie, unlike her atheistic husband, is devoutly religious and insists on
maintaining her schedule of prayers and devotions. In effect, this is the

one area of autonomy that she carves out for herself at Clarens, although the nature of this self-expression is itself quite restrictive. Prayer occupies a small portion of Julie's day, and religion generally serves as a restraining force on self-expression and willful acts, not as a rationale for revolution. Nevertheless, it is significant that Wolmar's atheism is the one barrier that Julie sees to her own perfect happiness and that this barrier manifests itself in precisely that area in which Julie achieves some autonomy for herself—albeit limited in character—an area that remains outside of her regular duties at Clarens. In general, however, Julie adheres to the belief that perfect transparency will guarantee her happiness. What Julie comes to realize on her deathbed is that transparency neither vouches for happiness as a moral criterion nor guarantees the attainment of happiness in terms of individual self-fulfillment. We, as readers, are further aware that this is because the transparency at Clarens was a sham to begin with. Julie's words on her deathbed—her admission of her love for Saint-Preux and her recognition that her life has not been a happy one—also hint at the acknowledgment that her categories of perception are themselves faulty. Till now, Julie had always based her choices on whether they would increase her happiness: for her, peace of mind remained a moral barometer. But her statements regarding her happiness now take on a contradictory quality. She declares that she is both happy and unhappy.[49] Even when she admits she is happy, she claims that her happiness bores her and that she would rather die.[50] Implied here is that Julie has come to recognize that language alone—in identifying concepts like happiness, for example—cannot help her identify moral categories, for language reflects the ambiguous nature of the concepts that it represents. In an inauthentic world, language is ambiguous because it parallels the malleability of symbols and images that can disguise inauthenticity as transparency. The disjunction between language and meaning points to the lack of meaning in Julie's own life. Forced to face this discrepancy, together with the ambiguity of the symbols that she mistook for solid guideposts to reality, Julie cannot survive.

The person at Clarens who can best understand the gist of Claire's message—that the inauthenticity of wearing masks brings with it a freedom of its own—is Wolmar. It is interesting that Wolmar's early life bears some resemblance to that of Saint-Preux: Wolmar changes his name and goes on to observe different levels of society.[51] Although it is never explicitly stated, it seems obvious that Wolmar, unlike Saint-Preux, is originally of high birth, because Julie's father never objects to his parentage.

Wolmar certainly comes from a wealthy family, although he loses most of his fortune right before his marriage to Julie. What most distinguishes Saint-Preux from Wolmar is their different characters. Saint-Preux, like Julie, needs to unify his personal life with his public persona. Wolmar, on the other hand, can choose to emphasize any realm of action that he wants, since he does not have to contend with any possible dissonance between the private and public aspects of his life. The ability of Wolmar to play a role can be attributed to his lack of anything truly personal in his life: he has no strong needs or desires. Consequently, while both Wolmar and Saint-Preux are "outsiders" of a sort, Wolmar can use his position of outsider to observe and manipulate other people unnoticed. Saint-Preux, on the other hand, winds up as the victim of a society that refuses to let him in. In effect, he "drops out," handing over the direction of his life alternately to Bomston and to Wolmar and filling his time with travel.

Both Wolmar and Claire are able respectively to create and cope with the inauthenticity of the surrounding environment—be it ostensibly perfect like Clarens or merely the received world of tradition—by wearing masks. But these masks have very different functions for the two characters. For Wolmar, the wearing of the mask propels his entire life. In his opinion, life is nothing more than a series of roles. He therefore engineers a part for himself that will allow him to sit on the sidelines and manipulate other people's actions and beliefs. Wolmer's genius is that he manages to dominate people's imaginations so that they think they spontaneously generate the image of him that his role-playing is designed to elicit. The irony is that Wolmar's audience mistakes his two-dimensional mask for a three-dimensional human being. For Claire, on the other hand, masks are a way to cope with a world she did not create and with which she is most emphatically unhappy. Unlike Julie, however, Claire accepts the need to cope with the world on its own terms. Thus, the use of masks to create an area of autonomy for herself is a necessary technique that enables Claire to preserve some sense of Self. To be sure, one can criticize Claire for having a rather shallow Self to begin with: she admits to Julie that she is incapable of truly loving any man, for example.[52] In that context, creating an area of autonomy—an area in which to express some measure of authenticity—may be no great feat as far as Claire is concerned. Certainly one cannot compare Claire's need for self-expression, which can be limited to discrete areas of her life, to Julie's yearning for total honesty and authenticity. On the other hand, Claire does manage to achieve one very great thing while living in an inauthentic world. She manages to survive with some sense of Self intact. Compared with Julie's fate, that is no inconsiderable accomplishment.

Claire comes out ahead of Julie not just in terms of sheer survival but in terms of the quality of that survival as well. While Claire's sense of Self is arguably rendered shallow by the masks that she wears, Julie's Self is totally crushed by them. Julie's existence in the world of masks is riddled with irony. Julie, who abjures the very notion of masks, is forced to live her life wearing one. Due to Wolmar's expert manipulation, she is not even aware that she is wearing a mask. This is accomplished while Julie thinks she has attained true transparency. Ironically, the result of complete consistency—Julie's actualization of Wolmar's dictum to act the same at all times[53]—is utter hypocrisy. Consumed by the need constantly to justify her actions and words as entirely virtuous and consistent, Julie never allows her real Self to come through.[54] Consequently, Julie's Self is destroyed, leaving only a mask as a reminder of the individual that once existed.

The Family as Philosophical Battleground

In their different ways, reactions to the tyranny of intimacy all center on the Self-destroying propensities of masks. Inasmuch as the tyranny of intimacy can take place only within the structure of private life, the family becomes the context in which important philosophical issues do battle. The family as depicted in La Nouvelle Héloïse exemplifies two tensions in Rousseau's thought. One is the contradiction between Self and Other, depicted in the theme of love as it is developed throughout the novel. The second is the opposition between the realms of private and public. The two issues are connected philosophically as well as structurally. Julie and Saint-Preux try to resolve the tensions within the various polarities by fusing them. They view a marriage based on love as the setting in which both oppositions can be combined, allowing the antinomies within them to coexist and flourish. The actualization of love in marriage would allow the Self and Other to survive coequally in combined form, while also providing a format for the simultaneous expression of both private and public authenticity. However, not everyone believes in fusion as the means toward achieving a resolution of the opposing forces of Self and Other, on the one hand, and private and public, on the other. Claire and Wolmar are examples of those who insist on the irrevocable dualism of life. According to this view, the choices that must be made are mutually exclusive. The opposition between Self and Other is seen as centering on nothing less than survival. Therefore, both Claire and Wolmar choose the primacy of the Self. In this context, the question of living on a higher, more exalted plane though love—the issue that is so central to the lives of Julie and Saint-Preux—is meaningless. Fusion for Claire is not an option: she views it as a synonym for being completely subsumed and rendered powerless by the Other.[55] As for Wolmar, his goal of giving life as an *oeil vivant* is not a denial but the strongest affirmation of the Self that exists in the novel. By remaining a spectator, he reduces everybody else to an Other—that is, an object of manipulation for Wolmar.

The delineation between the private and public realms follows from the opposition between Self and Other. Those who view the battle between Self and Other as a struggle of two morally worthy components that must be positively resolved in the best interests of all elements concerned—that is, with every person's autonomy essentially preserved—tend to consider the private, rather than the public, realm the source of moral values. Thus, Julie and Saint-Preux at the beginning of the novel speak of their love as ethically pure and capable of rendering the world around them a better place to live. On the other hand, those who consider the opposition between Self and Other to be a zero-sum game—that is, those who deny the possibility of a resolution through love—must inevitably valorize the public over the private realm. That appears to be problematic because, as seen in the examples of Wolmar and Claire, those who see the polarity of Self versus Other as a struggle for survival choose to strengthen the Self at the expense of the Other. How, then, can this choice be said to valorize the public over the private realm? On the contrary, the opposite would seem to be true: strengthening the Self would appear to emphasize the primacy of the private and not the public area. The answer is that the choice of Self that brings in its wake exploitation of the Other also winds up destroying that same Self. For all of Wolmar's manipulation of others, it is hard to grasp the essence of Wolmar as an individual. Wolmar himself admits that he is a person of few, if any, passions.[56] Regarding Claire, one has the sense of a woman struggling so hard to achieve autonomy despite her social constraints that in the end she remains with little, if any, Self at all. Despite Claire's own defense that she does the best she can to achieve autonomy within the limited sphere available to her, we never get enough of a feel of her as an individual to be able to extrapolate what she would have done with her life had her choices been truly free. Unlike Julie, and similar to Wolmar, Claire remains for the reader more of a figure than a whole person.

The consequences for people who have no Self left—or who have consciously deprived themselves of a Self—is that they must pour all of their psychic and emotional energy into the public realm. Their emphasis on the public mask that they wear—ostensibly as Self-protection—makes them unable to valorize the private dimension of life at all. Thus marriage, for Wolmar, is important not because of what it does to actualize the love of the couple for each other, but because it is a vehicle for them to contribute to society.[57] Similarly, the family is valued not for the psychic and emotional support that its members give one another, but for its contribution as a unit to the stability and continued existence of society.[58] If the private dimension of life has any value at all, it is to serve as the physical underpinning for the more important goals of the public realm—that is, of society as a whole. In this scheme, it is the public that valorizes the private.

Attempting to put these beliefs into practice at Clarens, Wolmar is faced with a problem. He must get people who are naturally more concerned with private satisfaction than with public goals to act according to his system of values. Moreover, consonant with his theory of ultimate—that is, unperceived—control, he must do so by convincing the people that they are acting in their own personal best interest.[59] To this end, Wolmar insists that private and public realms are one and the same. Wolmar's ideal in this context is the example of the Roman who opened up his private domicile to public view.[60] Wolmar tries to actualize that spirit of probity at Clarens by decreeing that everybody speak and act in the same way at all times, claiming that this will establish a society of perfect consistency and transparency. What he actually accomplishes is to render everyone so preoccupied with *seeming* transparent that they lose their sense of Self entirely.[61] Deepening the paradox is that the transparency ostensibly achieved at Clarens mimics perfectly the authentic transparency that can be attained only by honest personal and social interaction. As a result, it is hard, if not impossible, to distinguish between the inauthentic fusion of the private and public used to bolster Wolmar's social system at Clarens and the genuine fusion of private and public yearned for personally by Julie and Saint-Preux and depicted on the political level in Rousseau's portrait of the nurturing State in *Political Economy*.

The philosophical battles between Self and Other, private and public, that take place within the context of the family end in a deadlock. Neither Self nor Other, neither private nor public, achieves justification or definition in any positive sense. Instead, what emerges is a kind of stasis that is just an imitation of the true authenticity that the family is supposed to nurture. Far from helping its members to achieve any kind of personal or political authenticity, the family as depicted at Clarens cannot even succeed in enabling them to distinguish between authentic and inauthentic solutions to their dilemmas. Indeed, one could even argue that the family, whether in its stern patriarchal or its ostensibly benevolent paternalistic incarnation, actually helps to destroy any possibility of finding authentic and coherent solutions to the philosophical issues played out in its midst.

To be sure, it is possible to claim, in Rousseau's defense, that Rousseau does hint at one way of solving this dilemma. In his writings on the family, Rousseau seems to indicate that it is the women of the family who are responsible for teaching personal authenticity and for transmitting to their children an ethic that would also make them good citizens of the polis as adults. This means that women are, in effect, charged with defusing the philosophical contradictions between Self and Other and between private and public. However, several obstacles stand in the way of their fulfillment of this task. First, as we have seen in connection with the education of Sophie, women's own training leaves them bereft of a sense of Self. Thus, transmitting a sense of personal authenticity is something they are not particularly fit to do. Second, women's education is specifically not geared to affairs of public import.[62] Therefore, teaching their children about citizenship is not something they know much about. Third, inasmuch as women are effective in accomplishing any part of the above-stated goals, they are essentially working themselves out of a job. This is because educating their children to be devoted citizens according to Rousseau's understanding of that term means the denigration of the values of family life and personal relationships that women have come to stand for and esteem in their own lives. Finally, the double task that women are asked to perform proves to be inherently self-contradictory and impossible to fulfill. That is because political authenticity—the state of citizenship—is, as Rousseau understands it, based on the attainment of personal authenticity to which it is also antithetical. The fact that women are described by Rousseau in near-reverential terms as the moral centers of the family does not bestow upon them the tools they need to help people distinguish between Self and Other, and private and public, in a positive and authentic manner. In actuality, as seen in Rousseau's novelistic works, women's options come down to self-imposed obsolescence or being torn apart by the contradictions and impossibility of what they are asked to do. In this context, the death of Julie at Clarens and the rupture between Émile and Sophie appear less melodramatic than inevitable.

Given Rousseau's own emphasis on the family as an institution of great personal and political consequence, two questions must still be answered. First, why does it seem impossible for Rousseau to structure the family such that it would buttress instead of undermine his aims of personal and political authenticity? Second, is it possible at all for such a theory to be constructed? That is, can an understanding of the family be fostered that would encourage both the personal and political manifestations of authenticity?

The Family as a Theoretical Problem

It is, of course, always possible to review Rousseau's negative or contradictory answers as evidence of an incoherent or incomplete philosophical system.[63] More fruitfully, one can view Rousseau's seeming paradoxes and contradictions as confirmation that his analysis reflects the internal ambiguities of a given situation.[64] Using that method, one can attempt to trace the auto- and Self-destructiveness of Rousseau's families to internal contradictions present within his original theory of the family. If such theoretical contradictions do exist, they raise the question of whether and how Rousseau's theory of the Self, the family, and political society can overcome these contradictions to arrive at a dynamic theory of personal and political authenticity.

A review of Rousseau's theoretical writings on the family, especially in the *Discourse on Inequality*, reveals that for all his careful analysis of how the family develops in the State of Nature, Rousseau does leave one crucial question unanswered. Why does the family develop in the first place? Unlike the other discoveries and evolutions of the State of Nature, the appearance of the family seems to have little to do with man's survival. Rather, it is entirely the expression of man's creative and organizational ability: his power to effect changes in what the natural world offers him. Rousseau's narrative, although not explicit on that score, makes it appear that it was the man who initiated the formation of families by building individual huts. The support for this supposition lies in the fact that it was the strongest who built the huts (the weaker ones made do with the caves that had heretofore sufficed to provide shelter). Also, once families were established, it was woman's activities that became more sedentary and indoors-oriented, seeming to indicate a lack of active desire for, an indifference to, or perhaps even less of a capability for, active physical labor. Rousseau never states why women agreed to the notion of the family and the accompanying division of labor according to gender. What did they have to gain by this new state of affairs? Apparently, they had survived pretty well up till now: why would women entirely change the tenor of their lives? It is clear, as we have already noted, that those encouraging the choice of a new division of labor saw this as a great opportunity for themselves: it was their chance to alter Nature in a creative enterprise and to make their mark on Nature by introducing the structures of real and emotional property. Nothing, however, is stated to explain why women effectively agreed to alter their entire way of life.

One possible response to this difficulty is to suppose that women were forced to agree to this change. This would tally with Nannerl Keohane's contention that the genesis of the family is rooted in violence.[65] However, it is never made clear just what this violence was or whence it originated. Furthermore, although it appears likely that violence did exist in the State of Nature, it was generally engendered and resolved on a case-by-case basis. In other words, violence was a personal issue, suddenly occurring and quickly blown over. There would seem to be no precedent in the State of Nature for group subjugation through violence, and Rousseau gives no account of it in the genesis of the family.

The peaceful subjugation of an entire group of people is, however, a theme that does recur in Rousseau's theoretical writings. It even appears in the *Discourse on Inequality*. Toward the end of that essay, Rousseau describes the duping of the poor by the rich, who foist a false social contract upon the poor. This arrangement, as we have already seen, appears to guarantee basic liberties for the poor, while in effect legalizing and thus making permanent their subservience to the rich. From the textual context, it would seem logical that a similar sequence occurred with the establishment of the family. Women were persuaded that this change in lifestyle was in everyone's "best" interest. As Rousseau does state explicitly, "While each individual separately became less capable of combating savage beasts, it was on the other hand easier to assemble to resist them in common."[66] As in the case of the poor, however, deluding women about their real interests constitutes perpetrating on them false consciousness. In Rousseau's view of the world, an institution based on false consciousness must of necessity self-destruct. That is what happens to the unjust State at the end of the *Discourse on Inequality*. With that understanding, the inevitable breaking apart of the family and the destruction of its own members as seen at Clarens becomes comprehensible.

Given Rousseau's high hopes for the family as the guardian of the authentic spirit in inauthentic times, as well as the family's incarnation as the socializing agent for political authenticity, the seeming inevitability of the family's self-destruction would appear to set the final seal of doom on the possibility of ever transcending an existence of inauthenticity, whether personal or political. But the evidence can also be read, not as a prophecy of doom, but rather as a handbook for the options that can be actualized in inauthentic times. *La Nouvelle Héloïse* is particularly instructive in this regard. We have noted that Claire exemplifies the uses of inauthenticity in attempting to create enough space for a sense of Self to emerge. In our analysis, Claire's resultant sense of Self is not much in evidence, for it does not seem that Claire ever had much of a Self to begin with. But what if a person with a stronger, more moral notion of Self—like Julie, for example, but better able to weather the world of inauthenticity—were to make use of these same techniques? One could then envision a host of possibilities that would allow an authentic Self to flourish—albeit with difficulty—in an inauthentic world. This, in turn, could be the beginning of the authentic transformation that Rousseau was trying to achieve. In this case, moral sensitivity and the desire for authenticity would not have to preclude survival.

Rousseau's analysis of the possibilities of authentic transformation in an inauthentic world reveals an important source of hope for the future realization of his theory. That is Rousseau's sense that the root of transformation and revolution lies not with philosophical theories or political power but rather in the concrete minutiae of everyday life. This is particularly clear within the context of women's experiences. It is important to remember that it is specifically the women whom Rousseau charges with the education of the young so that they will be able to survive the upcoming revolution. True, Rousseau's limitation of women's education and concerns to the domestic sphere does not bode well for the realization of his ultimate goals of personal and political authenticity. On the other hand, this empowerment of women—emphasizing the personal and domestic roots of the coming political upheaval—reflects the importance of the seemingly trivial to Rousseau's understanding of the forces that move history. That these forces stem from the banality of quotidian concerns indicates how revolutionary Rousseau's perception of cause and effect in world affairs really was. Eventually, Rousseau's perception results in a revised understanding of the categories of the personal and the political, and of how to achieve authenticity in both of these areas.

Rousseau's appreciation of the central importance of the everyday to the larger concerns of political life is twofold. One aspect is familiar: it emphasizes the effect that the unspoken, unwritten customs of a people— their *moeurs*—have on their political life, and the influence that women in turn have in forming these *moeurs* in the first place. The second aspect of the centrality of the quotidian to the political is less obvious and emerges as a subsidiary message of Rousseau's literary works. That is women's ability to perceive and enact ways to survive in an inauthentic world. To be sure, these ways are not perfectly conceived, nor are they totally problem-free. But they indicate women's willingness to approach seemingly intractable problems in new and positive ways.

Rousseau's endowment of women with the ability to both cope with and transform the surrounding inauthenticity reveals a penetrating awareness of the complexity and ground-breaking dimensions of the tasks that women are called upon to do. The appreciation of the modern nature of this dilemma, exemplified with special clarity in women's lives, may appear surprising on the part of a critic who by and large wrote in the idiom of his time. Rousseau's rootedness in the intellectual constructs of his era—in this case, the mutually exclusive duality between public and private—is seen particularly in the way Rousseau structures the problem that he is trying to solve. In the beginning of *Émile*, for example, he phrases the issue as making either a man or a citizen—that is, as choosing between private or public education. Yet, in the development and resolution of this issue, it becomes apparent that no successful solution can exist if this dichotomous structure is slavishly upheld. In fact, the course of Émile's education proves that these two realms of public and private are not mutually impenetrable in real life. It is significant that this realization becomes clear at the point that Émile is ready to assume his adult duties and start a family, for it is when discussing the role and duties of the good spouse that Rousseau begins intellectually to formulate the extent of women's domestic influence over the surrounding political landscape.

Although Rousseau to a large extent in his theoretical writings maintains the dichotomy between the public and private realms that the liberal political theory of the seventeenth and eighteenth centuries upheld, a nascent awareness of the porousness of these categories is evident in the workings of his novelistic writings. This is seen particularly in the way Rousseau handles the lives of his fictional women. If women, working from the domestic sphere traditionally assigned to them, can be charged with coping with as well as transforming the inauthenticity that surrounds them in both the personal and political realms, it stands to reason that a theory that insists on the mutual exclusivity of the personal and political is both useless and misleading.[67] Furthermore, by implication, the beginnings of a new theory that can accurately describe the interrelationship of the personal and the political must have its genesis in reality as it is experienced by women, for it is their lives that serve as the source of the critique of the private/public dichotomy now exposed as artificial.[68]

This realization reveals in Rousseau's theory elements of sympathy and hope for the dilemma of contemporary women as emblematic of the quest of all people for personal and political authenticity. The sympathy is evident in Rousseau's description of the difficulties in the first of women's two special tasks: that is, coping with inauthenticity by trying to preserve an area of authenticity in an inauthentic world. Rousseau focuses on the dilemma of having to choose between various degrees of false consciousness, and on the effect that this may have on the larger goal of preserving authenticity in an inauthentic world. In Claire's case, for example, it is clear that all of the choices that Claire has before her are essentially inauthentic. Claire herself realizes that she will never be able to express herself fully in the constricted world that she inhabits. Her dilemma is that the alternative to picking one of the various degrees of false consciousness facing her is to do nothing at all: that is, to drop out. By consciously choosing to survive, Claire rejects Julie's passivity, but she also opens herself up to the constant realization of her life's shortcomings. Even if we suppose that Claire's sense of Self is shallow to begin with, it is clear that she is aware of the price she pays for her continued existence.

In thus outlining Claire's reaction to her own choice of living her life as a series of consciously chosen roles, Rousseau reveals his own awareness of the dilemmas facing women who must struggle to preserve their authenticity in a world that tries to subvert and ignore them. Implicitly, he indicates that there are times when survival demands choosing between various forms of false consciousness. The challenge for women trying to preserve their own authenticity is to make these choices without falling prey to the assumptions that underlie them. The tone of Claire's letters commenting on her own life reveals that this challenge is not easy, nor is its victory secure. The tactic of using inauthenticity in the fight to preserve authenticity can easily backfire, and as with all such ambiguous tactics, one can never be sure that the battle has been won. Coping with inauthenticity can tear women apart. Rousseau's sensitivity to that truth and to the amount of faith required nevertheless to accept that challenge is surprisingly prophetic of the problems faced by many women today who seek to maximize their own authenticity in a world that still clings to the old separation between the private (i.e., women's) realm and the public (i.e., man's) arena. Ironically, the grudging admission to the public arena brings with it the danger of being co-opted by the overarching constructs of the surrounding inauthenticity, with the result that women then lose the very authenticity that they have been struggling to preserve.

The faith to persist in this effort, notwithstanding the ambiguous appearances of the authentic and the inauthentic, reflects the second aspect of the legacy of Rousseau's theory. This is the element of hope. By positing women as the source of the education that would eventually sow the seeds of authenticity in the world at large (women's second special task), Rousseau demonstrates his own belief that coping with inauthenticity eventually yields fruitful results. It indicates that, for Rousseau, the revolution that would transform the inauthentic world might be incremental rather than cataclysmic. In either case, Rousseau's rooting of the coming revolution in the seemingly banal trivialities of everyday life—all of which are seen as the province of women—has two important consequences for his political theory. First, as we have seen, it serves as a further indication of the futility of artificially sundering the personal from the political. Second, it opens political action to everyone, regardless of gender or class. The powerful message of hope unleashed by this formulation has echoed through the ages. It recognizes the ability of everybody to take control of his or her own life, and the larger consequences that can flow from just that one individual act. It is this empowerment of the individual that for Rousseau guarantees the inevitability of the upcoming revolution that he never ceases to predict. This is due to an ironic reworking of Rousseau's own definition of absolute power. According to Rousseau, the most effective power is that which is least perceived. Locating power where it is least expected—by expanding the notion of power to include the regular individual and not just those of rank and fortune—

means that Rousseau already recognizes the existence of a vast reservoir of unperceived potential force whose mighty power, once unleashed, would indeed bring about a revolution.

Using women to exemplify the tensions and ambiguities in Rousseau's political theory by no means solves the contradictions that still exist in its intellectual and practical configurations. Still, Rousseau's examination of these oppositions reveals a sensibility that, given its historical provenance, is remarkably sympathetic to the vicissitudes encountered in attempting to realize personal and political authenticity in the modern world. Even in his novelistic descriptions of women's defeat in that pursuit, Rousseau also provides the tools for reconstructing those scenarios as alternatively providing the possibility for victory: that is, the realization of authenticity for everyone. Through the lives of these women, depicting the poverty of contemporary categories for effectively dealing with the problems of authenticity posed by modernity, Rousseau opens the way for different conceptions of reality that will take into account its ambiguity and, consequently, for the necessary porousness of categories that can adequately describe and also change it. More than any particular revolution that Rousseau predicts, it is the restructuring of these categories of reality and perception that provides both challenge and hope to future generations. With his understanding that women in their lives feel with full force the paradox and ambiguity of both inauthenticity and authenticity, Rousseau recognizes that women's experiences distill a central truth for human existence in general. Like Montesquieu a generation before him, Rousseau agrees that no matter who we are, we are finally, in essence, all women.[69]

Notes

1. *Confessions*, bk. 1, OC 1:31–32; bk. 3, 93ff.

2. *Émile*, bk. 4, OC 4:678–91; Bloom, 345–55.

3. In *Patriarchalism in Political Thought*, Gordon J. Schochet understands the patriarchal tradition to include this "genitive" understanding of family origins.

4. *Discours sur l'inégalité*, OC 3:160–61, 167ff., 139.

5. In the *Social Contract*, Rousseau calls the family "the first model of political societies" (*Du contrat social*, bk. 1, chap. 2, OC 3:352; my translation).

6. Julie writes to Saint-Preux: "[P]ourquoi tes lettres . . . viennent-elles contrister mon ame et troubler les premiers plaisirs d'une famille reúnie?" (*La Nouvelle Héloïse*, pt. 1, letter 20, OC 2:72).

7. Saint-Preux describes himself as "errant, sans famille, et presque sans patrie" (ibid., 73).

8. For example, Julie says, on discovering that she feels for her parents: "[J]'ai trouvé quelque sorte de consolation à sentir que les doux mouvements de la nature ne sont pas tout à fait éteints dans mon coeur" (ibid., letter 37, 114). On the other hand, love too is an emotion sanctioned by Nature and therefore good. Following one's heart is identified with "faith" and virtue. Consider, for example: "[V]eux-je être vertueuse? l'obéissance et la foi m'imposent des devoirs opposés. Veux-je suivre le penchant de mon coeur? qui préférer d'un amant ou d'un pere. Hélas, en écoutant l'amour ou la nature, je ne puis éviter de mettre l'un ou l'autre au desespoir; en me sacrifiant au devoir je ne puis éviter de commettre un crime, et quelque parti que je prenne, il faut que je meure à la fois malheureuse et coupable" (ibid., pt. 2, letter 4, 201). Also: "[Q]uels monstres d'enfer sont ces préjugés, qui dépravent les meilleurs coeurs, et font taire à chaque instant la nature?" (ibid., pt. 1, letter 63, 177). Similarly: "Depuis quand la vertu pese-t-elle ainsi les droits du sang et de la nature?" (ibid., pt. 2, letter 6, 208). Likewise: "[J]e serois à lui si l'ordre humain n'eut troublé les rapports de la nature, et s'il étroit permis à quelqu'un d'être heureux" (ibid., pt. 3, letter 18, 340–41).

9. Ibid., pt. 2, letter 6, 208.

10. The Baron d'Etanges speaks of someone marrying Julie as "s'allier à moi" (ibid., pt. 1, letter 63, 177).

11. "[S]i j'ai droit de disposer de moi contre le gré des auteurs de mes jours" (ibid., pt. 2, letter 6, 208).

12. "[C]ette idée horrible . . . me rendroit misérable au sein du bonheur" (ibid., 208–9).

13. "[M]on pere m'a donc vendue? il fait de sa fille une marchandise, une esclave, il s'acquite à mes depends! il paye sa vie de la mienne! . . . pere barbare et dénaturé!" (ibid., pt. 1, letter 28, 94).

14. "Celle qui deshonore sa famille apprendra-t-elle à ses enfans à l'honorer?" (ibid., pt. 2, letter 4, 202).

15. This approach fits neatly those critics who see Julie as a victim of her own class, a person who cannot and perhaps, at one level, does not want to overcome the structures that threaten to destroy her. On this topic, see Marshall Berman, *The Politics of Authenticity*, esp. "The Life and Death of Julie," 231–65.

16. "Combien de grands noms retomberoient dans l'oubli si l'on ne tenoit compte que de ceux qui ont comencé par un homme estimable? . . . Laissons, si vous voulez l'origine à part, et pesons le mérite et les services" (*La Nouvelle Héloïse*, pt. 1, letter 62, OC 2:169).

17. "Dequoi s'honore donc . . . cette noblesse dont vous êtes si fier? Que fait-elle pour la gloire de la patrie ou le bonheur du genre-humain?" (ibid., 170).

18. Ibid.

19. "Nos sages loix n'abrogent point celles de la nature" (ibid., pt. 2, letter 3, 200).

20. "L'approbation publique sera démentie incessament par le cri de la conscience" (ibid.).

21. "[V]ous serez honorée et méprisable. Il vaut mieux être oubliée et vertueuse" (ibid.).

22. Ibid., pt. 1, letter 62, 172.

23. "[P]reuve invincible que la volonté la plus générale est aussi toûjours la plus juste, et que la voix du peuple est en effet la voix de Dieu" (*Discours sur l'économie politique*, OC 3:246).

24. "On ne s'épouse point pour penser uniquement l'un à l'autre, mais pour remplir conjointement les devoirs de la vie civile" (*La Nouvelle Héloïse*, pt. 3, letter 20, OC 2:372).

25. "La servitude est si peu naturelle à l'homme qu'elle ne sauroit exister sans quelque mécontentement" (ibid., letter 10, 460). But the art of the master can fix that: "Tout l'art du maitre est de cacher cette gêne sous le voile du plaisir ou de l'intérêt, en sorte qu'ils pensent vouloir tout ce qu'on les oblige de faire" (ibid., 453).

26. "[C]hacun voudroit être le premier en faveur . . . [C]'est là leur unique plainte. . . . Dans les concurrences de jalousie et d'intérêt qui divisent sans cesse les gens d'une maison . . . ils ne demeurent presque jamais unis qu'aux dépends du maitre . . . il faut qu'ils soient ennemis ou complices . . . [ici] . . . l'union des membres y paroit venir de leur attachement aux chefs" (ibid., 460–62).

27. "[J]'osai croire à la vertu et vous épousai. . . . Je ne me suis trompé en rien; vous avez tenu

tout ce que je m'étois promis de vous." Also: "Si votre fidélité m'eut suffi, tout étoit fait du moment que vous me la promites" (ibid., letter 12, 494).

28. "Ce qui m'a d'abord le plus frappé dans cette maison, c'est d'y trouver l'aisance, la liberté, la gaité au milieu de l'ordre et de l'exactitude" (ibid., pt. 5, letter 2, 530).

29. "Tout le monde se met à table, maitres, journaliers, domestiques. . . . La présence des maitres si respectés contient tout le monde et n'empêche pas qu'on ne soit à son aise et gai. Que s'il arrive à quelqu'un de s'oublier, on ne trouble point la fête par des réprimandes, mais il est congédié sans remission dès le lendemain" (ibid., 608–9). Also: "[L]a douce égalité qui regne ici rétablit l'ordre de la nature, forme une instruction pour les uns, une consolation pour les autres et un lien d'amitié pour tous" (608).

30. "[L]a nature a tout fait, mais sous ma direction, et il n'y a rien là que je n'aye ordonné" (ibid., pt. 4, letter 11, 472).

31. "Je fus d'abord la dupe des noms pompeux qu'on donnoit à ces vins . . . [Julie m'a dit] . . . en riant. . . . Le rancio, le cherez, le malaga, le chassaigne, le siracuse dont vous buvez avec tant de plaisir ne sont en effet que des vins de Lavaux diversement préparés, et vous pouvez voir d'ici le vignoble qui produit toutes ces boissons lointaines" (ibid., pt. 5, letter 2, 552).

32. "[M]on imagination n'a plus rien à faire, je n'ai rien à désirer. . . . O mort, viens" (ibid., pt. 6, letter 8, 689). In that same letter, however, Julie adds: "Malheur à qui n'a plus rien à desirer! . . . vivre ainsi c'est être mort. . . . Je ne vois par tout que sujets de contentement, et je ne suis pas contente. . . . Cette peine est bizarre, j'en conviens . . . je suis trop heureuse; le bonheur m'ennuye" (693–94).

33. "[E]lle fait toujours les mêmes choses parce qu'elle . . . ne connoit rien de mieux à faire" (ibid., pt. 5, letter 2, 553).

34. "Le déjeuner est le repas des amis; les valets en sont exclus. . . . C'est presque le seul moment où il soit permis d'être ce qu'on est" (ibid., pt. 4, letter 11, 488).

35. "[I]l n'y avoit rien de bien qu'on n'obtint des belles ames avec de la confiance et de la franchise" (ibid., letter 12, 496).

36. "facile à subjuguer" (ibid., letter 14, 510). Wolmar's classification of Saint-Preux, together with Rousseau's appreciation of the very real effects of domination and exploitation, call into question Melzer's insistence on "intractability" as a central human characteristic (see, e.g., Melzer's analysis in The Natural Goodness of Man, 73ff.).

37. To an extent, even Julie is guilty of this. She uses her concern for her servants to get them to better serve her (La Nouvelle Héloïse, pt. 4, letter 10). Similarly, she teaches her children that they should be polite in order to get what they want: "[L]'enfant n'obtient jamais de ceux qui l'approchent qu'autant de complaisance qu'il a pour eux. Par là . . . il se rend docile et complaisant" (ibid., pt. 5, letter 3, OC 2:571). It is worth noting that in teaching her children to be polite as a way of getting what they want, Julie follows precisely those guidelines for bringing up children that are roundly condemned in Émile: "On voit d'abord que s'il vous plait signifie dans leur bouche il me plait, et je vous prie signifie je vous ordonne . . . Quant à moi qui crains moins qu'Emile ne soit grossier qu'arrogant, j'aime beaucoup mieux qu'il dise en priant faites cela, qu'en commandant je vous prie. Ce n'est pas le terme dont il se sert qui m'importe, mais bien l'acception qu'il y joint" (Émile, bk. 4, OC 4:312–13; Bloom, 86).

38. "Ne fais ni ne dis jamais rien que tu ne veuilles que tout le monde voye et entende . . . vivez dans la tête-à-tête comme si j'étois présent, ou devant moi comme je n'y étois pas" (ibid., pt. 4, letter 6, 424). Saint-Preux apparently accepts this directive unquestioningly: "M. de Wolmar commençoit à prendre une si grande autorité sur moi que j'y étois déja presque accoutumé" (425).

39. Richard Sennett, The Fall of Public Man, 338.

40. Rousseau also notes that the need to talk ceaselessly about the achievement of transparency, as the characters in La Nouvelle Héloïse do, indicates that they probably have not achieved it: "[C]elui qui le goute est tout à la chose, il ne s'amuse pas à dire: j'ai du plaisir" (Projet pour la Corse, OC

3:937). Similarly: "[E]ntre la chose même et sa jouissance il n'y en a point [d'intermédiaire]" (*Confessions*, bk. 1, OC 1:38). Also: "[L]e vrai bonheur ne se décrit pas, il se sent et se sent d'autant mieux qu'il peut le moins se décrire" (ibid., bk. 6, 236).

41. "Nos yeux se sont aussi rencontrés. J'ai senti à la maniere dont son mari m'a serré la main que la même émotion nous gagnoit tous trois" (*La Nouvelle Héloïse*, pt. 5, letter 3, OC 2:559). Certain commentators (e.g., Judith Still) have agreed that Wolmar's claim that he has erased Julie's love for Saint-Preux is indeed illusory, but they persist in seeing this illusion as benign. My reading of *La Nouvelle Héloïse* demonstrates that for the author of the *Social Contract* and *Considerations on Poland*, illusion and authentic freedom are incompatible. Consequently, to define an illusion as "benign" is to misunderstand Rousseau's critique of the harmful effects of theatrical inauthenticity, even in—or especially in—daily life.

42. Notable exceptions to this trend include Lester G. Crocker, "Julie ou la nouvelle duplicité"; Hans Wolpe, "Psychological Ambiguity in *La Nouvelle Héloïse*"; and Janet Todd, *Women's Friendship in Literature*, esp. the chapter "Manipulative Friendship."

43. "Je suis en femme un espèce de monstre" (*La Nouvelle Héloïse*, pt. 1, letter 64, OC 2:179). Claire confesses to Julie: "Je puis avoir des fantaisies, mais fort peu d'amour. Un mari . . . ne sera jamais pour moi qu'un mari" (ibid., pt. 2, letter 5, 206). Also, Claire writes: "[J]e n'étois point faite pour être femme. S'il eut dépendu de moi, je ne me serois point mariée" (ibid., pt. 4, letter 2, 407).

44. "[J]'avois des chagrins dans ma famille. Pour m'en délivrer, j'épousai donc M. d'Orbe" (ibid., pt. 4, letter 2, 407).

45. "[D]ans notre sexe, on n'achette la liberté que par l'esclavage" (ibid.).

46. "Durant sept années je n'ai pas ri sept petites fois à mon aise" (ibid., 408).

47. See, for example, Claire's letter on the political system in Geneva and on the situation of women there (ibid., pt. 6, letter 5), and the letter she elicits from Saint-Preux on French and Italian music (pt. 2, letter 23).

48. "Voila pourquoi les femmes les plus honnêtes conservent en général le plus d'ascendant sur leurs maris . . . et les empêchent de jamais se rassasier d'elles" (ibid., pt. 4, letter 13, 501).

49. "Je me rassasie de bonheur . . . je ne suis pas contente . . . je suis trop heureuse; le bonheur m'ennuye" (ibid., pt. 6, letter 8, 689, 694).

50. See notes 47 and 29 above.

51. "Je changeai de nom . . . je me jettai successivement dans les divers états que pouvoient m'aider à les comparer tous et à connoitre les uns par les autres . . . j'essayai d'une multitude de conditions" (*La Nouvelle Héloïse*, pt. 4, letter 12, OC 2:491–92).

52. See note 40 above.

53. "Ne fais ni ne dis jamais rien que tu ne veuilles que tout le monde voye et endentende . . . vivez dans la tête-à-tête" (ibid., pt. 4, letter 6, 424). Also: "On tient toujours le même language" (letter 10, 468).

54. Wolmar too, though from a more selfish point of view, is troubled by Julie's tendency to think about and doubt her own virtue. He fears—correctly, as it turns out—that her "cure" is not complete: "La seule chose qui me fait soupçonner qu'il lui reste quelque défiance à vaincre est qu'elle ne cesse chercher en elle-même ce qu'elle feroit si elle étoit tout-à-fait guérie, et le fait avec tout d'exactitude, que si elle étoit réellement guérie elle ne le feroit pas si bien" (ibid., letter 14, 509).

55. That is certainly one reason why Claire refuses to marry again. She describes her first marriage—which for her is symptomatic of the married state in general—as an emotional prison: "Je n'ai pas ri durant sept ans sept petites fois à mon aise" (ibid., letter 2, 408).

56. "J'ai naturellement l'ame tranquille et le coeur froid. . . . Si j'ai quelque passion dominante c'est celle de l'observation . . . c'est là toute la récompense de l'amour propre dans mes études continuelles. . . . Si je pouvois changer la nature de mon être et devenir un oeil vivant, je ferois volontiers cet échange" (ibid., letter 12, 490–91).

57. "L'amour est . . . peu convenable au mariage. . . . On ne s'épouse point pour penser unique-

ment l'un à l'autre, mais pour remplir conjointement les devoirs de la vie civile" (ibid., pt. 3, letter 20, 372).

58. "Quoique tous les domestiques n'aient qu'une même table, il y a d'ailleurs peu de communication entre les deux sexes. . . . Selon elle [Julie] la femme et le mari sont bien destinés à vivre ensemble mais non pas de la même maniere. . . . Le soir la famille se rassemble; chacun passe la nuit auprès de sa femme; la séparation commence avec le jour" (ibid., pt. 4, letter 10, 449–50).

59. Since Julie is to serve as the transmitter of these values, it is essential that she be convinced of their moral integrity: that they in fact contribute to maximize everyone's best interests. The best proof for Julie would be that she herself be happy at Clarens; hence the great emphasis placed by Wolmar on achieving Julie's happiness: "[J]e desirai d'avoir en elle une compagne aimable, sage, heureuse . . . j'espere que la troisieme ne nous manquera pas" (ibid., letter 12, 494).

60. "[J]'ai toujours regardé comme le plus estimable des hommes ce Romain qui vouloit que sa maison fut construite de maniere qu'on vit tout ce qui s'y faisoit" (ibid., letter 6, 424).

61. See note 54 above.

62. Thus, Sophie is not taught philosophy or theology. Rousseau holds up the intellectual woman—personified by Mlle L'Enclos—to ridicule (Émile, bk. 5, OC 4:736, 768; Bloom, 386, 409).

63. See Margaret Corcoran, "The Limits of Seriousness: Rousseau and the Interpretation of Political Theory."

64. See the section "Uses of Inauthenticity: Truth as Ambiguity" in Corcoran, Chapter 1.

65. Keohane, "But for Her Sex . . . ," 145.

66. "[S]i chacun séparément devint moins propre à combattre les bêtes sauvages, en revanche il fut plus aisé de s'assembler pour leur résister en commun" (Discour sur l'inégalité, OC 3:168; my translation).

67. Many of the oppositions that I have traced in Rousseau's political theory can be seen as a function of the perceived dichotomy between the private and public realms. For example, the discussion in the Social Contract regarding how much alienation is necessary to the political State can be understood as addressing the question whether private life can exist apart from the political. If those categories are porous, the question becomes meaningless. Of course, Rousseau does not tell us how this transformation might actually be accomplished.

68. In Gender and History, Linda J. Nicholson demonstrates the historical rootedness of the perceived impenetrability of the categories of private and public.

69. The citation is taken from Lionel Gossman's Empire Unpossess'd.

6

Developing a Feminist Concept of the Citizen

Rousseauian Insights on Nature and Reason

Alice Ormiston

How one judges the woman question in Rousseau hinges in large part on how Rousseau's concept of the *male* subject and citizen is interpreted. A proliferation of feminist interpreters have come to rely on what is essentially a Cartesian reading of Rousseau, where the male subject is seen to be constructed in a *relative* identity against the female.[1] In such a reading, the male is seen to constitute the abstract reasoner capable of taking up the most general perspective, while woman is emotionally imbedded in the particular; man is "creative and intellectual," while woman is "physical and sensual";[2] man is focused on virtue and the well-being of the whole, while woman represents the passion of lovers and particular attachments;[3] he represents law and she love;[4] he is the "self-identical identity," the "unified subject," while woman is the chaos of the maternal, submergence in nature; he is the voice of convention, while woman is that of nature;[5] he commands the realm of heroism and she that of intimacy.[6]

By playing the role of the other, according to this view, woman has in fact had projected onto her the other that exists within the male self, the other that constantly threatens to interrupt his masculine identity, and thus that must carefully be kept at bay. "[A] subversive feminine subjectivity is contained at the core of the male self."[7] She "upholds herself as referent, as the ground of masculinist self-representation" and "must guard him against whatever threatens to encroach on the fragile borders of his identity."[8] She is what he must struggle against "during the entire length of his personal history in order to become [and remain] separate."[9]

In terms of Rousseau's political theory, in this view, woman is central to the very being of the male citizen, and cannot be integrated into the public realm without undermining that being. If she ceases to play her role as other, he will cease to exist as virtuous male citizen. Coole puts it most plainly: "If women were active in the polity, the differentiations without which justice and liberty could not endure for Rousseau, would collapse. Compassion/self-love, particularity/generality, love/law, personal/impersonal, natural/conventional are all for him oppositions which are simultaneously sustained and harmonized only as long as women and men maintain their diffuse identities in an intimate relationship."[10] Hence, it is concluded, Rousseau's political theory is inherently and inescapably sexist. The idea of citizen and political community that he envisions necessarily entails the imposition of a subordinating identity upon women.

Against the sexism that is seen to be part and parcel of Rousseau's political theory, these feminist theorists seek to posit a vision that is more compatible with women's equality. The critique of Rousseau as a Cartesian, examined in terms of its implications for women, points toward a different conception of the citizen altogether. As Marso argues, in this view of Rousseau the citizen implicitly deconstructs itself and gestures toward a unity of the male and the female principle, of universality and particularity. Lloyd, although she has a different reading of Rousseau, nevertheless concludes her critique of the male tradition by pointing to the notion of a genuinely "transcendent reason" that does not rely on the *exclusion* of feeling for its own self-assertion. Zerilli calls for a new political theory founded on a recognition of the other that exists within the self, rather than a theory that projects that other onto women. And Okin, from a more pragmatic perspective, points to the need to restructure the public and the private sphere in order to accommodate the realities of women.[11] These critics of Rousseau join other feminists who have sought to counter the abstract, dominating conception of reason in the Western tradition of political thought with a more unified vision of the subject that takes into account its embodied status.[12]

While the attempt to move toward a non-Cartesian vision of the citizen is interesting and important, what is striking is that such a project is being undertaken as if it were entirely *against* Rousseau and most other male theorists of the Western tradition, as if it were an entirely new concept and theoretical objective, and a uniquely feminist project. That is why, it seems, it is first necessary to do a sweeping critique of the Western tradition, disposing of it in its entirety before one is able to put forth a new, feminist model of the self.[13] Rousseau's own political ideal, an ideal that has inspired the imagination of critical and alternative thinkers—including feminist thinkers—for more than two centuries, is lightly and easily done away with.[14]

While we can see that feminists might have a particular interest in the project of articulating an alternative model of the subject, given the traditional identification of women with the subordinated principle of nature, what I would like to argue in this essay is that it is nevertheless not the case that such a project is new, or that it is unique to feminism. What I would like to argue is that, well intended as these feminist approaches might be, they do themselves a grave disservice by attempting to sweep away the Western tradition as if it were fundamentally grounded on women's subjugation. For a thinker such as Rousseau has much in common with these feminists, in many ways was embarked upon a very similar project, motivated by similar concerns about abstract rationality and its implications for our relationship to nature and to one another. Indeed, it was Rousseau himself who realized that the separation from nature and reflection on ourselves as objects from an abstract standpoint had been the momentous occasion that had set us on the pathway toward inequality. That is, it sent us into a condition where we measure our entire identity in relativistic terms, as established always against an other to whom we compare ourselves, and thus to whom we are simultaneously beholden and hostile.[15] His notion of *amour-propre* embodies precisely this notion of identity. And his positive political philosophy is an attempt to establish a notion of self that could supercede or at least attenuate the domination of self by relations of *amour-propre*. Hence the notion that Rousseau *himself* was a Cartesian, or that his positive alternative is *itself* founded against an other—that of woman—in a dependency that Rousseau never saw, seems extraordinary.

This is not to suggest that the feminist critique has no basis or validity. Indeed, as I will argue here myself, there is a fundamental truth to the idea that Rousseau was hostile to a certain aspect of the self, and that his views of women can at least partially be explained in terms of this. But that this hostility can be construed as a hostility of reason toward nature, or of man toward woman, or that the two principles of reason and nature exist in a simple, relative identity to each other, reduces the complexity and richness of Rousseau's account of the self. What I would like to outline below is a more precise picture of the complicated relationship between reason and nature in Rousseau, and his own attempt to formulate a moral and political philosophy that incorporates this more comprehensive conception of self. It is only with this clearer picture of Rousseau's subject and what he was trying to accomplish, I would suggest, that we can begin to assess its significance for feminism, the ways in which he might be helpful in construing an alternative model of the citizen, and the ways in which it might indeed be exclusionary and repressive and thus where we must depart from it. It is not by dismissing Rousseau but by turning *back* and examining him from this different, more accurate perspective, and by *mining* the insights and implications of this perspective, that we can start to outline, in more than the sketchy manner that has been done, the conditions of an alternative way of thinking and being.[16]

Toward a More Accurate Reading of Rousseau's Citizen

Against the understanding of Rousseau as a Cartesian in the works noted earlier, there is another, more sympathetic and accurate view of his citizen available to us. Among feminist commentators, such a view can be found to some extent in Genevieve Lloyd.[17] As opposed to the notion that the male identity is constructed through the exclusion of nature and sentiment, Lloyd correctly points out that Rousseau's vision of the male citizen contains an ideal of *synthesis* and *harmony* between reason and feeling, universal and particular, head and heart. Reason must be seen as "a dynamic development from Nature," versus "an abstract scientific

knowledge, dominating Nature."[18] But in order to comprehend this reading of Rousseau, we must understand both what he means by nature and
what he means by reason.

In part I of the *Second Discourse*, Rousseau seeks to articulate the idea
of a "primordial" nature, a nature that is deeper than the understanding
found in the earlier social contract thinkers such as Hobbes and Locke.
These earlier thinkers had emphasized feelings of pride, envy, competition, and fear. But such emotions presuppose that the principle of reflective rationality, of separation and reflection on oneself from an abstract
perspective—the very standpoint of Cartesianism—is present in the
"natural" human being. It is this reflection on oneself and comparison
with others that stirs up emotions of pride and the struggle for recognition. While in some sense natural in that they are experienced as feeling,
pride and envy are nevertheless the product of reflective rationality and
participation in society. Hence they are factitious passions. In order to
comprehend our true nature, Rousseau seeks to go deeper—into *prereflective* consciousness, to an investigation of "the first and most simple
operations of the human soul" (*Second Discourse*, 35). And it is here that
he discovers the primordial passions of *amour de soi*—the "ardent interest
in our well-being and self-preservation"—and *pitié*—the natural repugnance to seeing any sentient being, especially our fellow man, perish or
suffer" (35).

While humans have become separated from their true nature due to
the influence of reflective rationality, we can nevertheless still find vestiges of the voice of nature within us. By examining our most immediate
emotional reactions to various situations, by seeking to retreat into our
prereflective self, we can see this nature at work within us. Against the
current political situation of Rousseau's time as characterized by "the
violence of powerful men and the oppression of the weak," he points to
the emotional responses that tell the truth of this situation. "The mind
revolts against the harshness of the former" (*pitié* for the weak), while
"one is inclined to deplore the blindness of the latter" (their failure to
act from *amour de soi*, to see their own true good) (36). Similarly, if we
look at our own emotional responses to the conjectural history of human
nature as Rousseau outlines it in the *Second Discourse*, these reveal the
true principle of *amour de soi* at work within us. Dissatisfaction with the
present state, with what it bodes for future generations, and the desire to
go backward to a simpler time, suggests Rousseau, "should be a hymn in
praise of your first ancestors, the criticism of your contemporaries, and

the dread of those who have the unhappiness of living after you" (39). These emotions of dissatisfaction and lament are the true judgment of our own situation, of what constitutes our real happiness. They are the voice of *amour de soi*.

Regarding the sentiment of *pitié*, Rousseau suggests that one can see it at work even in animals: "[O]ne daily observes the repugnance that horses have for trampling a living body with their hooves. An animal does not go undisturbed past a dead animal of its own species. There are even some animals that give them a kind of sepulchre; and the mournful lowing of cattle entering a slaughterhouse voices the impression they receive of the horrible spectacle that strikes them" (54). And even the most corrupt individuals are moved to tears at the fate of other human beings if they experience this in the theatre, where their own lust for power can cease for a moment to dominate them.

Through reason, however, the abstract reasoning of reflective rationality, the separation and reflection on ourselves from a distance, we have become alienated from the experience of our true nature.[19] Not only does this reason separate us from the primordial passions by giving us the capacity to take up a distance from them, but it confuses them by stirring up new and artificial feelings that are the product of comparison of ourselves with others from the abstract standpoint. As Rousseau says of primitive man, "the first glance he directed upon himself produced within him the first stirring of pride" (*Second Discourse*, 61). By comparing his own with other species and sensing the superiority of humans, "he prepared himself from afar to lay claim to it [that superiority] in virtue of his individuality" (61). Thus abstract reasoning or reflective rationality is not separate from the factitious passion of pride, but is in fact at the very source of such feelings.

Against the view of Rousseau as a Cartesian in the works noted earlier, then, we can see in this account that Rousseau does not simplistically divide nature and reason into two separate principles. Rather he articulates two types of nature—our original, primordial sentiments of *amour de soi* and *pitié*; and the passions of *amour-propre* that have developed *in and through* abstract reasoning and that thus can in no way be considered as a principle separate from reason. These two aspects of our nature are both present in the modern self and *both* are connected to reason but in different ways. While the factitious passions are intimately bound up with the abstract reasoning that distances itself from the self, in the modern human being the primordial passions of *amour de soi* and *pitié* also have an essential relationship to reason in their development into a larger sense of justice or conscience, as we see in Rousseau's crucial discussion of moral development in book IV of *Emile*.[20]

While abstract reasoning separates us from the emotions of *amour de soi* and *pitié*, and constitutes the principle of potential corruption in the self, it also allows us to rationally illuminate that self, to reflect on it and to make a distinction between one's genuine sense of one's own good and the artificial passions of *amour-propre*. That is, it allows us to *judge*. Furthermore, in the modern human, because of reason, we can extend our *pitié*—our sense of commonality with others—in an *imaginative* way. While in prereflective *pitié* I simply *feel* a repugnance to the suffering of the other, now with reason I can actually separate from myself and *imagine* myself in the shoes of that other. I can imagine things from the point of view of *their amour de soi*. Reason thus allows me to develop my *pitié* in a way that was unavailable to prereflective consciousness. Through *pitié* and reason, we can extend our own *amour de soi* to others. This is what the love of others actually is, according to Rousseau. And I become capable not just of judging what my *own* good is, based on my own *amour de soi*, but also of judging what the good of the whole is. The more developed our reason, the more generally we can extend our *amour de soi* to others, ideally to the whole of humanity.

Thus even in relation to the primordial sentiments, reason is not simplistically construed as a polar principle in Rousseau. It is bound up with the extension of those sentiments to others, and it is required for the rational judgment of right and wrong. Yet it requires conscience or "the love of the good," the developed passions of *pitié* and *amour de soi*, in order to motivate it toward the good—"as soon as his reason leads him to perceive it [the good], his conscience impels him to love it" (*Emile*, 253).

In spite of this complex interdependence between our primordial nature and reason, it is nevertheless possible for reason to separate itself from these sentiments, from conscience, and to run rampant. Rousseau characterizes such a thinking as "the unbridled understanding and a reason which knows no bounds" (254). An abstract reasoning that is not rooted in the primordial sentiments, that tears itself free from conscience, is at the source of man's *corruption* for Rousseau. Unhinged from conscience, it embroils itself in pursuing the self-interested passions of *amour-propre*; it develops, broadens, and deepens these passions until they take over nearly the entire substance of the self and threaten to stifle altogether the voice of conscience. This unbridled understanding, the separation of ourselves from the true nature within, is what Rousseau was so afraid of, what he saw as so disastrous for modern human beings, and what provides the philosophical explanation for a corrupt civil society where relations of *amour-propre* have run amok and injustice abounds. And it is in a reason *guided* by conscience, guided by a knowledge of our primordial nature, that the possibility of redemption lies. Only such a reason can allow the individual to resist the pervasive influence of *amour-propre*, and to act in accordance with the good of the whole. Rousseau's entire positive educational and political philosophy can thus be understood as an attempt to strengthen the voice of moral reason and conscience, on the one hand, and to diminish the passions of *amour-propre* and curtail the "unbridled understanding," on the other.

If the Rousseauian citizen is interpreted in this manner, not as being consistent with the abstract, calculating rationality of the early liberal thinkers, but as founding an altogether new conception of the subject in modernity, then it ceases to appear as one-sided and untenable as the feminists mentioned earlier have portrayed. The notion that Rousseau identified men with abstract reasoning and women with nature, conflates and obscures the more complex and interesting understanding of nature and reason that he is putting forth. Indeed, Rousseau's distinction between an artificial and a primordial nature parallels a distinction that many feminists have sought to make between emotions that might be seen as a product of social imposition—such as the female concern with physical appearances—on the one hand, and the deeper and more rewarding emotions associated with justice, love, and friendship on the other hand. Furthermore, the polarizing of the principles of reason and nature as if they existed in a merely relative identity to each other in the feminist commentary noted earlier, fails to grasp the essential relationship that Rousseau conceives as existing between reason and our moral nature. In the more complex view of Rousseau given here, the identity of the virtuous male citizen is not constituted against woman as other, but precisely as the synthesis of what has been constructed as a male and a female principle—reason and feeling, law and instinct—harmonized in a fully developed human being. Rather than being founded upon a denial and exclusion of the feminine principle of love and particularity, the male citizen seeks to cultivate the primordial nature within him. Nature is not left behind, or absolutely excluded, for it is the very filling, the substance, of the mature male identity. Without that substance he is merely a creature of *amour-propre*, with no foundation upon which to stand and resist the vicissitudes of the world of opinion and appearance.

Based on this more complex understanding of Rousseau's ideas on nature and reason, I would like to discuss some particular ways in which I think his analysis offers interesting and important insights for feminists in our attempt to conceive a different model of the citizen. First, his understanding of the role of reflective rationality in generating the factitious passions has great implications for women in their entry into a public sphere that is fundamentally *determined* by this type of rationality. That is, it means that women in entering civil society encounter new types of pressures and emotions that entail a fundamental change in our subjectivity, and that this existential change must be taken account of in any feminist attempt to reconceive the citizen. Second, Rousseau's ideas on the way that conscience, as the basis for resistance to *amour-propre*, is to be cultivated, have significant implications for feminist policy. His views on the role of love in the family in developing the basis of moral subjectivity points toward the need to take account of this work if women are to be integrated into the public world on an level equal with that of men. As well, his views on the censor and the civil religion further develop his conception of the importance of fostering the sensuous basis of morality, and thus are significant for feminists who seek to bring the dimension of emotion and intuition into considerations of citizenship. Finally, an analysis of the point at which some of Rousseau's institutions for moral cultivation do become disturbing brings into view exactly what is at the heart of feminist criticisms of Rousseau, and where we need to go beyond his model of the citizen.

Feminist Implications of the Rousseauian Model of the Citizen

Modern Women

Rousseau's analysis of reflective rationality and its development in relation to the passions of the modern subject highlight an essential characteristic of the public sphere into which women have entered. For modern civil society is *founded* on abstract self-consciousness and self-promotion, on relations of *amour-propre*. It was this relationship to oneself and others that undermined the peaceful state of prereflective consciousness, that embroiled humans in the dynamic of envy, pride, and competition that inevitably drove them out of the state of nature into a condition where competition and status could be regulated. Relations of *amour-propre* do not go away in a condition of civil society; there can be no retreat back to a prereflective realm. Rather, civil society becomes a sphere where one can assert one's individuality, establish one's identity at the expense of others, but in a legal, established manner.[21] It is only in Rousseau's ideal democracy, where individuals have a basis of independence from others that allows their moral conscience to flourish, and where the basic conditions governing individuals' lives are determined by the general will, that the relations of *amour-propre* can be prevented from dominating existence. In our own, much less perfect "democracies," civil society remains the realm where an individual can "lay claim" to assert his superiority "by virtue of his individuality" (*Second Discourse*, 61).

According to many feminists, however, as well as Rousseau himself, women develop a different type of subjectivity that is less dominated by *amour-propre*, and that shows more of a sense of connectedness to others.[22] Many feminists have sought to articulate and comprehend this difference, as the basis for a notion that women could, by their very presence, transform the public sphere. The idea is that women can and do *import* this different way of being directly into the public sphere, and that it is a difference that needs to be granted recognition and respect. But Rousseau's analysis of the nature of the difference of women, and of the public sphere, casts serious doubt upon this notion.

For Rousseau, the difference between men and women is not an *essential* one, for women show the same, if not a greater, propensity to *amour-propre*; women's difference rather is a product of their role in the family. Once she becomes responsible for looking after her husband and children, woman becomes more bound up with the principle of love. Hence she is less dominated by the abstract rationality that governs the public realm. In the development of their abstract rationality, men have increasingly become characterized by the rift within themselves between the primordial feelings that speak in a "nearly unrecognizable" voice and the passions that have developed as a result of abstract rationality, as a result of participation in civil society. Women also are determined by abstract self-consciousness and the recognition of others, as Rousseau clearly recognizes in his discussion of the education of Sophie (*Emile*, book V). Nevertheless, the training of women in concern for appearances is ultimately directed at binding their entire identity to the role of wife and mother, to the role of love.[23] Once they are in this role, then, Rousseau believes that their tendency to *amour-propre* will be subordinated to their ethical function as nurturer. Love, rather than concern for physical appearances, will become the primary filling of their existence,[24] and residing in the domestic realm they will be sheltered from the divisive effects of a civil society that is antagonistic to the principle of love. In this sense traditional women, even though they are also creatures of *amour-propre*, can be seen to be closer to the primordial nature from which we have broken.

But once women enter into a realm where the emphasis is on reflection on one's self and comparison with others, they as much as men become alienated from the primordial passions of *amour de soi* and *pitié*. Women as much as men become embroiled in the struggle for recognition, in the competitive struggle for identity that pits us one against the other, and that causes us to lose sight of our deeper, authentic impulses. Thus modern women, as much as Rousseau's male philosopher, are capable of covering their ears and arguing with themselves a little in order to quiet the voice of nature within (*Second Discourse*, 55).

In light of women's entrance into the public sphere, Rousseau's critique of modern subjectivity as fundamentally determined by reflective rationality and by the competitive relations of *amour-propre* bound up with that rationality applies now *as much* to women as it does to men. While women have gained enormously in being able to assert our individuality in the public sphere, Rousseau's critique of modern subjectivity shows us that we have also *lost*. The role of love in the family may well have kept women closer to their primordial passions, less impelled to separate from and reflect upon themselves in relation to others. But now that women no longer dwell exclusively in the realm of love, now that love becomes for women, as it has been for men, only one facet of our existence, no longer can we claim to be closer to nature. Indeed, the fact that so many women began to reject the domestic life, that on such a widespread scale women began to assert their dissatisfaction with that life, shows how tenuous was the claim that women are closer to nature.

Thus against those feminists who tout the notion of a "maternal thinking," a thinking that women can bring *with* them into the public realm in order to humanize that realm, Rousseau shows that the very step forth *into* that realm is founded upon a break with maternal thinking. Women cannot simply import their traditional subjectivity directly into the public realm. The very premise of the women's movement that pushed women to fight their way into the public sphere *was* the break from intuitive knowing, from the sense of one's immediate connection to others, with the reflection on one's own self as a separate individual with separate interests and rights. The very premise of the women's movement was the ascendance in women of the principle of reflective rationality that drove men out of the state of nature. And *once* this has been established, as Rousseau shows us, there is no going back. There is no way to recapture an intuitive knowing or traditional subjectivity *in the same way*, in its *immediate* fashion. Just as modern man was corrupted by the principle of abstract rationality when he asserted himself as an individual, so has modern woman been corrupted. The maternal mode of existence that used to dominate our subjectivity now becomes merely a part of it, a part that often finds itself in competition with our modern, public self.[25]

For feminists, as well as for others, Rousseau's understanding of the divisive principle of reflective rationality that characterizes modern subjectivity shows that any alternative to the Cartesian conception of the self must be a *post*-Cartesian conception, that it must take into account the reality of the principle of separation in the lives of modern men and women. It must be a conception that *reunifies* reason and feeling *after* the principle of separation has occurred, rather than seeking to retreat *back* to a prereflective or intuitive state. For modern women who have now to face the same existential reality as men, who also are characterized by the principle of division, such a pathway forward is instructive. There can be no nostalgia for the traditional self, only a movement forward in light of the reality of division, in light of the loss of a subjectivity that might have been considered to be closer to nature.

For Rousseau this movement forwards, this reunified self, is found in conscience. Conscience is post-Cartesian in exactly the sense mentioned above; it takes into account the separative principle of reflective rationality and the competing forces within the self, but nevertheless posits a ground of authentic feeling that reason can grasp as its true guide in a competitive public sphere. And his investigations into the conditions for the *nurturing* of this conscience are also peculiarly instructive for feminists.

Women's Work: Love in the Family

The development of conscience in Rousseau's thought, the realization of the full moral potential in human beings, requires as an essential basis for its development the role of love in the family, a role he assigns chiefly to women.[26] While the duties of women are manifold, as Rousseau discusses them in *Emile*, they can be basically comprehended in terms of their relationship to the two sides of the divided modern self—the moral self and the self that is dominated by the passions of *amour-propre*. On the one hand, women have an essential role in nurturing conscience through establishing the bond of love in the family. On the other hand, Rousseau places an enormous weight on women in containing the passions of *amour-propre*, both in herself and in the man. This is particularly true of the unruly sexual passions that threaten the integrity of the family.[27] But as well, the need for recognition and admiration is to be fulfilled by the moral judgment of women on male citizens' actions (*Emile*, 353, 356). The various duties that he articulates for women, then, can be comprehended as targeting or taking responsibility for one side of the self or the other.

What I think is valuable and extraordinary in Rousseau's thought generally and in relation to his views on the role of women in particular is the attention that he gives to the importance of the cultivation and sustaining of conscience in the modern self. But where he becomes disturbing and problematic, as I shall discuss more fully in the last section, is in his attitude toward the self of *amour-propre* and his sometimes drastic ideas for how that self is to be contained. What I would like to examine here is the importance of the recognition that he gives to the role of familial love in relation to the development of conscience, and the implications of that recognition for public policy in an age when women have also entered the public sphere and are taking on great responsibilities there as well.[28]

In fostering the bonds of love in the family, according to Rousseau, woman lays the "foundation in nature" for patriotism and virtue in the state. Love is seen by him to be a "natural" emotion, for as discussed earlier it is rooted in the primordial passion of *amour de soi*. Through the extension of *amour de soi* to others, one learns to care about them as one does for oneself. Hence love is the "first tie" that unites one to the species, that puts one in an ethical relationship to others (*Emile*, 194). By nurturing this emotion, then, woman lays the foundation for virtue, for the capacity to care for the community as a whole. For while individuals first experience love of those closest to themselves, in the family, the development of virtue entails that, with the aid of reason, one comes to extend love to the whole of one's own society (195). All human justice ultimately springs from *amour de soi,* gradually and increasingly extended to the object of the community as a whole. Plato's idea of eliminating the family in the name of engendering a stronger commitment to the community is a "subversion of all the tenderest of our natural feelings, which he sacrificed to an artificial sentiment *which can only exist by their aid*" (326, italics mine).

In a civil society that is centered around relations of *amour-propre,* furthermore, it is love that can "prevent the growth of envy, covetousness, and hatred." From the inclination of justice that is first cultivated in the home, Emile gains "clearness of judgement," "accuracy in reasoning," and a state where "noble feelings stifle the lesser passions" (215).[29] Woman's most essential function in relation to moral conscience, then, can be seen in the laying of the foundation of love.

Rousseau's confining of women to the role of love in the home is premised on his argument that women do not have the quality of rationality that could allow them to engage in subsequent moral development. While women are capable of extending *amour de soi* to the small circle of the family, and of nurturing this emotion in others, they are not capable of the abstract reasoning that enables the extension of love beyond this circle. They are not capable of a larger sense of justice. As Lloyd points out, woman is "the immature *stage* of consciousness, left behind by advancing Reason."[30]

Rousseau's sexist notion about women's rationality seems ludicrous now, since women have historically established their capacity for reasoning to be equal with that of men. Nevertheless, his attention to the work of traditional women in moral education has profound implications once women, as they have done, step forth and assert their right to participate in the public realm. It becomes transparently obvious, from this perspective, that a liberal feminism that seeks simply to integrate women into a public order that is founded on relations of *amour-propre* is highly inadequate. Such a feminism may well succeed in opening up the public sphere to women, but in failing adequately to acknowledge or address the work that traditional women did, it fails to address the issue of moral education in modern society. This is far from saying, as Rousseau would have done, that women should be kept in the home, or even that the role of love in the family requires one parent to stay at home full-time. It is rather to suggest that the integration of women into the public sphere *on an equal level* entails a recognition and *renegotiation* of this work that traditional women did.

If a *moral* society fundamentally relies on the work of women in the home, as Rousseau suggests, then this is as true of our own liberal, capitalist societies as it is of Rousseau's fictitious, ideal republic. The moral behavior of individuals in our own, extremely imperfect democracies entails at *minimum* a capacity for trust and mutual respect, and that capacity presupposes a moral education in the family.[31] Rousseau's extraordinary attention to the role of women in moral education points to the far-reaching need for structural changes at both the public *and* the private level if women are truly to be included.

At present, we can see the implications of not attending to the work that women have traditionally done, with the simple, formal opening up of the public sphere to women. Sociologists point out the irony that the liberal feminist movement has moved women into "the double day of labour."[32] In more-progressive families, the burden of playing two roles simultaneously is simply shifted onto both parents. The requirements of entry into public life remain as demanding, and in many cases even more so, than they were before women's entry, and there is an implicit failure to recognize that many people are playing two roles now. At the same time, child rearing continues to be seen by the state as a largely *private* responsibility. In North America at least, state subsidized child care is practically nonexistent. The lack of importance given to this work can be found in the terribly low rate of pay for child-care workers.

The strain of attempting to play dual roles can be found in the exhaustion that ordinary parents[33] experience on a day-to-day basis, an exhaustion borne particularly by women, who tend to share the heavier burden of the double load. Furthermore, without structural adjustment to public roles, individuals who do decide to have children cannot possibly compete on an equal level with those who do not, unless they decide to hand over the great bulk of the child-rearing responsibilities to paid help. Without structural adjustment, the strain will show itself in parents' relationships with their children, with each other, and most important of all, in the character of future citizens.

This is not to suggest that traditional families with a traditional division of labor between men and women provided a better environment for children. It is, however, to cast a shadow on the notion that shared parenting on its own, in the absence of structural adjustments to the public and private realms, can provide either a more nurturing environment for children, or provide the foundation for women's equality.

Rather than providing simply a model for women's exclusion, then,

Rousseau's attention to the family and women's role in moral education can provide us with a critical viewpoint on our contemporary situation, and a basis from which to begin to diagnose change. This is not to suggest, as Rousseau himself might have done, that women should be sent back to the home. His understanding of the role of women can also point to the conclusion that a society that is serious about women's inclusion in the public realm—*on an equal level*—must learn to concern itself much more adequately with the work that women have traditionally done, and *continue* to do, now in the face of other enormous pressures.

Some obvious adjustments that follow from this argument would include better pregnancy, maternity, and paternity leaves; part-time work in the professional world; revised expectations of what constitutes a good professional;[34] geared-to-income state-funded day care; better pay and recognition for child-care workers; subsidized activity programs for small children; the four-day workweek; and so on.

Only when parents are allowed time and tranquility with their children can the jobs of shared parenting and participation in public life be adequately managed. Critics might suggest that this is all very utopian. But if Rousseau is correct that love in the family is the foundation of any genuine citizen morality, then the bonds of a humane, peaceful, and egalitarian society can be forged under no less optimum conditions than these.

The Censor and the Civil Religion:
Moral Cultivation in the Adult Citizen

Rousseau's concern with love in the family as laying the foundation for moral conscience and virtuous citizenship in a good state is one essential aspect of his concern with moral edification, with strengthening the moral side of the self, that can be instructive for feminists in the struggle toward a more just society. But love in the family encounters its limit when individuals step forth into civil society, into the realm where abstract rationality predominates and where the emotions of pride, envy, and greed bound up with that comparative rationality proliferate. The antagonism that is encountered between these purely self-interested passions and our moral self creates the difficulties for modern men and women that have been pointed to above. And it is in Rousseau's prescriptions for a censor and a civic religion in particular that we can see his concern with this problem, his awareness of the danger that, even in a moral individual, the self-interested passions can crowd out or confuse the genuine moral sentiments and thus threaten the integrity of the moral community. Thus the fact that a maternal thinking cannot be directly imported into the public sphere because of the divisive character of that sphere, does not prevent Rousseau from sharing the concern of such feminists with the need to incorporate the emotional, intuitive aspects of the self into moral action, in order to counter the prevalence of *amour-propre*. However, he seeks to do so with a profound awareness of what he is dealing with, of the corruptive forces within the self of all modern individuals who participate in the competitive public sphere.

It is in his notion of the love of the laws in a just society, and the institutions that foster love of the laws, that we get a clearer sense of Rousseau's notion of moral edification in the adult citizen. In the notion of loving laws that are just, Rousseau recognizes that for individuals truly to be committed to the moral principles embodied in the laws and to be capable of standing up for those principles and sacrificing their own narrow self-interest when this is called for, they must be committed to the laws with the whole of their being, and not merely through an abstract, calculating rationality. Only a nonutilitarian devotion to the laws as sacred principles, principles that constitute the most essential aspect of one's own identity, can sustain a true political community. It is on the ground of these principles that citizens who at a personal level are largely anonymous can meet and feel their vital connection. The violation of a fundamental moral principle of the society in the case of one individual is experienced as a violation by all. Injustice toward one, the disregarding of the rights of and due respect toward a fellow citizen, will be felt in a deeply personal manner in the outrage of all.[35] True political community and the true bond of a healthy society is thus established on the ground of a shared conscience that has a lively existence in each citizen.

Putting aside for a moment the usual liberal reactions to Rousseau's doctrines of the censor and the civil religion, we can see the essential, positive function of these institutions in terms of the strengthening of the voice of conscience, in terms of the necessity of moral edification. The censor is not a body external to the democratic community, but is precisely the voice of that community, the expression of the public judgment on questions of what might threaten the essential mores that constitute the life of the community and the bonds that hold it together (*Social Contract*, 219). Hence the censor is to public opinion what the law is to the general will, merely the expression, the declaration, of the essential moral principles of the society. The role of the censor is one of *sustaining* the health of the mores of the society "by preventing opinions from becoming corrupt, by preserving their rectitude through wise applications" (219). Since the life of the community exists in and through these shared mores, the coming together of the community to reaffirm what it essentially stands for is a practice of edification; it stirs the sentiments and revitalizes the bonds of the members with one another. Furthermore, it seeks to maintain an environment within which those principles will be supported and promoted.

Identifying the positive function of the censor in sustaining the vitality of the community's most essential moral sensibilities is in no way meant to eclipse or deny the negative and troubling aspect of this institution, an aspect I shall attempt to account for below. It is, rather, to shed light on Rousseau's insight into the essentiality of practices of moral edification, practices that keep alive the citizens' experience of the basic principles that bind them together and that motivate them to moral action when this is called for.

Rousseau's doctrine of the civil religion can be analyzed from a similar perspective. He casts the dogmas of that religion as "sentiments of sociability" because they maintain the citizen's commitment to the moral principles that bind them together as a community. The absolute essentiality of the civil religion for sustaining moral conscience can be found in Rousseau's statement that without such beliefs, an individual is "incapable of sincerely loving the laws and justice, and of sacrificing his life, if necessary, for his duty" (226). The dogmas of the civil religion, limited as they might seem, are a powerful and essential basis for sustaining moral fortitude. Paralleling precisely the beliefs encountered in the "Creed of the Savoyard Priest," in *Emile*—"The existence of a powerful, intelligent, beneficent divinity that foresees and provides; the life to come; the happiness of the just; the punishment of the wicked; the sanctity of the social contract and of the laws" (*Social Contract*, 226)—these beliefs are what enable an individual to sustain their moral fortitude, to undertake moral action even when it requires the sacrifice of individual self-interest, and even when it might *appear* that the wicked are benefiting from wickedness and the just are being harmed by their own just action. The belief in some kind of a just moral order that will reflect just action is at bottom essential in order to avoid the fate of cynicism so common in our times.[36] It is necessary in order to keep reason tied to conscience and prevent the "unbridled understanding" from holding sway. Furthermore, the belief in the sanctity of the social contract gives the individual surety of conviction in undertaking moral action, silencing the nagging voice of skeptical rationality that would seek to cast doubt on everything and bring the individual to a state of moral impotence.

Rousseau's general concern in his notion of moral cultivation with the bringing of reason and conscience into harmony, through fostering the element of sentiment or emotion in moral judgment and activity, parallels the feminist concern to incorporate the "knowledge" of intuition and emotion in developing a more just public realm. Hence a study of these and other institutions of Rousseau's in terms of this question of moral edification can be extremely instructive to feminists. At the very least, they points toward the necessity of certain ideas and practices to sustain moral conscience in the face of a skeptical, questioning rationality that threatens to unhinge itself from conscience and to embroil the self in emotions of *amour-propre*.

Stifling Reflective Rationality and the Self of Amour-Propre: Beyond Rousseau's Theory of the Citizen

In spite of the positive insights that I think Rousseau's work holds for feminists—in his confrontation with the fundamentally divided self of the modern, between the moral self on the one hand and the passions of *amour-propre* on the other, and in his ideas on how the family and other institutions play an essential role in strengthening the moral self that must be recognized and accounted for—there inevitably comes a point when one must confront ideas in his thought that are galling or troublesome. We see these problematic aspects in the possibility that the majority could stifle unpopular views in its command of the censor, and in Rousseau's prescriptions for banishment and even the death penalty for those who refuse to believe in the civil religion (*Social Contract*, 226–27). And we encounter it in many other aspects of his moral and political philosophy. Feminist commentators have aptly illustrated the objectionable aspects of his views on the role of women. But as well is his curious ban on public discourse in the determination of the general will (156), the extraordinarily sheltered education of Emile, the emphasis on political withdrawal when one is living in a corrupt society (*Emile*, 437–39), as well as what I think is his ultimate political pessimism in the chapter on the civil religion.[37] While some of these characteristics might seem more objectionable than others, altogether they point to the need to confront the disturbing elements of Rousseau's thought.

I would like to suggest here that the problematic aspects of Rousseau's philosophy can all be comprehended in terms of a general and fundamental problem in his ontology of the self and his model for the ideal citizen, a problem that must push us beyond this conception and this model. This is a problem that feminists have been attempting to articulate, but I think in an overly sweeping and dismissive manner that fails to do justice to the complexity of Rousseau's thought, and fails to retain the extremely insightful and helpful aspects of his work. The difficulty with Rousseau, which manifests itself in the more illiberal or objectionable aspects of his philosophy, lies in his view of an unfettered abstract reasoning and of the passions of *amour-propre* as fundamentally *opposed* and *antagonistic* to the moral self. Furthermore, in viewing them as so opposed and so antagonistic, he views the moral self as a deeply fragile entity that must be carefully safeguarded. And it must be safeguarded not only through the positive institutions of moral edification, but also through the attempts to contain and reduce, and even excise where possible, the self of *amour-propre*. Rousseau is simultaneously terrified of and hostile toward abstract reflective reasoning and the passions of *amour-propre* that are bound up with that reasoning.

We can understand the various, troublesome aspects of his philosophy, then, in terms of this terrified and hostile attitude. In *Emile,* he introduces the Creed of the Savoyard Priest at the precise time when his pupil reaches the age of reason, when the doubting, questioning rationality becomes ascendant and all the dangers it represents come to the fore. The Creed is meant to satisfy but at the same time to contain reason within the confines of moral feeling, to *halt* it from any further progression. At a political level, Rousseau's prescription for a censor that would ultimately stifle unpopular views, his fear of any expression of dissenting belief in the dogmas of the civil religion, and his ban on public discourse prior to voting also point to his fear of letting rationality run free. An unfettered reason is *extremely* dangerous, for Rousseau, both because it can separate from and confuse individuals about what the right and the good are, but also because it does this in and through an appeal to the negative passions of *amour-propre*. Abstract reasoning let loose from conscience and a strictly moral thinking is sophistic—it plays on the desire for recognition; it emphasizes qualities of charisma, the need to fit in, or to distinguish oneself as special. Hence it must be strictly contained.

The passions of *amour-propre* that are bound up with the development of abstract reasoning must also be contained and, where possible, excised. In *Emile*, the sheltering of Rousseau's pupil from conventional society is designed to prevent altogether the development of the destructive desires that would cause one to admire pomp and splendor, false culture and empty beauty. Furthermore, Rousseau's choice for Emile as an adult citizen is political withdrawal. For in spite of Emile's strongly developed moral character and his resistance to the glamorous appearances of civil society, he might nevertheless succumb to the vices of that corrupt society if he were fully to engage with it. Only in a society of fellow Emiles, and where the ideal conditions of the social contract can be approximated, would political participation truly be safe (*Emile*, 439).

While in Emile's early education we see the attempt to reduce or excise the self of *amour-propre*, to the extent that this is not possible Rousseau puts much of the burden of dealing with this aspect of the self squarely onto women. The objectionable load that Rousseau places on women in containing sexual passion as well as in alleviating men's fears about their paternity can be understood in terms of the need to contain the passions of *amour-propre*. But as well there is the need to deal with the reality of individuals' need for recognition. This is to be contained by having women judge and award with recognition only actions that are noble and benefit the community. Thus women, given that the self of *amour-propre* is an inherent reality, play a fundamental role in *harmonizing amour-propre* with the moral self, in order to contain its inherently unruly tendencies.

For feminists seeking a model of the citizen that incorporates the elements of the self that women have come to be identified with, such as emotion and intuition, Rousseau's moral and political philosophy offers invaluable understanding and guidance. Yet it is in his fundamental attitude toward the self of *amour-propre* that we reach the limit of that guidance. Because he views the two sides of the self as largely antagonistic and opposed to each other, and because he seeks an ideal of harmony in the self (*Emile*, 9), his attitude toward the self of *amour-propre* is largely hostile. To the extent that he does seek to accommodate it, he imposes an objectionable set of responsibilities on women and prescribes some disturbingly illiberal political institutions. His model of the moral self and the good citizen is one that cannot abide the everyday weaknesses and vulnerabilities of modern individuals. It is a model that is essentially unforgiving toward an inescapable aspect of our humanity.[38]

In his hostility toward the self of *amour-propre*, Rousseau betrays his fundamental lack of confidence in the moral self. He may be right that abstract rationality is a potential antagonist to conscience. Yet it is only when the dictates of conscience have stood the test of that rational questioning that they deserve to become the guiding forces of a moral society. Hence unlimited exposure to such rationality might be seen as strengthening rather than merely threatening moral conscience. Similarly, his hostility toward the passions of *amour-propre* show his lack of faith in the moral self to hold its own in the face of our concerns with appearance, acceptance, and success. We see little notion that individuals can take responsibility for their own moral conflicts.

Feminists themselves must abandon the notion that we can ever achieve a fully harmonized moral subjectivity. Conscience itself will always have an uneasy peace with the self of *amour-propre*, and will at times be called upon to oppose the passions in the self that often threaten to compromise right action. But accepting this is a far cry from suggesting that the self of *amour-propre* must be excised or rigidly contained. Rather, moral reason and the conscience that sustains it must be seen as capable of standing up *in face of* the conflict with the potentially sophistic reasoning of abstract rationality and the passions of *amour-propre*. We must expect more from ourselves and from others. But beyond this, we must also recognize that conscience is not always and everywhere opposed to abstract reasoning and the self of *amour-propre*. Reason itself must ultimately vindicate the standpoint of conscience against its sophistic detractors. And as Rousseau himself saw, conscience itself needs to be fostered by the moral recognition of others.

Rousseau's ultimate inability to control the self of *amour-propre* is reflected in the incredible moment of political pessimism that we encounter in his discussion of the civil religion. Even a society of Emiles, he seems to suggest, in the "perfect" environment depicted in *The Social Contract*, will ultimately be betrayed and corrupted by the element of evil in the human spirit. It is this pessimistic conclusion, perhaps more than any other aspect of his philosophy, that must alert us to the problems with Rousseau's concept of moral subjectivity, and point us beyond it. A feminism that seeks to accept and forgive the self of *amour-propre*, while still requiring much from us as moral citizens, will be a feminism of hope rather than of pessimism.

Notes

1. See, for example, Diana Coole, *Women in Political Theory*, 2d ed. (New York: Harvester Wheatsheaf, 1993); Lori Jo Marso, *(Un)Manly Citizens: J.-J. Rousseau's and Germanin de Stael's Subversive Women* (Baltimore: Johns Hopkins University Press, 1999); Susan Moller Okin, *Women in Western Political Thought* (Princeton: Princeton University Press, 1979); Linda Zerilli, *Signifying Woman: Culture and Chaos in Rousseau, Burke, and Mill* (Ithaca: Cornell University Press, 1994). This Cartesian view comes by way of Simone de Beauvoir's appropriation and application of Hegel's master/slave analysis to the situation of women. But it has been greatly accelerated by postmodern analyses that repudiate the notion that identity could be established in any other way than through the relation of arbitrary signifiers (see especially Zerilli's analysis).

2. Okin, *Women in Western Political Thought*, 100.

3. Marso, *(Un)Manly Citizens*, 5–6.

4. Coole, *Women in Political Theory*, 90.

5. Zerilli, *Signifying Woman*, 23 and 52.

6. Marso, *(Un)Manly Citizens*, 3.

7. Marso, *(Un)Manly Citizens*, 3.

8. Zerilli, *Signifying Woman*, 47.

9. Zerilli, *Signifying Woman*, 54.

10. Coole, *Women in Political Theory*, 90.

11. See Susan Moller Okin, *Justice, Gender, and the Family* (New York: Basic Books, 1989), chap. 8.

12. See Wendy Brown, *Manhood and Politics: A Feminist Reading in Political Theory* (Totawa, N.J.: Rowman and Littlefield, 1988); Carol Pateman, *The Sexual Contract* (Cambridge: Polity Press, 1988); Genevieve Lloyd, *The Man of Reason: "Male" and "Female" in Western Philosophy* (London: Methuen, 1984); and Sara Ruddick, *Maternal Thinking: Towards a Politics of Peace* (New York: Ballantine Books, 1989).

13. Surely *this* tendency signifies a rather unfeminist will to mastery over the Western philosophical tradition.

14. Pateman, in *The Sexual Contract*, acknowledges that Rousseau is doing something different, but says he still keeps women subjugated and gives him no further consideration. Brown, in *Manhood and Politics*, draws on Marx in developing her alternative, but gives almost no consideration to Rousseau, even though he is clearly opposed to the tradition that she is criticizing. Lloyd, in *The Man of Reason*, although she has a more sympathetic reading of Rousseau, similarly dismisses him because he does not accord the possibility of moral development to women. There are exceptions, however. Lynda Lange, in "Rousseau and Modern Feminism," *Social Theory and Practice* 7, no. 3 (1981): 245–77, points to the importance of Rousseau, as does Mira Morgenstern, in *Rousseau and the Politics of Ambiguity: Self, Culture, and Society* (University Park: Pennsylvania State University Press, 1996).

15. Jean-Jacques Rousseau, "Discourse on the Origin and Foundation of Inequality Among Men," in *The Basic Political Writings*, trans. Donald A. Cress (Indianapolis: Hackett, 1988), 25–109 (henceforward *Second Discourse*).

16. Usually the notion of an alternative is put forth in the conclusions of these critical works on the Western tradition with little elaboration. (See Brown, *Manhood and Politics*; Lloyd, *The Man of Reason*; Marso, *(Un)Manly Citizens*; and Pateman, *The Sexual Contract*). Ruddick (*Maternal Thinking*) is an exception in making some attempt to elaborate what maternal thinking would entail in terms of the issue of peace.

17. See Lloyd, *The Man of Reason* and also, for a more developed discussion of Rousseau's concept of reason as different from the Cartesian one, "Rousseau on Reason, Nature, and Women," *Metaphilosophy* 14, nos. 3, 4 (1983): 308–25.

18. Lloyd, *The Man of Reason*, 58.

19. Rousseau discusses the development of this abstract rationality at the beginning of part II of the *Second Discourse*.

20. Jean-Jacques Rousseau, *Emile*, trans. Barbara Foxley (London: J. M. Dent and Sons, 1989) (henceforward *Emile*). See especially "The Creed of the Savoyard Priest," 228–78, as well as the first part of book IV.

21. In part II of the *Second Discourse* Rousseau discusses how the inequality between rich and poor was what became codified in a system of power that, while fundamentally unjust, established some sort of order.

22. For example, Ruddick, *Maternal Thinking*; Carol Gilligan, *In a Different Voice: Psychological Theory and Women's Development* (Cambridge: Harvard University Press, 1982).

23. This is the "natural" end that explains Rousseau's paradoxical statements about women and *amour-propre*, as Lloyd discusses in "Rousseau on Reason, Nature, and Women."

24. With the exception, of course, of concern for her reputation as faithful to her husband and children. There seems good reason to believe that Tolstoy's Natasha in *War and Peace* is based on this understanding of the nature and function of women, given the influence of Rousseau on Tolstoy. By nature a coquette, once Natasha finds her place as wife and mother she settles down to become plump, ethical, and satisfied.

25. Feminist discussions that promote the notion of a feminine difference too often fail to acknowledge the reality of the shift in the subjectivity of the modern woman, the difficulties and conflicts that this creates for women, and the ways in which it puts us in a position of much greater commonality with men. It is this shift, furthermore, that can explain the disappointments of the expectations that simply having more women in the public sphere would be transformative. Simply focusing on maternal thinking itself is not enough. The struggle at bottom is a struggle *within* the modern subjectivity that must take into account the rift between competing forces of the self.

26. Rousseau's discussions of the role of women are found chiefly in book V of *Emile*, in *Letter to d'Alembert*, in his novel *La nouvelle Héloïse*, as well as in the dedication to *The Social Contract*.

27. See *Emile*, 323, 335, 348. Woman must make herself simultaneously attractive yet elusive for her husband, keeping his sexual passion towards her aroused yet contained within the boundaries of the family. Furthermore, she must promote a modest and chaste appearance to outward society while being adequately attractive and coquettish with her husband.

28. The exclusion of the role of women from consideration in the main text of *The Social Contract* lends credence to the notion that the contract itself and Rousseau's ideal public realm already *presuppose* the work of women, a work that is thus rendered invisible from the standpoint of public life. That Rousseau nevertheless gives so much attention to the role of women *elsewhere* in his writing, however, signifies not that he is implicitly relying on the work of women in a type of invisible "sexual contract," but that he is extraordinarily *aware* of women's work in moral education. Indeed, I think that his thought can be seen as *highlighting* a work that usually does remain invisible, showing its importance and the need to take *political* account of it, even if Rousseau himself does not do so in *The Social Contract*.

29. Lynda Lange, in "Rousseau and Modern Feminism," *Social Theory and Practice*, 7, no. 3 (1981): 245–77, develops this point about the significance of the role of love if women are truly interested in transforming the public sphere.

30. Lloyd, *The Man of Reason*, 58, 64.

31. The liberal tendency to neglect the moral self, and to focus instead on a procedural rationality as if this could truly explain the nature of the social bond, has been well criticized by feminists and communitarians.

32. Pat Armstrong and Hugh Armstrong, *The Double Ghetto: Canadian Women and Their Segregated Work*, 3d ed. (Toronto: McClelland and Stewart, 1994).

33. Ordinary parents who cannot afford special nannies and babysitters on top of that, or who perhaps simply do not want to hand over so much of the care of their children to paid help.

34. The academic world provides manifold examples of the pressures that modern parents face. Rather than changing to better accommodate the realities of women, the environment is becoming more and more anathema to the realities of having and raising children. Not the least evidence of this is that *quantity* of publications is one of the chief determinants in the system of rewards. And the notion of a *half-time* academic position, which would suit many parents, is unheard of.

35. I think that this is the meaning of the idea of giving oneself up "whole and entire" to the community in Rousseau's idea of the social compact (*The Social Contract*, in *The Basic Political Writings*, trans. Donald A. Cress [Indianapolis: Hackett, 1988], 148). As he subsequently says: "As soon as this multitude is thus united in a body, one cannot harm one of the members without attacking the whole body. It is even less likely that the body can be harmed without the members feeling it" (*The Social Contract*, 150).

36. The absence of such a belief is responsible for Woody Allen's pessimistic conclusion in *Crimes and Misdemeanors*. Even the Platonic argument that the wicked are punished by the state of their own soul is unavailable to Allen, as the wicked or morally vacuous characters in his movie appear to achieve happiness, while Allen, the self-reflective moral person ends up not only losing his lover, but also becoming depressed, miserable, and cynical. Kant's concurrence with Rousseau on this notion that certain corresponding beliefs are necessary to carry out moral action can be found in his "Postulates of Practical Reason," in *Critique of Practical Reason*. These postulates bear an extraordinary resemblance to Rousseau's dogmas of the civil religion.

37. I refer here to two remarks: *The Social Contract*, 224: "[A] society of true Christians would no longer be a society of men"; and 225: "[L]eaving aside political considerations, let us return to right and determine the principles that govern this important point."

38. This is not to neglect the *practical* consideration that the control of information and ideas that would be required in Rousseau's ideal, and the homogeneous nature of his society, simply do not reflect the reality of our complex, contemporary societies in an age of information technology.

7

Empowerment Inside Patriarchy

Rousseau and the Masculine Construction of Femininity

Else Wiestad

Philosophers operating within a patriarchal framework have attempted to define and construct norms for women's exercise of power. Why does the male pattern of oppression prescribe certain modes of power for women? How does this concept of female power strategy operate inside a sexist system?

In what follows I will argue that such a neopatriarchal thinker as Rousseau has in reality provided a double set of rules for the exercise of power, one superior and masculine, the other subordinate and feminine. The two structures can be considered as not being in conflict or antagonistic. Instead they supplement and maintain each other, at the same time as they represent different and complementary normative standards.

It may be surprising to see that Rousseau, an advocate of women's subjection, not only tolerated, but even recommended and invited women to use certain informal power tactics, as is expressed in his ambiguous discourse on women. Indirectly Rousseau tells women that to some extent they should be active and take the initiative, if this is done within men's romantic dictates.

It has often been emphasized that women have at their disposal several power techniques, which give them more real influence than is evident from documentary sources. This kind of argument has until now been used to defend a gender-divided pattern in culture and society. In the 1880s such reasoning was used against the coming breakthrough of the European feminist liberation movement in the bourgeois class. But already in the mid-1700s the same type of argument was an integral part of Rousseau's neopatriarchal ideology.

In this essay I shall highlight the questions posed above through an interpretation and discussion of Rousseau's Sophie, or Woman, book V of Émile (1762), a central text on gender ideology in the eighteenth century. This famous book contributed decisively to the backlash against European feminism in the following decades.

Female power strategies is a constantly recurring theme in Sophie, or Woman. Implicitly Rousseau asks these questions: Which means of influence do women really have, and which do we want them to possess? What norms can both permit and restrict their exercise of power? What is the benefit to men if they allow women to use certain types of power techniques?

Some researchers have interpreted Rousseau as giving extended concessions of power to women (Burgelin 1963, 121ff.; Wexler 1976, 274, 281; Schwartz 1984, 37, 166–67; Green 1995). It has been claimed that Rousseau credits women with great sexual power, and therefore power in general (Schwartz 1984). From a different and relatively broad contextual reading I shall try both to put other nuances and counterarguments to this conception, and to partly reject it. I shall point at two parallel and gender divided power structures that are built into one another and into the same neopatriarchal system of domination.

This double power system displays a composite pattern, which in turn reveals an ambiguous technique of domination. Schwartz's interpretation draws attention to only one meaning, when he asserts that according to Rousseau sexuality gives men and women power over each other because of the mutual dependence it engenders. Although it divides and differentiates men and women, it also brings them together. Rousseau's teaching about sexuality, according to Schwartz, claims either liberation from sexuality through a radical individualistic male autonomy, or liberation through sexual interdependence. The latter is based on a reciprocity of sexual power, an interchange between men and women, of ruling and being ruled (Schwartz 1984).

However, Rousseau distinguishes between and emphasizes not only sexuality, but also a number of female power sources adapted to the same structure of male dominance, and he urges women to use all of them.

Michel Foucault argues that the exercise of power in Western society has gone through a profound transformation, tied to processes of reform that began starting in the period between 1760 and 1840. In *Discipline and Punish* he sees the prison as an expression of a technique of discipline that has been developed in the school, the hospital, the factory, and the army. Not the goodwill of reformers, but the emergence of a disciplinary society and a consequent new articulation of power, gave rise to the prison (Foucault 1975, 1979).

Although Foucault does not specifically focus on the social control of women, Sandra Bartky argues that women have their own experience of the modernization of power that in many respects follows the course outlined by Foucault. According to Bartky, the normative femininity is becoming more and more centered on women's bodies, through regulation of body size, weight, contours, and gestures (Bartky 1993, 115–16). In his book on women, Rousseau describes precisely and in detail a new, invasive, and nonviolent technique of control that aims at internalizing the constraint laid on women through a program of education.

In this connection we should keep in mind that *Sophie, or Woman* is a controversial book. It represented a counterattack on the emerging discussion and practice of gender liberation that Rousseau encountered in his own time and strongly resented. Both in *Lettre à d'Alembert* (1758) and later in *Émile,* he complains that modern life fails to respect the natural differences between the sexes (Rousseau 1967a, 113–16; 1966, 516), and he emphasizes the natural leadership of the male gender.

The arguments Rousseau presented in *Émile* and other writings were later repeated and used during the French Revolution and in the following decades to oppose women's participation in public and political affairs. It is therefore interesting to see which attitudes he explicitly admits to and recommends for women who want to influence their situation.

Although Rousseau points out several female power strategies, which I have discussed more thoroughly in another connection (Viestad [Wiestad] 1986, 1989), I shall briefly focus on and discuss only four of his prescriptions for the exercise of female power: those concerned with (1) virtues, (2) understanding, (3) eroticism, and (4) the romantic freedom of choice. I will try to show how these female strategies are built into and predominantly complement, and are subjugated to, a superior masculine power structure.

Interior Barriers and Male-Centered Care

To put the prescriptions for women's behavior into a broader perspective I will first emphasize two central features in Rousseau's gender ideology, that also reflects a transformation in the exercise of male power from this period on:

a) Rousseau contributes to and strongly points out the importance of shaping the female subject by setting up rules for her behavior. The suppression changes, from being expressed in an external, patriarchal mode to becoming an internalized coercion, attaching strong importance to the girl's internal barriers formed through socialization. This is in strong contrast to the training of Émile, who is the new, free model for men (Wiestad [Viestad] 2000).

b) Another ideological shift instigated by Rousseau consists in considerably extending the role of women as caretakers. Although breastfeeding and care for children was the practical "raison d'être" of the extended mothering role, the main shift and purpose for Rousseau was to train women to take care of men: "To satisfy them . . . making their lives pleasant and comfortable: This is the duty of women through all times." The entire education of women should therefore be planned through considering the needs of men (Rousseau 1966, 475).

The Power of Virtues

A woman's empire begins with her virtues, declares Rousseau. It is therefore interesting to look closely at the types of norms a woman should follow, to be described and appreciated as virtuous. According to Rousseau, woman's reign is one of gentleness, tact, and complaisance. Her commands are caresses, her threats are tears (Rousseau 1966, 511, 535). The woman should contrive to be ordered to do what she wants but never to usurp men's rights and take the command upon herself. This would be an inversion of the "proper order of things" and could only lead to misery and dishonor (511, 535).

A woman may thus obtain indirect influence if she pleases a man and does not openly threaten his dominant position. Her virtues are expressed through signs of friendly subservience. The good wife reigns through the sweetness of her disposition and the dignity of her modesty (511).

Woman's power in this case is based on the moral respect she gets from a man. To obtain his respect she must keep a low profile and practice virtues such as patience, modesty, and docility. But may the Virtuous Woman objectively influence her own position in this way? Can she gain more influence than any obedient child or servant may obtain?

Karen Green claims that Rousseau does not assume that women are by nature inferior to men, only that they are different. Reason will dictate different behaviors, and women should be trained to show other virtues and use different strategies from those of men to obtain what they want (Green 1995, 71–72). Furthermore, she points out that manipulation, ability to please, and obedience are among the Rousseauian methods they may use to be allowed their own way.

However, Rousseau's language of power and the forms of his strategies reveal an ambiguous and compounded gender model. If we look closely at his arguments, we note that women's methods as well as their goals refer to a dual and complementary power structure implying not only polarity, but also asymmetry.

First, according to a Rousseauian split value system, men are naturally free, independent, and self-sufficient, while women are naturally unfree, dependent, and made to obey a man and let herself be subjugated (Rousseau 1966, 466, 482, 534). Like Aristotle, Rousseau asserts that a man is woman's natural leader and master (529, 579, 627), and that her obedience arises from her inborn disposition for being dependent (482). In addition to natural reasons, he states rational reasons for placing men and women on an unequal footing. These reasons, however, point in their turn back to the man's uncertain position as a biological parent (470–71). In the end a physiological fact, which is to the man's disfavor, actually gives him a privilege, designed to secure his confidence as a biological father. Even these arguments for inequality therefore point back to natural differences.

Second, Rousseau asserts that although men and women are made for each other their mutual dependence is not of equal rank (*n'est pas égale*). Men depend on women because of their desires; women depend on men because of their desires and their needs. To obtain what is necessary for their station in life, they depend on men, to give it to them and to esteem them worthy of it (475). The unequal dependency between the sexes makes it possible for men to determine what are praiseworthy virtues and qualities in women (475, 482). We see that Rousseau's thinking presupposes not only natural differences, but also a hierarchical partition between the sexes that allows men to stipulate a value applied to women and their merits.

The asymmetric relation between men and women becomes still clearer when Rousseau further expands on which power strategies he imagines female virtue may exploit. For example, even if a man is brutal and insensitive, he says, it is strange if his character will not become gentler in the company of a thoughtful girl who says little, listens, has a modest bearing and a decent conversation (512).

This type of female influence works to the great benefit of men, Rousseau asserts. It "restrains the brutal husbands and maintains the good marriages," which would otherwise totter under matrimonial conflicts (485). Good marriages—for whom? For the brutal husbands? From a man's point of view, a wife's silence and evasive mildness may perhaps benefit and save his marriage. But can, under these circumstances, taciturnity and patience be considered a female tactic for gaining real power? Is it not more reasonable to see the appeasing behavior as a result of necessary self-preservation, to which women are compelled by a large measure of self-restraint?

The high moral esteem connected to the female virtues is dearly bought. Rousseau's indirect message is, The larger the loyalty shown for men's prescriptions, the more virtuous a woman is considered to be. If she gains moral respect this way, she may indirectly influence men.

The powerful usually take virtues to mean the qualities that are useful or convenient to themselves, Harriet Taylor Mill observes. For her this particularly is true with regard to women, who are still persuaded that the paramount virtue of womanhood is loyalty to men (Mill 1971, 108).

Female attitudes such as submissiveness and acceptance of constraint

will not challenge or provoke men. To some extent, the soft female virtues may neutralize, deny, or impede male aggressiveness. But through
such means a woman does not refuse to expose herself to, or to interact
with and indirectly continue to confirm, the supreme male patterns of
power.

A woman's acceptance of Rousseau's prescriptions for women's behavior implies that she is a captive. From them a woman learns that she is
not free to break her bonds and defend herself directly. She can evade
or soften brutality and insensitivity, but following these norms implies
acceptance of the role as one of suffering and victimization.

The profit obtained by woman is therefore a secondary gain compared
with man's primary gain, forcing a subjugation to his set of norms. His
dominant position is not decisively threatened by this type of indirect
and virtuous influence. On the contrary, it creates patterns of habit that
may operate internally and consolidate women's understanding of themselves as being unequally dependent and weak. In reality the asymmetric
and complementary norm system ensnares women in a defensive pattern
of behavior.

Understanding Men

In Rousseau's opinion woman's intellectual ability is her only true resource, and it should be used to compensate her lack of physical strength
(Rousseau 1966, 484). Without her cunning wit, woman would be a
man's slave, not his partner. To some extent the female intellect should
therefore be cultivated.

Nevertheless, Rousseau very soon outlines clear patriarchal limits to
women's abilities. Their talents should not be developed in the direction
of brilliant eloquence, of the type of wit that is highly valued in society
(484). A woman should not distinguish herself in any larger social context, since a brilliant wife is a plague to her husband as well as to everyone
else (536). Her intellect may rather be formed as a tool suitable to her
secondary position, in which she employs the art of making use of men's
position, and she will prevail through utilizing the special advantages that
men have (484–85).

She can influence her condition only through a man and through the
study of his mentality. Knowledge of a man's psychological inclinations

will therefore be decisive for her situation in life. To be able to influence men, privately and indirectly, a woman must first of all understand a man's *emotions*, Rousseau underscores. However, women should not study men in general. It is the particular man that she is at any time subjected to whom she must understand and, if possible, learn how to manipulate. Subsequently she may indirectly, through her own speech and actions, looks and gestures, instill those emotions in a man that she wants him to have, and without seeming to think of doing so (507).

The female knowledge of a man's feelings and nature, therefore, cannot be universalized. Every woman is self-taught, and if she learns something from the "book of the world," it belongs to her (508). Her insights remain private, situated, and particularistic, depending on her intuition and craftiness. Neither can this type of knowledge be transferred from one person to another; the art cannot be learned, because in women it is innate; they all have it (504). Besides, the power of her intuition rests on it being unarticulated and concealed. This in reality makes the individual man the norm and goal for any woman's spiritual efforts.

Even female cunning is, according to Rousseau, a talent to be cultivated, since virtue is not the same in men as in women. Lying may be accepted from women, because in contrast to men, women neither can nor should express themselves straightforwardly. When they follow the inclinations that in his opinion belong to their sex, they are not insincere even when they are lying (505).

By the aid of subconscious signals, self-taught and cunning women may indicate, and sometimes obtain, what they want. But by restricting women's mental resources to the individual, hidden, and specific, men's power interests benefit in at least two ways: (1) Women can neither develop generalized knowledge nor counter strategies based on a common understanding that give them power as a group, intellectually or in society. They operate in a dispersed fashion and as individual subjects in relation to men. (2) Men's private discharge of power, whether it be brutal or mild, is screened from outside control, and the wife's silence and discretion is secured.

The norms Rousseau set up for the use of female cleverness clearly reflects that, for good or bad, women depend on men. Their possibilities in life lie in a knowledge adjusted and responsive to the mentality of fathers and husbands, whose superior position they thus indirectly accept and confirm.

The key message in Rousseau's doctrine on women's intellectual capacity and craftiness is that it should be developed, but only within specific limits that enables them to manipulate individual men in order to get what they want through them. Women's cognitive powers as well as social feelings should be directed by the extremely narrow bounds that refer to their dependence on men.

Erotic Power Game

The ideal model of womankind, Sophie, meets Émile in rural surroundings, where he falls in love with her. The conquest of Sophie proceeds according to an ambiguous pattern. At the same time as his siege progresses and succeeds, he gives her increased power over his person. Finally, she consents to assume the same authority as a mistress. From this time on she prescribes what he shall do; she commands instead of requests (Rousseau 1966, 556).

In the courting phase, Sophie's sphere of authority appears to be considerably extended. Émile is described as her slave, toward whom she is imperious and exacting (576). To Émile the exchange of their superior and inferior roles is a male degradation (566). The masculine downfall brought about by the infatuation causes the male character to grovel before Sophie and obey her; the serious Émile is "a child's toy" (566).

What does Sophie's expanded area of influence as a mistress imply? When this is exemplified, we see that the privileges acquired are rather restricted and of a private kind. For instance, she decides the frequency of his visits; she forbids him to arrive before a certain day or to stay beyond a given hour (556–57). Sophie also notes with particular concern the care he takes to arrive at the prescribed hour; she wants him to arrive exactly on time (576).

Sophie's romantic influence remains limited to these kinds of trivia. And Rousseau comments with irony on her attentiveness when she enforces her power: "All this she carries out, not like some game, but very earnestly" (556). He indicates more than once that she acts like an immature person who cannot clearly distinguish between seriousness and play. To Émile this is a provisional arrangement, a game belonging to the introductory courting phase.

Her partial misapprehension of the erotic power game serves more than one purpose during the siege. The romantic age demanded mutual attraction and devotion, symbolically or for real, and the courting fore-play of the sentimental period allows woman to be fascinated by and return a man's emotions.

Rousseau was convinced that man's sexual and emotional dependence on women made it necessary to restrict and disadvantage them in other areas in order to restore the man's supposedly natural predominance, as is also pointed out by Okin (Rousseau 1966, 467; Okin 1979, 159). To the fear that female sexuality can enslave men should be added the Rous-seauian men's need for women's services (Martin 1985, 68). However, this dependency or need never appears as mutual in a symmetric fashion. Rousseau appears as a master builder of both gender-divided and asym-metric normative standards (Viestad 1989).

Broadening the contextual picture, one notes the conspicuous *equivo-cality* in Émile's subjection, causing the limits of female power during the courtship to emerge even more clearly. On one side he is subservient and compliant. On the other side he now discovers her inferior knowledge and vivid curiosity. Rousseau's ideal woman is ignorant and only prepared to learn from her husband when she reaches a marriageable age. Her mind should be like a prepared field ready to receive his sowing (Rousseau 1966, 538). As a pupil of the well-educated Émile she now can be shaped according to his interests and inclinations (538). From this moment on he becomes her spiritual model by virtue of his more extensive and thor-ough training.

Émile's ambiguous subordination is vividly illustrated when he kneels while teaching her. To Sophie this is embarrassing. He really enjoys his equivocal task, as "it is permissible for a lover to combine voluptuous pleasure with his teaching; it is permitted for him to be the master of his mistress" (557).

The man's dual role as adoring slave and spiritual leader discloses that the woman's subordinate position is not decisively changed when he falls in love. On the contrary, it uncovers some of the precautionary measures built into the double power structure. The male domination is not seri-ously threatened even when the woman's sexual attractiveness comes into effect. Sophie's ignorance is guaranteed by her lower level of learning. Her influence over Émile is restricted by his intellectual leadership and to matters within a limited emotional area, or to what Harriet Taylor Mill, ninety years later, characterized as the wife's sentimental priesthood in the family (Mill 1971, 120). Rousseau's strategy is to loosen the reins

in a controlled fashion inside the framework of the superior male dominion.

Generally, woman's erotic attraction can be used as a lever, claims
Rousseau, to stir man's passions (1966, 466–67, 507). Together with
clever calculation, this may put the young as well as the mature women in
a special power-strategic position. In Rousseau's novel *Julie; ou, la nouvelle
Héloïse* (1761), the tutor Saint-Preux desires and adores the elevated and
almost unobtainable Julie. In *Émile* Rousseau describes an obtainable,
average woman whom the man gets and lives an ordinary life with (1966,
532).

The power given by the woman's erotic influence depends, however,
on a considerable amount of constraint. Julie's power over both her husband, Wolmar, and her admirer, Saint-Preux, and Sophie's power over
Émile, depend on their capacity for self-discipline (Rousseau 1967b, 9ff.;
1966, 577). Their combined attractiveness to men and erotic self-control
enables them to fire and maintain men's desire.

Is it possible to avoid love's diminishing within marriage? Rousseau
raises the problem, and the means he proposes to the newly married
Sophie and Émile consist in having even husband and wife continue to
act as lover and mistress. To a man it is not so much the possession as the
subjection that leads to saturation, and usually he preserves the affection
for a mistress longer than for his wife (Rousseau 1966, 624). To Sophie it
is important to make her favors precious and scarce and thus highly valuable to Émile. By these means sexuality gives her a possibility to rule him.
She may control him if she can control herself (624, 627). While a man
may give free expression to his emotions, woman influences him by using
her greater capacities of dissimulation and self-restraint (561, 577). In
this way the larger part of the responsibility for the sexual morals and
constraints of both sides is attributed to woman. Even coquetry may be
used by the good woman instead of reproach in order to keep her husband
to the right conduct (627).

The double meaning in the text is striking when Rousseau admonishes
the newly married Émile to give his wife full powers of decision with
respect to intercourse, only to take them away a few days later. At first
the philosopher points out that it is mutual desire that confers rights.
Coercion and love go badly together and desire cannot arise by command. Émile finally grants Sophie the right to decide over her own sexuality: "Be my precious wife, she who is the master over my desire as well

as my life and my fate" (624). But when Sophie several days later makes use of the right, she is reprimanded by Émile's Mentor. Perhaps she had only comprehended that he wanted to teach her the art of moderation with pleasure, in order to make it more lasting. She must know that the Mentor's address had a more "deserving" purpose. When Émile became her spouse, he became her head: "you have to obey him, this is what nature intends" (626–27). When later the erotic attraction within marriage decreases, her freedom and right to reserve herself in the conjugal bed becomes even smaller: "No longer separate beds, no refusal, no caprices!" (626–27)

The self-contradictory argumentation in Rousseau's text on women typically weaves back and forth: First he makes concessions to women, and then he takes them back. Thus the woman's sexual power and freedom remains partly nominal and limited to the conception of the romantic love between the engaged or newly married. Even then it is narrowed down by a superior patriarchal demand of obedience. When her attractiveness gradually diminishes, the wife's right to decide over her own body decreases correspondingly, and she has to find other sources of power that may and should replace what is lost.

The doctrine of female power through eroticism contains an ambiguous message. It grants women the right to desire a man, since this may increase and prolong his pleasure over time. At the same time it assumes female self-restraint and implies that the woman should not seek erotic pleasure for herself, but as a means to prolong his desire in order to obtain something else, namely, a possibility to play upon a man. Rousseau does not argue that women should seek personal satisfaction, or share private or public power with men. Women should be prepared to take care of men and make them happy, never to be their equals or competitors. Sexuality gives no freedom or power to women beyond the intimate and private sphere, and even then it ultimately aims at giving better and more durable pleasure to the man.

Romantic Freedom of Choice?

Can Rousseau be considered a progressive eighteenth-century philosopher, stating that his female model is free to choose her own husband? One of the stories inside his text on women can be interpreted in this direction. In *Julie; ou, la nouvelle Héloïse*, published the year before *Émile*, one main subject was the conflict between love and the duty to the parental choice of marriage partner. Julie complains that her father turns her into an object for sale (Rousseau 1967b, 57). The conflict is solved in *Émile* by providing Sophie with progressive parents, who allow her to say yes or no to a suitor.

It surprises the prosperous Émile that he cannot just ask her parents for their consent to marry Sophie. In this matter she is her own master. To make him happy, she only has to want it herself.

What kind of freedom is Sophie given by her right to choose? The philosopher refrains from discussing the problem that Sophie has no socioeconomic alternative to marriage. Her limited training, for instance in needlework and housekeeping, is not aimed at making her able to provide for herself. In contrast to the woman, the new male model, Émile, receives a broad and versatile education, practical and intellectual, aimed at always enabling him to deal with any situation and to support himself.

Sophie's character illustrates the ideal female model for the bourgeoisie and upper middle class in the following century. The marriage, hoping and waiting for it, is the main event of her youth. She is reserved and modest, but also alluring and attractive. Since patriarchal norms demand restraint and allow her little freedom of expression, it is difficult to know whether it will be real affection or socioeconomical compulsion that decide her final choice.

The Rousseauian ideal woman is attractive, but all the same she remains unbetrothed for a long time. Sophie's parents do not pressure her directly to get married. Although several matches are presented to her and their attitude is one of patient waiting, they ask themselves: What is she waiting for? *What does she really want?* (Rousseau 1966, 529). Her understanding family admits, however, that a master for the rest of one's life is not easy to select (529).

The other story inside this text reveals the patriarchal premises of the situation, for instance, that Sophie's decision is about a lifelong master. The apparent freedom of choice, primarily based on emotions, could thus contribute to consolidating woman's greater consciousness of personal responsibility, both for entering into marriage and for its later content. She was now expected to be motivated by love and to feel personal guilt and deficiency if she became dissatisfied. Her eventual displeasure would become privatized, and the romantic freedom of choice could conceal her lack of real alternatives.

By her holding back her final yes for a while, Sophie's power over the amorous suitor increases, and he becomes uncertain, prudent, and shy. At times Émile gets impatient and almost annoyed, but it is enough that Sophie looks at him and he again becomes subservient. Émile understands that he has to exert himself even more to win her. He must please her personally and awaken her feelings.

On the one hand, this freedom of choice changes her position during the courting phase. From just being an object for a man's desire and men's family transactions she becomes a subject with her own feelings and possibilities of saying yes or no. To increase his own quality of life the man to some extent has to raise hers.

On the other hand, the conception of a freely chosen marriage based on romantic affection, but without real social and economic liberty, would serve to *internalize* a new set of male claims toward the woman. The new prescriptions dictated that the motive for her yes ought to be love, and that at least she should pretend that it was. Furthermore, she might now be expected to adjust to and satisfy the needs of her husband, not from duty or patriarchal restraint, but out of affection for his person.

The political consequences of the sentimental family have been observed by Okin. The new type of family in the eighteenth century served, in her opinion, as a reinforcement of patriarchal relations between men and women. Women increasingly came to be characterized as creatures of sentiment and love rather than through the rationality that was perceived as necessary for citizenship (Okin 1981, 74). The emphasis on affection within marriage had resulted in a situation in which claims from females for equal recognition as moral and political persons suffered rather than benefited from the newly idealized, sentimental family.

The restricted opening toward a sentimental liberation had, however, its positive effects and laid the ground for a female revolt on an emotional foundation in the 1800s. Female authors, such as the Rousseau-educated, early Norwegian feminist Camilla Collett (1813–95), complained about the gap between the contradictory demands of the romantic feelings they were expected to have and the compulsion to marry in order to be provided for.

However, this is a parallel narrative about regulation and female self-discipline. The premise of masculine romanticism represents an increase in male requirements as part of an internalized and normative strategy of subjugation. Romanticism redefined the role of woman by extending the task of offering empathy and care, subordinating the woman's own needs for those to her husband. This raises a mirror image of the apparently autonomous male model that Rousseau created and reveals the many-sided support functions required by the free and independent modern man.

Conclusion: Divided Power System

A philosopher who explicitly points out and accentuates the opportunities for women to exercise power, and who argues that it is desirable that they use them, may at a first glance seem to take a stand for the clever and cunning woman. Rousseau also admits that there is a *mutual relationship* of power. For the system to persist, both parties must to a certain extent collaborate as well as depend upon each other.

As we have seen, Rousseau makes it clear that woman is by nature made to obey a man and to be subservient (*être subjugee*), and to care for and please a man. In order for her to combine these two purposes her education should ensure that she becomes obedient without becoming unhappy. She always needs to feel the reins and be aware of her dependence, but without feeling too constrained or oppressed (Rousseau 1966, 466, 482, 483). In order to please she must also look merry, and like Nora in *A Doll's House* by Henrik Ibsen, she is supposed to be cheerful, to sing and dance (Rousseau 1966, 487).

The feat of education consists in getting women to combine being oppressed with a pleasing and happy tone. Indulgence in women's trickery and manipulation, dissimulations, and coquetries used not to gain satisfactory love for herself but to obtain power, is included in the same design. Within this frame the goal is to foster both woman's submission and her ability to please. As part of a romantic pattern of oppression these concessions finally aim at giving the man more benefits in terms of care and pleasure than what he may obtain through simple coercion.

Within an authoritarian power system the subjugated as a minimum must survive. But the master gender is better served if the survivor also retains a certain amount of vigor. Woman therefore has to be given some concessions to make her personally motivated to follow men's prescriptions for her behavior. She must gain something, and he has to invest something, to obtain both his goals. This investment, for example in the form of indulgence in cunning, sets the framework for woman's freedom of action and power inside the sentimental marriage in the following decades.

Insofar as a woman's goals in this way adapt to and ultimately are determined by the superior male power structure, this structure is not seriously threatened by woman's vices and various trickeries. When she morally degrades herself, for example by using despised methods such as lies, she indirectly confirms her weak position and his superior force. Correspondingly, if she departs from the role of being powerless, she makes herself deserve a man's contempt and rebuke. Indirectly she is expected to say: Because I confirm your superior position and value system and thus deserve your moral respect, I am able to influence you. But my power as a Good or Attractive Woman depends on and reflects our asymmetric power relation, our respective superior and subordinate positions within the gendered hierarchy.

The woman neutralizes countermeasures when she selects an area of influence that complements, without directly challenging, the masculine superior force. She may obtain minor concessions and goodwill that allows her to participate in a man's resources as far as he is willing to share them. But she obtains respect and goodwill only if she does not overstep the limits of her pleasing and subordinate exercise of power, set by the framework made by men.

The patriarchal system thus includes two domains of power, both made explicit in Rousseau's text: one superior and masculine, the other inferior and feminine. The two domains are in fact not contradictory or in conflict, but mutually depend on, supplement, and support each other. The feminine power structure can be described as a vital part of the male power system, the glue that holds it together. It is a pivotal condition if the superior power system is to be sustained and to function vitally over any length of time.

When Marilyn French, Catherine MacKinnon, and other feminists claim that the fundamental feminist problem is men's dominion over women, this largely is an adequate description of one part of a complex problem. But we have to take into account that the sexist power system has a dual, complementary, and asymmetric structure, where both parties play along and may obtain influence, but only within the dictates of the patriarchy.

For women there are many serious concerns with the application of the Rousseauian feminine power. One of them is the ambivalence resulting from a double set of open and closed rules. Another is the low value placed on the type of manipulations that are left for women to use. Although tolerated by men, they are at the same time exposed to contempt, condescension, and ridicule. This has serious results both for the individual woman's self-respect, and for women's general gender reputation and valorization.

The Good Women expose the "fair defects" and "amiable weaknesses" that male moral philosophers condescendingly referred to at the time of Mary Wollstonecraft. In her sharp criticism of Rousseauian norms, she observes that when women obtain power by unjust means and vice they loose the rank that reason would assign them, and must submit to being a *fair defect* in creation (Wollstonecraft 1975, 34, 45).

The indirect and evasive form may have a self-fulfilling effect, fortifying women's feelings of being abandoned to the arrangements and rules of male supremacy. Even when women obtain some indirect influence, their methods are designed to strengthen a pattern of dependence, which restricts and determines women's options, actions, and lives.

The female power allowed by the male construction of femininity may be regarded as a *counterstrategy* against a liberation exceeding the bounds of women's prescribed role. It enters as a part of a norm system that aims at exploiting women's resources and making them cooperate more actively with the premises of the male system, by relaxing demands and by offering some kind of reward to the Good Woman as she is defined by male society. The disciplinary power of patriarchy gradually ceases to operate directly and violently, and aims at a transformation of women's minds through normative regulation and socialization.

A neopatriarchal ideology hides the full picture. Historically it describes only a selected part of women's real possibilities to exercise power. At the same time it tells us much about the way male society for its own purposes has attempted to exploit, capture, and control women's potential power resources.

References

Abensour, Léon. 1923. *La femme et le féminisme avant la Révolution*. Paris: Éditions E. Leroux.

Agonito, R. 1977. *History of Ideas of Woman*. New York: G. P. Putnam's Sons.

Bartky, Sandra. 1993. "Foucault, Femininity, and the Modernization of Patriarchal

Power." In *Feminist Philosophies. Problems, Theories, and Applications*, ed. J. A. Kourany, J. P. Sterba, and, R. Tong. New York.

Burgelin, Pierre. 1952. *La philosophie de l'existence de J.-J. Rousseau*. Paris.

———. 1963. "L'éducation de Sophie." *Annales de la Societé Jean-Jacques Rousseau* (Geneva), 35 (1959–62): 113–37..

Disch, Lisa. 1994. "Claire Loves Julie." *Hypatia* 9, no. 3:19–45.

Foucault, Michel. 1975. *Surveiller et punir*. Paris.

———. 1977. *Discipline and Punish: The Birth of the Prison*. New York: Pantheon Books.

French, Marilyn. 1985. *Beyond Power: On Women, Men, and Morals*. New York.

Gillespie, Dair L. 1971. "Who Has the Power? The Marital Struggle." *Journal of Marriage and Family* 33, no. 3:445–58.

Green, Karen. 1995. *The Woman of Reason: Feminism, Humanism, and Political Thought*. New York: Continuum.

Lloyd, Genevieve. 1983. "Rousseau on Reason, Nature, and Women," *Metaphilosophy* 14:308–26.

MacKinnon, Catherine. 1987. *Feminism Unmodified*. Cambridge: Harvard University Press.

Martin, Jane R. 1985. *Reclaiming a Conversation: The Ideal of the Educated Woman*. New Haven: Yale University Press.

Mill, Harriet Taylor. 1971. "Enfranchisement of Women." (1851). In *John Stuart Mill and Harriet Taylor Mill: Essays on Sex Equality*. Ed. A. Rossi. London.

Okin, Susan Moller. 1979. *Women in Western Political Thought*. Princeton: Princeton University Press.

———. 1981. "Women and the Making of the Sentimental Family." In *Philosophy and Public Affairs* (Princeton University Press), 11, no. 1:65–88.

Rousseau, Jean-Jacques. 1966. *Émile; ou, De l'éducation*. Book 5, *Sophie; ou, La femme*. (1762) Paris: Garnier-Flammarion.

———. 1967a. *Lettre à d'Alembert sur les spectacles*. (1758). Paris.

———. 1967b. *Julie; ou, La nouvelle Héloïse*. (1761). Paris.

Schwartz, Joel. 1984. *The Sexual Politics of Jean-Jacques Rousseau*. Chicago: Chicago University Press.

Viestad [Wiestad], Else. 1989. *Kjønn og ideologi. En studie i kvinnesynet hos Locke, Hume, Rousseau og Kant* (Gender and ideology: An interpretation and critique of the view on women in Locke, Hume, Rousseau and Kant). Oslo: Solum Forlag.

Wexler, Victor G. 1976. "'Made for Man's Delight': Rousseau as Antifeminist." *American Historical Review* 81, no. 2:266–91.

Wollstonecraft, Mary. 1975. *A Vindication of the Rights of Woman*. (1792). New York.

Wiestad [Viestad], Else, ed. 1994. *De store hundreårsbølgene: Kjønnsdebatten gjennom 300 år* (The great hundred-year waves: Gender debate through the past 300 years). Oslo: Emilia Press.

———. 2000. "Gender Models in Europe in the Eighteenth Century." In Sofia Boesch, Kari Elisabeth Børresen, and Sara Cabbibo, eds., *Gender and Religion in Europe*. Rome: Dipartimento di Storia, Università Roma III.

8

The Politics of "Feminine Concealment" and "Masculine Openness" in Rousseau

Ingrid Makus

In a passage where Rousseau personifies both wisdom and nature as Woman, the theme that emerges is less that women represent Nature,[1] or disorder,[2] or the control of the passions[3] than that they represent the ability to hide things, knowledge in this instance, which imbues them with considerable power: "Peoples, know once and for all that nature wanted to keep you from being harmed by knowledge just as a mother wrests a dangerous weapon from her child's hands; that all the secrets she hides from you are so many evils from which she protects you."[4] The veil as women's particular accouterment is central to the metaphor: "The

An earlier versions of this essay was presented at the 1996 annual meeting of the American Political Science Association. I am grateful to Lynda Lange and Susan Okin for comments on that paper.

heavy veil with which she [eternal wisdom] covered all her operations seemed to warn us adequately that she did not destine us for vain studies."[5] To cover things up is to make them more enticing but also more fearful. The image of the veil appears frequently in Rousseau's writings, often as evoking fear.[6] In *La nouvelle Héloïse*, Saint-Preux has a nightmare foreshadowing Julie's death. Most terrifying to him is the part where he sees Julie covered with a veil that he cannot remove: "Always the mournful sight, always that same appearance of death, always that impenetrable veil eluding my hands and hiding from my eyes the dying person it covered."[7] In the *Discourses*, Rousseau refers to the "veil that covers so many horrors" in civil society.[8] And the horrors of advanced civil society, as Rousseau documents them, are fundamentally tied up with what comes out of covering things up—pretense, deception, and the exercise of behind-the-scenes power. At the same time, these are the very qualities that describe the machinations of the Governor and the Legislator—figures who are to undertake the regeneration and transformation of corrupt civil society.

Even more striking is that Rousseau consistently links women with such qualities. Indeed, at the heart of Rousseau's treatment of women, I want to suggest in this essay, is his association of women with concealment, deception, and behind-the-scenes power.[9] There is a sexual, maternal, and political dimension to this association. In part I of the essay, I explore the sexual dimension, showing how Rousseau's concern about women's biologically grounded ability to conceal and therefore to deceive men about sexual desire and arousal is at bottom of his insistence that modesty (*la pudeur*) is the 'natural' attribute of women and that love is the domain in which women reign. In part II of the essay, I explore the maternal dimension, suggesting that Rousseau's concern with women's potential to deceive men about paternity accounts for the peculiar way he depicts their proper role in the family: confined to private life but on public display. Most interesting is the political dimension of this association in Rousseau, which I examine in part III of the essay. At the same time as Rousseau attributes much of the political corruptions and decay of advanced civil society to the dominance of deception and pretense, linking them to the ascendancy of women themselves and the 'feminine' means they bring with them, he also invokes them—women, the 'feminine' principles of concealment, deception, and the exercise of behind-the-scenes power—as necessary components for civil societies' regeneration or transformation.

I

What are we to make of Rousseau's insistence that modesty is the 'natural' attribute distinguishing men from women, and that it is central to sexual relations between the two?[10] First, I think that running through his sometimes confusing and contradictory ruminations in his infamous chapter 5 in *Emile*, in sections of the "Letter to M. D'Alembert," and in *La nouvelle Héloïse*, is his concern that women's anatomical makeup means that they can conceal, and therefore deceive others about, either the presence or absence of sexual desire and arousal. Second, based on their biological capacity for such concealment, women have the edge on men when it comes to concealing and therefore deceiving men about their sentiments and their preferences.

The opposition between 'masculine' openness and 'feminine' concealment is suggested in the contrast between Emile and Sophie, whom Rousseau presents as the exemplary man and woman, both having been educated in a way that is compatible not only with the role they ought to play in the social and moral order but also with their bodily constitution.[11] Emile's most striking characteristic is that he hides nothing. He is an open book, acting the same in private as in public—"Emile is worse at disguising his feelings than any man in the world."[12] In contrast, Sophie has been educated to make proper use of her 'natural' talent for guile to disguise her feelings:[13] "Guile is a natural talent with the fair sex, and since I am persuaded that all the natural inclinations are good and right in themselves, I am of the opinion that this one should be cultivated like the others. The only issue is preventing its abuse."[14] "Preventing its abuse" for Rousseau is very much tied up with educating women to be virtuous. And the virtuous woman is above all modest.

Rousseau grounds modesty in biology—women's greater ability to conceal and therefore to deceive others about sexual desire and arousal and the biological requirement that men (but not women) be sexually aroused for conception to take place. But it is in civil society rather than in the original state of nature that these biological differences have any ramifications for the role of the two sexes.

Modesty is not 'natural' to women in the sense of being characteristic of their role in the original state of nature. Neither is it 'natural' to them in the sense of it being a characteristic present at birth.[15] But in what way is modesty "natural to the human species"?[16] It is a way of providing for the continuity of the species by ensuring in civil society that women act appropriately, that is, in ways that won't jeopardize male arousal.

Modesty is Rousseau's response to his perception of the power that accrues to women with the development of the moral element in love or romantic love as well as his perception of the increasing fragility of male desire, both of which characterize civil society for Rousseau. The predominance of the moral element in love in civil society means that sexual desire is fixed on one person[17] rather than being indiscriminate, as it is in the original state of nature.[18] Now, taste comes into play in the choosing of sexual mates. And only one particular woman will do. Moreover, she must choose one particular man in return.[19] But why would this development establish the ascendancy of women, as Rousseau insists it does? Rousseau claims that moral love is "extolled with much skill and care by women in order to establish their ascendancy and make dominant the sex that ought to obey"?[20]

The answer might be that, in the context of the importance he places on the desire for first place in the esteem and affection of others, and women's ability and propensity to conceal sexual desire, the woman can be more assured of the man's preference for her than he can be assured of her preference for him; this gives her the power that comes with knowledge of certainty and the man the disadvantage that comes with doubt.

As Rousseau describes them, men are motivated in love, as in other pursuits in civil society, by the desire to be preferred above all others, the effects of *amour-propre*. Rousseau gives no indication that women are any less motivated by such desires. But a man can less easily conceal his preferences. A woman can easily conceal and therefore deceive a man about her preference. It becomes more difficult, therefore to convince him that she prefers him to all others. Analogous to the need for assurance of paternity, men need assurance of sexual preference, but such assurance is difficult to obtain.[21] Yet, the conviction that she prefers him to all others is an essential component of male ardor or desire for a particular woman, in advanced civil society where *amour-propre* in the form of vanity is activated.[22]

Men cannot be assured that women are feigning desire that is absent rather than feigning not to have it when it is present. It is the former that Rousseau decries as being the practice of corrupt women. And it is the latter that Rousseau associates with modesty: "The species of dissimulation I mean here is the opposite of that which suits them and which they get from nature. The one consists in disguising the sentiments they have, and the other in feigning those they do not have. All society women spend their lives priding themselves on their pretended sensitivity and never love anything but themselves."[23] For Rousseau, the virtuous woman, the modest one, uses her ability to conceal desire when it is present. The corrupt woman pretends to have desire for the man when none is present.

The emphasis that Rousseau places on distinguishing between the two kinds of dissimulation is revealing. It suggests that women's vices and virtues both derive from their ability to conceal. The difference is that the virtuous woman uses her ability for beneficial ends, for one to ensure male arousal. If "[m]en will always be what is pleasing to women,"[24] if moral love gives the woman ascendancy because she can be more assured of the man's preference for her, than he can be assured of her preferences for him, then she needs to be made "virtuous," (not only so that she will esteem virtuous men)[25] but so that she will not abuse her power by wielding it in a fashion that Rousseau thinks is detrimental to the perpetuation of the species and the continuity of the political community.[26]

Male desire (for a particular woman) is more important for the reproduction of the species than is female desire (for a particular man). At the same time, the sexual instinct in general, like other instincts in civil society, according to Rousseau, is weakened. And as much as Rousseau refers to the need to moderate the desires, the impression one gets is that he is more worried that it is male desire and particularly male sexual ardor that are weak and fragile in advanced civil society. After meeting Sophie, Emile must take up hunting in order to prevent him from being too tender and languorous.[27] In La nouvelle Héloïse, Saint-Preux, Julie's lover, rarely acts with masculine audacity. Julie is the one who initiates their first sexual encounter, disguising her intention by pretending to be Claire. If the weakness of male desire and sexual ardor is threatening to the physical and political reproduction of the species and the community, its maintenance in civil society requires all sorts of devices and artifices. Sophie, the exemplary woman, is instructed to use them in regulating Emile's passions. One of them is keeping Emile at a distance, making her sexual favors rare and precious. This will cost Sophie some privation, we are told, interestingly enough, but it will keep Emile interested.[28] This becomes unnecessary, however, once Sophie has become a mother, that is, once reproduction has occurred. Then, the Governor counsels Sophie, "[I]n place of your former reserve, establish between yourselves the greatest intimacy."[29] Sophie's reserve is part of her modesty. Modesty entails women's concealing the presence of desire and strength,[30] or showing them only indirectly,[31] and in refraining from sexual aggression and sexual activity. It is also associated with bashfulness in the face of erotic matters and a delicacy toward matters of the body.[32] If it were otherwise, if women were the sexual aggressor, this would go against 'nature', Rousseau says, in the sense that it would be incompatible with the biological requirement that men be aroused in order for the species to be perpetuated.[33] "What would become of the human species if the order of attack and defense were changed?" Rousseau asks.[34] The species might be threatened, presumably, because if the woman assailed the man, she might do so at times when "victory would be impossible."[35] Instead, women must "let themselves be the vanquished."[36]

To be modest is to feign weakness. Women have the physical characteristics that make it easy for them to appear weak. But they are not in fact so weak by nature, Rousseau believes, that under normal circumstances, rape can take place, and it never ought to take place.[37] By making women appear weak, modesty encourages male desire in civil society, which is necessary to the perpetuation of the species. Modesty and coquetry, seemingly contradictory or opposites, derive from the same principle—concealment—and function to serve the same aim, maintenance of male ardor and desire. "The desires, veiled by shame, become only the more seductive; in hindering them, chasteness inflames them."[38] In her clothing and appearance, Sophie ought not to display all her charms; her modest clothes ought to cover them up, thereby making them more enticing. Her coquetry is in her modesty—"Her adornment is very modest in appearance and very coquettish in fact. She does not display her charms; she covers them, but, in covering them, she knows how to make them imagined."[39]

Modesty is what makes a woman sexually attractive, Saint-Preux says, but only when men believe that there is a genuine basis to it. Vulgar society women who feign modesty, Rousseau tells us in *La nouvelle Héloïse*, appear ridiculous. To be convincing, then, Sophie's modesty cannot simply be feigned, it must be incorporated into her very being, through education, so that it becomes 'natural' to her. Julie laments that modesty is felt as a constraint on young girls "to speak always otherwise than we think, to disguise all we feel, to be deceitful through obligation and to speak untruths through modesty."[40] Sophie, however, is educated to be used to such restraints from an early age, so that they becomes 'natural' to her.

But modesty is not a good in itself—it is an artificial device, albeit one grounded in biology, that is functional. When it serves no purpose, Rousseau suspends it. One incident in *Emile*, in which Sophie plays nurse to a strange peasant man who has broken his leg, is particularly illuminating. The seemingly fragile, weak, delicate, bashful Sophie, who can barely lift a plane (a carpentry tool), we are shown in one scene, has no trouble single-handedly rolling over and taking care of the intimate bodily needs of a helpless strange man, without making him feel this as an indignity:

> This extremely delicate girl is rebuffed neither by the dirtiness nor the bad smell and knows how to make both disappear without ordering anyone about and without the sick being tormented. She who always seems so modest and sometimes so disdainful, she who would not for anything in the world have touched a man's bed with the tip of her finger, turns the injured man over and changes him without any scruple, and puts him in a position in which he can stay more comfortably for a long time. The zeal of charity outweighs modesty.[41]

Sophie is above all virtuous—that is, she conceals her strength and desire, only when it is necessary and for beneficial ends—in order to ensure male arousal and male audacity and thereby the perpetuation of the species in civil society. She does not conceal and deceive, however, in ways that Rousseau believes are detrimental to relations between the sexes to the extent that they undermine the well-being of the community. For example, the virtuous woman does not conceal or deceive men about her sexual activity, so that paternity becomes questionable.[42]

II

The virtuous woman does not deceive about her virtue. This is compatible with 'nature,' Rousseau says, but in the sense, we can surmise, that 'nature' as biology, in making women the ones who bear the children, makes them the ones who must most openly display the likely consequences of sexual activity. Their biology (nature) makes it less easy for women to conceal the fact that they have had sexual relations, when pregnancy is the result. Rousseau's censure of abortion as going against

'nature' can be understood in this light. It goes against 'nature' for Rousseau not because it entails the taking of a life or potential life or works
against population increase,[43] but because it augments women's biological
ability to conceal on sexual matters. This explains why he seems to admire and prefer the Spartan practice of the outright exposure of weak
infants after birth,[44] (similar to what happens in the state of nature) to
the abortions and exposure of infants as practiced in the France of his
day. He prefers the former (which certainly worked against population
increase and which entailed the taking of a life) because it was done
openly in public for a publicly acclaimed collective good—it strengthened the stock and made the having of children less burdensome to parents.[45] The latter he describes as being done in secret (he refers to those
'secret abortions'), to cover up private vices.[46]

For Rousseau, the perniciousness of abortions is that they can be done
in "secret" and thereby increase women's powers of deception in sexual
matters. Women's potential to deceive about paternity and the power
that accrues to them from it is balanced by their greater inability to
conceal the frequent consequence of sexual activity—pregnancy. (He refers to this when he talks about the different results that sexual activity
has in men and women.) This balance is upset, however, by women's
access to abortions, which, done covertly, increase their ability to conceal
and therefore to deceive about their sexual activity, about whether they
have been promiscuous or faithful. By augmenting women's proclivity
and potential to pretend to be more virtuous than they really are, "those
secret abortions" not only take away paternity, but also increase uncertainty over it.

It is Rousseau's concern over women's biologically based potential to
conceal and deceive men about paternity (in contrast to women's biologically based certainty over maternity) rather than his perception of a natural maternal instinct that underlies his proposal for relegating women to
the private sphere of the family. Rousseau makes a weak case for the
presence of natural maternal instincts, but establishing this is less important than one might think, since these are not the grounds on which
Rousseau recommends and justifies the role he advocates for them.

Focusing on the themes of concealment and openness can draw our
attention to the peculiar way that Rousseau depicts women's place in the
"private" or family sphere. He advocates that they be removed from the
public stage, so to speak, quite literally in his discussion of the possibility
of a theater in Geneva[47] and placed on a private one. That is, they are to

remain in the private realm, performing their duties as mothers and wives, but they are not to remain hidden. Instead they are to be on public display at home. This is suggested by Rousseau's description of the ideal situation as one where the mother cares for and nurses the children, in her own home, for all to see. She does so in order to convince the husband that the children belong to him.

The mother who sends her children out to wetnurses is one who is hiding them. She is therefore suspect—"the mother whose children one does not see is less respected."[48] The rejuvenated family that will result when women assume their role as mothers and wives is described by Rousseau not as an entity enclosed to itself but as a "spectacle,"[49] something on display to outsiders, for the benefit of the father. Only through the eyes of others, of public opinion, is he able to convince himself of his wife's virtues and therefore of his paternity.

If the father could be assured of his paternity by biological means, as the mother is of maternity, or by means of his wife's word, such approval might be unnecessary. But biology and women's tendency to concealment and pretense work against paternal assurance. That women enjoy playing at games of concealment is intimated in a passage describing Julie and Claire's pleasure at concealing the maternity of Claire's daughter, Henriette, in public. Strangers are asked to guess whether the biological mother is Julie or Claire. The most discerning (wrongly) choose Julie. "It must be confessed that all appearances are in favour of the little mama, and I have perceived that this deception is so agreeable to the two cousins that it could well be intended sometimes and become a contrivance which suits them."[50]

The point that is also hinted at here in this scenario is that putting into doubt the maternity of Henriette may an amusing game because it can ultimately be verified. Julie and Claire do know who the real (biological) mother is. It would not be such an amusing game, however, if they played at concealing and deceiving strangers or the public about the paternity of the child. Doubt about the real (biological) father is not so easily verified. Moreover, it casts doubt on the virtue of the mother. Appearing virtuous in the eyes of others or in the eyes of public opinion therefore becomes a central part of women's duties.[51] Julie, the heroine of La nouvelle Héloïse remarks: "A virtuous woman must not only deserve her husband's esteem but also obtain it. If he blames her, she is to blame, and even were she innocent, she is in the wrong as soon as she is suspected, for even keeping up appearances is part of her duty."[52]

The crux of women's paradoxical situation in Rousseau, arising out of their potential to deceive men about paternity, is this: they ought to stay out of the public eye (in public) but they are more subject to it (even in private), since they must appear as well as be virtuous. The education that Rousseau advocates for them, therefore, is moved by paradoxical imperatives. It ought to make them desire public approval[53] but to prefer home life to public life.

Sophie, Rousseau's prototype of the ideally educated woman, rejects the kinds of activities he associates with the women of his day—activities in the arts and letters. Sophie, Rousseau emphasizes, must have intelligence but not the kind of brilliance displayed by society women.[54] She must be educated but not as a woman of letters. She must have the kind of wit that is compatible with her ability to use cunning and guile but not the kind wielded by women of the salons.[55] Why are such women so dangerous and undesirable? Rousseau's vociferous condemnation of them further illustrates his distinctive association of women with concealment and display, juxtaposed with his concern that they remain in the private realm on public display.

A female wit is a scourge for Rousseau because she uses her mind in a direct and aggressive manner to penetrate and uncover men's weaknesses (their dependence on women's esteem, for example). In doing so, she appropriates 'masculine' means (she "always begins by making herself into a man") and rejects what Rousseau considers as appropriate and distinctive 'feminine' means—being indirect, refraining from aggression, and concealing one's strengths in order to maintain the appearance of the others' dominance. Lacking modesty, the female wit cannot be trusted to conceal her powers of discernment or to use them in benevolent ways.

"A brilliant wife is a plague to her husband, her children, her friends, her valets, everyone. From the sublime elevation of her fair genius she disdains all her woman's duties and always begins by making herself into a man," he writes.[56] A woman of letters leaves the confines of her home or is not duly concerned with its care. She goes out into society to display her talents and compete with men for public honors (at the same time as her real power there is exercised covertly). More troublesome is that she has an undue influence over men in the form of her influence over public opinion. By determining who deserves praise, she deems what is meritorious. Her power is exercised covertly, undermining the overt power of the (mostly male) judges of the academies whose task it is to bestow public honors on talent in the arts.[57] In contrast to her, Rousseau upholds the woman of ancient times about whom little was said in public and who was seen in her home rather than in public. He asks us to be voyeurs, looking in on an ideal tableau: "What gives you a better opinion of a woman on entering her room, what makes you approach her with more respect—to see her occupied with the labors of her sex and the cares of her household, encompassed by her children's things, or to find her at her dressing table writing verses, surrounded by all sorts of pamphlets and letters written on tinted paper?"[58]

The fear of the damaging potential of a brilliant woman or a woman of the salons fits in with Rousseau's tendency to equate women with greater perceptive abilities than men. As Rousseau presents them, women are better at deceiving but less easily deceived. More observant than men, they are better able to see into the hearts of others. (Men generalize about the human heart, Rousseau contends). About women's powers of discernment, Rousseau writes: "They all possess it, and men never have it to the same degree. This is one of the distinctive characteristics of the fair sex. Presence of mind, incisiveness, and subtle observations are the science of women; cleverness at taking advantage of them is their talent."[59] Men's weaker powers of discernment make them more susceptible to being deceived by women. Considerable power accrues to women from men's weakness, coupled with their (women's) talent for guile.

One way of curtailing women's power, therefore, is to make men less deceivable. And much of Emile's education, as Rousseau prescribes it, is devoted to that goal. The greatest danger in being exposed to the outside world and becoming a member of society for Emile, Rousseau warns, is that he can be deceived by others, especially women.[60] Perhaps this is why Rousseau is so adamant that Emile ought to be educated to be simple rather than subtle: in the Social Contract Rousseau says, "Upright and simple men are hard to deceive by the very reason of their simplicity. Lures and plausible sophistries have no effect upon them, nor are they even sufficiently subtle to become dupes."[61] And this is also why Emile ought to develop the faculty of independent judgment; it enables him to see others as they are, not as they pretend to be.

If a central purpose of Emile's education is making him into someone who exercises independent judgment, so that he is less easily deceived by others, especially women, the central goal of Sophie's education is to make her virtuous, so that she will deceive others, men in particular, only for beneficial ends.[62]

III

As Rousseau describes it, the decline of civilized society, much of its corruption and degeneration, is accompanied and made possible by increasing deception. The problem is not only that *amour-propre* has been activated and that qualities such as beauty, strength, and talent become important and desired as means for acquiring the esteem of others, but also that one feels it necessary to deceive others about whether or not one has these qualities: "And these qualities being the only ones which could attract consideration, it was soon necessary to have them or affect them; for one's own advantage, it was necessary to appear to be other than what one in fact was. To be and to seem to be became two altogether different things; and from this distinction came conspicuous ostentation, deceptive cunning, and all the vices that follow from them."[63] One result is that the appearance of merit or superiority in strength, mind, and body are rewarded. By encouraging and providing the tools for giving "the semblance of all the virtues without the possession of any," the arts and sciences contribute to this dissimulation.[64]

Deceit exacerbates the disproportion between natural and political (civil) inequality and makes it easier to institute the latter.[65] The absence of compassion and concern for others, the desire to benefit from the misery of others, are all concealed.[66] In the most degenerate form of civil society, their opposites are feigned. We find "a secret jealousy all the more dangerous because, in order to strike its blow in greater safety, it often assumes the mask of benevolence."[67] Individuals or factions pretending to be concerned with the public interest are able to successfully pass laws that further their particular interests.[68] A state is ruined once all are "moved by motives unavowed," that is by self-interest. The real depravity, Rousseau implies, comes from self-interest being covered up. In former, less corrupted states, men and women may have been no less self-regarding. The difference was that they did not pretend to be otherwise—"human nature, basically, was no better, but men found their security in the ease of seeing through each other, and that advantage, which we no longer appreciate, spared them many vices."[69]

Pretense and deceit make discernment impossible, Rousseau complains. One can no longer tell the good from the bad, one's friends from one's enemies, the genuine from the artificial.[70] One can no longer know anything about oneself or one's place in the social and political order. Delusion takes the place of knowledge.

Rousseau's response to the depravity he thinks comes with conceal-ment, his most immediate reaction is to advocate bringing all into the open, on a psychological, social, and political plane. His enterprise, he tells us, is to uncover the "secret pretensions of the heart of every civilized man,"[71] and to reveal his real interests and preoccupations:[72] "Let us therefore perceive, through our frivolous demonstrations of good will, what goes on at the bottom of our hearts."[73]

On the one hand, Rousseau offers the principle of openness as a pana-cea for the corruptions of social life in civil society. In La nouvelle Héloïse, Wolmar tells Saint-Preux: "A single moral precept can take the place of all the others. It is this one: never do or say anything you do not want the whole world to see and hear. As for me, I have always regarded as the most estimable of men that Roman who wanted his house to be built in a way that people might see everything that was done there."[74] Everyone ought to act as if they lived in glass houses, open to the scrutiny of others. This way, they would have nothing to hide. "How pleasant it would be to live among us if exterior appearance were always a reflection of the heart's disposition," Rousseau muses.[75] Openness is the fundamental op-erating principle at Clarens, Rousseau's sketch of an ideal society. Julie and Wolmar talk and act in front of their servants as if they were alone. This is easy for them because they also do the opposite—talk and act when alone as if the servants were present. "All idle subtleties are un-known in this house, and the great art by which the master and mistress make their servants such as they desire them to be is to appear to their people such as they are."[76] There is no disjunction between the way the appear in front of others and the way they behave in private.[77]

In making deception more difficult, openness is also fundamental to a reformed political life. Rousseau speaks admiringly of the public open vote used by the primitive Romans, contrasting it to the secret ballot, which encourages corruption, and which is used in most regimes of his day.[78] The ideal state, Rousseau maintains, is small enough so that all citizens can know one another. In describing the birthplace he would choose, he writes: "all the individuals knowing one another, neither the obscure maneuvers of vice nor the modesty of virtue could be hidden from the notice and judgement of the public."[79] Pretense to merit would be more difficult in such a state.[80]

If Rousseau attributes much of what is most degenerate in advanced civil society to deception, pretense. and the hidden exercise of power, and if, as I have suggested, he associates these characteristics with women, it is not surprising that we find him equating the ascendancy of women themselves with much of the corruption and degeneration of advanced civil society, testimony of which he finds in the France of his day. The predominance of women signals the predominance of concealment, deception, pretense, and the wielding of hidden power—'feminine' means.

Rousseau refers to women as the "tyrants of their [men's] liberty" and "that half of the human race which governs the other."[81] "No one can do anything in Paris without the women" he complains.[82] He is critical of women's hidden influence in the arts and the sciences, which themselves use 'feminine' means in covering up rather than revealing truths. Although the judges of the academy are mostly men, it is women of the salons, Rousseau worries, who establish merit by inviting or refusing to invite individuals to their salons, thereby covertly acting as the real judges of talent. As the harbingers and purveyors of taste, women determine what is to be esteemed. And men, wanting to be esteemed by others, especially women, will choose what others esteem in the form of what public opinion has deemed worthy or desirable.[83] A central manifestation of women's ascendancy, Rousseau implies, is their impact on public opinion, which itself operates by means of 'feminine' principles, that is in a behind-the-scenes manner. "Opinion, queen of the world, is not subject to the power of kings; they are themselves her first slaves."[84] Women's influence over opinion is an influence over morals, manners, customs and public honors, over men's conduct and over their pleasures.[85]

Bringing things out into the open in Rousseau is identified with moving away from the ascendancy of women themselves and from the 'feminine' principles of concealment, deception, and the exercise of behind-the-scenes power and moving toward the 'masculine' principles of openness and the exercise of overt power. We find in Rousseau an aspiration to 'masculinize' society on the whole and 'men' in particular. Rousseau's concern for making men into warriors exemplifies this push. The soldier is a symbol of the exercise of overt power; his intentions are clear—the exercise of military power and ultimately victory over the enemy. In contrast, the arts and the sciences for Rousseau are the domain of the "feminine principles." He warns that engagement in the arts and sciences tends to "soften and enervate courage"[86] and that cultivating them is "harmful to warlike qualities."[87]

Rousseau's condemnation of modern civil life as 'effeminate' can be understand against this background. He describes the customs of the day, which are characterized by deceit and pretense, as "effeminate."[88] The predominance of women and of 'feminine' principles is likely to encourage men to become too much like women, he worries. For one, they may be induced to appropriate 'feminine' means. The danger of this happening is a recurring theme in Rousseau. Too much contact with women, he warns in "Letter to M. D'Alembert on the Theatre," will make men into women.[89] Given the increasing 'feminization' of modern civil life, the ascendancy of women, and the cultivation of the arts and the sciences, it is more difficult to make men than women, Rousseau seems to lament.

But Rousseau is ambivalent about the possibility and desirability of moving away from the power of women themselves in civil society.[90] Vanity, men's desire for women's esteem, moral love, all mean that "men will always be what women want them to be." This is why for Rousseau women need to be educated to be virtuous in sexual matters. Second, he is ambivalent about the desirability and the possibility of moving away from the 'feminine' principles of concealment, since they become necessary in his scheme for the regeneration or transformation of civil society. And this transformation is symbolized less in terms of masculine openness—exemplified by the warrior-soldier whose power is overt—than in terms of 'feminine' concealment—exemplified in the covert and deceptive manipulations of the Governor and the Legislator. If we pay attention only to the fact that Rousseau refers to both these figures as males, as "he," and not to their characteristics or the principles under which they operate, we might not see that they exhibit feminine principles more than masculine ones, and in the case of the Governor, in particular, maternal ones.

The Legislator has a number of characteristics.[91] "He" does not hold the overt power of the state—"he is neither magistrate or sovereign."[92] A good legislator must have two important qualities—the ability to see through others, to discern what is in their hearts; and the ability to transform their hearts through deception. The Legislator is a dissembler who hides "his" real intentions. Above all, the Legislator must be concerned with what Rousseau has characterized, metaphorically, as the domain which women control—public opinion: "I refer to manners, customs, and, above all, opinion. This is a field unknown to our politicians, yet on these things depends the success of all the rest. With them the great legislator is unceasingly occupied in private, even when he seems to be confining his attention to matters of detail which, at best, are merely the arch, whereas manners, slow in their growth, are the keystone without which it will not stand."[93]

The most important task of the Legislator is to transmute the hearts of citizens through opinion.[94] His power is creative and transformative. But it must be exercised covertly, so as not to be felt as either imposition or as manipulation. The Legislator "must work with full consciousness that he has set himself to change, as it were, the very stuff of human nature; to transform each individual who, in isolation, is a complete but solitary whole, into a part of something greater than himself, from which, in a sense, he derives his life and his being."[95]

The Governor has a similar task—to create from "his" pupil a virtuous man who is able to live in corrupt civil society.[96] Although Rousseau distinguishes among the tasks that different individuals such as the mother, father, nurse, and governor might perform in the care of the young pupil, he implies that this division of labor is undesirable, expressing a preference for, in modern terms, "one primary care-giver."[97] In fact the Governor is the primary caregiver who oversees all details of the infant's care.[98] "He" prepares for the infant's arrival as a mother might prepare for her newborn child, by overseeing the selection of a wetnurse. It is noteworthy that Rousseau assumes here that a wetnurse will be chosen, since he is so adamant elsewhere that women nurse their own children. It allows the Governor, who is to go live with the wetnurse and the infant, to establish himself, rather than the biological mother or the wetnurse whose actions and diet he oversees, as the primary "caretaker" of Emile. Reminiscent of the primary bond in which the mother and child are inseparable, the Governor and child are never to be parted without their consent—"that we never be taken from one another without our consent. This clause is essential, and I would even want the pupil and the governor to regard themselves as so inseparable that the lot of each in life is always a common object for them."[99]

Rousseau spells out the way in which the Governor must set up a carefully controlled environment, "child-proofing" the house, so that the child feels free and is unaware that he is being manipulated by an all-powerful entity:

> Let him always believe he is the master, and let it always be you who are. There is no subjection so perfect as that which keeps the appearance of freedom. Thus the will itself is made captive. The poor child who knows nothing, who can do nothing, who has no learning, is he not at your mercy? Do you not dispose, with respect to him, of everything which surrounds him? Are you not the mas-

ter of affecting him as you please? Are not his labors, his games, his pleasures, his pains, all in your hands without his knowing it? Doubtless he ought to do only what he wants; but he ought to want only what you want him to do. He ought not to make a step without your having foreseen it; he ought not to open his mouth without your knowing what he is going to say.[100]

Most important is that Emile must remain unaware of his complete dependence on the Governor.[101] Emile is to be taught that he is dependent only on things, not on persons (in order to give him a sense of independence and curb his desire to dominate those on whom he depends). This covers up the fact that he is in reality dependent on persons, since only persons, in the form of the Governor, can provide the kind of care that Rousseau advocates for the young pupil. It is an extensive all-encompassing, self-sacrificing kind of care. The difficulty in finding a governor, Rousseau says, is finding someone attentive enough to his charge. It is the kind of devotion that cannot be bought with money, we are told by Wolmar: "The respectable capacity of tutor requires so many talents which one would not be able to remunerate, so many virtues which have no price, that it is useless to seek one with money."[102] The ideal governor, according to Rousseau, has only one pupil in order that he may devote himself entirely to his pupil's well-being[103] and identify completely with his pupil's accomplishments.[104] The image of the Governor as exercising a kind of hidden feminine (maternal) power[105] is reinforced when one notes the similarity between what the Governor does with Emile and what Julie does in her garden. Just as Julie has cultivated her garden with an invisible hand, so too does the Governor cultivate Emile.[106]

The point at which the Governor relinquishes his hold over Emile is the point at which Emile passes from the Governor's to Sophie's control—"[t]oday I abdicate the authority you confided to me, and Sophie is your governor from now on."[107] Sophie carries on the role of behind-the-scenes arbiter of Emile's pleasures and needs.[108] Like the Governor, Sophie makes Emile feel he is powerful and free. Sophie takes over from the Governor in manipulating and regulating Emile's emotional needs.

IV

How useful is this interpretation of the place of women in Rousseau's scheme?

If we accept Rousseau's assessment of advanced civil society and the psychology that drives it, then we might have to pay attention to what he has to say about the 'naturalness' of modesty. It is helpful to distinguish at least four ways we can understand Rousseau's use of the term *natural*. First, what is natural is what we find in the original state of nature, as described in the Second Discourse. In a second sense, what is 'natural' is what is compatible with the body, one's biological attributes. Third, what is 'natural' is what is the result of adaptability to one's environment—it is what one can expect to happen given certain conditions. And fourth, what is 'natural' is simply what is good. Modesty is not natural in the first sense. It is natural in the second sense of being compatible with women's biological makeup. Yet Rousseau tells us that it is only in civil society that women's biological makeup has any ramifications for the role of the sexes. Modesty is natural in the third sense—adaptability to environmental circumstances, but only in response to the development of two conditions, moral love and the weakness of male desire—as well as to the psychological imperatives of *amour-propre*. And in the fourth sense, modesty is not natural. Rousseau deems it to be a means toward a more fundamental good—the perpetuation of the species and the political community—rather than a good in itself.

Indeed Rousseau's radical message is this: in advanced civil society we cannot be assured that a most fundamental requirement for the continuity of the political community—the very perpetuation of the species—is carried out. But the danger comes less from sexual relations among men and women, and the failure of female modesty, than from the infant's helplessness. Although it seems that Rousseau is saying that woman as sexual mate is more important than woman as mother—Sophie is introduced to facilitate Emile's second birth into a sexual being[109]—in fact what emerges is the opposite: woman as mother is paramount to woman as sexual mate. One does not die of celibacy, but the helpless infant dies without the care of an adult. Emile needs the Governor as "mother" before he needs Sophie as sexual mate. And the more extensive and complex the requirements of civil society, the more extensive that maternal care becomes. Indeed, the image of the Governor in Rousseau resembles the mother of mythical and exaggerated proportions, all-powerful, all-sacrificing, deemed to be the source of corruption and regeneration, as described by feminist object relations theory.[110] The themes of the feminization and masculinization of politics in Rousseau can illuminate contemporary concerns that it is the inherent masculinity of politics in liberal democracies that excludes women from political life. It may well be that politics is increasingly associated with feminine means, with the behind-the-scenes power of interest groups and the manipulation of public opinion through the media. Paradoxically, however, this does not benefit women when it comes to enjoying equal political status or representing their interests. Increasingly, men use these means to achieve political success.

Yet we also find in modern liberal democracies, as we find in Rousseau's ruminations, the fear that women are ascendant, that they are wielding too much power, that their influence is indeed all-pervasive, covert, and dangerous. Indeed it is striking that in modern liberal democracies we have, on the one hand the drive to curtail women's power, what some have called a "backlash," which is spurred not by the perception that women have achieved equal formal political rights but by the perception that they have too much covert influence on the political, intellectual agenda. On the other hand we have the drive not only to "make women into mothers," but to make them into mothers of awesome proportions— all-powerful and all-encompassing, self-sacrificing enough to rescue all from the degeneration and corruption of advanced civil society.

Notes

1. Variations on this theme are found in a number of commentaries on Rousseau's treatment of women. For example, Moira Gatens suggests that women are expected to provide the "natural foundation" of the civic sphere in Rousseau's framework (*Feminism and Philosophy* [Bloomington: Indiana University Press], chap. 1); Genevieve Lloyd suggests that women's affiliation with 'nature' serves to both elevate and denigrate them in Rousseau's thought (*The Man of Reason* [Minneapolis: University of Minnesota Press, 1984], 58–64, 74–79).

2. According to Carole Pateman, Rousseau deems women to be unable to control their passions, sexual or otherwise, through reason; women end up representing the disorder of incontinence, "'The Disorder of Women': Women, Love, and the Sense of Justice," *Ethics* 91 (1980), 20–34; Carole Pateman, *The Sexual Contract* (Stanford: Stanford University Press, 1988), 97–102.

3. Victor G. Wexler proposes that Rousseau attributes to women a greater ability than men to control their sexual passions ("'Made for Man's Delight': Rousseau as Antifeminist," *American Historical Review* 81 [1976]: 266–91).

4. Jean-Jacques Rousseau, *The First and Second Discourses*, trans. Judith R. Masters and Roger D. Masters (New York: St. Martin's Press, 1964), I:47. Roman numerals I and II indicate *First Discourse* and *Second Discourse*, respectively; Arabic numbers indicate page.

5. Rousseau, *Discourses*, I:46–47.

6. Jean Starobinski has written extensively on the importance of the image of the veil in Rousseau's writings, and related to it the themes of "transparency and obstruction." But Starobinski

does not connect this image to Rousseau's treatment of women themselves (*Jean-Jacques Rousseau: Transparency and Obstruction*, trans. Arthur Goldhammer [Chicago: University of Chicago Press, 1988]).

7. Jean-Jacques Rousseau, *La nouvelle Héloïse*, trans. Judith H. McDowell (University Park: Pennsylvania State University Press 1968), 365.

8. Rousseau, *Discourses*, II:198–99.

9. That Rousseau attributes to young girls manipulative tendencies has been noted by most commentators on the "woman question" in Rousseau, the most comprehensive of which include Susan Okin, *Women in Western Political Thought* (Princeton: Princeton University Press, 1979), chaps. 5–8; Lynda Lange, "Rousseau: Women and the General Will," in *The Sexism of Social and Political Theory*, ed. Lynda Lange and Lorenne M. G. Clark (Toronto: University of Toronto Press, 1979); Lynda Lange, "Rousseau and Modern Feminism," in *Feminist Interpretations and Political Theory*, ed. Mary Lyndon Shanley and Carole Pateman (University Park: Pennsylvania State University Press, 1991); Lynda Lange, "Women and Rousseau's Democratic Theory: Philosopher Monsters and Authoritarian Equality," in *Modern Engendering*, ed. Bat-Ami Bar On (Albany: State University of New York Press, 1994). But I am suggesting that the theme of concealment and deception takes center stage in the woman question in Rousseau. Examining it can allow us to take a somewhat different approach to understanding the debates and questions that emerge from these interpretations. One question is whether Rousseau confines women to the private realm on the basis of natural or conventional qualities, in particular whether he attributes to them a natural maternal instinct. Okin suggests that in failing to distinguish between what is natural and what is conventional in his depiction of women, Rousseau thereby ends up presenting them as having certain natural qualities such as a maternal instinct to justify the position he assigns to them. Lange suggests that women in Rousseau's framework simultaneously provide and siphon off what is humanly necessary but politically problematic—particularity and reproductive labor—both of which are associated with nature. In a different vein, Penny Weiss and Carol McMillan propose that Rousseau may want men and women to play different roles in society, but that he does not in fact deem them to have radically different 'natures'; he simply uses the language of 'nature' as a strategic tool or device. See Penny Weiss, "Rousseau, Antifeminism, and Woman's Nature," *Political Theory* 15 (1987): 81–98; Penny Weiss, "Sex, Freedom, and Equality in Rousseau's *Emile*," *Polity* 22 (1990): 603–25; Carole Mcmillan, *Women, Reason, and Nature* (Princeton: Princeton University Press, 1982).

10. In chapter 5 of *Emile*, Rousseau begins by saying that the difference between men and women is what is connected with their sex and then quickly moves to a discussion of the union of the sexes and the suggestion that modesty and shame are the peculiar attributes that nature has given to women (Jean-Jacques Rousseau, *Emile; or, On Education*, Allan Bloom, trans. (New York: Basic Books, 1979). In the "Letter to M. D'Alembert on the Theatre," Rousseau insists that shame, or bashfulness in reaction to erotic matters, and chasteness are not merely popular prejudices, or the result of education, or something that protects the rights of fathers and husbands. They are due to 'nature' (Rousseau, "Letter to M. D'Alembert on the Theatre," trans. Allan Bloom, in *Politics and the Arts* [Ithaca: Cornell University Press, 1960], 83).

11. Sophie, Rousseau writes, "ought to be a woman as Emile is a man—that is to say, she ought to have everything which suits the constitution of her species and her sex in order to fill her place in the physical and moral order" (*Emile*, 357).

12. Rousseau, *Emile*, 415.

13. The governor remarks of her—"Women are skilful and know how to disguise themselves. The more she grumbles in secret against my tyranny, the more attentive she is in flattering me" (*Emile*, 449).

14. *Emile*, 370. Rousseau proceeds to tell the story of a young boy and a young girl at the dinner table and the different ways they go about getting something they want—the boy asking for it directly, the girl using cunning to make her wishes known.

15. Children, Rousseau says, do not have modesty or shame in sexual matters (*Emile*, 217). In fact, they are sexless, not much interested in or even aware of sexual differentiation. Emile before puberty "does not feel himself to be of any sex, of any species. Man and woman are equally alien to him" (*Emile*, 219). Rousseau suggests that for both Sophie and Emile some shame comes with their first experience of sexual desire (*Emile*, 331).

16. Rousseau, *Emile*, 217.

17. The development of the moral aspect of love, Rousseau says, "determines this desire and fixes it exclusively on a single object" (*Discourses*, II:134).

18. In the original state of nature, any woman will do (as will any man). Love is strictly a physical sexual encounter. In the original state of nature, there is "one appetite that invited him to perpetuate his species; and this blind inclination, devoid of any sentiment of the heart, produced only a purely animal act" (Rousseau, *Discourses*, II:142).

19. Rousseau writes: "By contrast, in species in which one male is united with one female, in which mating produces a sort of moral bond—a sort of marriage—the female belongs by her own choice to the male to whom she has given herself, and commonly resists all others. And the male, who has this affection founded on preference as a guarantee of her fidelity, is thus less anxious at the sight of other males and lives more peacefully with them" (*Emile*, 429).

20. Rousseau, *Discourses*, II:135.

21. Allan Bloom misinterprets Rousseau on this point, among others. Bloom claims that doubt about whether or not he is preferred above all others is what motivates him to pursue his love and to pursue virtue in order to "win" his love. But Bloom mistakes a problem Rousseau would like to ameliorate or get around—uncertainty—for something that Rousseau deems to be desirable. It is the assurance, not the doubt, that she prefers him to all others that motivates the man to be virtuous (Allen Bloom, *Love and Friendship* [New York: Simon and Schuster, 1993], 102).

22. In a discussion of jealousy, Rousseau remarks—"If he fears that he is not the only object of her attentions, it is the effect of that *amour-propre* whose origin I have showed, and he suffers far more out of vanity than out of love" (*Emile*, 430).

23. Rousseau, *Emile*, 430. Social institutions, Rousseau laments, have made women dissembling in a negative fashion, that is they disguise their preferences so that "one can hardly count on their most proved attachment and that they can no longer demonstrate preferences which reassure a man against the fear of competitors" (*Emile*, 430).

24. Rousseau, *Discourses*, I:52.

25. One result of Sophie's love of virtue is that she will esteem only a man who has merit, *Emile*, 439. Rousseau writes: "[I]f you want them (men) to become great and virtuous, teach women what greatness of soul and virtue are" (*Discourses* I:52–53).

26. Rousseau writes: "I am very far from thinking that this ascendency of women is in itself an evil. It is a gift given them by nature for the happiness of the human race" (*Discourses*, I:52).

27. Rousseau, *Emile*, 320, 323.

28. The Governor says to Sophie—"It will cost you some painful privations, but you will reign over him if you know how to reign over yourself; what has happened already shows me that this difficult art is not beyond your courage. You will reign by means of love for a long time if you make your favors rare and precious, if you know how to make them valued" (*Emile*, 478–79).

29. Rousseau, *Emile*, 479.

30. Women and men may have similar sexual desires, Rousseau indicates, but not the same "faculties for their satisfaction" ("Letter to M. D'Alembert," 83, 84). In *Emile*, Rousseau refers to the women as having "unlimited desire to which this shame serves as a brake" (359).

31. Rousseau, *Emile*, 385.

32. Rousseau, "Letter to M. D'Alembert," 83.

33. It is summed up in a passage from *La nouvelle Héloïse*—"The attack and the defense, the audacity of men, the modesty of women—these are by no means conventions, as your philosophers

think, but natural institutions which are easily accounted for and from which all the other moral distinctions are readily inferred. Besides, the purposes of nature not being the same in each sex, its inclinations, perceptions, and sentiments must be directed according to its own views; opposite tastes and constitutions are required for tilling the soil and for nursing children. A taller stature, a stronger voice, and features more strongly marked seem to have no necessary bearing on one's sex, but these exterior modifications indicate the intentions of the creator in the modifications of the spirit. The souls of a perfect woman and a perfect man must not resemble each other more than their appearance" (108).

34. Rousseau, "Letter to M. D' Alembert," 84.

35. Ibid.

36. Ibid, 86.

37. There are certain instances, says Rousseau, where differences of strength and age are such that rape takes place, but in general the strength of the sexes is so equal that this is unlikely (*Emile*, 360). The man must be audacious but not brutal ("Letter to M. D'Alembert," 85). He must have the consent of the loved one. Rousseau's presentation of what counts as consent is highly problematic, but he does insist that it is essential. Emile is instructed that Sophie is the master of her own body and that Emile must never impose himself on Sophie—"Let each of you always remain master of his own person and his caresses and have the right to dispense them to the other only at his own will. Always remember that even in marriage pleasure is legitimate only when desire is shared" (*Emile*, 477).

38. Rousseau, "Letter to M.D'Alembert," 84.

39. Rousseau, *Emile*, 394.

40. Rousseau, *La nouvelle Héloïse*, 180.

41. Rousseau, *Emile*, 441.

42. For example, what causes Julie, the moral heroine of *La nouvelle Héloïse*, the most suffering is deceiving her parents, chiefly her father, about her affair with Saint-Preux and keeping it secret from her husband, Wolmar.

43. Population increase is a sign of good government for Rousseau, although excess population also leads to a state's decline.

44. Rousseau, *Discourses*, II:106.

45. The benefits, as Rousseau presents them, are that parents, knowing they do not have to care for the weak ones, do not feel their children to be a burden and are more eager to have them. By letting only the strong live, the species as a whole is strengthened. Not knowing which is strong and which is weak before birth, abortion eliminates both indiscriminately, thereby weakening the species.

46. The relevant passage reads: "How many shameful ways there are to prevent the birth of men and trick nature; either by those brutal and depraved tastes that insult its most charming work, tastes that neither savages nor animals ever knew and that have arisen in civilized countries only from a corrupt imagination; or by those secret abortions, worthy fruits of debauchery and vicious honor; or by the exposure or murder of a multitude of infants, victims of the misery of their parents or the barbarous shame of their mothers; or, finally, by the mutilation of those unfortunates, for whom a part of their existence and all posterity are sacrificed to vain songs" (Rousseau, *Discourses*, II:197).

47. Rousseau, "Letter to M. D'Alembert," 47–49.

48. Rousseau, *Emile*, 46.

49. Ibid.

50. Rousseau, *La nouvelle Héloïse*, 357.

51. Sophie then makes Emile concerned with public opinion. This is how she facilitates his second birth. He has been raised to be self-regarding, now he must regard social opinion, because Sophie's honor depends on her social reputation. The Governor reminds Emile that he must now care about what others think of both his and Sophie's action—"Your honor is in you alone, and hers

depends on others. To neglect it would be to wound your own honor; and you do not render yourself what you owe yourself if you are the cause of her not being rendered what is owed her" (*Emile*, 418).

52. Rousseau, *La nouvelle Héloïse*, 206.

53. Rousseau writes: "Their honour is not only in their conduct but in their reputation; and it is not possible that a woman who consents to be regarded as disreputable can ever be decent. When a man acts well, he depends only on himself and can brave public judgement; but when a woman acts well, she has accomplished only half of her task, and what is thought of her is no less important to her than what she actually is. From this it follows that the system of woman's education ought to be contrary in this respect to the system of our education. Opinion is the grave of virtue among men and its throne among women" (*Emile*, 364–65).

54. Rousseau, *Emile*, 396. Women can think, but they ought not to, Rousseau says (426).

55. Rousseau distinguishes between the two when he writes: "Wit alone is the true resource of the fair sex—not that stupid wit which the social world values so highly and which is of no use for making women's lives happy, but the wit which suits their position and consists in an art of exploiting man's position and putting our peculiar advantages to their use" (*Emile*, 371–72).

56. Rousseau, *Emile*, 409.

57. Rousseau refers to the "salonierres'" of his day when he writes, "With us, on the contrary, the most esteemed woman is the one who has the greatest renown, about whom the most is said, who is the most often seen in society, at whose home one dines the most, who most imperiously sets the tone, who judges, resolves, decides, pronounces, assigns talents, merit, and virtues their degrees and places, and whose favour is most ignominiously begged for by humble, learned men" ("Letter to M. D'Alembert," 49). For a discussion of women's role in the salons in eighteenth-century Europe and France and their relation to the academy, see Bonnie G. Smith, *Changing Lives: Women in European History Since 1700* (Lexington, Mass.: D. C. Heath, 1989), 78–82.

58. Rousseau, *Emile*, 409.

59. Rousseau, *Emile*, 385.

60. In an unfinished sequel to *Emile*, Sophie has a child by another man. Emile, undeceived by her attempt to hide the paternity of the child and her faithlessness, finds out, and it destroys their marriage (Jean-Jacques Rousseau, "Emile et Sophie; ou, Les solitaires," in *Oeuvres complètes*, vol. 4 [Editions Gallimard, 1969], 881–924.

61. Jean-Jacques Rousseau, *The Social Contract*, trans. Sir Ernest Barker (London: Oxford University Press, 1977), bk. 4, chap. 1, 269.

62. Sophie has been trained so that her dominant passion is her love of virtue: "She loves it because there is nothing so fine as virtue. She loves it because virtue constitutes woman's glory and because to her a virtuous woman appears almost equal to the angels. She loves it as the only route of true happiness and because she sees only misery, abandonment, unhappiness, and ignominy in the life of a shameless woman" (*Emile*, 397).

63. Rousseau, *Discourses*, II:155–56.

64. Rousseau, *Discourses*, I:36.

65. Rousseau, *Discourses*, II:101, 172.

66. "There is perhaps no well-to-do man whose death is not secretly hoped for by avid heirs and often his own children" (*Discourses*, II:194). One finds "always the hidden desire to profit at the expense of others. All these evils are the first effect of property and the inseparable consequence of nascent inequality" (II:156).

67. Rousseau, *Discourses*, II:156.

68. Rousseau describes the end result: "Last stage of all, when the State, now near its ruin, lives on only in a vain and deceptive form, when the bond of society is broken in all men's hearts, when the vilest self-interest bears insolently the sacred name of Common-Weal, then does the general will fall dumb." Then "unjust decrees, aiming only at the satisfaction of private interests, can be passed under the guise of laws" (*The Social Contract* bk. 4, chap. 1, 270).

69. Rousseau, *Discourses*, I:37.

70. Rousseau, *Discourses*, I:38.

71. Rousseau, *Discourses*, II:195.

72. According to Judith N. Shklar, Rousseau may be setting an example in his own *Confessions*: "In a world where men hide their inner selves no one can know himself or another. By presenting the history of his own soul to other men he hoped to liberate them from their self-deceptions and to bring them to that self-knowledge which alone is worthy of the name of wisdom" (*Men and Citizens* [Cambridge: Cambridge University Press, 1985], 41).

73. Rousseau, *Discourses*, II:194.

74. Rousseau, *La nouvelle Héloïse*, 291.

75. Rousseau, *Discourses*, I:37.

76. Rousseau, *La nouvelle Héloïse*, 302.

77. This concept also addresses Rousseau's concern with the divided self, a characteristic of modern civil life. If one acts the same in private and public, then one does not develop one in contradiction to the other. There is no disjunction then between inner and outer self. Self-censorship thwarts a division between the two. This theme is captured in Wolmar's proposed solution to publicly unacceptable passion between Julie and Saint-Preux. They are to act alone as if Wolmar were with them and in the presence of Wolmar as if they were alone (Rousseau, *La nouvelle Héloïse*, 291).

78. Rousseau, *The Social Contract*, bk. 4, chap. 4, 286.

79. Rousseau, *Discourses*, II:79.

80. A similar theme is expressed in "Considerations on the Government of Poland" where he advocates an arrangement in which all citizens feel they are constantly under public scrutiny. This functions to bring their behavior out into the open so that judgment is immediate and public. It also makes the desire for public esteem the regulating force of their actions. Public scrutiny and the desire for public esteem combine to bring patriotism to its highest pitch (Jean-Jacques Rousseau, "Considerations on the Government of Poland," in *Political Writings*, ed. Frederick Watkins [Madison: University of Wisconsin Press, 1986], 244).

81. Rousseau, *Discourses*, I:52.

82. Jean-Jacques Rousseau,. *The Confessions of Jean-Jacques Rousseau*, illus. Hedouin (London: Bibliophilist Society), part 2, 14.

83. Judith N. Shklar notes that, for Rousseau, the desire for the esteem of others makes public opinion a ruling force: "The moment that sees the birth of AMOUR-PROPRE is the instant in which opinion becomes the dominant psychological force in human life" (*Men and Citizens*, 76).

84. Rousseau, "Letter to M. D'Alembert," 73–74.

85. Rousseau writes: "In all the countries of the world, it is opinion, not nature, that decides men in the choice of their pleasures. Reform their opinions, and their morals will automatically be purified. . . . Whoso judges of manners, judges of honour; and whoso judges of honour makes opinion his touchstone" (*The Social Contract*, bk. 4, chap. 7, 294).

86. Past events teach us, Rousseau contends, that "the study of the sciences is much more apt to soften and enervate courage than to strengthen and animate it" (*Discourses*, I:55).

87. Rousseau, *Discourses*, I:56.

88. Rousseau, *Discourses*, I:45.

89. Rousseau, "Letter to M. D'Alembert," 100.

90. The great paradox of Clarens, described in Rousseau's *La nouvelle Héloïse*, is that although openness is espoused as the principle making it a model of an ideal form of society and way of life, there is a great deal of concealment and deception going on there. Julie keeps secret from Wolmar her passion for Saint-Preux. Wolmar hides his atheism from Julie.

91. Rousseau, *The Social Contract*, bk. 2, chap. 7, 204–5.

92. Rousseau, *The Social Contract*, bk. 2, chap. 7, 206.

93. Rousseau, *The Social Contract*, bk. 2, chap. 12, 220.

94. The Legislator addresses a Catch 22—for individuals in civil society to accept the legitimacy of good laws, they must already have been born and raised in a place where good laws have made them into individuals capable of loving the laws. The problem is to persuade them to accept laws before they have been socialized (by the prior existence of such laws) to feel them and acknowledge them as legitimate.

95. Rousseau, *The Social Contract*, bk. 2, chap. 7, 205.

96. That the Governor's position is odd and that one might have difficulty explaining where such a person could be found has been noted by several commentators. For example, Judith N. Shklar comments that "Rousseau doubted whether any man was really fit for it" (*Men and Citizens*, 146).

97. "A child ought to know no other superiors than his father and his mother or, in default of them, his nurse and his governor; even one of the two is already too many. But this division is inevitable, and all that one can do to remedy it is to make sure that the persons of the two sexes who govern him are in such perfect agreement concerning him that the two are only one as far as he is concerned" (Rousseau, *Emile*, 57).

98. Rousseau, *Emile*, 57–59.

99. Rousseau, *Emile*, 53.

100. Rousseau, *Emile*, 120.

101. "It is true that I leave him the appearance of independence, but he was never better subjected to me; for now he is subjected because he wants to be. As long as I was unable to make myself master of his will, I remained master of his person; I was never a step away from him. Now I sometimes leave him to himself, because I govern him always" (Rousseau, *Emile*, 332).

102. Rousseau, *La nouvelle Héloïse*, 328.

103. "My young friend, when I took you in my arms at your birth and, calling the Supreme Being to be witness of the commitment I dared to contract, dedicated my days to the happiness of yours, did I myself know what I was committing myself to? No, I only knew that in my making you happy, I was sure to be" (Rousseau, *Emile*, 442).

104. "Remember that your honor is no longer in you but in your pupil" (Rousseau, *Emile*, 246).

105. In *La nouvelle Héloïse*, Rousseau makes reference to women's unsuitability for tutoring, when Wolmar speaks to Claire of his plan to make Saint-Preux the tutor of his children: "Your sex [female] is not suited for these duties" (328). But he also suggests the opposite when Claire says to Saint-Preux: "You are a child. You still need a tutor, and I shall be yours" (154).

106. Great pains are taken to conceal Julie's handiwork. Saint-Preux marvels: "It is that a place so different from what it was can become what it is only with cultivation and care, yet nowhere do I see the slightest trace of cultivation. All is green, fresh, vigourous, and the gardener's hand is nowhere to be seen" (Rousseau, *La nouvelle Héloïse*, 311).

107. Rousseau, *Emile*, 479.

108. She is to be the "arbiter of his [Emile's] pleasures," in order to "reign over him" (Rousseau, *Emile*, 478).

109. This is the emphasis in Joel Schwartz's interpretation of Rousseau on the sexes, *The Sexual Politics of Jean-Jacques Rousseau* (Chicago: University of Chicago Press, 1984). According to Schwartz, sexual relations between men and women are a training school for overcoming an important political problem for Rousseau—dependence. I suggest that the infant's dependence on a 'mother' figure is a more fundamental prototype for dependence. Indeed it is the latter that we find in Rousseau.

110. For example, see Dorothy Dinnerstein, *The Mermaid and The Minotaur* (New York: Harper-Perennial, 1991) and Nancy Chodorow, *The Reproduction of Mothering* (Berkeley and Los Angeles: University of California Press, 1978).

9

Rousseau and the Politics of Care

Melissa A. Butler

In the past quarter century, feminist scholarship has not only led us to seek a more complete, more inclusive understanding of human experience, it has also forced scholars to rethink familiar ways of looking at their fields. Sometimes the new understandings made possible through feminist analysis amount to Gestalt switches. One such dramatic shift occurred through Carol Gilligan's reexamination of the process of moral development and her identification of an alternative to the "ethic of justice" that had become paradigmatic in psychology. Interest in Gilligan's new model, an "ethic of care," spread rapidly in psychology and women's studies and soon passed into other disciplines as well. In political theory, Joan Tronto has noted the indispensability of both the care and justice perspectives and has argued that the contemporary tendency to split the two apart was historical and culture-bound. She suggested that the split had roots in the eighteenth century and traced this shift in moral and political thinking back to the philosophers of the Scottish Enlightenment.

In this essay, I examine the treatment of care and justice in the thought of Jean-Jacques Rousseau, a contemporary of those eighteenth-century writers, and a man who had a stormy acquaintance with one of those Scots, David Hume. At first glance, perhaps, the creator of the asocial Noble Savage would seem a strange source for commentary on the "politics of care," yet I argue that issues of care and connection were important in Rousseau's thought. Although these issues suffuse most of Rousseau's works, I focus in this essay on several of his most directly, explicitly political works—*Political Economy*, *Constitution of Poland*, and the *Social Contract*. In a nutshell, I claim that in these works Rousseau offered a solution to the problem of accommodating both justice and care, a different solution from the one proposed in other works such as *Emile* or *La nouvelle Héloïse*. In these two works, Rousseau relied on a rigid public/private distinction. Care became the domain of women confined in the home, and justice the province of men who went out into the world. Care and justice could come together in men who returned home to be revitalized for their next foray into the public sphere but the possibilities for women's full development were sacrificed. In the more political works, however, the state took on the role of establishing justice through the social contract, but also assumed responsibility for many aspects of care. In these accounts, the state became a "maternal state" and women seemed to "wither away."

The Care Perspective

The focus on a care perspective in political theory grows out of issues raised in psychology by Carol Gilligan in her iconoclastic book, *In A Different Voice*, and continued by feminists interested in the subjects of moral development and political theory.[1] To summarize briefly, here are key elements of the tale thus far: Gilligan noticed that Lawrence Kohlberg, whose model of moral development dominated the field of psychology, had based his work on the experiences of male research subjects.[2] From work on these young men, he devised a model of the stages of human development in moral reasoning. Kohlberg believed that his model identified universal structures. According to the model, as moral reasoning advanced from lower to higher stages, it referred less to the particular consequences of actions on specific individuals or communities and focused more on abstract and universal principles. (See table.)

When Kohlberg's model was applied, women tended to score lower on its scales than did men. Carol Gilligan began interviewing women and concluded that Kohlberg's model had, in effect, oversimplified the picture of moral development. As she interviewed women about their moral lives, she discovered an emphasis on relationships, connectedness, and interdependence rather than on the rules, abstraction, and autonomy that Kohlberg had found in his work with male subjects. Drawing on the work of Nancy Chodorow, Gilligan suggested that the difference she had discovered between men and women had its roots in the different developmental requirements boys and girls faced.[3] Girls, able to retain their early identification with their mothers, grew up encouraged to value connectedness; boys, forced to sever that primary connection, came to value autonomy. Kohlberg's model was skewed toward those values associated with male development, rather than those characteristic of female development. This eroded Kohlberg's claim of universality for his model. An-

Kohlberg's Stages of Moral Development

Stage I	Heteronomous morality	Individual avoids punishment—amoral
Stage II	Individualistic, instrumental morality	Individual acts, expects like response
Stage III	Interpersonally normative morality	Individual seeks approval of those closest.
Stage IV	Social system morality	Individual extends concern for approval to larger community
Stage V	Human rights and social welfare morality	Individuals accept rules because they have agreed to their creation
Stage VI	Morality of universalizable, reversible and prescriptive general ethical principles	Individual commits to fairness, to understanding moral dilemmas from the standpoint of all concerned.

Note: From Kohlberg, Appendix A, "The Six Stages of Justice Development," in *Essays*, 2:621–39.

other perspective had to be taken into account. Kohlberg's "ethic of justice" relied on rules, rights, and abstract principles. It prized rationality and fairness. Yet, Gilligan argued, there was a need to recognize another type of moral reasoning built around relationships, responsibility, and attention to concrete situations. In this version, empathy and commitment were important. An account of moral development that disregarded the possibility of an ethic of care did not really tell the full story.

The influence of Gilligan's work would be difficult to exaggerate. For me, it calls to mind Thomas Kuhn's *Structure of Scientific Revolution,* on two counts; first, for the huge amount of criticism and new research it stimulated in its own field; and second, for its impact on other fields.[4] Like the Kuhnian notion of "paradigm shift," Gilligan's recognition of a "different voice" invited scholars in a variety of disciplines to reexamine their fields in light of her insights. Kuhn's concept of "paradigm shift" itself became a kind of paradigm shift in the history/philosophy of science, and Gilligan's emphasis on two ethics, an ethic of justice and an ethic of care operated in similar fashion. Gilligan's work raised enormous issues for psychologists, feminists, and other scholars in far-ranging fields. Included among these issues are whether or not the differences Gilligan observed truly differentiate the sexes; whether they are biological and essential or results of socialization; whether the "different voice" Gilligan heard was itself a white, heterosexual, well-educated voice of privileged women; why the number of different voices must stop at two; and, whether the ethic of justice and the ethic of care are truly separable.

What is significant to me about Gilligan's contribution as it has filtered over into political theory is that it brings the perspective of care in from the periphery, where, at least in contemporary political thought outside of feminist analysis, it tended to be privatized, devalued, or ignored. Gilligan's insights invite us to look at the issues raised from the standpoint of care *as political issues.*

In political thought, as feminist scholars have pointed out, political theorists writing about justice have generally excluded private/family/female concerns from their consideration; justice wasn't about these and they weren't about justice. Susan Okin's *Justice, Gender, and the Family* did a superb job of discrediting this approach and demonstrating the importance of establishing justice as a "family value."[5] The separation between the spheres was breached. So, if justice entered the household, did "care" enter the political sphere? Here, Okin suggested that we might be dealing with a false dichotomy. Justice and care were closely joined together. She illustrated this contention through a discussion of the requirements of Rawls's original position.[6] The thought experiment at the foundation of Rawls's theory would simply become unworkable unless those in the original position were capable of empathy as well as rationality. Okin's point was well taken; yet, as she noted, the implication she drew was not something Rawls himself had noticed. Even if justice always rested on a foundation of care, the fact remained that much of the time that foundation was overlooked.

In her work *Moral Boundaries*, Joan Tronto moved toward remedying that oversight by putting care front and center in her approach to political theory.[7] She argued that a political theory or a politics that disregarded care was not really telling the full story of political life. She underscored the importance of both justice and care perspectives in informing politics. Tronto argued that the division by gender roles in patterns of moral development was historical as well as culture-bound. She undermined "the idea that moral sympathy is exclusively a 'woman's sphere'" (20). By examining works of the Scottish Enlightenment, Tronto exposed the similarity between so-called women's morality and the theory of "moral sentiments" of eighteenth-century philosophers. She traced a shift away from a morality rooted in feeling and context to one based on reason and abstraction. As the range of human contacts expanded, philosophers confronted the need to deal with the problem of "otherness." Their responses exalted the universal and devalued the particular. Before the eighteenth century, according to Tronto, "feeling was an important quality of the virtuous man" (52). But as that century wore on, increasingly "it fell to women to provide the automatic sentiments of sympathy, benevolence and humanity" (55).

Rousseau and the Care Perspective

A good bit of the responsibility for helping sentiment find "a home at home" went to none other than Jean-Jacques Rousseau, through his enormously popular epistolary novel, *La nouvelle Héloïse*, as well as his treatise on education, *Emile*. I am impressed with Tronto's book and accept most of her comments on Rousseau; but in the remainder of this essay I will look at his work in greater detail to show that there is more to be gleaned by rereading this part of the canon in terms of considerations raised by the care perspective.

Why Rousseau? First of all, he is contemporaneous with, and apparently a contributor to, the shift Tronto discussed. Second, because quite possibly more than any other writer in "the canon" of political theory, Rousseau obviously *cared* about *care*. He problematized matters of care, connection, and relationship in ways that were new and original in the history of political thought. Rousseau, more than most political theorists, took care seriously as something central, not as something marginal.

Why was care so important to Rousseau? His autobiographical works shed some light on that question. No doubt one of the major insights feminists have brought to political theory is the claim that "the personal is political." Anyone who has studied Rousseau, however, has had this insight brought home with particular force. The problems Rousseau confronted in his theories were the problems he himself lived with. (And if they were not, he made them so!) Why is it that researchers who listened to women came to notice the care perspective? Because issues about care and relationships occupied center stage in the lives of those women. Ditto, Rousseau.

So, in this essay about Rousseau's contribution to a political theory of care, I begin my analysis by stepping back to look at Rousseau himself from the perspective of care.

Care played a ubiquitous and problematic role in Rousseau's life. In his extensive autobiographical writings, he provided voluminous information about himself cast in the roles of care receiver and caregiver. We know he was unsuccessful in both these roles. As a receiver of care, the first thing he did was kill the mother who bore him![8] (*Unintentionally*, but it did seem to set the pattern of his life.) Unlike many other theorists whose lack of personal acquaintance with women led them to overlook women's concerns, Rousseau was neither "cleric . . . [n]or puritan bachelor."[9] He spent his whole life surrounded by women. For much of his life, this apostle of independence lived largely "on the kindness of others," notably a string of protectresses, ranging from Mme de Warens to Mme d'Epinay. He became involved in a series of relationships with male and female friends—virtually all of which ended disastrously, and ended in large measure because of Rousseau's difficulty as a care *receiver* in reconciling his need for independence with his other needs.

The *Confessions* also show Rousseau summoned to the role of caregiver; and we see him shamefully inadequate in answering these calls. At one point in his youth, when he found his great expectations would result only in yet another in a string of positions in domestic service, he railed against his fate: "What, always a lackey?" he remarked to himself (*Confessions*, 78). In the role of servant, Rousseau was deeply, personally aware of the social inequality between caregivers and care receivers—an inequality he found oppressive since it had no basis in true merit. Yet his greatest failures as a caregiver came not in employer/employee or patron/client relationships; rather they were to be found in situations involving friends and family. The examples could be multiplied almost endlessly, but two should be cited here. In book III of the *Confessions*, Rousseau admitted abandoning his stricken friend, Le Maitre. At the moment of his friend's greatest need, Rousseau left this unfortunate man on the street in a strange town, writhing and foaming at the mouth in an epileptic seizure (*Confessions*, 108; OC, 1:129). Most dramatically, of course, Rousseau failed at care as a father. He abandoned each of his five newborn children to a foundling home. In his account of these acts he was desperate to salvage his image as a tender man full of goodwill for his fellows. He excused himself as follows:

> If I was one of those low born men, deaf to the gentle voice of nature, inside of whom no true feeling of justice and humanity ever sprouts, this hardening would be very simple to explain. But that warmth of heart; that very lively sensitivity; that facility of forming attachments, that strength with which they subject me, those cruel wrenchings when it is necessary to sever them, that innate good will for my fellows, that ardent love of the great, the true, the beautiful, the just; that horror of evil of every sort, that impossibility of hating, of doing harm and even of wanting to; that pity that lively and sweet emotion that I feel at the sight of all that is virtuous, generous, lovable; can all this ever be reconciled in the same soul which caused the sweetest of duties to be trampled underfoot without a scruple? No, I feel it and say it loudly; that is not possible. Never for a single moment of his life could J.-J. have been a man without feeling, without innermost emotions [without morals], a denatured father. (*Confessions*, 299; OC, 1:357)

How did this most caring of men explain the fact that, not once, but five times over, he abandoned his own helpless children? By claiming to have acted under the influence of reason, which deceived him:

I might have deceived myself, but not hardened myself. . . . [M]y reason was such that by abandoning my children to public education for lack of power to bring them up myself; by destining them to become workers and peasants rather than adventurers and fortune hunters, I believed I was performing an action of a Citizen and father and I looked at myself as a member of Plato's *Republic*. More than once since then, the regrets of my heart have taught me that I deceived myself, but my reason has been far from giving me the same admonition. (*Confessions*, 299; OC, 1:357)

His argument (disingenuous though it may be) that in abandoning his children he acted as a citizen of Plato's *Republic* found echoes in the design of his maternal state.

Rousseau took great pains to portray himself as a man of feeling and emotion. Indeed, others were convinced that he was so. Consider, for example, David Hume's account of Rousseau, written near the beginning of their stormy acquaintance:

This man, the most singular of all human beings, has at last left me. . . . He has read very little during the course of his life, and has now renounced all reading: He has seen very little; and has no manner of curiosity to see or remark. He has reflected, properly speaking, and studied very little; and has not indeed much knowledge: He has only felt, during the whole course of his life; and in this respect, his sensibility rises to a pitch beyond what I have seen any example of; but it still gives him a more acute feeling of pain than of pleasure. He is like a man who were stript not only of his clothes, but of his skin, and turned out in that situation to combat with the rude and boisterous elements, such as perpetually disturb this lower world.[10]

Hume then gave an account of the last evening he spent with Rousseau before his departure. In the course of that evening, Rousseau became annoyed with Hume and their mutual friend, Davenport:

[Rousseau] sat down very sullen and silent; and all my attempts were in vain to revive the conversation. . . . At last, after passing nearly an hour in this ill-humour, he rose up and took a turn about the room. But judge of my surprise when he sat down suddenly on my knee, threw his hands about my neck, kissed me with the greatest warmth, and bedewing all my face with tears, exclaimed, "Is it possible you can ever forgive me, my dear friend? After all the testimonies of affection I have received from you, I reward you at last with this folly and ill behaviour; but I have notwithstanding a heart worthy of your friendship; I love you, I esteem you, and not an instance of your kindness is thrown away upon me." I hope you have not so bad an opinion of me as to think I was not melted on this occasion; I assure you I kissed him and embraced him twenty times, with a plentiful effusion of tears. I think no scene of my life was ever more affecting.[11]

There we have it! Abandon his children to a foundling home, well he might have done; but never would Rousseau give up feeling, emotion, or sensitivity to the moral domain of women. He devoted considerable attention in his works to the subjects of care, connection, and relationships. Care played a central role in two of his major works, *Emile* and *La nouvelle Héloïse*. Both works may be read as responses to what had gone on in his life. *Emile* redeemed Rousseau, the "deadbeat dad," and transformed him into the Dr. Spock of his century. *La nouvelle Héloïse* allowed him to work out in fantasy a happier version of his relationship with Sophy d'Houdetot and develop his vision of perfect (albeit unsustainable) family life at Clarens.

Before moving on to specific consideration of the *politics* of care, I believe that two other aspects of Rousseau's thought relevant to the care perspective deserve to be mentioned. First, there is the form that his work often took. He was given to the use of genres especially suited to the exploration of interpersonal relationships. Not only did the writing of novels make him influential with women, as Tronto suggested, but the use of the epistolary form challenged him to let his characters speak for themselves, and to develop their relationships through their own words. It allowed him to speak, as it were, in different voices. Rousseau resorted to dialogue not only in *La nouvelle Héloïse*, but also at several points in *Emile*, including dialogues between Emile and his tutor, "Jean-Jacques," as well as the profession of faith of the Savoyard Vicar. Finally, and perhaps even more intriguingly, Rousseau resorted to dialogue in an autobiographical work, where he featured the characters "Rousseau" and a "Frenchman" standing in judgment of Jean-Jacques.[12]

Second, turning to the substance of his work, there was the primacy of feeling, especially of pity, in his portrait of natural human beings. In contrast to the long tradition of political theorists who emphasized rationality as the key to what was distinctively human, Rousseau's account of the state of nature was geared to bring issues of care to the forefront. While it is true that he pictured humans living there as asocial, he also zeroed in on two original passions, *amour de soi* (an unreflective self-love, self-satisfaction, or sense of self-preservation), and natural pity. Human beings did not have to reason through to a categorical imperative, nor did they need rational choice theory to help them decide on a course of action. Indeed, for Rousseau, the "man who meditates is a depraved animal."[13] His Noble Savage naturally felt the other's pain. But this natural empathy did not necessarily lead to any action or intervention to alleviate suffering.

Rousseau's philosophy revolved around the problems that occurred when self-sufficient and asocial beings found their contacts increased and their needs multiplied but not their personal capacity to satisfy these needs. The result was inequality, dependence, and oppression, which crowded out, distorted, and corrupted the two original passions. Recognizing that it was not possible to return to the lost innocence of natural state, Rousseau sought solutions in society. In *Emile* and *La nouvelle Héloïse*[14] Rousseau solved problems of care by championing a rigid public/ private distinction that relegated matters of care largely to the home, which was largely the province of women (or servants, though managing servants also became the responsibility of women). Care happened in private, through close adherence to a gendered division of labor; care, provided at home by women, made men ready for public life. Others have written about the details of this solution, so I'll confine myself here to three brief comments.

First, Rousseau did not simply privatize care as a way of dismissing it in order to concentrate on "more important things" in the public sphere. He devoted considerable attention to even tiny details of care. Unpalatable though his solution may be, it was not offered by a man who trivialized care or denigrated private life.

Second, though women (and servants) played key roles as caregivers, we find some examples of men assuming caregiving roles as well. The most fully developed, fully human example was probably Jean-Jacques/the tutor in *Emile*, who was not a servant but an equal of Emile's (deceased) parents. His care for Emile consisted of exercising total control over his charge without stifling the boy's sense of his own independence. There were other male figures in whom aspects of both justice and care perspectives came together—Wolmar in *La nouvelle Héloïse* and the Legislator in the *Social Contract*. Both of these figures were, in a sense, superhuman. They demonstrated the attentiveness and sensitivity to context required from a care perspective but they also established rules for a social order and were themselves characterized by their personal immunity from human passions.

Third, Rousseau was pessimistic about the feasibility of the solution summarized above. Even in fictional works where his own pen controlled the behavior of his characters, the family life of Emile and Sophy as well as that of Julie and Wolmar failed to live up to his expectations, as Julie's death and the unfinished sequel to *Emile*, *Emile and Sophy*, demonstrated.

Rousseau's Maternal State

Rousseau offered another solution, however—a more exclusively public and "political" one, detailed in the state of the *Social Contract*, as well as in *Political Economy* and *On the Government of Poland*. In this solution, the caring functions played by women elsewhere in Rousseau's work were performed by the state. The state itself became a kind of maternal state. A distinctive feature of this solution was that women were essentially absent from it. This, perhaps, should come as no surprise given Rousseau's criticism of Plato's *Republic*. As Rousseau charged in *Emile*, "Plato . . . having removed particular families from his government and no longer knowing what to do with women, was forced to turn them into men."[15] Rousseau, by contrast, fell back on a more common response in the history of political thought. He simply ignored women.

At first, Rousseau's political associations would seem to offer little promise to anyone looking to them for elements of an ethic of care. For example, Judith Shklar 's reading of Rousseau, detailed in *Men and Citizens*, located two ideal societies in Rousseau's works.[16] The first, a "Golden Age," was an essentially antipolitical nuclear-family-oriented model where people were independent, contact was rare, and the separation of male and female spheres could be maintained. The second model was Sparta, in which "the family disappears while the city is everywhere."[17] This alternative was explicitly built on the destruction of the family and its emotional and social gratification. Sparta, Shklar maintained, was no extension of the family. She argued that "nothing in Rousseau's vision of Spartan community life suggests the extended family group. There is nothing cozy about Sparta."[18] In Shklar's reading of Rousseau, family had limited political relevance, and state had no familial relevance.

Yet this approach underestimated the range of familial tasks and functions Rousseau assigned to the state as well as the role he expected the state to play in the emotional lives of its citizens. At different points in his work, Rousseau offered two apparently contradictory statements concerning the relationship of family and state. In the *Social Contract*, he wrote, "[T]he family is first model of political societies,"[19] while in his *Political Economy*, he claimed that "the state has nothing in common with the family" (OC, 3:244). In the first statement, Rousseau followed a Lockean lead in his search for an answer to the question posed at the beginning of the *Social Contract*—what could legitimize freeborn man's apparently inescapable headlong rush into chains? He considered a family grounded in consent (not simply rooted in nature) as a "first model of political societies." Families and states had one difference, however, which consisted in this: "in the family, the father's love for his children rewards him for the care he provides; whereas in the State, the pleasure of commanding substitutes for this love, which the leader does not have for his people" (OC, 3:352) Rousseau found consent to be a necessary, but not a sufficient, condition for a legitimate state. The contractual state lacked a key ingredient found in a contractual family and needed to seek a substitute. In ordinary (illegitimate) states, the "pleasure of command" could substitute for a "father's love" as motivation for leadership. Yet the legitimacy of the society of the *Social Contract* was based on popular sovereignty and egalitarianism, which seem incompatible with the type of leadership just described. Rousseau dealt with this by retaining the compact as the basis of political authority but also by introducing a kind of love into the relationship between citizen and state. Rousseau's solution thus depended on changing both the rulers and their motivation. Sovereignty would rest with the people, who would prescribe laws for themselves based on the General Will and united by common interest.

As for the second passage, presented in the *Political Economy*, this was largely Rousseau's effort to distance himself from the patriarchal theory of Robert Filmer. Rousseau maintained that the state had nothing in common with the family *except* the obligation of the head to render each of them happy (OC, 3:244). Despite that claim, Rousseau went further in the *Political Economy* than any other work in stripping the family of its functions. Furthermore, it was in the *Political Economy* that he most frequently used familial language to refer to the state. He clearly tried to shift the affective qualities associated with family life to the state.

Although Rousseau never abolished the family, he did shrink its sphere. Like Plato, Rousseau offered a vision of the state as the family writ large.[20] Given Rousseau's explanation for abandoning his children, it probably should not surprise us to find that his own designs for political institutions would include versions that transferred familial responsibilities to the state. How was Rousseau's vision of a state comparable to the family-state of Plato's *Republic?* The short answer is that Rousseau designed a model that turned over to the state practical responsibility for education, as well as significant responsibility for nurturing the emotional health of its citizens. The state acquired affective dimensions that Rousseau often associated with the family.[21]

Claiming that "all peoples become what the government makes them," he outlined the task of the state in socializing its population (OC, 3:251). The state played a creative role in the formation of the people, indeed, it should make its own men: "make men if you would command men" (OC, 3:251). In this Rousseau seemed to follow Aristotle's notion of good laws instilling good habits, as Rousseau pointed to sumptuary laws and other laws regulating conduct. But more than legal prescriptions were needed, for as Rousseau noted, "it is not enough to say to citizens be good, they must be taught" (OC, 3:254). Furthermore, the educational process was "not the work of a day," but must begin early in childhood (OC, 3:259). Rousseau explicitly recognized the role of public education as "one of the fundamental rules of popular or legitimate government" (OC, 3:260–61). Some of his readers might have thought of education as a central task of the family, but Rousseau was at pains to point out that education was more important to the state than to the family: "As it is not left to the reason of each man to be the unique arbiter of his duties one ought even less abandon to the lights and prejudices of fathers the education of their children since that is still more important to the state than to the fathers because according to the course of nature the death of a father steals from him the fruit of that education but the state sooner or later feels the effects of it. The state lives and the family dissolves" (OC, 3:260). Furthermore, the family lost nothing by allowing the state to take on the responsibility: "As for public authority taking the place of the father and taking charge of this important functions, it acquires his rights by fulfilling his duties, but he has little cause to complain since in this regard they have only properly made a change of name and they still have in common under the name of citizen the same authority over their children which they had separately under the name of father" (OC, 3:260).

Rousseau clearly tried to carry the relationship between citizen and state far beyond anything implied by a Lockean contract. The work of the state in forming citizens created a special bond between people and state, one in which citizens regarded themselves as parts of the state and the country as the common mother of its citizens (OC, 3:258). Rousseau compared state and family most fully in this passage in *Political Economy*:

> If children are brought up in common in the bosom of equality; if they are imbued with the laws of the state and the precepts of the general will . . . if they are surrounded by examples and objects which constantly remind them of the tender mother who nourishes them, or the love she bears them, of the inestimable benefits they receive from her and of the return they owe her, we cannot doubt that they will learn to cherish one another mutually as brothers ... and become in time defenders and fathers of the country of which they have been for so long the children. (OC, 3:261)

In *Emile*, the authentic nuclear family acted as an incubator of civic attachment: "as if it were not through the little fatherland that is the family that one's heart becomes attached to the great one; as if it were not the good son, the good husband, the good father who makes the good citizen" (OC, 4:700). In *Political Economy*, by contrast, the state appropriated that role for itself, crossing the boundary of the family as an affective community.

The state may have taken on the educational and affective roles of families, but the family still retained an economic role. In essence, Rousseau returned to the idea of family narrowly construed as economic entity (OC, 3:241). Rousseau, unlike Plato, did not take the step of eliminating private property. He admitted that a society ruled by the General Will could choose to do so, but nonetheless, he himself still believed that private property constituted a key element of social stability. In the *Political Economy*, the one role Rousseau did not transfer to the state was the family's role in property inheritance. There was less contention, less room for social unrest, where property was passed down through families (OC, 3:263–64).

In moving away from the ideal and toward the practical to sketch out a plan of government for Poland, Rousseau acknowledged that practical constraints might limit the application of what was so desirable in theory. As he pointed out in the *Social Contract*, plans needed to be tailored to the specific context (*Social Contract*, 163; OC, 3:393). Some Polish parents, he realized, might resist turning the task of education over to the state. Rousseau bent somewhat to this potential pressure but still required, at minimum, that parents send their children to public exercises.

In the Polish case, Rousseau still saw his goal as reaching hearts, and making them love the fatherland (OC, 3:955). Just how early this task would begin became clear in the plan for Poland, in which Rousseau suggested that "when he first opens his eyes, an infant ought to see the fatherland and up to the day of his death he ought never to see anything else . . . he should drink love of country with his mother's milk" (OC, 3:966).

In this work, he even suggested creating a specific status for scholarship children: "children of the state" for offspring of those who had served the state well (OC, 3:967). He criticized other reformers who relied on coercion and punishment and instead saw the value of using children's games as tools to "move the hearts of men and make them love the fatherland and its laws" (OC, 3:955). He exhorted his readers to "have many public games where the good mother country is pleased to see her children at play. Let her pay frequent attention to them, that they may pay constant attention to her" (OC, 3:962). Later, when men reached adulthood, they should practice drilling with arms; these drills should take place in front of their families and the people (OC, 3:1016). While Rousseau thus acknowledged a role for the family, that role was shared with the general public. Furthermore, Rousseau left no doubt that the public's judgment was to be preferred to the approbation of family members, as his advice to the legislators was to "arrange things so that all citizens will feel themselves to be incessantly under the public eye, that no one will advance or succeed save by favor of the public . . . all shall be so dependent on public esteem that nothing can be done, nothing acquired, no success obtained without it" (OC, 3:1019).

As Rousseau approached his ideal political association the family role shrank, for as he once noted, "The better the state is constituted, the more does public rather than private business preoccupy the minds of citizens. The amount of private business will ever be greatly reduced for the aggregate of common happiness will constitute a larger fraction of the happiness of each individual and he will therefore have less happiness to seek on his own account" (OC, 3:492).

If, as Rousseau suggested, the similarity between family and state consisted in the common obligation of the head of each to make members happy, then as the state approached perfection, and thereby accounted for a greater share of the happiness of each individual, the task of the family ought to shrink proportionally. If the task of the family shrank, what became of women? There was, of course, the model of the Spartan woman, more interested in the outcome of a battle than in the fate of her sons. Yet Rousseau was not very comfortable with that alternative. He was sure that a withdrawn life nurturing husband and family and serving as a guardian of morals was the right life for a woman. But that worked well only in his Golden Age solution. What happened to women when the state became the common mother of its citizens? What happened to women when the state took on the role of caregiver, nurturing and educating its citizen children? Plato responded to the questions by making citizens of women; Rousseau avoided the issue. When the state became more involved in a politics of care, women dropped out of view.

Notes

1. Carol Gilligan, In a Different Voice: Psychological Theory and Women's Development (Cambridge: Harvard University Press, 1982).

2. Lawrence Kohlberg, Essays in Moral Development, 2 vols. (New York: Harper and Row, 1981–84). For an extensive bibliography of literature on Kohlberg's work, see James S. Leming, Foundations of Moral Education: An Annotated Bibliography (Westport, Conn.: Greenwood Press, 1983).

3. Nancy Chodorow, The Reproduction of Mothering: Psychoanalysis and the Sociology of Gender (Berkeley and Los Angeles: University of California Press, 1978).

4. One rough-and-ready indicator of a work's influence is the number of times it is cited in other works. A quick look at The Social Science Citation Index (SSCI) gives a sense of the huge impact both these works have had. The SSCI records 1,957 references to Kuhn's Structure of Scientific Revolution from its date of publication through 1982 and 5,406 from 1983 to 1996. Gilligan's In a Different Voice has been cited 3,049 times from publication to 1996.

5. Susan Moller Okin, Justice, Gender, and the Family (New York: Basic Books, 1989).

6. Susan Moller Okin, "Reason and Feeling in Thinking about Justice," Ethics 99 (January 1989): 234ff.

7. Joan Tronto, Moral Boundaries: A Political Argument for an Ethic of Care (New York: Routledge, 1993).

8. Jean-Jacques Rousseau, Confessions, in The Collected Writings of Rousseau, ed. Christopher Kelly, Roger Masters, and Peter Stillman, vol. 5 (Hanover: University Press of New England, 1995), 6; for the French, see the Pleiade edition: Rousseau, Oeuvres complètes, ed. Bernard Gagnebin and

Marcel Raymond (Geneva: Editions Gallimard, 1964–95), 1:7. *Oeuvres complètes* will be cited as OC.

9. Annette Baier, "Trust and Anti-Trust," *Ethics* 96 (January 1986): 247. The word omitted from Baier's phrase is "misogynist," a description often applied to Rousseau—but one which also continues to spark controversy among readers of Rousseau.

10. John Hill Burton, *Life and Correspondence of David Hume*, vol. 2 (New York: Burt Franklin, 1967; originally published Edinburgh, 1846), 313–14.

11. Burton, *Life and Correspondence of David Hume*, 314–15.

12. Rousseau, *Rousseau: Judge of Jean-Jacques: Dialogues*, in *The Collected Writings of Rousseau*, ed. Christopher Kelly, Roger Masters, and Peter Stillman (Hanover: University Press of New England, 1995), 1:657ff.

13. Rousseau, *Discourse on the Origin and Foundations of Inequality Among Men*, in *The Collected Writings of Rousseau*, ed. Christopher Kelly, Roger Masters, and Peter Stillman (Hanover: University Press of New England, 1995), 3:23; OC, 3:138.

14. Other works that include discussions of care could be added to this list—the *Letter to D'Alembert*, for example.

15. Jean Jacques Rousseau, *Emile*, in OC, IV:699–700.

16. The two societies are roughly equivalent to what I have described here as two different solutions. Judith Shklar, *Men and Citizens: A Study of Rousseau's Social Theory* (Cambridge: Cambridge University Press, 1969, 1985).

17. Shklar, *Men and Citizens*, xii.

18. Shklar, *Men and Citizens*, 193.

19. Rousseau, *The Social Contract*, in *The Collected Writings of Rousseau*, ed. Christopher Kelly, Roger Masters, and Peter Stillman (Hanover: University Press of New England, 1995), 4:132; OC, III:352.

20. Other commentators have recognized a greater resemblance between state and family. Marshall Berman has previously described Rousseau's political ideal as a "maternal state." See *The Politics of Authenticity* (New York: Atheneum, 1970), 203. Lynda Lange cited the mother-child bond as the basis for all affective relations including those between citizens and the state. See "Rousseau and Modern Feminism" in Carole Pateman and Molly Shanley, eds., *Feminist Interpretations in Political Theory* (Oxford: Polity Press, 1990), 105. Susan Okin spotted several ways in which Rousseau's ideal state acquired the attributes of a family. See *Women in Western Political Thought* (Princeton: Princeton University Press, 1979), 187–88.

21. Where Rousseau did not follow Plato concerned economic arrangements. Property remained private and the family retained an important role in this connection.

10

Rousseau's Phallocratic Ends

Sarah Kofman

Translated by Mara Dukats

Everybody knows it: Rousseau is very free in calling on Nature, on good Mother Nature. It's always in Her name that he couches his claims. Just as he identifies with his mother who died bringing him into the world;[1] and just as he attempts to supplant that one indispensable woman,[2] to bring her back to life by himself becoming woman and mother;[3] so in the same way he tries to speak in the place of Nature, the mother of us all, the Nature who is not dead even though her cries have been muffled by the philosophy fashionable in the cities, that is, by an artificial and falsifying culture.[4] It appears that Rousseau alone, in this depraved century, has understood her voice, and has rushed to the rescue in order to protect her from the fashionable philosophers, who have joined forces with those citified and denatured women, women in name only, for they have become dolls and puppets, and have decked themselves out as a bastard sex. They are no longer women since they deny their one and only natural destiny: childbearing. Therefore, it is necessary to resuscitate and disseminate nature's suppressed voice, reminding these "women" of their one and only duty: motherhood. "Women have ceased to be mothers; they no longer will be mothers; they no longer want to be mothers."⁵ The family and the whole moral order of society depend on this duty. "As soon as women become mothers again men will quickly become fathers and husbands" (*Emile*, 48). This single but fundamental duty thus has multiple implications. Rousseau claims to deduce from it the entire temperament, the entire physical and moral constitution of women, as well as an entire educational program. For, in order to conform to nature, the education of women would have to differ radically from that of men.

Thus, natural teleology alone would legitimate all the inequalities of development, all the dissymmetries attributed to sexual difference. However, insofar as these dissymmetries favor the masculine sex, as they always do, we might wonder if good Mother Nature doesn't serve as a mere pretext here, if the ends of Nature don't in fact dissimulate the ends of man (*vir*), rationalizing his injustices and violences.

Several of Rousseau's texts come close to acknowledging this. In the "Entretien sur les romans" ("Reflections on the Novel"), which precedes the second edition of *La Nouvelle Héloïse* (The New Héloïse), he writes: "Let us give women their due: the cause of their disorder is less in themselves than in our faulty institutions." In "Sur les femmes" ("On Women"), his unfinished essay on the "Evénements importants dont les femmes ont été la cause secrète" ("Important events of which women were the secret cause"), Rousseau accuses men of having prevented women from governing and thereby, from doing everything that they could have done in politics, morals, and literature. In all areas of life, the law of the strongest has enabled men to exercise a veritable tyranny over women, preventing them from evincing their true virtues.

> Relatively speaking, women would have been able to present more and better examples of noble-mindedness and love of virtue than men, had our injustice not deprived them of their liberty, and of the opportunity to manifest these qualities to the world . . . [I]f women had had as large a share as we've had in handling affairs and governing empires, they might have carried heroism and cour-

age to greater heights and more of them might have distinguished themselves in this regard.[6]

Rousseau's story "La Reine fantasque" ("The Capricious Queen") shows, in a comic vein, how men always exclude women from power. They prefer the stupidest man, even an animal, "a monkey or a wolf," to the wisest woman, since they think women should always be subject to men's will.

It is probably not just a coincidence that such writings remained unfinished, are considered "minor" and are usually ignored. Rousseau usually adopts a very different language, a language of Nature which partakes of the most traditional phallocratic discourse.[7] This is especially the case in *Lettre à d'Alembert* and *Emile*, where he is "hardest" on women, as opposed to *La Nouvelle Héloïse* where he adopts a more conciliatory tone.[8] Thus, at the very moment when he claims to speak in the name of Nature, to oppose the "philosophers" and their prejudices, he can only repeat the most hackneyed and symptomatically masculinist philosophical discourse. For example, that of Aristotle, who also claimed, of course, to write neutrally and objectively and to found an intellectual, moral, and political hierarchy on a natural ontological hierarchy. At the top of this hierarchy is divinity, followed by the philosopher and men in general. As for woman, she ranks below the child of the masculine sex, for whereas he is male in potentiality, if not yet in actuality, she remains branded throughout her entire life with an "indelible inferiority" because of her sex. She is and always will be a "mutilated male," even a "monster," a flaw of nature, a male manqué.

Rousseau repeats the discourse of Aristotle as well as that of the Bible, which, although it stems from another tradition, is no less phallocentric.

So, in Book V of *Emile*, he purports to provide a rational deduction of the temperament, constitution, duties, and education of women. A sophistic argument, actually, in which the pseudo-voice of Nature becomes the vehicle for the expression of Rousseau's prejudices. It is significant that the question of women and their education is not approached until Book V. In the dramatic fiction of *Emile*, women are granted only one act of the play, the last one. This gesture is emblematic of the subordination of woman—the weak sex, the second sex—to the strong sex—the sole referent and prototype for humanity. It reenacts the gesture of divine creation in which the first woman is made from the rib of the first man, in which she is derived from him and is created *for* him. "It is not good for man to be alone; I shall make for him a companion similar to him" (*Genesis* II, 8). "It is not good that man be alone. Emile is a man; we promised him a companion; now we must give her to him" (*Emile*, 465).

As a pedagogical novel, *Emile* sets out to re-create women so as to perfect and improve upon divine creation. An appropriate education, one in conformity with nature, should beget the sort of woman who can now only be found in some mythical natural preserve, untouched by civilization—a wise and perfect woman, Sophie, a woman who knows how to stay within the limits Nature has assigned to her, in the place befitting her sex, subordinate to man, the one and only king of creation. Rousseau takes Sophie, not Eve or Lilith, as this model woman. Certainly not those corrupt and seductive Parisian women who are the source of all of men's woes, those women who have failed to respect the natural hierarchy between the sexes, who have abandoned their place and their reserve, who have aspired to Knowledge, and who have not hesitated to show themselves in public and to mix with the other sex. According to Rousseau, all disorders, abuses, and perversions originate in the "scandalous confusion" of the sexes.

Thus, Rousseau, in his divine magnanimity, gives Emile a companion and a helpmeet "made for him" but not "similar to him." No, she must certainly not be "similar to him," and it will be up to education to see to that, on pain of the direst disasters. For if it is true that "in everything not having to do with sex, the woman is a man," and that she contains within herself a divine model just like he does, it is no less true that "in everything that does have to do with sex, . . . man and woman always have both similarities and dissimilarities" (*Emile*, 465–66). Thus, if it is to fulfill its natural destiny in the physical and moral order, each sex must be subject to its own sex-specific model. "A perfect man and a perfect woman must no more resemble each other in mind than in face, and there is no such thing as being more or less perfect" (*Emile*, 466).

Although in *Genesis*, woman's name (*icha*) derives from that of man (*ich*), Rousseau is careful not to derive the name of the perfect woman from that of the perfect man. Her name is not Emilie, but Sophie. In his overt discourse, he never claims to establish any derivation or hierarchy, only differences. Neither sex is to be superior to the other, nor even comparable to the other. Each is to be perfect of its own kind, incomparable to the other insofar as they differ, equal to the other insofar as they are similar. If each remained in the place nature assigned to it, perfect harmony and happiness would reign, just like at Clarens. The two sexes would then be like a single person: "Woman would be the eye and man the arm. They would be so dependent on one another that woman would learn from man what should be seen and man would learn from woman what must be done. . . . Each would follow the impetus of the other; each would obey and both would be masters" (*Emile*, 492).

Although, shades of Aristotle, the temperaments, tastes, inclinations, tasks, and duties of the two sexes vary as a function of their respective natural destinies, they nonetheless "participate in a common happiness" albeit by different routes (*Emile*, 466). "This division of labor and of responsibilities is the strongest aspect of their union."9

"Common happiness," he says. Yet this alleged equality surely conceals a profound hierarchical inequality, a profound unhappiness which can only be interpreted as happiness if one postulates that women enjoy sub-ordination, subjection, and docility. And in fact, Rousseau does not recoil from asserting this. Following Aristotle, he contends that women are made to obey. "Since dependence is women's natural condition, girls feel they are made to obey" (*Emile*, 482).

The rigid segregation of sexes and the sexual division of labor result in the extensive confinement of women. In the name of their natural des-tiny, they are condemned to a sedentary and reclusive life in the shadows of domestic enclosure. There they are excluded from knowledge and pub-lic life. The latter are reserved for men who are destined for the active life, life in the open air and in the sun. Thus Rousseau, as early as Book I of *Emile*, deems that, if a man were to engage in "a typical stay-at-home and sedentary occupation" like sewing or some other "needle trade," he would be reduced to a cripple or a eunuch because these occupations "feminize and weaken the body." They "dishonor the masculine sex" for "the needle and the sword cannot be wielded by the same hands." (More-over, in Book V, Hercules, forced to spin near Omphale, is deemed, de-spite his strength, to be dominated by a woman.)

How, then, does Rousseau justify the domestic lot of women and their confinement? He claims to ground these in the feminine temperament as he deduced it, in the most natural way, in the beginning of Book V: "In the union of the sexes, each contributes equally to the common goal, but not in the same manner. From this diversity comes the first major differ-ence between our moral relation to the one and to the other. One should be active and strong, the other passive and weak. It follows that the one should be willing and able; that the other should not resist too much" (*Emile*, 466).

And it seems obvious that it is the woman who must be passive and weak and not the reverse. So obvious, in fact, that only the authority of Aristotle can guarantee it. "Once this principle is established,"—but is it?—it would follow naturally that woman's specific function is to please man and to be subjugated. From that, in turn, it would follow that woman should "resist" his advances in order to be agreeable to man and to arouse his strength. Man, however, turns out not to be that strong since an elaborate feminine strategy is required to actualize his potentiality, to awaken the flames of a rather feeble fire.

Hence the audacity of the masculine sex and the timidity of the other sex, "the modesty and the shame with which Nature armed the weak in order to subjugate the strong" (*Emile*, 467).

Timidity, modesty, decency, or again, reserve and a sense of shame (*pudeur*). These are the natural virtues, the cardinal virtues, of women. This premise is essential to Rousseau's argument. From it he infers—not without a certain slippage—the necessity of confining women. From their pseudo-natural reserve he deduces their forcible relocation to a reservation.

Here, a sense of shame is cast as a brake given to the feminine sex in order to make up for the animal instinct it lacks, an instinct which naturally moderates animals' sexual avidity. Once "the cargo is loaded" and "the hold is full," female animals reject their mates. Human women, by contrast, can never get enough, and if it were not for this sense of shame, they would pursue these poor men to their deaths. For although men are held to be the strong and active sex, they have no real sexual need; whereas women, supposedly the weak and passive sex, have a lust which knows no bounds.[10]

> Given the facility women have for exciting men's senses and for awakening, deep in their hearts, the remnants of a most feeble disposition, if there existed some unfortunate climate on earth where philosophy might have introduced a practice [whereby women initiate aggression], especially in hot climates where more women than men are born, men would be women's victims, tyrannized by them, and they would all end up dragged to their death without any means of defense. (*Emile*, 467)

Nature would thus have granted women a supplement of shame not so much to compensate for their weakness as to compel man to "find his strength and use it," that is, in order to give him the illusion that he is the strongest. The point is not so much to prevent the downfall of both sexes and to save the human race, although without this feminine reserve the species would "perish by the means established to preserve it" (*Emile*, 467). It is rather, above all, to save the male sex. This whole economy of shame is aimed at sparing the male some loss or narcissistic wound.

If it were indeed "Nature" that had "given" women a sense of shame, then the generosity of Nature would be entirely at the service of man. But is this sense of shame really a gift of Nature? Doesn't Nature's generosity rather serve as a pretext and a cover for the phallocratic aim of Rousseau's discourse? The demonstration of the natural character of shame, whether in *Emile* or in *Lettre à d'Alembert*, is highly shaky. In vain does Rousseau multiply his arguments and respond to the *philosphes'* objections; he remains caught in a web of sophisms. Thus, in *Lettre à d'Alembert*, he tries to show that, contrary to the fashionable option of the *philosophes*, shame is not a prejudice but a natural virtue. Natural because necessary to the sexual economy of the two sexes! Necessary to preserve feminine charm so that man can be sexually aroused without ever being fully satisfied. The sense of shame, then, would be the natural veil that introduces a beneficial distance into the economy. It would be the shared safeguard that Nature provided for the sake of both sexes in order that they not be subject to indiscriminate advances when in a "state of weakness and self-forgetfulness." It would be the sense of shame that hides the pleasures of love from the eyes of others, just as the shade of night conceals and protects sexual relationships.

But why, if it is a matter of a shared safeguard, is it woman who must have a sense of shame? Why, if it is a matter of natural virtue, is there a difference between human and animal behavior?

Pushed into a corner, Rousseau responds to the first objection with a true *petitio principii*: only Nature, the Maker of the human race, could answer this, since it is She who has endowed woman, and only woman, with this sentiment. Then, taking the place of Nature, identifying himself with Her, as always, Rousseau tries to supply the natural reasons for this difference: both sexes have equal desires, but they don't have equal means to satisfy these. If the order of advance and defense were changed, then chance would rule. Love would no longer be the support of Nature, but its destroyer and its bane.

Equal liberty of the two sexes, by overcoming every obstacle, would suppress amorous desire.

Finally, and above all, shame is reserved for woman because the consequences are not the same for the two sexes: "A child must have *one*
father."

Because women's proper destiny is to bear children (even if they don't
always do so), because the lot of women is motherhood, Nature and manners must provide for this by general laws such as that of shame. In *Émile*
it is this same "lot" of women which justifies the view that the duty of
conjugal fidelity, and that of a reputation for fidelity, fall upon women
only. It is on women that Nature has conferred exclusive responsibility
for protecting natural family ties; it is to women that Nature has confided
the sacred trust of children: "when a woman gives a man children who
are not his own, she betrays both of them, she combines perfidy with
infidelity." All "disorders" and "crimes" are linked with this one. Thus,
a woman must be "modest, attentive and reserved"; she must display to
the eyes of the world the "evidence of her virtue" so that children can
esteem and respect their mothers. "Honor and reputation are no less
necessary than chastity."[11]

It is indeed Nature, then, who intended to adorn women with the veil
of shame and it is a crime to stifle Her voice. Once this constraint is
removed, women will cease to have any reticence whatever. Woman can't
attach any importance to honor, she can't respect anything anymore, if
she doesn't respect her own honor.[12] Just look, says *Emile*, at Ninon de
Lenclos!

Experience would confirm this reasoning: the closer women are to
their natural state, the more susceptible they are to shame. Don't think
that the nakedness of savage women disproves this, for it is not the sign
of an absence of shame. On the contrary, it is clothing that arouses the
senses by exciting the imagination. As pointed out in *Emile*, nakedness,
that of children, for example, is always a sign of innocence. Lacedaemon-
ian maidens used to dance naked: this is a scandal only for depraved
modern man.

> Do we really believe that the skillful finery of our women is less
> dangerous than an absolute nakedness which, if habitual, would
> soon turn first impressions into indifference, maybe even into dis-
> gust! Don't we know that statues and paintings offend our eyes
> only when the combination of clothes renders nakedness ob-
> scene? The greatest ravages occur when imagination steps in.[13]

Do not assume, however, that Rousseau condemns clothing and finery. On the contrary, they are necessary in order that woman preserve her charm, that she continue to excite man's imagination. In this sense, "clothing" is part of sexual strategy. It is in the service of shame and its ends. The taste for finery, ornament, mirrors, and jewels is part of feminine nature. A girl "has more hunger for finery than for food" (*Emile*, 479).

In this argument, aimed at demonstrating the natural character of shame, clothing has a complex function and plays a strategic rôle. Rousseau still has to justify the difference between human and animal behavior with respect to shame. At this point, he resorts to a true "cauldron argument."[14]

On the one hand, man is precisely not an ordinary animal like any other; he alone is capable of conceiving of honesty and of beauty. On the other hand, animals are more susceptible to shame than one would think, even though they too, like children, are naked. . . . In any case, even if we grant to d'Alembert and the other *philosophes* that shame is not a natural sentiment but, rather, a conventional virtue, the same essential consequence remains: women ought to cultivate the virtues of shame and timidity. Their lot is to lead a secluded domestic life, a life hidden in a cloister-like retreat. Woman should not be showy nor should she put herself on show. Her home is her ornament; she is its soul. Her place is not in public. For her to appear there is to usurp man's place and to debase him, to degrade both her sex and his.

If you object that Rousseau imprisons women in the home, that he demands from them an excessive reserve, he will respond like Lucrèce to Pauline: "Do you call the sweetness of a peaceful life in the bosom of one's family a prison? As for me, my happiness needs no other society, my glory needs no other esteem, than that of my husband, my father and my children."[15]

It's no coincidence that, when Rousseau does concede that shame might be a cultural prejudice, there is a slide in his logic. He slides from an insistence on women's reticence to a demand for female seclusion, from feminine reserve to the confinement of the feminine on a reservation. In this slippage Rousseau repeats a familiar social operation of masculine domination. Under the pretext of giving back Nature her suppressed voice and of defending Nature's ends, what is really being advocated, as always, are the phallocratic ends of man. It is the voice of man (*vir*)—stifled by women, those wicked and degenerate women—that Rousseau restores.

These maxims, these natural or conventional maxims which demand the isolation and domestic confinement of women, would be doubly confirmed by experience: wherever women are free, low morals are rampant; conversely, wherever morals are regulated, women are confined and separated from men. This separation of the sexes is necessary for their pleasure and their union. Indeed, there is no union without separation. Every communication, every commerce between the sexes is indiscreet, every familiarity is suspect, every liaison dangerous! Thus, it is in order to insure a lasting bond between them that Emile is separated from Sophie. Thus, the "admirable" order maintained by Julie at Clarens is based on the separation of the sexes. In this well-run domestic economy, there is little commerce between men and women. They live apart from one another like men and women everywhere, be they civilized or savage. The very universality of this practice proves its conformity to nature. "Even among savages, men and women are never seen indiscriminately mixed. In the evening the family gathers, every man spends the night with his woman; the separation resumes with the light of day and the two sexes have nothing but meals, at the most, in common."[16]

Lettre à d'Alembert privileges the people of Antiquity (for they are the closest to nature): Rome and Sparta would be the best models of this admirable domestic economy where, when men and women do see each other, "it is very briefly and almost secretly."[17]

Thus, nothing justifies the natural character of shame, the slippage from feminine reserve to the confinement of the feminine on a reservation, and the strict segregation of the sexes, unless it is Rousseau's phallocratic aim. But isn't the latter itself based on Rousseau's libidinal economy, on a certain paranoiac structure? Isn't it based on his desire to be confused with women, and at the same time, on his fear of being contaminated by women, the very women to whom he feels himself so very close? Isn't it this very proximity which compels him to erect barriers, to emphasize the differences and the separations? Consider the passage in *Lettre à d'Alembert* where, for once, Rousseau declares that if women are brave enough they should, like Spartan women, imitate the masculine model. This passage is symptomatic of his desire/fear of becoming woman. It shows that this whole discourse is motivated by that desire/fear. Now we see what is really at stake in the segregation of sexes: the point is not so much to avoid the general confusion of the sexes; it is rather to avoid the contamination of the masculine by the feminine and a general effeminization. "Among barbaric peoples, men did not live like women because women had the courage to live like men. In Sparta, women became robust and man was not enervated. . . . Unable to make themselves men, women make us women, [a frightening perversion, degradation, and denaturation] especially in a Republic where men are needed."

The thesis that Rousseau defends is always already anticipated by his libidinal drives; the voice of Nature is equally the echo of *his* nature. That the singularity of his nature resonates with the universality of traditional philosophic discourse is not an objection to, but rather a proof of, the complicity or, as Freud would say, the secret kinship between philosophic Reason and "paranoiac" madness.[18] On this subject, we must proceed with caution. Let's restrict ourselves here to emphasizing the "kinship" between the apparently non-biographical texts and the *Confessions* or the *Dialogues*.

The "theoretical" insistence on virile mobility and activity is inseparable from Rousseau's fantasies of being suffocated, paralyzed, and imprisoned in the maternal womb. We can read this fantasy when Rousseau describes the doll-woman, the Parisienne, who illegitimately reverses the relation of domination. "[F]ragility, sweetness of voice and delicate features were not given to her in order that she may be offensive, insulting or disfigure herself with anger."[19] Thus, when she assumes the right to command, woman fails to heed the voice of the master; seeking to usurp his rights, she unleashes disorder, misery, scandal, and dishonor. Far from guaranteeing his freedom, the new empire of women enslaves, deforms, and emasculates man. Henceforth, woman confines him in chains in the darkness of her enclosure. Instead of being a mother, of *bringing him into the world*, into the light of day, she tries to keep him in her cave, to put him back into her womb, to *suffocate* him by denying him air and mobility.

Terms like these abound in *Lettre à d'Alembert*, *Emile*, and *La Nouvelle Héloïse*. So "unnatural" and perverse is this stifling and paralyzing "feminine" operation that, even as it feminizes man, it cannot obliterate every "vestige" of his real nature and destiny. His virility reasserts itself in his desire for mobility, in the involuntary agitation and anxiety he experiences whenever woman, by nature sedentary and indolent, reclines tranquilly on a chaise lounge, suffocating him behind the closed doors of some over-stuffed parlor. This, as Rousseau describes in *Lettre à d'Alembert*, is especially true in Paris, where women harbor in their rooms a true seraglio of men (more feminine than masculine) whose automatic instinct struggles incessantly against the bondage they find themselves in and drives them, despite themselves, to the active and painstaking life that nature imposes upon them.

Likewise in the theaters of Paris, "men stand in the orchestra stalls as if wanting to relax after having spent the whole day in a sitting room. Finally, overwhelmed by the ennui of this effeminate and sedentary idleness, and in order to temper their disgust, to involve themselves in at least some sort of activity, they give their places to strangers and go looking for the women of other men."[20]

However, these vestiges of man's former nature are laughable. They express only a half-hearted desire to reclaim his nature. They don't prevent him from dribbling away his strength in the idle and lax life of a sex-junkie, nor from keeping to the "abode and repose of women," where he is enervated and loses his vigor.

Such passages from *Lettre à d'Alembert*, *Emile*, or *La Nouvelle Héloïse*, which depict the sadistic spectacle of the male paralyzed, suffocated, and imprisoned, call to mind certain passages of the *Confessions*. How can one not think, for example, of the passage where Jean-Jacques states that for him to remain seated in a room, arms crossed, inactive, chatting with others, "moving only his tongue," is an "unbearable torture"?[21] How, in general, can one fail to recall Rousseau's claustrophobia, his taste for the outdoor life, his hikes, his disgust at traveling in a poste chaise, which he likens to a small, locked cage where one is bound and blinded, an obscure prison which no free man could tolerate?

> One does not acquire a taste for prison by virtue of residing in one. . . . Active life, manual work, exercise, and movement have become so necessary that man couldn't give them up without suffering. To suddenly reduce him to an indolent and sedentary life would be to imprison him, to put him in chains, to keep him in a violent and constrained state. No doubt his disposition and health would be equally altered. He can scarcely breathe in a stuffy room. He needs the open air, movement, and fatigue . . . ; he is disturbed and agitated; he seems to be struggling; he stays because he is in chains. (*Emile*, 567–68)

These are the words of Emile's private tutor. But they betray all the fantasies of Jean-Jacques as endlessly repeated in the *Dialogues*: his fear, his horror of the dark, the belief that his persecutors have surrounded him with a "triple enclosure of darkness," entombed him behind impenetrable walls of darkness; his fantasy of being weighed down with chains, of being unable to say a word, take a step, move a finger without the knowledge and permission of his enemies; of being enclosed in an immense labyrinth where tortuous and subterranean false paths lead him further and further astray; and finally, the fantasy of being buried alive. All of these persecution fantasies express not only horror but also desire: the desire "to be beaten." Caught in the grip of his persecutors, he barely tries to escape. Surrounded by falsity and darkness, he waits, without a murmur of protest, for truth and light. Finally, buried alive in a coffin, he lies still, not even thinking of death. Is this the tranquility of innocence? Or the tranquility of masochistic pleasure at being punished, immobilized, possessed like a woman and by women, the pleasure of being suffocated and humiliated by women, of being made into their thing, their property?

In the *Confessions*, we learn that the episode with Mlle Lambercier determined the shape of the remainder of Jean-Jacques' love life. Her severity was for him a thousand times sweeter than her favors would ever have been. She treated him "as a thing that belonged to her," possessing him as one possesses private property. Their encounter becomes a prototype: to kneel before an imperious mistress, obeying her orders, begging her forgiveness—these always remain very sweet pleasures for him. Mlle Goton, who deigns to act the school mistress, showers him with joy. On his knees before Mme Basile, silent and still, afraid to do or say anything, Jean-Jacques finds this state ludicrous but delightful. "Nothing I ever experienced in possessing a woman could rival the two minutes I spent at her feet without even daring to touch her dress."[22] It's the same with Sophie d'Houdetot who, for six months, floods his heart with a delight he defies any mere sensualist to match. "Am I not your possession? Have you not taken possession?" he writes to her.[23]

Now, all of these captivating women, these castrating women, are also maternal figures, figures of and substitutes for the mother who died bringing him into the light of day. It is perhaps in order to still the reproaches for this death "which cannot be atoned," that Rousseau effects an inversion. Man will no longer be the cause of the death of women or mothers. Rather, women will be responsible for the death of man. By refusing motherhood, refusing to put themselves entirely at his service, to be filled with pity and tenderness for him, women will be responsible for his degeneration, perversion, emasculation, and depropriation. This masterful inversion displaces all aggression onto the "dolls." At the same time, it preserves, or rather constructs and internalizes, the image, intact and pure, of an idealized and divine Mother, a Mother who could only be the best of mothers—even if she nearly suffocated him in her womb, causing him to be born "disabled and sickly."

Thus, there is a split between two mother figures—the whore and the Virgin—between public women unafraid to trespass the domestic enclosure (the comediennes, the Dolls, the prostitutes, the Parisiennes, all "public women" in Rousseau's eyes) and the women who live within the shadow of the enclosure, the respectable Mothers, surrounded by their husbands and children (can there be a more pleasing sight?). This split suggests that the phallocraticism of Rousseau is also, as always, a *feminism*.

The sense of shame, whose corollary is the enclosure of women, is in effect responsible for the "natural" inversion of domination: through it, the strongest become dependent on the weakest, the weakest truly rule over the strongest. The respectable woman, reserved and chaste, the woman who knows her place, incites a love which verges on enthusiasm, on sublime transports of emotion. Admittedly, she does not govern, but she reigns. She is a queen, an idol, a goddess. With a simple sign or word she sends men to the ends of the world, off to combat and to glory, here, there, wherever she pleases. A note in *Emile* cites the case of a woman who, during the reign of François I, imposed a vow of strict silence upon her garrulous lover. For two-and-a-half years he kept it faithfully. "One thought that he had become mute through illness. She cured him with a single word: speak! Isn't there something grand and heroic in such love? Doesn't one imagine a divinity giving the organ of speech to a mortal with a single word?" (*Emile*, 515).

The empire of women—these women, the "true" women, the respectable mothers—is not feared by men because it doesn't debase them. On the contrary, it enables them to fulfill their duties, to prove their heroism and their virility. For men, there is "no sweeter" or more respected "empire." If only women really wanted to be women and mothers, their uncontested power would be immense. Mothers, "be all that you should be and you will overcome all obstacles."[24]

Women are thus wrong to demand equal rights and the same education as men. If they aspire to become men, they can only fail. They would surely be inferior men and in the bargain they would lose the essential thing—the empire in which they naturally reign.

Obviously, this reign is conditional upon women's natural qualities, their submission, docility, and gentleness. It is given to them on the condition that, from childhood on, they be schooled in constraints and permanent discomforts, since their "natural state" is to be dependent, to be subjected to man and at the service of man.

Since men are, from the beginning, dependent on women, the education of women must be relative to men. Here in a nutshell is the sophism.

> The formation of children depends on the formation of mothers, the first education of men depends on the care of women; the manners, passions, tastes, pleasures and even happiness of men depends on women. Thus the entire education of women must be relative to men. To please men, to be useful to them, to be loved and honored by them, to raise them when they are young, care for them when they are grown-up, to console them, to make their lives agreeable and gentle—these are the duties of women in all times and this is what they must be taught from childhood. Unless we return to this principle, we will stray from the goal, and all of the precepts we give to women will serve neither their happiness nor our own. (*Emile*, 475)

No confession could be clearer: he who claims always to "follow the directions of Nature," is really following the best of guides. In fulfilling his own "nature" to the maximum, he serves the interests and ends of man (*vir*).

Notes

1. "I was born disabled and sickly; I cost my mother her life, and my birth was the first of my misfortunes." *Confessions*, éd. Livre de Poche, t. I, 8. This and all other translations of Rousseau are my own—M. D.

2. On the death of Julie's mother he writes in *La Nouvelle Héloïse*, Part III, Letter VI: "a loss which cannot be restored and for which one never finds consolation once one has been able to reproach oneself for it." And in *Emile*, Book I: "Maternal solicitude cannot be supplied."

3. See S. Kofman, *Le Respect des femmes*, Galilée, 1980.

4. See, for example, *Lettre à d'Alembert*, "At this very instant the short-lived philosophy that is born and dies in the corner of a great city, this philosophy that seeks to suppress the cry of Nature and the unanimous voice of humankind is going to rise up against me." ["à l'instant va s'élever contre moi, cette philosophie d'un jour . . . (Garnier-Flammarion, 168)], and further: "Thus it was willed by nature, it is a crime to suppress her voice" ["Ainsi l'a voulu la Nature, . . . 171)].

5. *Emile*, éd. Garnier-Flammarion, 48. All page numbers in this text for *Emile* refer to the Garnier-Flammarion edition. Translations are my own—M. D.

6. "*Sur les femmes*" in *Oeuvres complètes*, Pléiade, t. II, 1255.

7. One could find this contrast between "major" and "minor" texts, between texts of "youth" and those of "maturity" in other philosophers. This is the case with Auguste Comte, another phallocrat, whose early letter to Valet, dating from Sept. 24, 1819, espouses a position which will later be that of his adversary, John Stuart Mill. See S. Kofman: *Aberrations, le devenir-femme d'A. Comte* (Aubier-Flammarion, 230 and following).

8. See Kofman, *Le Respect des femmes*, Galilée, 1980.

9. *La Nouvelle Héloïse*, Part IV, Letter X.

10. The Rousseauistic description is the opposite of that of Freud for whom libido is essentially "masculine." See Kofman, *The Enigma of Woman*, Cornell University Press, 1985. Despite this difference, both appeal to the same "Nature" to justify the sexual subjugation of women, the essential point of the whole argument.

11. *Emile*, 470–71. See also *La Nouvelle Héloïse*, Part II, Letter XVIII, where Julie writes to Saint-Preux about the married woman: "She not only invested her faith, but alienated her freedom. (. . .) It is not enough to be honest, it is necessary that she be honored; it is not enough to do only what is good, it is necessary that she refrain from doing anything that isn't approved. A virtuous woman must not only merit the esteem of her husband, but obtain it. If he blames her, she is blameful; and if she were to be innocent, she is wrong as soon as she is suspect—for appearance itself counts as one of her duties."

12. Lucrèce, who preferred death to the loss of honor, is quoted by Rousseau as being among the heroines comparable and superior to male heroes. (See "*Sur les femmes*" and *La Mort de Lucrèce*, O.C., II).

13. *Lettre à d'Alembert*, éd. Garnier-Flammarion, 246.

14. See Nancy Holland's "Introduction" to the volume of *Hypatia* in which this essay appeared, for an explanation of this reference to "cauldron" logic (tr.).

15. *La Mort de Lucrèce*.

16. *La Nouvelle Héloïse*, Part IV, Letter X.

17. It would be interesting and very enlightening to compare Rousseau's discourse on decency with that of Montesquieu in *L'Esprit des lois* (Books XVI, X, XI, XX). In particular, one would find clarification for the allusion to warm countries where climate renders feminine sexual avidity fearsome. Montesquieu overtly grounds decency and the domestic confinement of women in the sexual danger that these represent for men in warm countries. In contrast, where climate is temperate, it is unnecessary to confine women. Men can "communicate" with them for the pleasure and "entertainment" of both men and women.

18. See *De l'intérêt de la psychanalyse;* in *Aberrations, le devenir-femme d' A. Comte* (Aubier-Flammarion, 1978) Kofman offers a detailed analysis of the possible relationships between a philosopher's delirium and his philosophical system.

19. *Emile*, Book V.

20. *La Nouvelle Héloïse*, Part IV, Letter X.

21. *Confessions*, Book XII.

22. For Mlle Lambercier, see Book I and *L'Ebauche des Confessions*, 13. For Mlle Goton, Book I. For Mme Basile, Book II.

23. Letter of October 15, 1757.

24. *La Nouvelle Héloïse*, Part V, Letter 111.

11

Rousseau's Subversive Women

Lori J. Marso

It is possible that there are in the world a few women worthy of being listened to by a serious man; but, in general, is it from women that he ought to take counsel, and is there no way of honoring their sex without abasing our own?

—Jean-Jacques Rousseau, *Letter to D'Alembert*

Why does Rousseau consider "manliness" to be at risk when women speak? Women's "chatter" is so threatening that we dare not let women voice their ideas in public. Banished from the space where male citizens conduct their serious business, woman is theorized as the ominous presence, the dangerous *supplément*, the remainder: she is the intermediate body against which the male citizen is defined, but she is easily and quickly forgotten.[1]

Or is she? Such an extreme position directs my attention to the women Rousseau describes in his work. If Rousseau's women are safely ensconced at home, why does it remain so difficult for Rousseau's men to forget the feminine? It is almost as if neither male public space *nor* men's confidence in their masculinity is ever totally secure from threat of encroachment by women. What is so dangerous about what women might say? What is it about women's education, women's ways of knowing, the things women like to do, the ways in which women communicate with others that makes the feminine such an immanent threat?

In the argument that follows, I will advance a reading of *Emile* and *La nouvelle Héloïse* that maps Rousseau's attempt to constitute identity in terms of the manly citizen.[2] Rousseau's manly citizen is taught to realize his identity as manifest in the projection of the free will of each as the general will of all. But from the perspective of Rousseau's women, a van-tage point that I will argue Rousseau implicitly invites us to adopt, at-tempts to construct manly citizenship and forge a unanimous general will result in a complete and utter failure of identity. Mapping Rousseau's failure sheds light on the source of his difficulty: the feminine presence as constant disruption, as continual reminder of the inability to efface difference and project each as a coherent and stable self. Focus on this subversive feminine presence points the way toward recognition of an alternative democratic principle at the heart of Rousseau's work.

I

Feminists have rightly criticized the misogynist Rousseau who defines woman as he might like her to be, a mirror opposite of the male image. Susan Okin remarks that Rousseau was "not at all interested in discover-ing what women's natural potential might enable her to achieve, but was simply concerned with suiting her to her role as man's subordinate complement in the patriarchal family."[3] Choosing certain passages that describe Sophie as Emile's perfect mate, Sophie has been typically read as a mouthpiece of masculine desire. One of the first analyses and condemnations of Rousseau's description of woman appears in Mary Wollstonecraft's 1792 *Vindication of the Rights of Woman*. Wollstonecraft singles out Rousseau's description of young girls where he cites their natu-ral inclination towards adornment, being pretty, and being thought pretty:

> Observe a little girl spending the day around her doll, constantly changing its clothes, dressing and undressing it hundreds and hundreds of times, continuously seeking new combinations of or-

naments—well- or ill-matched, it makes no difference. Her fingers lack adroitness, her taste is not yet formed, but already the inclination reveals itself. In this eternal occupation time flows without her thinking of it; the hours pass, and she knows nothing of it. She even forgets meals. She is hungrier for adornment than for food. . . . In fact, almost all little girls learn to read and write with repugnance. But as for holding a needle, that they always learn gladly. They imagine themselves to be grown up and think with pleasure that these talents will one day be useful for adorning themselves. (E, V:367–68)

It seems that here Rousseau is attempting to argue that differences between the sexes are based in nature. Clearly it's a weak attempt; Rousseau did not consider either nature or science to be judicious and reliable determinants for gender difference. At times he readily infers that sexual difference is merely a product of social expediency: women must be seen as chaste to preserve the reputation of their husbands; fathers must think that their children are their own; men and women must be each incomplete in order that they become interdependent. Certain women might claim that women's ways are a direct reflection of the education they've been given by men; Rousseau accuses that it is women *themselves* who teach young girls the art of performing their femininity: "Is it our [men's] fault that they [women] please us when they are pretty, that their mincing ways seduce us, that the art which they learn from you attracts us and pleases us, that we like to see them tastefully dressed, that we let them sharpen at their leisure the weapons with which they subjugate us?" (E, V:363). Wollstonecraft responds that indeed it is, that because Rousseau had his own unruly passions, he placed them onto women in order to justify the men's use of women, both sexually and politically. According to Wollstonecraft: "[Rousseau's] imagination constantly prepared inflammable fuel for his inflammable senses; but, in order to reconcile his respect for self-denial, fortitude, and those heroic virtues, which a mind like his could not coolly admire, he labours to invert the law of nature, and broaches a doctrine pregnant with mischief and derogatory to the character of supreme wisdom."[4] Wollstonecraft reflects that Rousseau not only has got it all wrong but he's got it wrong precisely because his personal desires dictate his "philosophical" reflection: he remarks that women are a certain way (sexually promiscuous and powerful over men and the family) only in order to legitimately deny women any public power and any access to man's world. On this account, Rousseau's remarks on the nature of women are simply a mirror image of his own desires for and about women. This criticism is repeated in Jean Bethke Elshtain's analysis of Rousseau: "Rousseau believed that women already possessed power on so many levels vis-à-vis men and children, simply by virtue of their being what they were, that they neither 'needed' nor could be trusted with power of a public, political sort. Women were volatile and must be reined in, forced to be content to wield their power 'privately.' "[5]

As is clear from Elshtain's comments, Wollstonecraft's early writings on Rousseau's description of femininity have informed subsequent feminist critiques. Rousseau's depiction of the feminine, particularly as embodied in Sophie, his ideal woman, have been deemed a caricature of woman, a truncated version of anything a woman might desire or achieve.[6] Sophie desires only to be a helpmate to Emile. As Rousseau himself puts it: "Thus the whole education of women ought to relate to men. To please men, to be useful to them, to make herself loved and honored by them, to raise them when young, to care for them when grown, to counsel them, to console them, to make their lives agreeable and sweet—these are the duties of women at all times" (E, V:365).

Confirmation of this interpretation of Rousseau whereby the feminine is solely determined by male desire is readily available throughout Rousseau's oeuvre. Countless passages describe women as meek, unquestioning, and quick to please men, desiring solely to admire and serve their husbands/lovers. Rousseau's two well-known descriptions of woman's nature, the dangerous coquette and the subjugated wife, are seemingly just complementary versions of male desire. Men easily master both kinds of women: if masculinity itself has a secure basis, femininity is merely its opposite, able to be manipulated and controlled at man's behest. Yet, if this were the only version of the feminine represented in Rousseau, why would men need to be fearful?

II

Since gender is learned, it is never complete. "Man," "woman," and "citizen" are each fragile constructions in Rousseau's oeuvre. Identity is never as stable as Rousseau desires. The feminine is never quite as contained as he would like it to be. Sustained analysis of the feminine in Rousseau produces a surprising result: Rousseau's women really are subversive of the kind of polity Rousseau seeks to create. Moreover, Rousseau is ever aware of, constantly flirting with, this danger. What is, after all, so dangerous about Sophie? In which ways does she exceed man's imagination, his controllable other? What might her actions reveal about a democratic alternative in Rousseau's politics?

Sophie is educated to be the ideal woman for Emile. Sophie's nature is "good"; she has a "very sensitive heart"; her face is "ordinary but agreeable"; her "expression gives promise of a soul and does not lie; one can approach her with indifference but not leave her without emotion" (E, V:393). As Rousseau describes her, it is the combination of qualities in Sophie that makes her character so appealing; moreover, she even knows how to turn her defects into virtues. For instance, though Sophie has no talent for music and cannot read a note, she has a taste for music that makes her remarkably able to feel the "charms of expression" and "love music for itself" (E, V:394). Although she is a glutton by nature, loving all sweets and tending to eat them excessively, Sophie has learned that sugar spoils her teeth and fattens her figure. Guided by virtue, she eats only very moderate amounts of everything (E, V:395). Although gaiety and spontaneity come naturally to Sophie, if she is seen enjoying herself too readily, she blushes modestly (E, V:396). When her feelings are hurt, which they often are, because of her sensitive heart, Sophie does not pout, but her heart swells. She rushes to get away to cry so as not to burden others with her sadness (E, V:396).

Sophie's knowledge does not derive from books or from intellectual rigor. Her mind has been formed through interactions with others, attention to detail, conversations with her mother and father, her own reflections, and the observations she has made in "the little bit of the world she has seen" (E, V:396). Sophie is not entirely exempt from caprice, but when she falters, her shame stems from the knowledge of the offense she has committed, rather than the punishment exacted (E, V:396). Even if nothing is said to her, she will hasten to make amends for her offense in an attempt to recover her virtue. The "need to love" devours Sophie (E, V:397). Most important, she treats others with respect and commitment. "She would kiss the ground before the lowliest domestic without this abasement causing her the least discomfort . . . in a word, she suffers the wrongs of others with patience and makes amends for their own with pleasure" (E, V:396). So far, this is hardly the description of a dangerous woman. Yet, when we compare ideal woman to ideal man,

Sophie to Emile, we begin to see the ways in which Sophie's art of interaction directly challenges Emile's view of the world.

In her education as a woman, Sophie has been taught to watch for
subtle gestures that indicate how other people perceive any given situation. She lives outside herself for the most part, sensitive to the hurt
feelings or exclusion (perceived or real) of those unlike herself. Emile, in
contrast, has been taught to isolate his own experience and place it onto
others as the common experience of all. Consider, for example, Rousseau's description of the different ways a man and a woman behave at a
dinner party:

> I go to parties at which master and mistress jointly do the honors.
> . . . The husband omits no care in order to be attentive to all. He
> goes; he comes; he makes his rounds and puts himself out in
> countless ways; he would like to be all attentiveness. . . . [As for
> the woman] . . . nothing takes place that she does not notice; no
> one leaves to whom she has not spoken; she has omitted nothing
> that could interest everyone; she has said nothing to anyone that
> was not agreeable to him; and without in any way upsetting the
> order, the least important person among her company is no more
> forgotten than the most important. . . . Dinner is served. All go
> to the table. The man, knowledgeable about who gets along with
> whom, will seat them on the basis of what he knows. The woman,
> without knowing anything, will make no mistakes about it. She
> will have already read in their eyes and in their bearing, every-
> thing about who belongs with whom, and each guest will find
> himself placed where he wants to be. I do not say that when the
> food is served, no one is forgotten. But even though the master of
> the house may have forgotten no one when he passed around the
> food, his wife goes further and divines what you look at with
> pleasure and offers you some. In speaking to her neighbor, she has
> her eye on the end of the table; she distinguishes between the
> guest who does not eat because he is not hungry, and the one
> who does not dare to help himself or to ask because he is awkward
> or timid. On leaving the table each guest believes that she has
> thought only of him. (E, V:383–84)

This quote distinguishes Rousseau's model of man's and woman's gendered roles in community. Able to see what is common in all based on

what he knows of himself, the man "omits no care to be attentive to all" and seats persons in a satisfactory way. In other words, the man is fair, impartial, and knowledgeable and applies a universal standard (again, based in what he knows of himself) to all at the party. He tries to speak to each and for the same amount of time. But some might be forgotten in the process. The woman, however, makes certain that "the least important person among her company is no more forgotten than the most important." She is extremely attentive to the slightest gesture. She can distinguish between the one who does not eat because she is not hungry and the one who doesn't eat because she is too shy to ask for food. Because the man is looking to see what is common in all, he cannot see, cannot hear, those who are different or those who have life experiences that require them to express themselves in ways unfamiliar to the man. The woman, in contrast, who has made a "profound study of the mind of man—not an abstraction of the mind of man in general, but the minds of the men around her" (E, V:387), is able to decipher the languages of those who speak differently. The woman has honed observing and listening to an art. She "has seen what was whispered at the other end of the room; she knows what this person thought, to what this remark or that gesture related" (E, V:384).

From this description of the dinner party, we can extract what looks to be two different models for citizenship. As I have already indicated, the model based on Emile's behavior is one in which the community will, or the general will, is located by the male citizen who looks deep inside himself; he seeks to find what is common to all within himself and then to uniformly apply this to everyone at the party. I contend that this model forces everyone to speak in the same language in order to be heard. Some commentators have said otherwise. For example, in an analysis of the "politics of the ordinary" in Rousseau, Tracy Strong has remarked that Rousseau is *not* a theorist of the unified self—human beings are, rather, composite in Rousseau's mind.[7] "Our commonalty—the stuff of humanity—requires difference and there is no identity that is not that of difference."[8] Strong paints a portrait of Rousseau as sensitive to diversity, advancing a model of political space as the location for living with inequality in a way that allows all to remain free. But what of the political context, here the sexual politics, which structures what counts as common, what counts as community, how each person negotiates his or her relationship to that political space? It remains the case that Rousseau solely advances *man*, not woman, as citizen, and that man is taught certain characteristics (denying or suppressing other characteristics) that make him (through a very particular and controlled education) the best kind of citizen. From Rousseau's description of the dinner party, the man is the one who in knowing himself, *assumes* that he knows others: he is fair, he is impartial, he treats each equally. In seeking the common in himself and in all, Rousseau's man is able to tap into our feelings of human solidarity, of being ourselves with others in a community. Yet this same man cannot detect the voices/gestures of those actually unlike himself. Hannah Arendt also accuses Rousseau of looking only within himself to read the needs of others: "While the plight of others aroused his heart, he became involved in *his* heart rather than in the sufferings of others, and he was enchanted with its moods and caprices as they disclosed themselves in the sweet delight of intimacy which Rousseau was one of the first to discover and which from then on began playing its important role in the formation of modern sensibility."[9] Deepening our sense of commonalty and community in this particular case requires that all be alike in order to participate in conversation.

And what of the woman in this description? She knows nothing, but is able to read the subtle gestures of each. She is attuned to discord and seeks out those who, for whatever reason, are *in* but not *of* the dinner party. From what we are told, it almost seems as if the woman can read the mind of each of the guests. She "divines what you look at with pleasure and offers you some"; each guest leaves the table believing that "she has thought only of him." Were we to use the woman as a model for citizenship, we would be edging dangerously close to advocating what Iris Marion Young has called the "Rousseauist dream of transparency." This dream is one in which democratic space is structured so that we can privilege face-to-face relations and see in another person exactly what they desire; we can communicate immediately and transparently. In speaking of theorists of community who advocate these relations, Young argues: "Immediacy is better than mediation because immediate relations have the purity and security longed for in the Rousseauist dream: we are transparent to one another, purely copresent in the same time and space, close enough to touch, and nothing comes between us to obstruct our vision of one another."[10] Young goes on to point out that this ideal is a metaphysical illusion. Even more damning, though, is the notion that this ideal, if advanced by the woman in the dinner party description, could possibly be merely the flip side of the male ideal. While the man arrogantly projects himself onto others, the woman just as arrogantly assumes that she can empathize to such an extent as to read the longings of others. If we read the models in this way, it seems that both ultimately erase others and deny alterity.

If the woman in this passage can be read as merely offering a model that is a mirror opposite of the male, we have not come any distance toward an alternative. Were this the case, we would remain trapped within the logic of identity, the metaphysics of presence, the myth of the stable self. Although the woman described in this passage flirts with the myth of the immediate present and unmediated communication, when read in the context of Rousseau's awe and fear of the feminine, her behavior points elsewhere. As Rousseau mentions, the woman at the dinner party does not know the mind of man in general, but the minds of those around her. In this sense, it may be that she would be willing to confront the other, whether outside or within herself. Recall, also, that the woman lives outside of herself. She looks around to others to understand herself and the situation. Emile can only look inside himself; he can only see those who conform to the vision of his own desire. Sophie disrupts his thought in a violent way.

From the very inception of his education, Emile was taught that "a truly happy being is a solitary being" (E, IV:221). When Emile reaches adolescence, he has no emotional attachment to any other living being aside from his tutor. Only the onset of puberty arouses his passions, threatening the development of *amour-propre*, for "to be loved, one has to make oneself lovable" (E, IV:214). At this critical stage, Jean-Jacques manipulates Emile's potentially dangerous sexuality by attempting to incorporate an ideal of beauty and spirituality into Emile's vision of an object of love. Emile will long for a beautiful, spiritual, virtuous woman to satisfy his sexual desire, binding his lust with the need for true love. If Emile were in the state of nature, any and every woman would be equally able to fulfill his sexual desires (E, II:78). In the submission to sexual desire, interpreted as a direct need for another human being, a possibility is created for both tyranny and slavery. Rousseau wants to bypass both options (of tyranny and slavery—conditions he finds definitive in intimate relationships of mutual dependency) by making the conditions of autonomy available to Emile.

Emile learns to love, not through an attachment to a real human being outside himself, but rather by loving an internal image, one supplied to him by his tutor. At Rousseau's insistence, Emile learns the value of autonomy through learning to love an object. In order for Emile's integrity as man and citizen to remain intact, Sophie can only be a "holy image," one to which Emile must initially submit in order to develop the authentic autonomy that is absolutely essential to Rousseau's masculine version of citizenship. When Emile's growing attachment to the flesh-and-blood Sophie threatens to destroy his autonomy, he must retreat. In the following vignette, Rousseau makes it clear that one cannot be happy if dependent on another human being: "One morning, when they have not seen each other for two days, I enter Emile's room with a letter in my hand; staring fixedly at him, I say, 'What would you do if you were informed that Sophie is dead?' He lets out a great cry, gets up, striking his hands together, and looks wild-eyed at me without saying a single word" (*E*, V:442). Emile's response to this false information initiates a conversation in which Emile is warned that his passion for Sophie has threatened all his education meant to achieve, mainly his independence and his preparation for citizenship: "How pitiable you are going to be, thus subjected to your unruly passions! There will always be privations, losses and alarms. . . . The fear of losing everything will prevent you from possessing anything. . . . How will you know how to sacrifice inclination to duty and to hold out against your heart in order to listen to your reason? . . . Learn to become your own master. Command your heart, Emile, and you will be virtuous" (*E*, V:444–45).

To remedy his too intense commitment to the woman he loves, Emile is forced to delay his marriage in order to travel through Europe. His trip teaches him to endure life without Sophie. Emile learns his lesson well, carefully guarding his independence and autonomy. He learns to confirm what he knows of himself and deny all that challenges that identity. In order to guard against a confrontation with difference, Emile practices the art of embracing in others only what is the same as what he knows within himself: "He loves men because they are his fellows, but he will especially love those who resemble him most because he will feel that his is good; and since he judges this resemblance by agreement in moral taste, he will be quite gratified to be approved in everything connected with good character" (*E*, IV:339). Good character consists of looking deep inside the masculine self to will what he finds there onto humanity. When Emile is confronted with Sophie's difference (the feminine subversive) this picture of the world falters. For example, during Emile's and Sophie's courtship, Emile and his tutor come to visit Sophie and her parents almost every day. One day they fail to come. Their absence sends Sophie into a state of extreme anxiety and worry. Later, to explain their negligence, Jean-Jacques tells the story of a gallant Emile who saved an injured man and assisted a woman in labor. Emile turns to Sophie to say: "Sophie, you are the arbiter of my fate. You know it well. You can make me die of pain. But do not hope to make me forget the rights of humanity. They are more sacred to me than yours. I will never give them up for you" (E, V:441). Although deeply in love with Sophie, Emile finds it necessary to remind both himself and Sophie that though he is tied to Sophie as a lover, his duties as citizen take priority over his love. In short, Emile manages to maintain his autonomy both as man and as citizen though engaged in an interdependent and intimate relationship. In saying to Sophie that the "rights of humanity" (whatever they may be) are "more sacred" to him than his love for Sophie, he ranks in order what he perceives as conflicting duties. Willing what is best for the common good will always take priority over his love for Sophie.

Singling out the conflict between duty and inclination, however, is only *one* possible way to interpret this story. We might identify with Emile and see his actions as completely justified, even honorable, had we not the benefit of an alternative perspective. In the person of Sophie, however, Rousseau offers the alternative perspective. Sophie does not accept the rules of the game as Emile lays them out. She fails to see a contradiction in her duty to the rights of humanity and the needs of those most dear to her. Sophie is moved by Emile's story of sacrifice, promises to love him forever, and suggests (to Emile's surprise) that they immediately visit the people whom Emile had helped. Once they arrive, Sophie knows exactly what to do:

> Her gentle and light hand knows how to get at everything that hurts them and to place their sore limbs in a more relaxed position. They feel relieved at her very approach. One would say that she guesses everything which hurts them. . . . She has the appearance and the grace, as well as the gentleness and the goodness of an angel. Emile is moved and contemplates her in silence. Man, love your companion. God gives her to you to console you in your pains, to relieve you in your ills. This is woman. (E, V:441–42)

Again, this passage could be read as yet another example of an excessively gendered portrayal of the roles of man and woman in the good society: man is a citizen who helps his fellow-citizens, while woman waits silently, comforting all after the fact. Yet, although it is that, it is also much more. For though Sophie's place is constantly one of the shadows, in the background, and at the margins, her actions implicitly (and some-times explicitly) challenge the model being put forth by Rousseau in his recommendation that Emile be considered the best citizen. When we read this passage, we have to wonder at Emile's dismissal of Sophie's worry, his immediate announcement that no matter how close the two of them might be or become, the "rights of humanity" will always over-ride his love for his future wife, future mother of his children. This an-nouncement plants a seed of doubt in the reader's mind about whether one must, indeed, rank these priorities. Is it necessarily the case that to intimately love another person automatically conflicts with one's duties as a citizen? Does an acknowledgment of love for a particular other (in this case Sophie) automatically threaten the duty we have toward others whom we don't know very well at all? Emile consistently puts abstract others (those whom he knows by recognizing the common in himself as the common in all) first, while Sophie looks for the peculiarities that distinguish people and make each unique, lovable or not.

III

Sophie's way, what Sophie knows, becomes even more dangerous as the story of Emile and Sophie continues. In *Emile,* mirroring the argument Rousseau makes about the city as theater in his *Letter to D'Alembert,*[11] Emile and Sophie are constantly warned to avoid the big city. In fact, Emile and his tutor had already visited Paris searching for the ideal woman. Of course, their search was fruitless: Paris is no place for a virtu-ous woman. They came home unsatisfied, disappointed, and restless: "We are sad and dreamy as we leave Paris. This city of chatter is not the place for us. Emile turns a disdainful eye toward this great city and says resentfully, 'How many days lost in vain searches! Ah, the wife of my heart is not there. My friend, you knew it well'" (*E*, V:410). Like love that fosters mutual dependency, the "city of chatter" threatens Emile's vision of himself, his autonomy, his authenticity. The big city is full of people who might cause Emile to question his own vision of himself: "In a big city, full of scheming, idle people without religion or principle, whose imagination, depraved by sloth, inactivity, the love of pleasure, and great needs, engenders only monsters and inspires only crimes; in a big city, . . . morals [manners] and honor are nothing because each, easily hiding his conduct from the public eye, shows himself only by his reputation and is esteemed only for his riches" (*LD'A*, 58–59).

In an urban environment, people are known by what others think of them. Their "reputation" proceeds them. One is forced to live outside one's self, like a woman, in the opinion of others. Richard Sennett has remarked that though Rousseau hated urban public life, he was the most constant student of the city, arriving "at the first complete and probing theory of the modern city as an expressive milieu."[12] Here people are free from the duties of survival: they seek entertainment and leisure; they interact on the streets, in the cafés, on the boulevards. They are extremely sociable: they speak, listen, pay the greatest attention to one another's gestures and the way ideas are expressed. According to Rousseau, style seems almost as important as content in this milieu. The "art of conversation" blossoms.

Iris Marion Young commends the urban atmosphere as offering an alternative to the impasse between liberal individualism and communitarianism. Defining subjectivity as multiple and heterogeneous, as opposed to stable and transparent, Young argues that people cannot ever be fully autonomous or visibly transparent to others. We are always living and working in response and in connection with others in a way that makes "misunderstanding, rejection, withdrawal, and conflict" certainly as viable as outcomes to social being as are mutual understanding and reciprocity (Young, *Justice*, 231). It is these possibilities which arise from the interactions of people with multiple understandings of themselves and multiple ways of expressing those desires (and multiple ways that they can be understood) that is the heart of political relations. Young describes and embraces the diversity of city life as an alternative to either liberal autonomy or community identity in words that are reminiscent of Rousseau's warnings *against* city life (and the *feminine* as the principle at the heart of city life). As Young puts it:

> City life is a vast, even infinite, economic network of production, distribution, transportation, exchange, communication, service provision, and amusement. City dwellers depend on the mediation of thousands of other people and vast organizational resources in order to accomplish their individual ends. City dwellers are thus together, bound to one another, in what should be and sometimes is a single polity. Their being together entails some

common problems and common interests, but they do not create
a community of shared final ends, of mutual identification and
reciprocity. (Young, *Justice*, 238)

In his condemnation of city life and his singling out of salon life as
microcosm of the connections between femininity, urbanity, and difference, Rousseau vilifies this atmosphere as inauthentic, as completely
lacking in seriousness. In the *cercles*, men have serious conversation: "By
themselves, the men, exempted from having to lower their ideas to the
range of women and to clothe reason in gallantry, can devote themselves
to grave and serious discourse without fear of ridicule. They dare to speak
of country and virtue without passing for windbags; they even dare to be
themselves without being enslaved to the maxims of a magpie" (*LD'A*,
105). Here again, Rousseau advances his often repeated mantra that
women undermine seriousness, and thus, should *not* be taken seriously.
Simultaneously, though, he defies his own warning: *Rousseau himself takes
women very seriously*. In Rousseau's descriptions of women's ways, of wom-
en's connections to the theater, to city life, and to an affirmation of
difference, women *are* a serious threat to the kind of community Rousseau
is ostensibly attempting to create. Women's knowledge, Sophie's actions,
directly challenge all that Rousseau argues is good, authentic, virtuous,
even democratic. As Dena Goodman reminds us of the philosophes and
salonnières: "The Enlightenment was not a game, and the salonnières
were not simply ladies of leisure killing time. . . . Like the philosophes
who gathered in their home, the salonnières were practical people who
worked at tasks they considered productive and useful. They took themselves, their salons, and their guests very seriously."[13]

Just as Sophie does, we might add. Had the story of Emile and Sophie
ended with Rousseau's *Emile*, we might believe that Rousseau actually
bought his own precepts and conclusions: that gender boundaries ensure
a good community, that autonomy is absolutely essential in order to make
decent moral and political choices; we might believe that his masculine
vision of democracy (one where the general will rules all and each is
forced to be free) is the one he finds most viable and desirable.

The story of Emile and Sophie does not, however, end so tidily. Rousseau reveals, even more powerfully than in *Emile* itself, his deep ambivalence about his own solutions in his tragic "conclusion," *Emile et Sophie,
ou Les solitaires*.[14] Only two chapters of *Les solitaires* were actually completed by Rousseau; these chapters take the form of letters written by

Emile to his tutor. Judith Shklar explains the significance of this work in stating that "not a single theme of real importance to Rousseau is left out in these thirty-odd pages."[15] We learn immediately that Emile and Sophie have suffered many hardships, most important, the death of their young daughter and both of Sophie's parents. Sophie is devastated by these events. Her misery leads Emile to contemplate that which he had been so severely warned against: to travel to Paris to distract Sophie from her pain. As Rousseau had predicted, coming to Paris proves to be their downfall. The city has a poisonous effect on Emile's soul and his fate. Emile writes that upon their establishing themselves in Paris, he began to undergo a revolution in himself that he found impossible to forestall. He was so worn by frivolous amusements that his heart lost strength, becoming, as he put it, incapable of heat and force (that is, he ceased to have an honest inner life). He was only happy where he was not and sought out everything only to quickly become bored. All his affections became tepid; he let go of his attachments, including his attachment to Sophie.

Tempted by Parisian women, Emile has an affair. Sophie, discarded by Emile, finds herself pregnant by another man. Emile, taught to love Sophie's honor more than Sophie herself, cannot accept Sophie's mistake (which was merely a response to Emile's own adultery) and blames her tyrannical power over him for his own subsequent misery. He rejects Sophie and plans an even sweeter revenge in having Sophie separated from their son. Rejected by Emile, separated from her son, and consumed by grief, Sophie gives up on life and dies.

Attempting to digest this story, one might argue that it merely confirms Rousseau's edicts: the city and certain kinds of women in the city (even Sophie in the city) threaten community. Even the small trio of Emile, Sophie, and their son fail to survive in such a corrupt environment. Scholars have argued that Rousseau's bias against the customs and manners of city life turn on his desire to preserve authenticity.[16] Underpinning this interpretation is a particular reading of the *Second Discourse* that indicates that for Rousseau, modern life always entails loss—we were once authentic and natural beings; we could communicate in an unmediated and transparent fashion; we were not slaves to *amour-propre*. Rousseau's goal in creating Emile is to create both a natural man and a citizen—a citizen who can know himself, communicate authentically, and legitimate a political arrangement that, as best as possible, preserves our original freedom. This argument, however, presumes that Rousseau

thinks his goal is possible and that he's actually done it, that he's succeeded at some level in constructing such an authentic community in
the midst of the modern world.

I contend, in contrast, that Rousseau's work points elsewhere. The
dominant model put forth by Rousseau for the way citizens should act is
Emile as manly citizen. But even Emile ends up unhappy. He is only able
to preserve the precarious balance between his role as man/citizen and
his interactions with others in the world by projecting what he knows of
himself onto others. In the city, he is unable to do this: his fellow-citizens
are not so easily read. At the same time, Rousseau presents us with an
alternative model, that of Sophie. Sophie also comes to her demise in
the city: Emile, unable to shoulder the challenge to his identity once
Sophie is pregnant by another man, completely cuts her off emotionally.
Most important, neither Emile's nor Sophie's identities, even their most
"natural" sexual identities, are either stable or authentic. Emile's performance as a man (and likewise Sophie's performance as a woman) is
presumably critical for achieving republican community, yet the community completely disintegrates once the unnatural status of their identity
lies exposed.

IV

Let me turn now to *La nouvelle Héloïse* in order to extend and deepen the
argument I have made about the subversive potential of Rousseau's
women. Julie is a Sophie in flesh-and-blood terms, a woman who actually
could become Rousseau's exemplary (alternative) citizen. In *La nouvelle
Héloïse*, the feminine presence disrupts all that Rousseau (in other pieces,
especially the *Social Contract*, *The Government of Poland*, and the *Letter
to D'Alembert*) advocates as best for republican community: male solidarity, the festival as education for citizenry, rules against a "too intimate
commerce" between men and women—all of which direct Rousseau
toward advocating a unilateral, provincial, and univocal public sphere
that dictates to everyone about proper behavior. Exploring the feminine
in Rousseau allows me to more fully expand on Rousseau's ambivalence
concerning the price of such a community.

In *Emile; or, On Education*, one of Rousseau's goals was to educate
Emile from an early age to be both man and citizen. We have noted the

failure of both identities. In *La nouvelle Héloïse*, Rousseau tries something even more difficult: rather than start with an uncorrupted boy child as his raw material for citizenship, he looks to a man at the margins of society, Saint-Preux, and a man already considered an upstanding citizen (but not of the ideal society), Wolmar. Neither of these men are able to be convincing or compelling citizens because neither knows how to love. Recall that the personal and the political are intricately connected in Rousseau's oeuvre, and that Rousseau finds stories of love far more convincing than moral tales. This is why, in his *Letter to D'Alembert*, he opposes the introduction of a theater in Geneva: citizens who have been taught good morals and virtues, to keep their gender identities "straight," and to love their fatherland above all else, would be far too affected by the love interest in the theater. The personal appeals to us above all else; when we see and identify with a person in love, we are apt to sympathize with their dilemmas even if fulfilling passion means that we must defy gender rules and the dictates of the fatherland. Rousseau writes that "the harm for which the theatre is reproached is not precisely that of inspiring criminal passions but of disposing the soul to feelings which are too tender and which are later satisfied at the expense of virtue" (*LD'A*, 51).

That being the case, what are we to make of the fact that Rousseau's men inspire nothing but contempt, while his women inspire sympathy? What are we to learn from the fact that his men do not know how to love, that they consistently sacrifice love for duty, and that his women suffer immeasurably for these "manly" decisions in favor of virtue and duty? None of Rousseau's men are able to truly love in a way that inspires the tender feelings of heart that Rousseau so admires, to love in a way that would inspire great sacrifice without hesitation, to love in such a way that the whole world is changed in light of that love. Rather, Rousseau's men love their women only as projections of their own imagination.

Linda M. G. Zerilli calls the chaste image of woman that replaces actual women the "celestial object." She explains this via reference to Alfred Binet's credit to Rousseau for "a form of fetishism that substituted the relic for and preferred it to the woman to whom it originally belonged."[17] This fetishism is brilliantly displayed by Saint-Preux as part of his performance of manliness. As it turns out, the education needed for becoming a man does not include knowledge of how to love another person. Julie accuses Saint-Preux of only being able to love her in the abstract, as the object of *his* desire. This can be seen, for example, when Julie sends Saint-Preux "a sort of amulet that lovers are wont to wear" (*J*,

II:XX, 216). In Saint-Preux's letter to Julie recounting his fascination with her gift, he reports that "a sort of sensuality" seized his imagination; he shifted the object from hand to hand such that "one would have thought it was burning them" (J, II:XXII, 228). He rushed home from the post, fondling the object all the way, dreaming of its "volume," its "weight," and the "tone of [Julie's] letter" (J, II:XXII, 228). Opening the object, feeling his "heart throb," Saint-Preux ends his engagement with the day's mail collapsing in an orgasmic swoon onto the bed (J, II:XXII, 229).

In another instance, Saint-Preux writes to Julie that "a frantic love feeds on fantasies," and that it is quite possible, even "easy," to "decoy intense desires with the most frivolous objects!" (J, II:XVI, 197). He claims to receive Julie's letters with the "same transports [her] presence would have evoked, and in the exaltation of my joy a mere piece of paper stood me in stead of you" (J, II:XVI, 197). Appalled by her lover's delight in his solitary experiences of her, Julie admonishes Saint-Preux: "I fear these deceiving raptures, so much the more dangerous when the imagination which excites them has no limits, and I am more afraid that you are insulting your Julie in your very love for her. . . . What do you enjoy when you are the only one to enjoy it? These solitary, sensual pleasures are lifeless pleasures. . . . Sensual man, will you never know how to love?"[18] Saint-Preux thinks only of what he desires, mapping it onto the "objects" around him. When he is not imagining Julie as a lover in the form of an amulet or piece of paper, Saint-Preux imagines Julie as property.

Warned to avoid mutual dependency that is fostered through love, Rousseau's men imagine women as objects, shaping their desire into a fantasy of woman. This process makes attachment to real women virtually impossible. Rousseau had cautioned Emile that a too close attachment to Sophie would threaten his autonomy, especially in terms of his ability to make good judgments. Emile was educated to avoid mutual dependency in his relationship with Sophie. Recall that when Emile's tutor felt Emile had become too close to Sophie, he insisted that Emile travel around the world to assure himself that he could live easily without the one he loved.

In contrast, Rousseau's women find that the ability to make good moral judgments is intractably tied to our commitments to others. Confused by the dilemma the lovers find themselves in, Saint-Preux and Julie wonder what to do: defy the father in the name of their love, or suppress their passion to conform to society's version of virtue? Julie begs Saint-Preux to follow her lead in making a decision in this matter: "I admit that I am the younger; but have you never noticed that if reason is generally weaker and sooner to wane in women, it is also formed earlier, just as a frail sunflower grows and dies quicker than an oak. We find ourselves, from the tenderest age, assigned such a dangerous trust, that the responsibility of preserving it soon awakens our judgment, and an excellent way to see clearly the consequences of things is to feel intensely the risks they cause us to run" (J, I:XI, 45). Claiming that her reason is more fully developed than his, Julie explains in even more compelling terms why Saint-Preux should allow her to steer their relationship: Saint-Preux should defer to his lover because it is Julie who is able to think of both of them, and their commitments to their family and society, *all at the same time*. Saint-Preux is only able to think of himself. Julie argues that "the opinion of whichever of us least distinguishes his own happiness from the other's is the one to be preferred" (J, I:XI, 45).

Julie's cousin Claire also makes judgments that factor in her responsibility to others. When Julie first informs Claire of her love for Saint-Preux, Claire expresses extreme anxiety about the situation, but promises not to betray Julie's confidence. She acknowledges that "many people would find it more honest to reveal it; maybe they would be right" (J, I:VII, 37). It would be more honest in that it is the naked truth, but, Claire reasons, it is a truth that would harm a number of people, her beloved Julie included. Claire wants no part in an "honesty which betrays faith, trust, friendship" (J, I:VII, 37). This kind of contextual model for moral reasoning is clearly an alternative, and a subversive one at that, to the autonomous decision-making required of manly citizens. Later on in the novel, learning that Julie has taken sick because of the absence of her lover, Claire is the one willing to call Saint-Preux back to her side. When Julie questions her own worth in society's eyes, Claire assures her that just because she has lost her virginity, this does not make her less worthy in the eyes of her friend:

> Is genuine love meant to degrade the soul? Let not a single fault that love has committed deprive you of that noble enthusiasm for honesty and beauty, which always raised you above yourself. Is a spot visible on the sun? How many virtues do you still possess for one that has become tainted? Will that make you any less sweet, less sincere, less modest, less generous? Will you be any less wor-

thy, in a word, of all our praise? Honor, humanity, friendship, pure love, will these be any less dear to your heart? (J, I:XXX, 81)

Further expounding on the politics of love, Rousseau indicates that women's way of loving as expressed through contextualized reasoning could even be considered a demonstration of better judgment. Recall that Julie, not Saint-Preux or Wolmar, consistently knows how to love, and in doing so, makes good decisions. Early on in their exchange of letters, Saint-Preux complains to Julie that though he has written to his beloved Julie and there has been plenty of time for her to respond, he has not received any word. He claims that "there is no possible dire reason for its delay that [his] troubled spirit does not imagine" (J, I:XIX, 57). Julie replies that Saint-Preux's imagination has forged far ahead of his reason:

> Your two letters reached me at the same time because the Courier, who comes only once a week, set out only with the second. It takes a certain amount of time to deliver letters; it takes more for my agent to bring me mine in secret, and the Courier does not return from here the day after his arrival. Thus all told, we need eight days, when the Courier's day is well chosen to receive replies from each other; I explain this in order to calm once and for all your impatient petulance. While you are declaiming against fortune and my negligence, you see that I am adroitly gathering information about whatever can assure our correspondence and anticipate your uncertainties. I leave you to decide on which side the most tender care is to be found. (J, I:XX, 58)

Loving care, for Julie, means attention to assuring their love and happiness. This is manifested most concretely in maintaining correspondence between the two lovers if necessary, but ideally in arranging for their physical proximity. Just as Julie arranges the rendezvous for their first kiss and manipulates circumstances to provide for subsequent amorous engagements, she constantly erodes barriers and seeks pathways in order for their love to continue. Saint-Preux, in contrast, busily occupies himself with imaginary raptures of Julie and the never-ending task of preserving his own "honor." Rousseau's men define love in a way that eschews relationship, pits duty against inclination, the heart and reason "endlessly at war" (J, I:XXVI, 73).

Saint-Preux's practice of "loving" Julie prepares him well for his eventual acceptance into the community at Clarens. Despite her love for Saint-Preux, Julie eventually is persuaded by her father (in light of her mother's death) to marry Wolmar and attempt to live a conventional life as wife and mother. Many years after Julie's marriage to Wolmar, he "tests" the passion of Julie and her former lover by asking Saint-Preux to live at Clarens as tutor to Wolmar and Julie's children. Unlike Julie, who is never able to fully conform to her husband's authority, Saint-Preux quickly learns Wolmar's ways and is "cured" of any residual passion he might have had for his lover. When Saint-Preux is initially summoned to Clarens, he doubts his ability to suppress his love for Julie. He worries aloud in his letter to Claire: "How am I to think of her as a friend whom I never saw but as a lover? (J, IV:III, 341). Surprisingly, then, the "cure" works almost immediately. When Saint-Preux sees Julie, the initial sight is not one of his former lover, but of Madame de Wolmar, Monsieur de Wolmar's wife: "It was a materfamilias I was embracing; I saw her surrounded by her Husband and children; this awed me. I saw in her a dignified mien that had not struck me at first; I felt obliged to have a new sort of respect for her; her familiarity was almost a burden; as beautiful as she seemed to me I would have kissed the hem of her dress more willingly than her cheek. From that instant, in a word, I knew that neither she nor I were the same, and I began in earnest to augur well for myself" (J, IV:VI, 348).

V

Scholars have noted that if we take Clarens as representative of Rousseau's ideal community, Rousseau's commitment to democratic practice is far less convincing than it might otherwise be. Jean Starobinski, for example, notes the contrast between the "democratic ideal of *The Social Contract* and the still feudal structure of the community at Clarens."[19] Joel Schwartz points out the obvious in this case: "Clarens is a highly inegalitarian society . . . in fact a despotism, as Rousseau makes perfectly evident."[20] The most important distinguishing characteristics of Clarens include presumption of transparent conversation between all (Wolmar says the society must be completely "open"—no hidden secrets); rules against a too intimate commerce between the sexes (we see this most clearly in the separation of male from female servants, who come together only for festivals and the like); suppression of romantic love in favor of arranged marriage (exemplified between Julie and Wolmar, as well as in arrangements made for servants); and the enforcement of a model of reasoned dialogue and political/moral judgment that claims to treat all the same yet makes traitors of those who do not share the common experience.

Wolmar is the patriarch of this community. He reasons that since he observes "composedly and disinterestedly" he "scarcely err[s] in [his] judgments" (J, IV:XII, 403). Wolmar's philosophy is such that "[a] single precept of morality can do for all the others; it is this: Never do nor say anything that thou does not wish everyone to see and hear" (J, IV:VI, 349). Saint-Preux describes the effect that this single moral precept has on the conduct of everyone who lives at Clarens:

> All these vain subtleties are unknown in this house, and the great art of masters to make their domestics as they wish them is to show themselves to them as they are. Their conduct is always candid and open, because they do not fear lest their acts belie their words. As they do not have for themselves a moral different from the one they wish to impart to others, they have no need to be circumspect in what they say; a word that foolishly escapes them does not overturn the principles they have endeavored to establish. They do not indiscreetly reveal all their business, but they freely state their maxims. At table, out strolling, in private or in front of everyone, they always maintain the same language. (J, IV:X, 385)

Everyone at Clarens is forced to act as if their hearts and minds were completely on display. All privacy has been effaced; all is openly revealed. The "openness," however, obscures all the secrets being kept. Forced to speak in a language that does not express her thoughts, feelings, or desires, Julie becomes unable to speak or listen at all; in fact, she kills herself in the end. As Lisa Disch notes, when one considers Wolmar's cool reason in light of its effect on Julie, it begins to look far more like punishment, discipline, and "cruel disregard for Julie's feelings" than it does like "perfect impartiality" or justice.[21] "The authority [Wolmar] wields is perverse both for its universalism, which erases Julie's feelings, and for its dogmatism, which makes it impossible for her to resist Wolmar's test without incriminating herself" (Disch, "Claire Loves Julie," 38). Had

Julie chosen to recognize Claire's friendship as replacement for the love
of a husband, Disch argues, Wolmar's cruel authority over Julie might
have been subverted.

Both Starobinski and Schwartz emphasize that the success of Clarens
as a community is dependent on the state of mind of its inhabitants such
that though they are unequal and differentiated, they believe they are
equal contributing members. Most surprising in their analyses, though, is
the interpretation that Julie "rules" this society and holds it together. Joel
Schwartz's analysis of Rousseau's sexual politics rests on this assumption:
Rousseau believes women to be both sexual and political (far more inclined to interest themselves in theatricality and domination—politics
being our attempt to dominate one another), while men, or at least a few
good men, might be able to "transcend the domination characteristic of
politics and sexuality" (Schwartz, *Sexual Politics*, 7). For Schwartz, Julie
"rules" Clarens due precisely because of her sexuality. He points out that
Rousseau's ambivalence concerning sexuality dictates that women have
lots of sexual power, and thus, contact between the sexes should be vigor-
ously policed. According to Schwartz: "*Julie* tells the story of a woman's
employment of authority. Women such as Julie use their authority to
fashion men according to their feminine desires" (Schwartz, *Sexual Politics*, 115).

Yet how can we assert that Julie's desire "fashions" Clarens in light of
the fact that her unfulfilled desire leaves her unable to fight for her life?
Soon after learning that Wolmar has invited her ex-lover into their home
to live permanently, Julie plunges into an icy lake to save her child. She
never recovers from the fever brought on by the "accident." How are we
to read the centrality of Julie's role, both before and after her death? Julie
certainly is the "glue" that holds Clarens together. She is the pivotal
figure at Clarens: the servants, the children, Wolmar, Saint-Preux, and
Claire all direct their attention and concern to Julie. Even the structure
of the letters and the title of the book place Julie as the main event.
Before her death, she elaborates explicit and detailed rules concerning
the direction and maintenance of the household in her absence. In one
of the last letters of the novel, Wolmar explains at length the "long
monologue" in the course of which Julie "wrote her testament" into his
heart (Rousseau, *Julie, or the New Eloise*, VI:XI, 581). This influence over
the household and the emotions of those within the household suggests
that Julie exerted some control over important aspects of her own life
and the lives of others.

At the same time, however, the image of woman as well as the labor of women maintains the community as male-centered without any acknowledgment of women's autonomous desire and subjectivity—indeed, without women's autonomous participation. Julie is passed from her father to Wolmar and used as a suture between Wolmar and Saint-Preux. Because Schwartz emphasizes the perspective of Rousseau's men, he argues that women have sexual power. When we focus on Rousseau's women, however, we notice women's lack of agency and control over the situation. I find it fascinating that Rousseau writes so convincingly about Julie's *discontent*. Once Julie marries Wolmar and becomes a part of the community of Clarens, she is forced to change her way of interacting with others. Instead of listening to each person alone, considering each perspective, and making everyone feel as if he or she each was uniquely important to her, Julie is forced to take on the ways of Wolmar and the rules of conduct imposed at Clarens. I maintain that Julie *herself* recognizes that she is unhappy at Clarens and that Rousseau's story demands that we strongly empathize with her grief. Although it goes against the rules of society and the rules of Wolmar, Julie sustains her desire for Saint-Preux while simultaneously trying to displace this desire onto passionate love for her children. Although Julie writes to Claire that her "status of wife and mother uplifts" her soul and sustains her "against the remorse" of her "earlier condition" (J, IV:I, 330), she also complains that Wolmar "does not respond enough to me for my fancy" (J, IV:I, 328). Julie says to Claire that she desires "a friend, a mother who is as dotty as me about my children and her own" (J, IV:I, 328).

From these statements, it seems clear that Julie is completely aware that her desire as a woman is not being fulfilled within the confines of Clarens. She tries to fill the gap with the love of her children, yet she remains unhappy and listless. Luce Irigaray writes that this is a typical response for a woman within the economy of male desire:

> If woman is asked to sustain, to revive, man's desire, the request neglects to spell out what it implies as to the value of her own desire. A desire of which she is not aware, moreover, at least not explicitly. But one whose force and continuity are capable of nurturing repeatedly and at length all the masquerades of "femininity" that are expected of her. It is true that she still has the child, in relation to whom her appetite for touch, for contact, has free rein, unless it is already lost, alienated by the taboo against touching of a highly obsessive civilization. Otherwise her pleasure will

find, in the child, compensations for and diversions from the frustrations that she too often encounters in sexual relations per se. Thus maternity fills the gaps in a repressed female sexuality.[22]

But for Julie, love for the children, especially when not shared with Wolmar, is not enough. Wolmar seems to suspect (and certainly fear) Julie's discontent. It is as if any recognition of her autonomous feminine desire would lead explicitly and undeniably to a subversion of the Enlightenment order Wolmar has worked so diligently to create at Clarens. When Julie admits to Wolmar that she had loved Saint-Preux, Wolmar, in keeping with his cruel punishment of openly revealing all to everyone, invites Saint-Preux into their home to live with them and be tutor to their children. It is as if when he recognizes Julie's desire and frustration, rather than listen to her, he punishes her. This is the final act that proves too much for Julie to bear.

Notice again that Wolmar's values and way of understanding others is quite similar to Emile's. He takes what he knows of himself, assumes that it is common to all, and places it onto all around him. Any hint of difference is tinged with darkness, intrigue, secrecy, and chaos. As Saint-Preux observes of Clarens, at the table Wolmar (and Julie forced to act like Wolmar in his presence) "openly proclaim all their maxims"—no matter what the situation, no matter who is speaking—"their language is always the same." Wolmar invites Saint-Preux into their home to "cure" the lovers of their passion and to keep "open" conversation alive in the same, univocal, spirit. Anyone who speaks differently, or who disrupts the conversation as structured by Wolmar, must necessarily be banned from the community. Wolmar is inherently suspicious of what takes place outside his vision, untouched by the order he imposes by his presence. When Julie, during her last few days of life, requests that Claire sleep with her in the same bed, Wolmar is crazed by the fear of their potential intimacy. "As for me, I was sent off," he recounts (J, VI:XI, 582). Despite the fact that he "genuinely needed rest," Wolmar remained uneasy all night long. Explicitly he proclaims his worry over Julie's health; implicitly he worries about what exactly transpired between the two women:

> I was up early. Anxious to learn what had taken place during the night, at the first sound I heard I entered the bedroom. From Madame d'Orbe's condition the night before, I gauged the despair I would find her in and the rantings I would witness. Upon entering I saw her seated in an armchair, haggard and pale, or rather

livid, her eyes leaden and almost lifeless; but she was gentle, quiet, she spoke little, and did all she was told, without answering. As for Julie, she appeared less weak than the night before, her voice was steadier, her gestures more animated; she seemed to have taken on her Cousin's animation. I easily recognized from her color that this apparent improvement was the effect of fever: but I also saw glimmering in her eyes I know not what secret joy that might have contributed to it, the cause of which I could not determine. (J, VI:XI, 582–83)

Could the "secret joy" glimmering in Julie's eyes be attributed to a lesbian liaison with Claire? Wolmar starts to worry that he has never known Julie, that she has never been herself in his presence. It is odd that this should worry such a man as Wolmar, given his own rules. With Julie lying on her deathbed, Wolmar accuses her of secretly welcoming her death: "Julie, my dear Julie! Your have cut me to the heart: alas, you waited until very late! Yes, I continued, seeing that she looked at me with surprise; I have figured you out; you are delighted to be dying; you are more than happy to be leaving me" (J, VI:XI, 590).

Julie chooses death as a better option than the closed community of Clarens. She singles out her friendship with Claire as the one blessing that she alone was granted by heaven. "I was a woman, and a woman was my friend. . . . I have kept her my whole life long, and her hand closes my eyes. . . . What would I have been without her?" (J, VI:XI, 594). Claire, sadly, is left behind. She is devastated at the prospect of life without Julie. Left alone in the world of men, Claire loses herself in the process. Her grief is profoundly alien to Wolmar. Describing Claire's reaction to Julie's death, Wolmar writes: "When I entered, I found her completely out of her mind, seeing nothing, hearing nothing, recognizing no one, rolling around on the floor wringing her hands and biting the legs of the chairs, murmuring some extravagant words in a muted voice, then at long intervals uttering piercing cries that made one start" (J, VI:XI, 602).

VI

In analyzing women's relationship to communities, Susan Bickford has suggested that "an antifoundational thinker like Foucault, who is explicitly concerned with 'how human beings are made subjects,' might prove useful for feminists and others concerned with subjugation and transformation."[23] In Rousseau's oeuvre, human beings are made subjects by their enacting and embodying the traits of their gender. In placing masculinist discourse in the public, and feminine discourse in the private, realm, Rousseau seems to believe that he has secured the smooth functioning of the social contract. We don't have to listen to women, or listen to women listening to others, à la the *standard* interpretation of Rousseau, because women simply don't count in public discourse. Foucault claims, in contrast, what makes the excluded and the marginal *worth listening to* is precisely their difference from, and marginalization in terms of, the dominant discourse: "[F]or there to be a sense in listening to them and in searching for what they want to say, it is sufficient that they exist and that they have against them so much which is set up to silence them."[24]

Yet though Rousseau claims that women aren't worth listening to, he gives them a lot to say, and he frames what women say in a way that makes their statements quite compelling as an alternative to his own arguments. Just as in listening to what Sophie says, we begin to sketch an alternative way of thinking, knowing, and judging, in listening to Julie and Claire we do the same. Describing herself, Claire claims that she is a "sort of monster" (J, I:LXIV, 146), ignoring the ways she is supposed to behave in favor of defining her own course. Like Sophie, both Julie and Claire are products of their social and cultural history. They have been taught, for better or for worse, to "perform" their gender (with Claire defying the rules she finds most obnoxious). Also like Sophie, Julie is an actress: she works at seeing and listening and responding to those around her. Recall that Sophie lives in the opinions of others; she deliberately makes other people feel recognized; everyone leaves the dinner party thinking that Sophie has thought only of them. Julie has developed some of these same skills of communication, making everyone feel that they are her private and intimate friends. In the first letter that Saint-Preux writes to Julie, the one in which he reveals his love for her, he exclaims: "No, fair Julie; your charms had dazzled my eyes, never would they have led my heart astray without the stronger charm that animates them. It is that touching combination of such lively sensibility and unfailing gentleness, it is that tender pity for all the sufferings of others, it is that sound judgment and exquisite taste that draw their purity from the soul's own, it is, in a word, that attractions of the sentiments far more than those of the person that I worship in you" (J, I:I, 26). Likewise, Claire notes that it is not Julie's beauty or her grace or the talent of pleasing that makes Julie the center of any community and draws others toward her. Claire says that it is the "gift of loving" that makes Julie loved, "something undefinably seductive that is not merely pleasing, but affecting, and attracts all hearts" (J, II:V, 166).

Everyone seeks to be near Julie as part of her immediate community. Saint-Preux complains to Julie that while she is the center of a community, he has no one:

> You are surrounded by people you cherish and who worship you; the attentions of a tender mother, a father whose unique hope is in you; the friendship of a cousin who seems to breathe only through you; a whole family of which you are the ornament; an entire town proud to have known you from birth, everything occupies and shares your sensibility, and what remains for love is but the least part of what is claimed by the rights of blood and friendship. But I, Julie, alas! Wandering and without family, and almost without fatherland, I have no one on earth but you, and love alone stands me in stead of everything. (J, I:XXI, 60)

Despite Saint-Preux's worry that Julie will have nothing left over for him due to all the others who have claims on her heart, we have seen that Julie has plenty of love to give to him. Julie is able to understand her identity in multiple ways: loving an "other" intimately, for her, does not mean that she cannot love her family or her community, or indeed, that she cannot be responsible to others whom she has not met, or even will never meet. Rousseau shows us that Julie loves *better* than her lover does, and that in loving better she has better judgment. Because she does not maintain an identity as manly citizen of the fatherland who must sacrifice individual ties for the "general will," Julie is able to seek out various perspectives (including of those usually not heard), to juggle conflicting opinions, and to contribute to collective decisions that recognize human responsibility for each and all members of community, even those marginalized from the dominant discourse. In her role as mistress of Clarens, Julie convincingly argues *against* many of the prescriptions mandated in the *Social Contract*, *The Government of Poland*, and *Letter to D'Alembert*. Julie's constant frustration at the inability to express her passion within the "open" society, her advocacy of public gatherings of the servants where the sexes mix in an "intimate" commerce, her dismay over male control of women, the love and friendship she shares with her cousin Claire, and her willingness to die all point to Rousseau's sympathies with

Julie and his unwillingness to fully embrace manliness as a good model for citizenship. We can safely conclude that Emile, Saint-Preux, and Wolmar do not make good citizens. How could they be citizens of a polity required to make good decisions for all when they are so pathetically *unable* to do what is best even for those closest to them? Yet the nagging question remains: Does Rousseau really intend for us to conclude, then, that the women he describes (Sophie, Julie, and Claire) might be models for a better kind of citizen?

What constitutes democratic and participatory citizenship as opposed to passive or tacit citizenship? When we concentrate on Rousseau's women, the dangers of manly citizenship are highlighted. Within the model of manly citizenship, women are completely excluded,[25] while the reason and sentiment of *one man* (with Emile, Saint-Preux, or Wolmar searching for the common in himself to apply as the general will for all) is taken to stand for all men. This common will within men is exemplified in the office of the legislator in the *Social Contract*. Rousseau notes that "in order to discover the rules of society best suited to nations, a superior intelligence beholding all the passions of men without experiencing any of them would be needed."[26] Although this office "nowhere enters into the Constitution" and "has nothing in common with the human empire" (SC, 214), when we look closely at the gender politics in Rousseau's oeuvre, we clearly see that this superior intelligence is merely the "common" will of all *men*. As I have noted, when we look to Rousseau's sympathetic depiction of women, the text invites an interpretation of Rousseau as unwilling to sacrifice his women (even his men) for this version of passive citizenship inconsistent with principles of justice. In an analysis of Levinas's work on the dangers of reducing diverse and other voices to the same or the common in all, Wendy Farley has argued against the kind of politics exemplified in the standard interpretation of Rousseau's general will: "The primordial error in Western philosophy is that . . . it reverses the proper roles of particulars and universals: it ontologizes universals and reduces particulars to mere exemplars. . . . With this erasure of the reality of beings in their actual, fragile livingness comes a deafness to their claims to justice. The epistemological primacy of being over beings has as its ethical corollary a trivialization of actually existing creatures: an indifference to their beauty and inoculation against their suffering."[27] When we read Rousseau from the vantage point of his women characters, this "primordial error" of Western philosophy is not reinscribed. In pointing to the effects that this common will has on women, the marginalized, and the speechless, Rousseau reveals his own dissatisfaction with a society that is *above* politics.

Allowing and encouraging Rousseau's women to speak clearly and forcefully in the words of their own desire would constitute a more active and participatory (and dare I say, *unruly*) politics. Bringing passion and desire (exemplified in the feminine) back in to the polity would significantly complicate things. As we have seen, none of Rousseau's women are willing to rank in order various priorities; none are willing to disregard the sometimes unpopular opinions of the marginalized; none are willing to put the good of the whole above the grief of the one; none are willing to count and measure and number items that are clearly incommensurable; none are willing to put a clear and identifiable name on their conflicting identities and passions. The unwillingness of Rousseau's women to reduce the confusing reality of everyday life and decisions of justice to fit an orderly grid is reminiscent of the confusion that Rousseau finds within the city among diverse groups of people who simultaneously hold varying opinions, alter their identities, and confront one another in public places. In this milieu, you can never really predict, or maybe never even know, what another person is thinking; one is never really sure of another's earnestness, authenticity, devotion to the nation. This tragic loss (though indeed there was *nothing* to lose) of authenticity and identity in modern life so permeates all aspects such that one can never even know what one's *lover* is thinking.

In his impulse to heal the wounds created by the inequalities of the Old Regime, Rousseau seems to advocate a fraternal brotherhood based in male will. But when we shift our perspective to the women this fraternity excludes, Rousseau's trust in his own solution begins to quake. Although he does not *fully* develop a solution to the modern dilemmas wrought by the "loss" of identity, authenticity, and transparency, the voices of his women gesture toward a more active and participatory political ideal that recognizes the demands and desires of the marginalized. This ideal can only begin to be realized via abandoning strict gender boundaries tied into the politics of will and generality.

VII

No matter from which perspective we read Rousseau, the personal and the political are inextricably bound: we learn to be citizens in our most intimate relationships with our families, friends, and lovers. When we read Rousseau from the perspective of his women, gender boundaries, identity, and authenticity are radically subverted. Saint-Preux articulates the paradox at the heart of Rousseau's texts: "Julie, ah, what would I have been without you? Cold reason would have enlightened me, perhaps; a tepid admirer of the good, I would at least have loved it in others. I shall do more; I shall know how to practice it with zeal, and imbued with your wise lessons, I shall one day make those who have known us say: Oh what men we all would be, if the world were full of Julies and our hearts knew how to love them!" (J, II:XIII, 188).

Rousseau's texts remain the site of critical negotiation concerning the role that women could and should play in society, particularly as potential citizens. Sophie and Julie invite questions about the legitimacy and value of that from which they are excluded. They also gesture toward an alternative future, one that moves beyond "the economy of the same" in an attempt to recognize feminine desire.

Notes

1. The idea of a *supplément* is Jacques Derrida's from *On Grammatology*, Trans. Gayatri Chakravorty Spivak (Baltimore: Johns Hopkins University Press, 1976), 156–57. Here Derrida speaks of Thérèse as supplement for Jean-Jacques, in other words, as necessary to create his identity, yet quickly denied or maybe forgotten. What Derrida calls the "immediate presence" or in Rousseau's system a "metaphysics of presence" is created through an infinite chain of supplements—in Derrida's reading of the *Confessions*, he notes that Mamma is the supplement for an unknown mother, that Thérèse is the supplement for Mamma: "That all begins through the intermediary [woman] is what is indeed "inconceivable [to reason]."

2. Unless otherwise indicated, all quotes from *Emile* are from Jean-Jacques Rousseau, *Emile; or, On Education*, trans. Allan Bloom (New York: Basic Books, 1979), cited as *E*, followed by book and page number). Quotes from *La nouvelle Héloïse* are from Rousseau, *Julie, or the New Heloise*, trans. Philip Stewart and Jen Vaché (Hanover: University Press of New England, 1997), cited as *J*, followed by part, letter, and page number.

3. Susan Okin, *Women in Western Political Thought* (Princeton: Princeton University Press, 1979), 132.

4. Mary Wollstonecraft, *A Vindication of the Rights of Woman*, ed. Carol H. Poston (New York: W. W. Norton, 1988), 42.

5. Jean Elshtain, *Public Man, Private Woman* (Princeton: Princeton University Press, 1981), 159.

6. The most recent version of this interpretation of Rousseau appears in Joan Wallach Scott's *Only Paradoxes to Offer: French Feminists and the Rights of Man* (Cambridge: Harvard, 1996): "For Rousseau, the way finally to manage, if not to eliminate, the dangers of erotic excess in both sexes was to restrain it in women. Thus Sophie's education aims at making her a modest, selfless creature whose only goal is to serve her husband; her job is to confirm Emile in his vision of himself, not to

seek through him a self of her own. The key to her education lies in the control if not the repression of her imagination" (28).

7. Tracy Strong, *The Politics of the Ordinary* (Thousand Oaks, Calif.: Sage University Press, 1994), 84.

8. Strong, *The Politics of the Ordinary*, 54.

9. Hannah Arendt, *On Revolution* (New York: Viking Press, 1963), 83, my emphasis.

10. Iris Marion Young, *Justice and the Politics of Difference* (Princeton: Princeton University Press, 1990), 233.

11. Rousseau, *Politics and the Arts: Letter to D'Alembert*, trans. Allan Bloom (Ithaca: Cornell University Press, 1960), cited within the text as *LD'A*, followed by page number.

12. Richard Sennett, *The Fall of Public Man* (New York: Vintage, 1974), 115.

13. Dean Goodman, *The Republic of Letters: A Cultural History of the French Enlightenment* (Ithaca: Cornell, 1994), 74.

14. Jean-Jacques Rousseau, *Emile et Sophie; ou, Les solitaires*, vol. 4 of *Oeuvres complètes*, vol. 4 (Paris: Gallimard, 1969). I thank Roger Hagedorn for his skill in helping me to translate this piece.

15. Judith Sklar, *Men and Citizens* (Cambridge: Cambridge University Press, 1969), 235.

16. Marshall Berman, *The Politics of Authenticity: Radical Individualism and the Emergence of Modern Society* (New York: Antheneum, 1972) and Alessandro Ferrara, *Modernity and Authenticity: A Study of the Social and Ethical Thought of Jean-Jacques Rousseau* (Albany: State University of New York Press, 1993).

17. Linda Zerilli, *Signifying Woman: Culture and Chaos in Rousseau, Burke, and Mill* (Ithaca: Cornell University Press, 1994), 44–45.

18. This quote is taken from Rousseau, *Julie, or the New Eloise*, trans. Judith McDowell (University Park: Pennsylvania State University Press, 1968), II:XV, 198.

19. Jean Starobinski, *Jean-Jacques Rousseau: Transparency and Obstruction*, trans. Arthur Goldhammer (Chicago: University of Chicago Press, 1988), 99.

20. Joel Schwartz, *The Sexual Politics of Jean-Jacques Rousseau* (Chicago: University of Chicago Press, 1984), 125.

21. Lisa Disch, "Claire Loves Julie: Reading the Story of Women's Friendship in *La Nouvelle Héloïse*," *Hypatia: A Journal of Feminist Philosophy* 9, no. 3 (1994): 37.

22. Luce Irigaray, "This Sex Which Is Not One," in *This Sex Which Is Not One*, trans. Catherine Porter (Ithaca: Cornell University Press, 1985), 27.

23. Susan Bickford, "Why We Listen to Lunatics: Antifoundational Theories and Feminist Politics," *Hypatia* 8, no. 2 (1993): 104–23; at 114.

24. Michel Foucault, "Is It Useless to Revolt?" *Philosophy and Social Criticism* 8, no. 1:3–9, quoted in Bickford, "Why We Listen to Lunatics," 15.

25. Unless, of course, we agree with Joel Schartz that women's passive and indirect citizenship (their contribution to the private sphere) is just as important and highly valued as the male contribution as public and active citizenship (Aristotle lives!).

26. Rousseau, *The Social Contract and Discourses*, trans. G. D. H. Cole (London: Everyman's Library, 1973), 214, hereinafter cited as *SC*.

27. Wendy Farley, *Eros for the Other: Retaining Truth in a Pluralistic World* (University Park: Pennsylvania State University Press, 1996), 50.

12

"Une Maitresse Imperieuse"

Woman in Rousseau's Semiotic Republic

Linda Zerilli

Nature's most charming object, the one most able to touch a sensitive heart and to lead it to the good, is, I admit, an agreeable and virtuous woman. But where is this celestial object hiding itself? Is it not cruel to contemplate it with so much pleasure in the theatre, only to find such a different sort in society?

—*Letter to D'Alembert*

To quest for the celestial object, to unmask its earthly referent, such was the task for the writer whose texts bear the manly signature "Jean-Jacques Rousseau, citizen of Geneva." The former he found in the imaginary world of reverie, the latter everywhere else, and above all in the theater—representational site of the unauthentic, performative site of female power. Indeed, for Rousseau the theater is a woman in masquerade, a cunning coquette who courts the look of a captive male audience bewitched by the spectacle of female self-display. Thus fixated on the simulacrum of womanly virtue, thus beguiled by a "counterfeited sweetness," men are lured away from their civic duties and toward that other sort of woman in society: the disorderly and disordering woman who is without modesty, utterly without shame, and whose illicit desire for mastery confounds the natural order of an active masculinity and a passive femininity.

The theater is a female space in which nothing is as it seems, a topsy-turvy world of disguise and deception presided over by "the sex that ought to obey."[1] And yet gender inversion on the stage, says Rousseau, is but a dramatic rendering of the everyday scene of the salon, where a similar overvaluation of the feminine object translates into a counter-spectacle in which it is the man who masquerades, the man who plays to the female gaze, the man who loses his "constitution" by "amusing women."

> Every woman at Paris gathers in her apartment a harem of men more womanish than she. . . . But observe these same men, always constrained in these *voluntary prisons*, get up, sit down, pace continually back and forth to the fireplace, to the window, pick up and set down a fan a hundred times, leaf through books, glance at pictures, turn and pirouette about the room, while the idol, stretched out motionlessly on her couch, has only her eyes and her tongue active.[2]

In the very next sentence, Rousseau contains this "perversion of natural relations" by reading his own representation of counterfeit masculinity as clear evidence of the gallant's "restlessness," of this rustic virility in revolt against the "sedentary and homebound life" that nature imposes on woman, and that woman then imposes on man. The natural man is still discernable under the vile ornaments of the courtier, says the Genevan, still visible under the feminine artifice of our vaunted urbanity. This is the citizen who refuses the command of a female idol and heeds only the call of Mother Nature. Not content to be passive and beautiful, he wants to be active and useful. Perhaps. Then again—the phrase "voluntary prisons" suggests an alternative meaning: the male voyeur in the female space of the theater shares with the exhibitionist in that of the salon a "feminine" passivity and even subservience all the more terrifying to the extent that it is not in fact refused but rather desired.

That men might take no little pleasure in gender inversion and in submission to a dominatrix was the remarkable psychological insight of a theorist who confessed his own mixed delight in self-display, not to mention his "strange taste" in erotic fantasy: "To fall on my knees before a

masterful mistress, to obey her commands, to have to beg for her forgiveness, have been to me the most delicate of pleasures." Could it be that,
just as the autobiographer "was preserved by that very perversity which,"
as he says, "might have been my undoing,"[3] a crime against nature that
gave rise to the godsend of his sexual temerity with women and his over-
active imagination, so too might the man or the citizen be saved by keeping him on his knees before the one who gives the law in love? But saved
from what? From women, it would seem. On his knees before whom? Not
before women but before woman: that celestial object, that magnificent
fetish, the imperious and mute woman of the male imaginary who protects man against that other sort of woman and all her sex, against the
speaking woman of the theater and the salon, but also, indeed especially,
against that uncanny other woman in himself.

Exploring the possibility that it is not fidelity to nature but a crime
against nature, a perverse desire, that emerges as the central issue in
Rousseau's political theory, I should at once highlight his challenge to
the binarism of masculinity and femininity and his quick retreat into a
rigid conception of sexual difference. What Rousseau teaches and fears is
that natural man and woman are pedagogical constructions and highly
unstable ones at that. There is a profound sense in his writings that gender boundaries must be carefully fabricated and maintained because they
have no solid foundation in nature, because what announces "man" or
"woman" is not anatomical difference but instead an arbitrary system of
signs that stands in permanent danger of collapsing into a frightening
ambiguity of meaning and a loss of manly constitution.[4] For what haunts
the writer Rousseau above all else is the similitude of his sexual other, his
dread of becoming woman—his own terrible recognition that, to borrow
Shoshana Felman's words, "femininity inhabits masculinity, inhabits it as
otherness, as its own disruption."[5]

Rousseau's repeated and familiar warnings against the "disorder of
women" evince his fear that, if the code of gender difference is not
strictly adhered to at each and every moment, all is lost.[6] There will not
be any citizens because there will not be any men. Contesting the critical
consensus that Rousseau presents us with the choice of making either a
man or a citizen (since one cannot make both at once), I show that to
be the latter one must, in the first place, be the former, and that to be a
man is to be no more a product of nature than is to be a citizen to be a
"denatured" man.[7] To represent themselves as members of the republic,
men must first contract to represent themselves as members of their own

sex. They must renounce the elegant discourse and elaborate dress of the demimonde, those signifiers of class privilege and counterfeit masculinity. The social contract, it turns out, is a linguistic and sartorial contract, an agreement about the proper symbolic forms of communication among citizens. Simple attire and direct speech are to function as outward signs of men's devotion to each other and to the universalistic principles of the patrie.

Excluded from the social contract, of course, is woman. But her absence is the foundation of the social pact. For woman is the "scapegoat," in Kristeva's words, "charged with the evil of which the community duly constituted can then purge itself."[8] Even as the trope of the disorderly woman carries powerful rhetorical effects that lend urgency to Rousseau's case for the contract, the figure who leads mankind into the abyss, I argue, is a scapegoat precipitated by the disorder in men: that feminine other within the citizen-subject who, despite his almost phobic avoidance of woman, "will always be marked by the uncertainty of his borders and of his affective valency as well."[9]

There is something curious about the frontispiece to the *Discourse on the Origin and Foundations of Inequality Among Men*. The image is of a Hottentot male, scantily dressed, carrying a large cutlass at his side and wearing a long V-shaped necklace. Beneath it stand the words "He goes back to his equals."[10] The Hottentot is departing, as Rousseau explains in a note to the reader, from the Dutch missionaries who had raised him at the Cape of Good Hope as a Christian and in the practice of European customs. "He was richly dressed, he was taught several languages." Then comes the day when, while visiting Hottentot relatives, he makes "the decision to divest himself of his European finery in order to clothe himself in a sheepskin." He returns to the mission, hands over to the governor of the Cape a bundle that contains the vile artifice of his past and makes this speech: "Be so kind, sir, as to understand that I renounce this paraphernalia forever. . . . The sole favor I ask of you is to *let me keep the necklace and cutlass* I am wearing; I shall keep them *for love of you*" (my emphasis). To which Rousseau adds, the civil-savage awaited no reply but immediately ran away and "was never seen again at the Cape" (225–26).

The frontispiece captures in an image what Flugel calls "The Great Masculine Renunciation" that occurred toward the end of the eighteenth century: man's abandonment of his claim to be beautiful—his renunciation of "all the brighter, gayer, more elaborate, and more varied forms of ornamentation"—in favor of being useful.[11] Foregrounding this association of democracy with the democratization of dress, Rousseau tells us that men must eschew the luxurious attire that is a divisive and dissimulating signifier of rank, status, and wealth. Whereas the sartorial signifiers of excess "announce a wealthy man," says Rousseau, "the healthy, robust man is known by other signs. It is in the rustic clothes of a farmer and not beneath the gilt of a courtier that strength and vigor of the body will be found."[12] To communicate proper political meaning, the body of the citizen must be clothed in simple and functional attire. As Flugel observes, "the whole relatively 'fixed' system of his clothing is, in fact, an outward and visible sign of the strictness of his adherence to the social code."[13] Immorality attaches to the man who retains a taste for finery, but it is woman, as we see next, who comes to stand for the self-display that is the driving force behind dissimulation in human affairs.

The Field of Female Voice and Vision

The *Letter to D'Alembert on the Theatre* is obsessed with the dissimulatress who puts sartorial and linguistic signifiers in the service of other than referential functions. Realm of deception, the theater is the field of female voice and vision. Voice is crucial. It is only through "the successive impression made by discourse, striking with cumulative impact," as the *Essay on the Origin of Languages* argues, that "the scenes of tragedy produce their effect. The passions have their gestures but also their accents; and these accents, which cause us to shudder, these accents to which one cannot close one's ear and which by way of it penetrate to the very depths of the heart, in spite of ourselves convey to it the [e]motions that wring them [from us], and cause us to feel what we hear."[14] Invasive and irresistible, the voice carries to our ears sounds we are unable to shut out (as unable, as *Emile* shows, as the infant is to shut out the voice of the mother). As the vehicle of staged tragedies, the voice heard in the theater is the antithesis of the gentle voice: it communicates not genuine sentiments but rather "feigned miseries."[15] Artificial and secondary, the female voice stands in the *Letter* for the degeneration of "natural" language into the counterfeit meanings Rousseau associates with civilization, commerce, and luxury, with an excess he tries to contain by depriving women of any discursive authority.[16]

The female signifying practices of the theater and the salon "pose a sort of problem" for Rousseau. The ancients "had as their maxim that the land where morals [manners] were purest was the one where they spoke the least of women, and that the best woman was the one about whom the least was said."[17] They preserved the value of women, of the sign, by restraining the circulation of women as signs. In an age when "what was said most vividly was expressed not by words but by signs,"[18] to speak of women was to rob them of their intrinsic value, namely, their purity or virtue.[19] To talk about women is scandalous. Far more scandalous, however, is the woman who talks, who steps out of her function as sign, as the signifier of a "common brotherhood." "It is possible that there are in the world a few women worthy of being listened to by a serious man," concedes Rousseau, but the question is whether it is possible to listen to women without "abasing" one's own sex (47). Masculinity dissipates in the acoustic field of female voice.[20] The "most esteemed woman" among us moderns, says Rousseau, is the one "about whom the most is said" and the one who says the most: "who most imperiously sets the tone, who judges, resolves, decides, pronounces, assigns talents, merit, and virtues their degrees and places, and whose favor is most ignominiously begged for by humble, learned men" (49).

Rousseau's complaint against this "perversion of natural relations" (50) was hardly novel. As Joan Landes argues, Montesquieu and Fenelon (among numerous others) had criticized the salon as the site of bourgeois ennoblement and the salonnières as the instructors of aristocratic values. In an age in which "not birth but commerce, venality of office, and intrigue at court became the new coins of power," she writes, "salon women were particularly important in teaching the appropriate style, dress, manners, language, art, and literature" to non-nobles who sought entry into the culture of polite society. If Rousseau linked the salon to the theater, moreover, it was because the line between them was indistinct. "In this aristocratic world of spectacular relations," Landes observes, "where seeing and being seen was an overriding concern, a favorite sport was to play dress up," to stage "amateur theatrical productions," and generally to revel in the art of the masquerade.[21]

Although Rousseau's critique of the salon merely extends these denouncements of women as the arbiters of aristocratic culture and as the driving force behind luxury, and although his attack on the theater advances well-known arguments about women as the agents of masquerade and imposture, he complicates these debates by infusing them with a sense of urgency that belies his recognition that performance is crucial in the constitution of social and sexual identity, and that it has everything to do with political identity. What Rousseau sees and fears, moreover, is that the "perversion of natural [sexual] relations" is possible because pleasurable. Apart from the woman who assumes a position of mastery in the salon, the men who "weep like women" in the theater and throw themselves at the feet of women outside it are a political problem of the highest order. The major threat to the man and the citizen, in short, is the masculine desire to give oneself over to the imperious woman who seeks to overturn the system of exchange between men.

To explain how it is that a man becomes a woman's "thing," Rousseau shows that identity, especially masculine identity, dissipates in the fields of acoustic and scopic pleasure. The theater is condemned because the spectator loses himself in the spectacle: "Who does not himself become a thief for a minute in being concerned about him" (46)? Such identification is possible because "the stage is, in general, a painting of the human passions, the original of which is in every heart" (18); it is dangerous because we spectators do not have to account for our vicarious pleasure. But such pleasure is itself unthinkable without imagination, the faculty that transports us outside ourselves. Imagination is what makes us human and, Rousseau being Rousseau, what makes us perverse. It is not only that some men "pervert the use of this consoling faculty"[22] but also that perversion attends the imagination when it guards the masculine subject against the female and the abyss.

The imagination protects this subject against what Rousseau's prose constructs as a universal female threat to masculinity and social order. Female desire, as we are told in *Emile* and the *Letter* confirms, is an excess that "drag[s] [men] to death without ever being able to defend themselves."[23] To change the natural "order of attack and defense," to remove the "veil" of female chastity, Rousseau warns, is to unleash the fury of female desire, before which the male goes instantly and utterly limp. What is this chastity, this veil? It is a ruse, a fake, an imaginary good that substitutes for the real good that has never the power to excite but always the power to horrify and destroy. It is the uneasy solution to male performance anxiety and a certain lack of desire. "The apparent obstacle, which seems to keep this object at a distance, is in reality what brings it nearer. The desires, veiled by shame, become only the more seductive; in hindering them, chasteness inflames them. Its fears, its tricks, its reserves, its timid avowals," says Rousseau, "say better what chasteness thinks to hide than passion could have said it without chasteness." So male desire is created in the space of the imagination, which is also the female space of the theater; both require props, masks, veils, obstacles. To be a (certain kind of) woman is to say no so that man can say yes—can say anything—to love. It is to create male desire by hiding that one is a subject of desire; it is to misrepresent oneself. The modest woman is like the actor. "What is the talent of the actor? It is the art of counterfeiting himself, of putting on another character than his own, of appearing different than he is." If the actor "annihilates himself" in a role, the woman who does not act annihilates everything: "Love would no longer be the support of nature but its destroyer and plague" (79–84).

Yet not even the feminine artifice of modesty can ward off the threat of disorder. Perversion inheres in the very faculty of the imagination, "which scandalizes the eye in revealing to it what it sees not only as naked but as something that ought to be clothed. There is no garment so modest that a glance inflamed by imagination does not penetrate with its desires." The irrepressible scopophilic drive will always seek to reach its erotic object: the "absolute nudity [of the female sex]" which, we are told, would create "indifference and perhaps [that is, certainly] distaste"— another way of saying that danger attaches to the immodest woman who hides "part of the object. . . . only to set off what is exposed," but also to the modest woman who must play at the game of the veil (134–35). Whatever Rousseau says about the modest woman, she (like the immodest one) is in the last instance an actress implicated in that greatest of crimes. Supplementing herself ("the real good"), the modest woman puts the sign in place of the thing, the signifier in place of the signified. Then, since on this reading the chaste woman herself is nothing but a simulacrum, she opens up the abyss of signification: the copy that is really a copy of a copy of . . . Enter the professional actress, that "counterfeited sweetness" who lures her unwitting admirer to his destruction at the hands of that other simulacrum of womanly virtue in society. If the *Letter* all but spins out of control, as it so often does, it is because danger (the danger of appearing other than one is, of using all manner of signs to effect a no when one wants to say yes) is written into the Rousseauist ideal of woman. The modest woman as masquerade, the actress as masquerade, the idol of the salon as masquerade. Where does the woman-as-spectacle end?

In the circles, in the space where there is no masquerade because there are no women. (They too have their little societies but—thank heaven—one does not often find men there, and the man who does frequent them is a disgrace to his sex.) Where there is no woman there is no female voice to excite unmanly emotions. The circles preserve a space in which men, because they do not have "to clothe reason in gallantry, can devote themselves to grave and serious discourse" (105). They are the site, in Landes's words, where Rousseau can uphold "the fiction of a 'natural language' against the artificial stylized discourse [of le monde]" and its feminized culture. The salonnières—and let us not forget that they, like actresses, existed as public women outside the institution of marriage—are guilty, in the Genevan's view, of tampering with language and thus with the natural order.[24] Whereas women of the salons employ artificial signifiers that do violence to truth, the men of the circles, as Thomas Crow puts it, speak "the language of the truth . . . [as found] dans la Nature toute seule."[25] Still, even though the "citizen of Geneva" projects all that is culturally debased onto the female voice, he knows that this voice commands and the masculine subject all too happily obeys. That is why, for Rousseau, "the two sexes ought to come together sometimes and to live separated ordinarily." In "a commerce that is too intimate," he warns, men "lose not only their morals [manners], but we lose our morals [manners] and our constitution; . . . the women make us into women" (100).

Such is the danger, such is the scandal. But how exactly does the theater figure in the loss of manly constitution? Once again, by means of a spectatorial identification (as with the thief), only now with the simulacrum of a simulacrum: the modest woman played by the actress in a romance. Her art is to "dispos[e] the soul to feelings which are too tender"—much too tender. Since "however love is depicted for us, it seduces or it is not love," cautions Rousseau, one admires "decent love" in the theater only to find oneself in the grip of "criminal love" in society. "The theater is a treasury of perfect women," and therein lies the danger (51–56). Indeed the power of the actress is at its height when she appropriates the signs of the modest woman and sends out, as it were, false messages from the theatrical place of virtue. In this chaste disguise she effects the most profound subversion of the moral order. For, by the time the male spectator discovers the fake (if he ever does), he is already at the mercy of that other fake in society. But the problem runs even deeper, for the man puts himself at the feet of the imperious woman outside the theater not only because he mistakes her for the passive feminine figure on stage but also, if not precisely, because he identifies with that figure.

Consider Rousseau's reading of Racine's Berenice. Here, says the "citizen of Geneva," we have a Roman (Titus) who sways between his duty to country and his love of a mistress. Although the spectator leaves the theater "pitying this sensitive man whom he despised," it is Berenice who claims his heart. At the moment when Berenice can cry no more, the spectators usurp her place and shed volumes of tears at her fate. The result: "The queen departs without the leave of the audience. The Emperor sends her away *invitus invitam* [against his will, against hers]; one might add *invito spectatore* [against the spectator's will]. Titus can very well remain a Roman; he is the only one on his side; all the spectators have married Berenice" (53). One might add, all the spectators have become Berenice, including the male spectators.

Only the sex-segregated circles and societies can protect the masculine subject against his feminine double. "But the moment there is drama, goodby to the *circles*, goodby to the societies!"—more exactly, goodby to the citizen because goodby to the man. "In a republic, *men* are needed" (100—101, my emphasis). That is why the theater must never be allowed inside the gates of Geneva, city of Calvin, of the circles of sumptuary laws.

The mere institution of a theater in Geneva would destroy the republic. The moment actors and actresses so much as enter the city, "the taste for luxury, adornment, and dissipation" will take hold. Not only are sumptuary laws useless in uprooting luxury where it already exists, the mere sight of "the costumes and jewelry of the players" will immediately introduce luxury as excess where it does not yet exist, an excess that no law could ever contain (57). Then, since luxury is a woman,

> the wives of the Mountaineers, going first to see and then to be seen, will want to be dressed and dressed with distinction. The wife of the chief magistrate will not want to present herself at the theater attired like the schoolmaster's. The schoolmaster's wife will strive to be attired like the chief magistrate's. Out of this will soon emerge a competition in dress which will ruin the husbands, will perhaps win them over, and which will find countless new ways to get around the sumptuary laws. (63)

Danger threatens from inside the walls of the republic: in a flash, wives will want to be seen, men will want to see them, "all the rest is easy to imagine" (63). It appears at first that only constant motion, strenuous work, and strict adherence to the laws can keep this excess at bay, but it turns out that to vanquish the desire for woman-as-spectacle the republic must erect another kind of spectacle.

Rousseau outlines a variety of entertainments (*spectacles*) that would be fitting for citizens. For one thing, socially sanctioned forms of pleasure are necessary so that men "fulfill their duties better, that they torment themselves less over changing their stations" (126n). Rousseau criticizes extreme differences in wealth, but it is less material equality than the sentiment of equality he endorses and wishes to nurture in the republican festivities. Since woman is the master signifier of rank according to the "citizen of Geneva," it is she who must be recoded in the *Letter* as a signifier of fraternity. In the place of the sumptuous idol of the salon stretched out on her couch and the actress passing herself off as the modest woman, Rousseau puts the "Queen of the Ball": the young girl who, at the yearly gathering that brings young persons together to dance under the eyes of the public, is crowned for having "comported herself most decently, most modestly." Since every girl will naturally aspire to be Queen, "the attentions to the adornment of their daughters would be an object of amusement of the women which, in turn, would provide diversion for many others"—pleasure, that is to say, for the men. In this way, observes Rousseau, one "can content vanity without offending virtue" (130–31).

Whose vanity? Women's vanity certainly, but also if not especially men's. Rousseau retains and contains not only feminine but also masculine narcissistic and exhibitionist desires in the festivities he recommends: "Why should we not found, on the model of the military prizes, other prizes for gymnastics, wrestling, runnings, discus, and the various bodily exercises? Why should we not animate our boatmen by contests on the lake? Could there be an entertainment in the world more brilliant than seeing, on this vast and superb body of water, hundreds of boats?" So "magnificent" is this spectacle of men, that it will extinguish man's fatal desire to gaze at that other blazing magnificence: the sumptuous body of the salonnière or the actress (127).

The most appealing image of manly pleasure for Rousseau, however, is without doubt the military spectacle he rememorates from his childhood. The scene is in the square of Saint-Gervais where, after a day of military exercises, officers and soldiers have begun to dance together around a fountain: "A dance of men would seem to present nothing very interesting to see," he writes,

> however, the harmony of five or six hundred men in uniform, holding one another by the hand and forming a long ribbon

which wound around, serpent-like, in cadence and without confusion, with countless turns and returns, countless sorts of figured evolutions, the excellence of the tunes which animated them, the sound of the drums, the glare of the torches, a certain military pomp in the midst of pleasure, all this created a very lively sensation that could not be experienced coldly. It was late; the women were in bed; all of them got up. Soon the windows were full of female spectators who gave a new zeal to the actors; . . . they came down; the wives came to their husbands. . . . *The dance was suspended.* . . . My father, embracing me, was seized with trembling which I think I still feel and share: "Jean-Jacques," he said to me, "love your country. Do you see these good Genevans? They are all friends, they are all brothers; . . . You are a Genevan." (135n, my emphasis)

In this image of hundreds of men in uniform, holding hands, dancing in a serpentlike (necklacelike) formation around a fountain—recall that other fountain, that other scene of unbounded desire in the *Essay on the Origin of Languages*—in a state of orderly rapture we have the republican spectacle par excellence. Here the author Rousseau reenacts the moment his father spoke his fraternal name and promotes a spectacle in which "the spectators become an entertainment [*spectacle*] to themselves." Instead of being "suffocat[ed] . . . in sound rooms well closed" (the salon, 102), instead of being buried alive in the "gloomy cavern" of the theater (deadly maternal space), men will take part in festivities "in the open air, under the sky" (125–26). Uniforms, swords (cutlasses), and whatever else accompanies a "certain military pomp" will guard against the feminine threat yet preserve the masculine pleasure in self-adornment and self-display. At once spectator and spectacle, man sees himself seeing himself.

What of the female spectators peering out their windows? It is the female gaze, as Rousseau tells us, that animates the male pleasure in self-display. And so it does. But it is a gaze whose power is circumscribed by the domestic sphere, a domesticated gaze that knows its proper place and specular function, which, like the ruse of chastity, is to reflect man back to himself at twice his original size. And let us not neglect that the presence of the women who come down to join the men (each woman joins her husband) guards against another threat: the manly dance that might very well have transgressed itself in homoerotic ecstasy. The dance was halted at the moment women entered the square, as Rousseau himself says, and could not be taken up anymore.

The *Letter* would efface the gap between spectacle and spectator, representor and represented, signifier and signified. Yet it is inadequate to assert, as Derrida does, that the text evinces Rousseau's "dream of a mute society, of a society before the origin of languages."[26] His dream, rather, is of a society without female voice, one in which woman remains within her proper function as sign. Rousseau's critique of the signifier, in fact, explicitly links the deadly play of signification (the effacement of the referent or the speaker in the signifier) to woman as signifying subject. That the modest woman masquerades, indeed must masquerade, however, means that there is, finally, no stable referent outside the play of signification that could possibly ground woman as (unified, stable) sign and therefore the natural binarism of masculinity and femininity Rousseau claims to be essential to moral order. This is why the pedagogical construction of gender difference in *Emile* is supplemented by the image of woman in the male imagination: the celestial object that has no earthly referent and, for that very reason, protects man against woman and all her sex.

Making a Man

The educational project of *Emile* is straightforward: to raise a child who "will, in the first place, be a man."[27] Perhaps Emile will be a citizen as well. But he has not the slightest chance of becoming a member of the political community if he does not first become a member of his own sex. Noticeable immediately in the text, as Mary Jacobus observes, is that the man-child "comes into being on the basis of a missing mother."[28] Rousseau himself declares, "Emile is an orphan" (52)—or, more exactly and for all pedagogical purposes, he is orphaned by being placed in infancy in the hands of the tutor. Emile has a mother (as fictive as her son), but apart from her biological function she is redundant. Even her first and most sacred duty to nurse (should she consent to it) is supplemented with a Rousseauist script: "She will be given written instruction, for this advantage has its counter-poise and keeps the governor at something more of a distance from his pupil" (56). The mother-child dyad, in other words, can be overclose, dangerous.

Thus emerges the other face to the nursing mother whom Rousseau raises to the status of a secular idol and contrasts to those big-city mothers who deposit their children with a wet nurse in the country. Rousseau rails for pages in Book I against the "mercenary" practice of wet-nursing, which symbolizes the economy of the supplement and the cash nexus.[29] The child who is farmed out to a hired nurse is swaddled, "hung from a nail like a sack of clothes," and deprived of the maternal breast. And lacking this real good (which Rousseau credits as the source of all felicity, peace, and morals), the child will cry and then fantasize: he will substitute the first of an endless number of imaginary goods that mark the gap between his desires and powers. But if Rousseau holds neglectful mothers to be the cause of all unhappiness, he is just as, if not more, worried by loving mothers who carry their first duty to excess. "Plunging their children into softness," these equally "cruel mothers" prepare them for the sedentary life of a eunuch, lived with women or in their manner (44, 47).[30]

In the place of all mothers, Rousseau puts "Thetis [who], to make her son [Achilles] invulnerable, plunged him . . . in the water of the Styx" (47), then puts himself as tutor in the place of the mythical mother. This "lovely" fable is the subject of the frontispiece of *Emile*. It depicts Rousseauist pedagogy as military strategy. To make a man, the sacred mother-child bond must be closely supervised, if not drastically and symbolically severed, in order to prepare the child for battle with "the enemy" who will appear in Book V: the desire for a woman, to be at the feet of a woman if not to be a woman. But just as the mythical Achilles had one weak point (his heel, by which his mother held him when she dipped him in the water, which connected him to his maternal origin), so too is Emile at risk by virtue of being born of woman. The tutor/ author, however, knows his mythology well enough to devise safeguards to delay the impending disaster.

The first of these deferral strategies is to replace the mother with a wet nurse, whom the tutor then subjects to relentless visual surveillance in order to ensure that the child be made dependent on things and not on wills. For the very first thing the helpless infant encounters is, of course, absolutely inseparable from human will—that is, a woman's will: the breast is inseparable from her who gives or withholds it and who is, for that reason, the child's first master. Double danger: the infant is not only dependent on the will of a woman but also caught in the sonorous envelope of the (substitute) maternal voice. "I do not disapprove of the nurse's entertaining the child with songs and very gay and varied accents," remarks Rousseau. "But I do disapprove of her making him constantly giddy with a multitude of useless words of which he understands nothing other than the tone she gives them." The child who listens "in swaddling clothes to the prattle of his nurse" confuses the words uttered by the female speaker with reality and soon comes to speak like a woman. The nurse or mother "serve[s] as an interpreter for the city child," whose voice she reduces to mimicry.[31] It is a weak and indistinct voice: "A man who learns to speak only in his bedroom will fail to make himself understood at the head of a battalion," warns the "citizen of Geneva." "First teach children to speak to men; they will know how to speak to women when they have to" (70–73).

The maternal voice is disorienting. "I would want the first articulations which he [the child] is made to hear to be rare, easy, distinct, often repeated," advises the tutor, "and that the words they express relate only to objects of the senses which can in the first place be shown to the child" (70). The child who is taught representative signs before he understands their relation to things loses his originary wholeness in the arbitrary relation between signifier and signified. Thus weakened, he is doomed to become a mouthpiece or actor and to take up his place in the salon or theater amusing women: he can be made to "say whatever one wants" (250)—whatever women want. Double maxim: keep the maternal voice at a distance and keep the child away from books. There is only one book the child needs to learn, "the book of the world" (451). If "we absolutely must have books," says Rousseau, "there exists one which, to my taste, provides the most felicitous treatise on natural education" (184): *Robinson Crusoe*—"that bourgeois parable of masculine self sufficiency," as Jacobus puts it.[32] Let Emile imagine that "he is Robinson himself, . . . dressed in skins, wearing a large cap, carrying a large saber and all the rest of the character's grotesque equipment," muses Rousseau, "with the exception of the parasol, which he will not need" (185)—of course.

And so (properly attired like that other manly civil-savage of the *Discourse on Inequality*) the child is ready to be taught the value of manual labor. "I absolutely want Emile to learn a trade," declares the tutor. "I do not want him to be an embroiderer, a gilder, or a varnisher, like Locke's gentleman." He should be given a trade that suits his sex and forbidden any that would soften his body. Since we have a choice, says Rousseau, let us choose a trade for its "cleanliness." Let us choose, then, carpentry:

"It is clean; it is useful." Whatever trade one prefers, always remember that big manly hands were not made to handle "ribbons, tassels, net, and chenille." So contaminating is such paraphernalia, so fragile is the whole pedagogical code of gender difference by trade, that such crimes against nature should be forbidden by royal decree: "If I were sovereign," declares Rousseau, "I would permit sewing and the needle trades only to women and to cripples reduced to occupations like theirs"; or, if necessary, such crimes should be punished by castration: "And if there absolutely must be true eunuchs, let men who dishonor their sex by taking jobs which do not suit it be reduced to this condition" (197–200).

Immersed in the book of the world, Emile's powers and desires are kept in equilibrium. Another maxim: "the real world has its limits; the imaginary world is infinite. Unable to enlarge the one, let us restrict the other, for it is from the difference between the two alone that are born all the pains which make us truly unhappy" (81). Then, since language operates in the realm of the imagination (the child needs words to signify the real objects it lacks), "in general, never substitute the sign for the thing except when it is impossible for you to show the latter, for the sign absorbs the child's attention and makes him forget the thing represented" (170). Still, it is not quite accurate to say, as Starobinski does, that in *Emile* "discourse . . . follows encounters with real objects."[33] There is one crucial exception to the Rousseauist rule governing the related uses of discourse and the imagination. Not every thing can be shown more safely than the sign, not every "real good" is less dangerous than the imaginary one; one sign is of value precisely because it absorbs the child's attention: "Sophie or the woman."

In Book IV, Emile comes into danger. The moment of crisis has arrived, the decisive moment of his confused sexual awakening. Let us note that this was the moment when the autobiographer's own objectless desires "took a false turn"; the moment when the young Jean-Jacques developed his abject wish to be beaten by a masterful mistress.[34] Warns the tutor, if the child's "pulse rises and his eye is inflamed; if the hand of a woman placed on his makes him shiver; if he gets flustered or is intimidated near her—Ulysses, O wise Ulysses, be careful. The goatskins you closed with so much care are open. The winds are already loose. No longer leave the tiller for an instant, or all is lost." Not about to jump ship, the tutor will play midwife at "the second birth" (212).

Let us reflect on the first appearance of the mythical Ulysses at this point in the text, where *amour-propre* (or "the relative I," 243) comes into play. Everything in Emile's education has thus far been addressed to his *amour de soi* alone. "He has said, 'I love you,' to no one" (222); "He does not feel himself to be of any sex, of any species. Man and woman are equally alien to him" (219). In love only with himself but unable to recognize himself (because he recognizes and is recognized by no other), Emile is, so to speak, like the mythical Narcissus, who is entirely within himself and, as Kristeva writes, "does not, in fact, know who he is": "He Loves, he loves Himself—active and passive, subject *and* object."[35] But the ego of narcissism, says Kristeva, is fragile and uncertain because it lacks an object, indeed only barely maintains its borders in relation to a nonobject (the maternal voice, gaze, breast).[36] Emile was dipped in the Styx, but he is not invulnerable. Narcissus, as the fable says, drowned in the pool of his own reflection, fell into the watery maternal element. Ulysses too is on a quest, not of his own image but rather, as Kristeva quotes the *Enneads*, of "the 'fatherland,' for 'it is there that dwells our Father.'" The trajectory "from Narcissus to Ulysses," she writes, "proceeds through *love* and the exclusion of the impure"—the abject.[37] Ulysses does not heed the seductive voice of the Sirens that lured others before him into the abyss, and, as the symbolically appropriate frontispiece to Book V of *Emile* shows us, he triumphs over Circe, who gives herself to the one man she could not debase.[38] Emile too will be sent on a quest for the fatherland, but first he must confront the enemy in himself.

Emile's objectless desires do not arise out of hormonal changes, they "are awakened by the imagination alone. Their need is not properly a physical need. It is not true that it is a true need. If *no lewd object* had ever struck our eyes, if *no indecent idea* had ever entered our minds, perhaps this alleged need would never have made itself felt to us, and we would have remained chaste without temptation, without effort, and without merit" (333, my emphasis). It is true that *Emile*, as Allan Bloom maintains, advances the idea of sublimated sex, but what is sublimated is no instinctual drive; it is rather a perverse desire that is excited by "the memory of objects" from childhood (the nurse, books, women).[39]

"You do not know the fury with which the senses, by the lure of pleasure, drag young men like you into the abyss of the vices," the tutor tells Emile. "Just as Ulysses, moved by the Sirens' song and seduced by the lure of the pleasures, cried out to his crew to unchain him, so you will want to break the bonds which hinder you." To be saved by his guardian, the pupil must first give his duly considered consent. Once "he has, so to speak, signed the contract," the tutor sets about reinforcing the fortress around his young charge. "Removing dangerous objects is nothing, if I do not also remove the memory of them." The tutor comes thus upon the idea of sending Emile on the hunt. "He will lose in it—at least for a time—the dangerous inclinations born of softness. The hunt hardens the heart as well as the body. It accustoms one to blood, to cruelty" (326, 320). It purges the male subject, as Kristeva would say, of the feminine, the abject.

The primary means for erasing the kind of memories that "engend[er] monsters" (325), however, is to plant in Emile's imagination the chaste image of woman. The search for the celestial object begins thus:

> It is unimportant whether the object I depict for him [Emile] is imaginary; it suffices that it make him disgusted with those that could tempt him; it suffices that he everywhere find comparisons which make him prefer his chimera to the real objects that strike his eye. And what is true love itself if it is not chimera, lie, and illusion? We love the image we make for ourselves far more than we love the object to which we apply it. . . . The magic veil drops, and love disappears. (329)

Few knew better than Rousseau that, thanks to the imaginary object, one sex ceases to be anything for the other. In the *Confessions*, the auto-biographer tells us that the image of the mother substitute (Madame de Warens) "safeguarded me against her and all her sex." "Fondling her image in my secret heart," writes Rousseau, "and surrounded at night by objects to remind me of her" was not "my undoing" but rather "my salvation."[40] Alfred Binet credits Rousseau with the invention of a form of fetishism that substituted the relic for and preferred it to the woman to whom it originally belonged.[41] Rousseau himself admitted: "It's not at all the vanity produced by estate or rank that attracts me, its sensual delight; a better preserved complexion; a finer, better-made dress, a dain-tier shoe, ribbons, lace, hair better dressed. I would always prefer the less pretty one as long as she had more of all of that."[42]

Binet's observations help explain why the author Rousseau is im-mersed in "voluptuous reveries," as Mary Wollstonecraft so astutely put it, "when he describes the pretty foot and enticing airs of his little favour-ite,"[43] and why Sophie must master "the art of dressing oneself up" (368), of "getting looked at" (373). Sophie "loves adornment" (393). Her natural desire to please begins, as does every girl's, with

> what presents itself to sight and is useful for ornamentation; mirrors, jewels, dresses, particularly dolls. . . . Observe a little girl spending the day around her doll, constantly changing its clothes, dressing and undressing it hundreds and hundreds of times, continuously seeking new combinations of ornaments. . . . you will say, she adorns her doll and not her person. Doubtless. She sees her doll and does not see herself. . . . She is entirely in her doll, and she puts all her coquetry into it. She will not always leave it there. She awaits the moment when she will be her own doll. (367)

If *Emile* can be read as foregrounding "the Great Masculine Renunciation" (and all the psychic inhibitions it entailed for the citizen-subject), then it is more than female vanity that is being gratified in this scene. The narcissistic pleasures the masculine subject denies himself (the tutor forbids his pupil) are projected onto the feminine other who is compelled to love adornment, to make herself a fetish, to become "her own doll." Woman must bear the double burden of *his* desire to see and to be seen, must gratify *his* pleasure in looking and self-display.

Since the pedagogical project of *Emile* is to make a man who renounces aristocratic affectation, not just any kind of female adornment will do. The doll-woman who struts in her elaborate and rich finery stands accused of trafficking in counterfeit goods, of trying "to hide some defects": "I have also noticed that the most sumptuous adornment usually marks ugly women" (372), informs Rousseau.[44] These fakes deceive men and impose the class law of fashion on beautiful women. Attractive or not, the dangerous woman, it turns out, is not so much dissembling as self-sufficient: caught up in her own image, she only appears to please the men who must please her. She is the aristocratic idol who holds court "in the ceremony of the dressing table" surrounded by "the merchants, the salesmen, the fops, the scribblers, the poems, the songs, the pamphlets" (373). Then, since all women are natural coquettes, proper femininity too operates in the realm of deception. But there are two "species of dissimulation," says Rousseau: natural and unnatural, chaste and unchaste, dependent and independent. Women who practice the former kind are commended for "disguising the sentiments that they have";

those who practice the latter are condemned for "feigning those they do not have" (430n).[45] What fascinates and terrifies Rousseau are the narcissistic women who dress up and gaze at their own image but are indifferent to male desire, who "never love [or desire] anything but themselves" (430n). That these women are nothing but the scapegoats of "the Great Masculine Renunciation" is suggested by Flugel's remark that "men with strong exhibitionist desires"—like the autobiographical subject of the *Confessions*—"admire women and at the same time envy their opportunity for bodily and sartorial self-display."[46] That is why the little girl who dresses her doll must be inscribed in the economy of male pleasure, and why Sophie must be made into a dependent coquette who is solicitous of Emile's gaze.

The author/tutor proceeds with his reverie on the imaginary object, telling both reader and pupil that Sophie's "adornment is very modest in appearance and very coquettish in fact." The man whose eyes "roam over her whole person," muses the tutor, cannot help but think that her "very simple attire was put on only to be taken off piece by piece by the imagination" (394). And so female self-representation plays (once again) to the male gaze, to the perverse scopic drive, which means (once again) that it carries the risk of exciting unpleasure. The chaste woman must sustain the endless play of sartorial signifiers, for they alone inhibit the drive from reaching (as we saw in the *Letter*) its erotic object. Female presence is tolerable only as a kind of absence; there must always be one more piece of clothing, one more veil, yet one more obstacle to keep alive the lifesaving economy of the fetish, the signifying chain of synecdoches.

Even though the modest woman's great art of the lie is her sacred duty,[47] she may never signify herself as subject, as speaking subject, as a producer of signs—that is, if she is to remain in her function as sign.[48]. Thus woman must conceal the production of her femininity, of herself as coquette. Sophie's "art is apparent nowhere" (394), she makes artifice appear natural.[49] So it is that woman effaces herself as subject and thereby upholds herself as referent, as the ground of masculinist self-representation.[50] Men find in Sophie not a radical speaking other, as Joel Schwartz would have it,[51] but rather, as Rousseau tells us time and again, "more or less what they find in their own minds."[52] Indeed Sophie, to borrow Luce Irigaray's account of woman's function in a masculinist symbolic economy, is "the foundation for this specular duplication, giving man back 'his' image and repeating it as the 'same'."[53]

To reflect back to the masculine speaking subject the stable, self-identical image of himself, the symbolic oneness of the I, Sophie must guard him against whatever threatens to encroach on the fragile borders of his identity: the chaste woman must secure the borders of the clean and proper. Proper femininity keeps at bay the abject: that which is opposed to I, that which, in Kristeva's words, "establishes intermixture and disorder," that frightful mingling or confusion.[54] This is why Sophie, as Rousseau tells us, is obsessed with cleanliness. Learned from her mother, she demands it in her "person, her things, her room, her work, her grooming." Sophie's first maxim is to do everything "cleanly," but without any trace of "vain affectation or softness." Of course, Emile too likes things clean, likes his wife-to-be clean. After all, "nothing in the world is more disgusting than an unclean woman, and the husband who is disgusted by her is never wrong."[55] Sophie, fortunately, "is much more than clean. She is pure" (395).

When Emile finally encounters his imaginary object in all her pure and fictive flesh, he barely notices her (although she is sitting at the dinner table with him)—that is, until the mother utters Sophie's name. It is love not at first sight but at first sound. In a matter of moments Emile is ready to camp out in a ditch near her abode, to give "his lessons on his knees before her," to crawl before her. He wants to adorn her, "he needs to adorn her": "As the idolater enriches the object of his worship with treasures that he esteems and adorns on the altar the God he adores, so the lover," writes the tutor, "constantly wants to add new ornaments to her [his mistress Sophie]" (425). Then again, perhaps he wants to add a few of those ornaments to himself. Having renunciated masculine self-adornment as a disgrace to his sex, the Rousseauist lover settles for vicarious pleasure, indeed rechannels his desire to be seen into the desire to see.[56] There is always the possibility, however, that the lover may find himself caught in a kind of psychic cross-dressing, that is to say, in a destabilizing identification with his own woman-as-spectacle.[57]

"Dear Emile," implores the tutor, "it is in vain that I have dipped your soul in the Styx; I was not able to make it everywhere invulnerable. A new enemy is arising which you have not learned to conquer and from which I can no longer save you. This enemy is yourself" (443). Emile "lets himself be governed by women" and is becoming one of them, "softened by an idle life" (431). The tutor has tried all manly means at his disposal to hold off the fatal metamorphosis. But woman's "empire" consists precisely in her power to turn man into his sexual other: "Hercules who believed he raped the fifty daughters of Thespitius was nevertheless constrained to weave [and, in fact to dress as a woman] while he was with Omphale" (360–61). Rousseau leaves little doubt that the only way to avoid Hercules' fate (not to mention Narcissus's) is to follow the example of Ulysses, and thus to set out on a quest for the fatherland. "Do you know what government, laws, and fatherland are?" the tutor asks his pupil. The answer is clear, the consequence obvious: "Emile, you must leave Sophie" (448).

And so the reluctant pupil is dragged off on a two-year journey and given a crash course in the social contract. He learns the meaning of the body politic, the people, the sovereign, the laws. But he does not, in fact, find the fatherland because it does not exist. Emile declares his choice to remain a man to whom place is irrelevant; a nomad in spirit, he is equally at home among men or without them. The young man has his passions, however, and thus implores the tutor to give him back his "one chain," Sophie (472). The governor restrains his pupil, reminding him that, even though the "social contract has not been observed," "he who does not have a fatherland at least has a country." Should the state call him he must "fulfill the honorable function of citizen" (473–74).

Even though *Emile*, as Judith Shklar rightly argues, is primarily about making not a citizen but rather a man, domestic education would be doomed in the absence of some civic education.[58] Indeed, the chimera of the fatherland comes to the rescue at the moment Emile is most vulnerable (ready to marry and take to the nuptial bed); it is a supplement to that other chimera, the celestial object; and both chimeras are imaginary props whose purpose is to ensure that Emile attain the status of a man— that is, a non-woman. The man and the citizen (like domestic education and civic education) are, in fact, two sides of the same coin to the extent that both entail the renunciation of that which signifies at once the feminine and the aristocratic, and to the extent that neither can succeed in that renunciation alone. Each requires the supplement of the other. Sophie is no Spartan mother, but her modest attire and natural speech are the bedrock of Emile's own forswearing of luxury and strict adherence to the abstract principles of the fatherland, even in its absence: the values of work, duty, and simplicity and the sentiments of fraternity and equality.[59]

What *Emile* teaches, finally, is that cohabitation with women can be lived only with woman: that fiction within a fiction, the chaste image of Sophie that protects Emile against Sophie and all her sex. But the celestial object's earthly referent remains the wild card in Rousseau's pedagogical project. Quite apart from Sophie's unsurprising infidelity in the unfinished sequel to *Emile*—which leads her, as Susan Okin has shown, to the familiar, suicidal "fate of Rousseau's heroines"[60]—her status as a kind of compromise solution to the masterful mistress of the *Confessions* places "the woman" beyond the law. Indeed male pleasure and danger attend the "imperious Sophie," "the severe Sophie," as Rousseau repeatedly describes her. Having learned that the man wants to be on his knees at her feet and how to keep him there, that "imperious girl" (478) makes poor Emile sleep in a separate bed on their wedding night. She is admonished by the tutor for giving her husband cause to complain of her "coldness" (478–79). Her empire, in other words, might very well turn into that of those big-city women, who practice a false species of dissimulation and never love anything but themselves. Whatever its species, however, dissimulation is always just that. There is never any guarantee that men will correctly read the signs of femininity qua coquetry. The latter may be sincere or insincere, put in the service of woman's "natural empire" or "unnatural" female power. The whole foundation of the man or citizen stands on nothing but quicksand. Then again, there is always the social contract: chimera of the fatherland made sacred law.

The Semiotic Republic

Why is woman missing in the *Social Contract*? Leaving aside, for a moment, her unsurprising absence as citizen, let us reflect on her remarkable absence as a topic for political debate in a text that was published almost simultaneously with *Emile*.[61] Indeed, of woman (for once) hardly a word is said; the word itself appears only three times in the entire text.[62] And if we consider that the opening line addressed to men in this treatise on political right ("Man was/is born free, and everywhere he is in chains"; 46) finds its analogue in a line addressed to mothers in that treatise on education ("The first gifts they receive from you are chains"),[63] it seems even more incredible that a blank should mark the place of man's very first master. Taking up the analogy, however, we may speculate that the *Social Contract*, which argues that chains can be made "legitimate" (46), works surreptitiously on the problem of those other chains in *Emile* (and in the *Letter* and the *Discourse*). The Rousseauist citizen-subject will be in "a [desired] condition of bondage," as Hilail Gilden aptly puts it.[64] But the question is, who will be his master? with whom will he contract? with "une maitresse imperieuse" or with other men?

With the preceding remarks in mind, we may speculate that the absence of woman marks her spatial exclusion from the political site of meaning (the enactment and reenactment of the sociosymbolic pact, of legitimate chains), and that woman's permanent exile constitutes an absent presence, and a potentially disruptive one at that. To locate the paradigmatic and unnamed feminine threat, we have only to turn to the second chapter of the text, "On the First Societies": it is Circe, the sorceress. Contesting Aristotle's claim that "some [men] are born for slavery and others for domination," Rousseau observes: "Aristotle was right, but he mistook the effect for the cause. Slaves lose everything in their chains, even the desire to be rid of them. They love their servitude as the companions of Ulysses loved their brutishness. If there are slaves by nature, therefore, it is because there have been slaves contrary to nature. Force made the first slaves; their cowardice perpetuated them" (48). The reference to Ulysses, as Gilden notes, is taken from a work by Plutarch in which the hero "asks Circe to liberate his companions as well as other Greeks whom she had bewitched and transformed into brutes. Circe refuses to do so without their consent. She restores the power of speech to one of her victims and leaves Ulysses alone to speak to him. The beast to whom he speaks argues for the superiority of his transformed condition and refuses to become a man again."[65] Because Ulysses remains a man, says Gilden, he is the model mortal who points to the legislator. Perhaps. But clearly his contented companions—if not the "men as they are" who point to the Rousseauist problem of forming "laws as they can be" (46)— are the men as they might easily become (i.e., as speechless as infants) who point to the very necessity of the laws. And before accepting Gilden's suggestion that the lawgiver is a man like Ulysses, let us not forget that, in Homer's telling at least, even the famed hero is not invulnerable to Circe's charms and in fact barely escapes with his life. He all but forgets his goals of return, Ithaca and the fatherland. If he had not been later tied to the mast, moreover, he would have most surely succumbed to the sweet voices of the Sirens and fallen into the abyss. This feminine call from the beyond can be kept at bay only by the most extraordinary means, including that most extraordinary of human beings, the lawgiver.

Simply put, the sacred task of those whom Rousseau calls "Pères de Nations" is to make men aware of what they themselves desire but are often unable to discern; it is to articulate the unified inner voice of reason in every man's heart: the general will that is immutable, impartial, and never errs. The lawgiver is a quasi-divine figure who, because he knows all men's passions but feels none of them, can serve as the "organ" with which the body politic can "enunciate its will" (67). He is neither Robert Filmer's patriarch nor Thomas Hobbes's sovereign; he does not have that kind of monopoly on power and meaning. Let us be clear as well that the wholly conventional voice of the lawgiver bears no resemblance whatsoever to the original maternal voice. Indeed "Nature's voice" is now deemed, as the first version of the Social Contract (Geneva Manuscript) tells us, a "false guide, working continuously to separate him [the lawgiver] from his people, and bringing him sooner or later to his downfall or to that of the State."[66]

Rather than heed Nature, then, the lawgiver must oppose her, separate his people from her: in short, codify the social pact or "oath" such that the voice of duty replaces physical impulse, right replaces appetite.[67] What looks like the Freudian superego is a fragile achievement at best. Because men are "constantly reminded of their primitive condition by nature,"[68] all it takes is a small miscalculation on the part of the legislator as to the type of laws a people can bear, or the slightest division in the "artificial social body," for the whole political edifice to collapse, whereby "invincible nature" regains her "dominion" (76). And if we now note that the "sacred right that serves as a basis for all the others" (47) assumes but does not name the sacred law we found buried in the Essay on the Origin of Languages,[69] we can glimpse the magnitude of the lawgiver's sacred task. To separate men from their "common mother," to wrest from each individual the moi humain and transform it into the moi commune, the lawgiver must, as the Geneva Manuscript puts it, "in a sense mutilate man's constitution in order to strengthen it,"[70] substitute "a partial and moral existence for the physical and independent existence we have all received from nature." He must, so to speak, build a fortress around the citizen-subject by ensuring that "natural forces are dead and destroyed" (68).

The importance of this act, first of separating and then of keeping separate (that is, of establishing and maintaining a series of symbolic and psychic oppositions: inside/outside, citizen/foreigner, culture/nature, masculine/feminine) can be seen clearly in Rousseau's unbounded admiration for Moses. In The Government of Poland—where the author tries his own hand at the role of the great legislator, in accordance with many of the principles of the *Social Contract*—Moses is celebrated for having transformed a "herd of servile emigrants ['wandering about in the wilderness'] into a political society, a free people." Just as the Genevan would secure the Poles against the impending Russian domination and cultural intermixture, so did Moses secure the Israelites against the hostile Philistines, pagan reengulfment:

> Determined that his people should never be *absorbed* by other peoples, Moses devised for them customs and practices that could not be *blended* into those of other nations and weighted them down with rites and peculiar ceremonies. He put countless prohibitions upon them, all calculated *to keep them constantly on their toes*, and to make them, with respect to the rest of mankind, outsiders forever. Each fraternal bond that he established among the individual members of his republic became *a further barrier, separating* them from their neighbors and keeping them from *becoming one* with those neighbors.[71]

The rites, ceremonies, and prohibitions that kept the Israelites vigilant or "on their toes" kept them distinct and separate, prevented the kind of cultural intermingling whereby their identity would have dissipated (as it often came close to doing) into the indistinct pagan environment. These rites included, among numerous others, circumcision (the sign of the covenant for which women cannot be marked and which symbolically separates men from the feminine, the maternal)[72] and the taboo on idols (representation of an invisible God). As Kristeva writes, Moses imposed on his people "a *strategy of identity*, which is, in all strictness, that of monotheism": aimed "to guarantee the place and law of the One God." And "the place *and* law of the One," she adds, "do not exist without *a series of separations* . . . [which relate in the last analysis] to fusion with the mother." Those rites testify to "the harsh combat Judaism, in order to constitute itself, must wage against paganism and its maternal cults." What is more, they carry "into the private lives of everyone the brunt of the struggle each subject must wage during the entire length of his personal history in order to become [and remain] separate, that is to say, to become [and remain] a speaking subject and/or subject to Law."[73]

Like Moses, Rousseau's secular lawgiver must create a subject who consents to law, a subject who unites himself with others to create the one: the unity of the artificial social body, its common ego and vice. That is why it is not enough for the great legislator to draft the laws; he must also communicate them such that they penetrate to the very hearts of the citizens, who will then preserve them in their cultural practices. This he does, in part, not by employing force or reason, both of which Rousseau strictly forbids him, but rather by speaking in the mute eloquence of Signs, those "crude but august monuments of the sanctity of contracts."[74] The Jews' prophets, says Rousseau, were masters of this archaic language,[75] but the political uses of Signs are not in any way exclusive to biblical or ecclesiastical communities. Indeed, as Rousseau indicates in *Emile*, the Sign is the very lifeblood of monarchies and, not least, of republics. To cite one example, the genius of Antony was to eschew the letter for the Sign when he had the bloody corpse of Caesar "brought in" for all to see: "What rhetoric!"[76]

Of particular interest, however, is a less gruesome version of the Sign, in which the law is engraved on the hearts of citizens, the image of the fatherland kept constantly before their eyes, through "spectacular display,"[77] better known as the secular ceremonies and rites of manly passage in which the social is secured through the sartorial contract: "How great was the attention that the Romans paid to the language of signs! Different clothing according to ages and according to stations—togas, sagums, praetexts, bullas, laticlaves; thrones, lictors, fasces, axes; crowns of gold or of herbs or of leaves; ovations, triumphs. Everything with them was display, show, ceremony, and everything made an impression on the hearts of citizens."[78] The hierarchic features of dress mark and sustain differences among men in the midst of unity; the individual identifies with but is not lost within the manly crowd; the masculine pleasure in self-adornment is indulged without betraying any effeminacy. Finally, let us note and reserve comment on a more sexually ambiguous version of the Sign: "The Doge of Venice [is] without power, without authority, but rendered sacred by his pomp and dressed up in a woman's hairdo under his ducal bonnet."[79]

One place where the semiotics of the Roman republic and those of the Jewish state meet those of the social contract, where the Sign prevents the kind of mingling that is the death of the body politic and the citizen-subject, is in Rousseau's detailed proposal for preserving Poland against the foreign threat. Above all, the citizenry must develop "an instinctive distaste for mingling with the peoples of other countries." Therefore, Rousseau advises, all national customs must "be purely Polish." For example, "the Poles [should] have a distinctive mode of dress. . . . See to it that your king, your senators, everyone in public life, never wear anything but distinctively Polish clothing."[80] And, to guard against class mingling, "I should like each rank, each employment, each honorific reward, to be dignified with its own external badge or emblem. I should like you to permit no officeholder to move about *incognito*, so that the marks of a man's rank or position shall accompany him wherever he goes."[81] And so forth.

Even as this amazingly precise semiotics evinces the "dream of a transparent society, visible and legible in each of its parts," in Michel Foucault's words, it also contests inherited class position, the signifying economy of landed property.[82] All "active members of the republic," advises Rousseau, are to be divided into three classes, each of which is to have "a distinctive emblem that its members will wear on their persons." These emblems, however, are to "be struck out of distinct metals, whose intrinsic value would be in inverse proportion to the wearer's rank." Then, since signifiers of aristocratic privilege are also those of counterfeit masculinity, "the ribbons and jewels" that have served as the insignia of "knighthoods"—and were conferred on the basis of "royal favor"—are to be strictly forbidden: they "have overtones of finery and womanish adornment that we must avoid in the institution we are creating."[83]

In the place of such unmanly marks, Rousseau puts "the stamp of the knightly tournaments," which are to reconfigure the male body as the spectacular site of republican virtue and individual merit. Because "delight in physical exercise discourages the dangerous kind of idleness, unmanly pleasures, and luxury of spirit," Poland should promote a variety of "open-air spectacles" in which men of all classes compete for prizes (yet other emblems) and display their "bodily-strength and skill." These public games—in which "different ranks would be carefully distinguished," "the people never actually mingle with the rulers"—would challenge those of noble birth to prove their worth in a communal scopic field. All claims to superior rank would be evidenced by "external signs," which must be legible enough to be read by the people, public enough to prevent those who govern from becoming "unmanly and corrupt."[84]

"Spectacular display," then, makes at once the man *and* the citizen; the citizen *and* the man are produced at once through the republican spectacle.[85] This is why the masculine pleasure in self-display is not in any way forbidden by Rousseau but rather strictly regulated: "Let us look with a tolerant eye on military display, which is a matter of weapons and horses [not to mention the rest of the martial paraphernalia that characterized the festive scene in the square of Saint-Gervais]. But let all kinds of womanish adornment be held in contempt. And if you cannot bring women themselves to renounce it [or rather men to renounce their vicarious pleasure in it], let them at least be taught to disapprove of it, and view it with disdain, in men."[86] At stake is "The Great Masculine Renunciation," which is to say the man, the citizen, the republic. Sumptuary laws alone are powerless against the masculine desire for sumptuous self-display. No law could possibly contain that kind of excess, that kind of disorder in men; not even the prohibition on "gambling, the theater, comedies, operas—everything that makes men unmanly."[87]

To be in any way effective—effective at keeping the feminine other at bay—sumptuary laws and the taboo on disgraceful spectacles must be combined, at each and every moment, with hard work, strict adherence to the laws, constant vigilance, in a word, obstacles to dangerous idleness and unmanly pleasures. That is why freedom for Rousseau, as Benjamin Barber writes, "entails permanent and necessary tension, ineluctable conflict. It requires not the absence but the presence of obstacles; for without them there can be no tension, no overcoming, and consequently, no freedom."[88] In the absence of all obstacles there is only the permeability of the ego or, as the Social Contract tells us, of the "moral and collective body," its "unity" and "common self" (53).

Thus, in addition to the natural obstacles to self-preservation that bring men together in the first place, there is the obstacle of private wills: "If there were no different interests, the common interest, which would never encounter any obstacle, would scarcely be felt" (61). Invincible Nature would take its place; the abject feminine other would take its place. Then there is the obstacle of the weather that guards men against the ravages of luxury: "In climates where seasonal changes are abrupt and violent, clothes are better and simpler" (94). A certain deprivation is necessary in the republic, not so much to foment revolution, but enough to keep men on their toes.[89]

Above all, the republic must regulate the use of money, that secular idol—the other being woman—that "merely supplements men." For one thing, "that which supplements is never so valuable as that which is supplemented."[90] For another, what is supplemented soon ceases to exist. "Is it necessary to march to battle? They [the citizens] pay troops and stay home. Is it necessary to attend the council? They name deputies and stay home." Money promotes "softness and the love of comforts." It is the beginning of the end: "Give money and you will soon have chains." With his purse in the place of himself, the masculine subject vanishes as a citizen, vanishes as a man. He forgoes active participation in the public duties and ceremonies that alone safeguard against the feminine threat: military service (masculinist self-display) and the "periodic assemblies" (reenactment of the contract, 106–7). Money breeds the fatal economy of the representative, the parasite that is the "death of the body politic." Fact: The moment a people allows itself to be represented, "it is no longer free, it no longer exists." Reason: "Sovereignty cannot be represented. . . . It consists essentially in the general will [the one, the I], and the will cannot be represented. Either it is itself [the one, the I] or it is something else; there is no middle ground." None at all—that is, nothing short of the something else, the chaos or abyss of the unmanly passions. Indeed, the slightest spacing between the citizen-subject and his political voice introduces a momentary noncoincidence that is nothing less than calamitous: "The general will becomes mute" (98–109).

The republic, then, must be small, tight, fortresslike. Since any slackening of the social bond spells disaster, each citizen must remain, as Derrida observes, "within earshot" of all the others, within the acoustic field of the one, the celestial voice.[91] A man is either with the community or against it, a citizen or a foreigner. There is nothing in between short of the dissolution of the social pact. And let us not forget, "Whoever refuses to obey the general will shall be constrained to do so by the entire body; which means only that he will be forced to be free. For this is the condition that, by giving each citizen to the homeland, guarantees him against all personal dependence" (55). This contentious Rousseauist maxim makes profound sense inasmuch as one state of bondage substitutes for another; compared to enslavement to a feminine authority, not to mention one's own femininity, it is an act of secular grace when the republic compels a man to be free—to be a citizen qua man.

Woman is not simply missing in the *Social Contract*; she is, rather, the absent presence that constitutes but mostly unsettles the boundaries of the semiotic republic. She is, in fact, as dangerous as money (if not more so): a supplement, simulacrum, or idol. Inscribed in the very crime of representation, compelled to make of herself a fetish, woman always exceeds the Rousseauist terms of her containment. Like money, woman is that which, in Kristeva's words, "impinges on symbolic oneness,"[92] the I of the masculine speaking subject, the I of the *moi commune*. The celestial object undercuts the celestial voice. Inhabiting the citizen-subject as otherness, woman haunts a social (sartorial/linguistic) contract which is as unstable as the masculinist signs that constitute it are arbitrary. Rousseau may insist that "we are not our clothes,"[93] but his version of "The Great

Masculine Renunciation" teaches just that. And, "if it is clothes alone, i.e., a cultural sign, an institution, which determine our reading of . . . masculinity and femininity and insure sexual opposition," as Shoshana Felman asks; "if indeed clothes make the *man*—or the woman—, are not sex roles as such, inherently, but travesties?"[94] "Jean-Jacques Rousseau, citizen of Geneva," has already given us his insightful if fearful answer to that very rhetorical question.

Notes

1. Jean-Jacques Rousseau, *Discourse on the Origin and Foundations of Inequality among Men*, in *The First and Second Discourses*, ed. Roger D. Masters, trans. Roger D. Masters and Judith R. Masters (New York: St. Martin's Press, 1964), 135.

2. Jean-Jacques Rousseau, *Politics and the Arts: Letter to M. D'Alembert on the Theatre*, ed. and trans. Allan Bloom (Ithaca: Cornell University Press, 1977), 101, my emphasis. As Paul Thomas interprets this passage, "the eroticism of female idleness is unmistakable and implies that women are at all costs to be kept busy. The alternative is too horrible to contemplate." "Jean-Jacques Rousseau, Sexist?" *Feminist Studies* 17 (Summer 1991): 213.

3. Jean-Jacques Rousseau, *The Confessions*, trans. J. M. Cohen (Harmondsworth: Penguin Books, 1953), 27–28. There are variations on this figure of a masterful mistress throughout Rousseau's work. Following Gilles Deleuze's study of masochism, one could argue that it is not the father but rather the mother who gives the law in Rousseau's thought. The masochist, argues Deleuze, aligns himself with the mother against the father. He "experiences the symbolic order as an intermaternal order in which the mother represents the law under certain prescribed conditions," whence the notion of the contract that is crucial to the masochism. *Masochism*, trans. Jean McNeil (New York: Zone Books, 1991), 63. For a study of Rousseau's masochism from within the political theory tradition, see William H. Blanchard, *Rousseau and the Spirit of Revolt* (Ann Arbor: University of Michigan Press, 1967). Blanchard argues convincingly that Rousseau's desire to give himself over to a masterful mistress shaped his entire social thought. For a psychobiography of Rousseau's personal relations to women, see Maurice Cranston, *Jean-Jacques Rousseau: The Prophetic Voice, 1758–1778*, vol. 2 (New York: Macmillan, 1973), and *Jean-Jacques: The Early Life and Work of Jean-Jacques Rousseau, 1712–1754* (New York: Norton, 1982). Whereas these works focus on the writing self, Huntington Williams has treated Rousseau's autobiographical writings as constructions of the written self. *Rousseau and Romantic Autobiography* (Oxford: Oxford University Press, 1983). For a convincing reading of the *Confessions* as a work of political theory, see Christopher Kelly, *Rousseau's Exemplary Life: The Confessions as Political Philosophy* (Ithaca: Cornell University Press, 1987).

4. The reading I advance draws on and departs from those offered by Joel Schwartz and Penny Weiss, both of whom have done much to situate gender at the center of the scholarly debate on Rousseau. Although Schwartz rightly argues that sexual difference is a political issue, he errs in asserting that Rousseau is a "materialist" who believes that "the bodily differences between men and women unalterably differentiate women from men." *The Sexual Politics of Jean-Jacques Rousseau* (Chicago: University of Chicago Press, 1984), 85. For a similar, if somewhat more qualified and critical, version of this argument, see Jean Bethke Elshtain, *Public Man, Private Woman* (Princeton: Princeton University Press, 1979), 160–161. On the contrary, for Rousseau anatomical difference is nothing apart from the signifiers of sexual difference, from linguistic and sartorial signifiers. In con-

trast to Schwartz, Penny Weiss has shown that for Rousseau gender difference is not in any way natural but rather "should be created, encouraged, and enforced because of what he considers to be their necessary and beneficial consequences." She correctly insists, moreover, that "Rousseau's rhetoric [about "natural" sexual difference] is consistently undercut by his theoretical argument." "Rousseau, Antifeminism, and Woman's Nature," *Political Theory* 15 (February 1987): 83, 94. His rhetoric is undercut as well, I argue, by the vicissitudes of male desire and by his own claim that gender is performative: nothing more than a way of speaking and of dressing, simply a cultural matter of words and clothes.

5. Shoshana Felman, "Rereading Femininity," *Yale French Studies* 62 (1981): 42.

6. Rousseau, *Letter to D'Alembert*, 109.

7. The best-known example of this argument is given by Judith Shklar, who maintains that Rousseau presents us with the man and the citizen as two possible models for living, "and the two were meant to stand in polar opposition to each other." The citizen is the radically denatured man. *Men and Citizens: A Study of Rousseau's Social Theory* (Cambridge: Cambridge University Press, 1969), 3. Shklar's thesis has been accepted (or has remained uncontested) throughout most of the scholarly literature. Susan Okin has suggested that in *Emile* Rousseau tries to create the man and the citizen at once. *Women in Western Political Thought* (Princeton: Princeton University Press, 1979), 168–69. In the pages that follow, I take up and complicate this insight.

8. Julia Kristeva, "Women's Time," in *The Kristeva Reader*, ed. Toril Moi (New York: Columbia University Press, 1986), 202.

9. Julia Kristeva, *Powers of Horror: An Essay on Abjection*, trans. Leon S. Roudiez (New York: Columbia University Press, 1982), 63.

10. Rousseau, *Discourse on Inequality*, 76.

11. J. C. Flugel, *The Psychology of Clothes* (New York: International Universities Press, 1930), 110–11.

12. Rousseau, *Discourse on the Sciences and the Arts*, 37.

13. Flugel, *The Psychology of Clothes*, 113.

14. Rousseau, *Essay on the Origin of Languages*, 242, 243.

15. Ibid.

16. Women are blamed for the degeneration of "natural" language, "the plain tongue of common sense," as Norman Jacobson puts it, into "metaphysical double-talk." *Pride and Solace: The Functions and Limits of Political Theory* (Berkeley: University of California Press, 1978), 107. Paul Thomas argues that, for Rousseau, "women, in their capacity as bearers or agents of civilization, are also necessarily the bearers or agents of corruption too." Thomas shows that women are "in effect stand-ins or surrogates for civilization and [human] perfectibility." "Jean-Jacques Rousseau, Sexist?" 212.

17. Rousseau, *Letter to D'Alembert*, 48. Further page references are cited in the text.

18. Jean-Jacques Rousseau, *Emile, or On Education*, trans. Allan Bloom (New York: Basic Books, 1979), 322.

19. "It is on this principle that a Spartan, hearing a foreigner singing the praises of a lady of his acquaintance, interrupted him in anger: 'Won't you stop,' he said to him, 'slandering a virtuous woman?'" *Letter to D'Alembert*, 48.

20. As Elshtain rightly notes, "The depth of Rousseau's mistrust of women is apparent in the fact that those closer to original nature, by his own logic, are not allowed to speak in the always-to-be trusted voice of that nature." The result is an attempt to shut up not only salon women and actresses but also the natural woman par excellence, Sophie. *Public Man, Private Woman*, 164.

21. Joan Landes, *Women and the Public Sphere in the Age of the French Revolution* (Ithaca: Cornell University Press, 1988), 24–25. On gender inversion and the masquerade, see Terry Castle, *Masquerade and Civilization: The Carnivalesque in Eighteenth-Century English Culture and Fiction* (Stanford: Stanford University Press, 1986).

22. Rousseau, *Rousseau juge de Jean Jaques—Dialogues*, *Oeuvres Complètes*, 1:815 (my translation).

23. Rousseau, *Emile*, 359.

24. See Landes, *Women and the Public Sphere*, 30; Domna Stanton, "The Fiction of Préciosité and the Fear of Women," *Yale French Studies* 62 (1981): 129. On women's place in the public spaces of the theater and the salon, see Barbara G. Mittman, "Women and Theater Arts," in *French Women and the Age of Enlightenment*, ed. Samia I. Spencer (Bloomington: Indiana University Press, 1984), 155–169. On public debates about actresses as agents of cultural chaos, see Kristina Straub, *Sexual Suspects: Eighteenth-Century Players and Sexual Ideology* (Princeton: Princeton University Press, 1992).

25. Thomas Crow, "The Oath of the Horatii in 1785: Painting and Pre-Revolutionary Radicalism in France," *Art History* 1 (December 1978): 442.

26. Derrida, *Of Grammatology*, 240.

27. Rousseau, *Emile*, 42. Further page references are cited in the text.

28. Mary Jacobus, *Romanticism, Writing, and Sexual Difference* (Oxford: Oxford University Press, 1989), 242.

29. Rousseau's critique of wet-nursing was neither wholly novel nor accurate. As George Sussman has shown, the overwhelming majority of the children who were given over to wet nurses came not from the nobility (that is, not, as Rousseau would have it, from families in which the mothers "devote themselves gaily to the entertainments of the city"; *Emile*, 44) but rather from the preindustrial urban class of independent artisans and shop-keepers. It was, moreover, especially poor but not indigent urban families who were most affected by "the polemical campaign against wet-nursing that began around 1760." *Selling Mother's Milk: The Wet-Nursing Business in France*, 1715–1914 (Urbana: University of Illinois Press, 1982), 24, 30.

30. The result of such cruel mothering? Nothing less than the chaos of intermingling or intermixture which opens *Emile*: "Everything is good as it leaves the hands of the Author of our being; everything degenerates in the hands of man. He forces one soil to nourish the products of another, one tree to bear the fruit of another. He mixes and confuses the climates, the elements, the seasons. He mutilates his dog, his horse, his slave. He turns everything upside down; he disfigures everything; he loves deformity, monsters" (37).

31. The peasant child, in contrast, is kept at a distance from, and therefore does not imitate the voice of, the mother, who is hard at work in the fields. Peasant children, says Rousseau, speak in a clear and accented voice, their speech is that of "sentiment and truth." *Emile*, 71, 72.

32. Jacobus, *Romanticism, Writing, and Sexual Difference*, 246.

33. Starobinski, *Jean-Jacques Rousseau*, 146.

34. Rousseau's first masterful mistress was his childhood governess, Mlle Lambercier. *Confessions*, 26.

35. Kristeva, *Tales of Love*, 107, 116. Kristeva observes further that primary narcissism (what Rousseau calls *l'amour de soi*), "being far from originary," is rather a "supplement" to the "autoeroticism of the mother-child dyad" (22). It therefore marks the very first stage of primal differentiation. Narcissism, she argues, is necessary to maintain that space of "emptiness" between self and mother, "lest chaos prevail and borders dissolve" (24). Rousseau, in his own way, knows this too, which is why distancing the child from the nurse/mother and strengthening his love of self are the pedagogical goals of Books I–III, indeed, why *l'amour de soi* is for Rousseau the very source of man's strength.

36. See especially Kristeva, *Powers of Horror*, 62–63.

37. Kristeva, *Tales of Love*, 109–10.

38. On the frontispiece to Book V of *Emile*, see Patricia Parker, *Literary Fat Ladies: Rhetoric, Gender, Property* (New York: Methuen, 1987), 207.

39. Allan Bloom, Introduction to *Emile*, 15–16. Even though Bloom recognizes that the imagination plays a large part in Rousseau's discussion of sexuality, he also assumes that sexual desire is merely a rechanneling of sexual instinct. Bloom's reading of Rousseau fits the familiar image of the

political theorist as the tamer of eros. Once so-called heterosexual instinct is posited as just that, an instinct, it can be treated as if it were a universal and potential chaos that has to be contained in the interests of social order. Rousseau himself shows that all sexual desire, indeed any form of desire, is culturally created through the boundless play of the imagination; it has nothing to do with instinct. "I am persuaded that solitary man raised in a desert, without books, without instruction, and without women, would die there a virgin at whatever age he had reached" *Emile*, 333).

40. Rousseau, *Confessions*, 109.

41. Writes Binet: "Amorous fetishism has a tendency to detach completely, to isolate (the object) from anything separating it from its cult-worship, and when the object is part of a living person, the fetishist tries to render this part an independent entity." "La Fetichisme dans l'amour" [1887], quoted in Emily Apter, *Feminizing the Fetish: Psychoanalysis and Narrative Obsession in Turn-of-the-Century France* (Ithaca: Cornell University Press, 1991), 21. Deleuze observes that "fetishism, as defined by the process of disavowal and suspension of belief, belongs essentially to masochism. . . . There can be no masochism without fetishism in the primary sense." The masochist employs the fetish to preserve the masterful mistress, the phallic mother, the mother who lacks nothing. The fetish is also crucial to the world of reverie and the art of delay that characterize Rousseau's amorous accounts. See *Masochism*, 32.

42. The citation from Rousseau is quoted by Binet. See Apter, *Feminizing the Fetish*, 21.

43. Mary Wollstonecraft, *A Vindication of the Rights of Woman*, ed. Miriam Brody Kramnick (Harmondsworth: Penguin, 1975), 107.

44. Rousseau's strict semiotics for female adornment relate to the place of the fetish in this thought. The purpose of the fetish, on the psychoanalytic account, is to disavow female sexual difference. See Apter, *Feminizing the Fetish*, esp. 13; Deleuze, *Masochism*, 31. Even though woman in Rousseau's texts is duty-bound to conceal her lack (with the adornment he prescribes), she is also duty-bound to reveal it (in ways that uphold rather than undercut the masculine subject, of course). The trick is to find the right quality and quantity of adornment: a disguise that signifies that woman lacks, in order for the masculine subject to deny his own symbolic castration and affirm symbolic wholeness; but also a disguise that does not signify that she lacks too much, in order not to confront the masculine subject with castration (the sin of the "ugly woman").

45. Rousseau's logic yields such mind-boggling statements as the following: "We are told that women are false. They become so. Their particular gift is skill and not falseness. According to the true inclination of their sex, even whey they are lying they are not false." *Emile*, 385.

46. Flugel, *The Psychology of Clothes*, 119. On Rousseau's penchant for self-display and exhibitionism, see Starobinski, *Jean-Jacques Rousseau*, 170–77.

47. As Nannerl O. Keohane puts it, "In fitting Sophie for her fate, Rousseau employs a panoply of artifices indistinguishable from those he excoriated in the second *Discourse*: dissimulation, dependence, reliance on the opinions of others as a guide for behavior and as a source for one's very own sense of self." " 'But for Her Sex . . .': The Domestication of Sophie," *University of Ottawa Quarterly* 49, nos. 3–4 (1979): 397. Wollstonecraft argued the same point in the *Vindication*.

48. This is one reason the natural woman must remain, as Clément argued and as Rousseau himself says, a child all her life (*Emile*, 211)—speaking little but causing men's talk.

49. For another example of woman's duty to efface the trace of her own artifice, see Rousseau's description of Julie's garden in the novel *La nouvelle Heloise*, *Oeuvres Complètes*, 2:472.

50. "The moral of Sophie's education," as Jacobus puts it, "is that women must be the guarantors and safe-keepers, not only of masculinity, but of language made chaste, naturalized, and brought into imaginary correspondence with reality." *Romanticism, Writing, and Sexual Difference*, 249.

51. Schwartz argues that Rousseau creates Sophie as a complement to Emile and as a subject in her own right. Contrasting Emile with the hero (Valere) of Rousseau's play *Narcisse, ou l'amant de lui-même*, Schwartz writes that, whereas Valere "falls in love with a girl whom he can only imagine," Emile falls in love with a girl who "actually *is* a girl, and not Emile's male self dressed to resemble a

girl." It is Emile who, when he does love, "loves another." *The Sexual Politics of Jean-Jacques Rousseau*, 81. On the contrary, I maintain that, inasmuch as Sophie is the scapegoat of the masculine desire to dress like a girl (not to mention to play with "jewels, mirrors, and dolls"), she is not Emile's sexual other but his specular double.

52. The "whole art [of coquetry] depend[s] . . . on sharp and continuous observations which make her [woman] see what is going on in men's hearts at every instant, and which dispose her to bring to each secret movement that she notices the force needed to suspend or accelerate it." *Emile*, 385.

53. Luce Irigaray, *Speculum of the Other Woman*, trans. Gillian C. Gill (Ithaca: Cornell University Press, 1985), 54. If it is true that Sophie or the woman is the specular double of Emile or the man, then the argument advanced, albeit in different ways, by Weiss and Schwartz (i.e., that Rousseau aims to create interdependence between the sexes) seems highly debatable to say the least.

54. Kristeva, *Powers of Horror*, 98, 99.

55. Like uncleanliness, "extreme ugliness" in a woman is "disgusting," and both are at bottom the relation with the abject, that is, with death: "Ugliness which produces disgust is the greatest of misfortunes. This sentiment, far from fading away, increases constantly and turns into hatred. Such a marriage is hell. It would be better to be dead than to be thus united." *Emile*, 409. On the subject of Sophie's cleanliness, see Keohane, " 'But for Her Sex,' " 396.

56. Flugel writes, "In the case of the [male] exhibitionistic desires connected with self-display, a particularly easy form of conversation may be found in a change from (passive) exhibitionism to (active) scoptophilia (erotic pleasure in the use of vision)—the desire to be seen being transformed into the desire to see. This desire to see may itself remain unsublimated and find its appropriate satisfaction in the contemplation of the other sex, or it may be sublimated and find expression in the more general desire to see and know." *The Psychology of Clothes*, 118. That it is the powerful and dangerous desire to be seen that subtends the masculine subject's desire to see helps to explain the character of Wolmar, in *La Nouvelle Héloïse*, who wanted to "become a living eye," seeing without being seen; *Oeuvres Complètes*, 2:491. It also explains why Rousseau, in the *Reveries*, expressed his wish to own the magic ring of Gyges, which would have given him the power to render himself invisible at will; ibid, 1:1057–58.

57. Flugel again: "In such cases there is clearly some element of identification with the woman. . . . We incline in general to identify ourselves with such persons as we admire or envy [for their opportunity for bodily and sartorial display]." This identification is obviously dangerous for the masculine subject, but not nearly as threatening as the following: if the woman does not accept her role as adorned object, then the man's desire for exhibitionism could seek satisfaction in transvestitism, whereby "the man may consciously seek to identify himself with a woman by wearing feminine attire." *The Psychology of Clothes*, 118–19.

58. Shklar reads *Emile* as the model for making a man and associates it with Rousseau's ideal of the Golden Age. See *Men and Citizens*, esp. 11, 147–48. Okin argues, "Rousseau clearly tries to make of Emile a citizen, as well a natural and independent man." *Women in Western Political Thought*, 168.

59. If Emile has to travel to avoid becoming his sexual other, why does he have to fall in love before he travels? This question is answered by Rousseau himself, who tells us that he got the idea while visiting the governor of a young Englishman. The governor was reading a letter to his pupil (Lord John) when suddenly, says Rousseau, "I saw the young man tear off the very fine lace cuffs he was wearing and throw them one after the other into the fire." *Emile*, 470. It turned out that the cuffs were a present given to Lord John by a "city lady," and that the letter described his country fiancée hard at work making him a quite different set of cuffs with her own hands. This incident reveals, once again, the place of Sophie or the woman in the masculine renunciation of aristocratic finery, not to mention his own femininity.

60. Okin argues that Rousseau places incompatible demands on his female characters. The chaste coquette is doomed right from the start because she must excite and restrain male desire.

What is more, "no woman educated and confined as Julie [of La Nouvelle Héloïse] and Sophie are would ever be able to behave like the Spartan mother whose patriotism Rousseau so much admired." These women are "even more vulnerable than men to the conflicts of loyalties" that Rousseau showed to exist between the state and the family. And thus women as mothers become a problem for men as citizens. Women in Western Political Thought, 193. Likewise, Zillah Eisenstein maintains that, in Emile, the dependent woman creates significant problems for the independent man. The Radical Future of Liberal Feminism (New York: Longman, 1981), 80–83.

61. Okin (Women in Western Political Thought), Elshtain (Public Man, Private Woman), and Pateman (The Sexual Contract) have shown quite clearly that women cannot be added to the social contract. As Landes puts it, "the very generality of the [general] will is predicated on the silent but tacit consent of women." Women and the Public Sphere, 66. Schwartz, for his part, has tried to track women down in the supplement to written law: the morals, customs, and public opinion that form the basis of the impersonal authority Rousseau seems to credit as the ultimate source of social stability. "Because Rousseau acknowledges the necessity of hidden and personal rule, he can also acknowledge and admire the political power of women (even as he advocates their formal political powerlessness)." Rousseau's Sexual Politics, 43–44. On the contrary, as we see in this section, this informal power is not the good to be preserved but rather the problem to be solved by the social contract.

62. Jean-Jacques Rousseau, On the Social Contract, published together with Geneva Manuscript and Political Economy, ed. Roger D. Masters, trans. Judith R. Masters (New York: St. Martin's Press, 1978). Further page references are cited in the text. Actually, it is not the word "woman" but "women" that appears three times in Rousseau's text: twice in connection with the fecundity of a people (73, 74) and once in connection with "foreigners," "children," and "slaves" (99).

63. Rousseau, Emile, 43.

64. Hilail Gilden, Rousseau's Social Contract: The Design of the Argument (Chicago: University of Chicago Press, 1983), 27.

65. Ibid., 23.

66. Rousseau, Geneva Manuscript, 171; see also 158.

67. See Shklar, Men and Citizens, 155.

68. Rousseau, Geneva Manuscript, 177.

69. On this point, see Derrida, Of Grammatology, 264–65.

70. Rousseau, Geneva Manuscript, 180. "Qu'il mutile en quelque sorte la constitution de l'homme pour la renforcer." Oeuvres Complètes 3:313.

71. Jean-Jacques Rousseau, The Government of Poland, trans. and ed. Willmoore Kendall (New York: Bobbs-Merrill, 1972), 6, my emphasis.

72. Kristeva writes: "Circumcision would thus separate one from maternal, feminine impurity and defilement; it stands instead of sacrifice, meaning not only that it [circumcision] replaces it [sacrifice] but is its equivalent—a sign of the alliance with God. . . . [What] circumcision carves out on his [the masculine subject's] very sex, is the other sex, impure, defiled." Powers of Horror, 99–100.

73. Ibid., 94.

74. Rousseau, Emile, 321.

75. Rousseau, Essay on the Origin of Languages, 242. Rousseau gives a particularly telling example from the Old Testament, which reveals the use of woman as Sign, the Sign that transforms a fleeting bond into something durable, the oath into a people, the voices of the many into that of the one: "When the Levite of Ephraim wanted to avenge the death of his wife he did not write to the Tribes of Israel; he divided her body into twelve pieces which he sent to them. At this ghastly sight they rushed to arms, crying with one voice: No, never has anything like this happened in Israel, from the day when our fathers left Egypt until this day! And the Tribe of Benjamin was exterminated. Nowadays it would have been turned into lawsuits, debates, perhaps even jokes; it would have dragged on, and the most ghastly crime would finally have remained unpunished" (ibid.).

Actually—and this must have been known to Rousseau—what spurred the eleven tribes of Israel to revenge against the twelfth (the Benjamites) was the mutilated body of the concubine (the second or third wife) of the polygamous Levite, who had given her over to a mob of Benjamite men to save himself from being sodomized. It was her raped and brutalized corpse that the Levite then cut into pieces and sent to the other tribes, who promptly put aside their differences and united as a people to avenge her murder. Out of the Benjamite tribe, as Rousseau says, "only six hundred of its men, without any women or children, were left" (ibid.). These men fled into the desert and, in time, were called back by the Israelite elders, who grieved deeply for them and felt duty bound to ensure their continued existence. Fratricide led to mourning and then to reparation through another bloody act: having vowed never to give their daughters to any of the Benjamites, the elders sent an army to Jabash-gilead, which seized four hundred virgins and slaughtered the rest of the population. Then, because there were still not enough women for the Benjamites, the elders advised the remaining bachelors to go to the town of Shiloh where each should abduct a girl at the annual festival. This they did and were thus saved from extinction (see Judges 19:2–21:35).

The Book of Judges, which concludes with the line, "In those days Israel had no King; everyone did as he saw fit" (21:25), points up the moral depravity, intertribal disputes, and pagan ways into which the Israelites had fallen since the deaths of Moses and Joshua. The story Rousseau cites also shows that woman is the visible sacrifice that recalls to the Israelites the fading memory of their covenant with an invisible God. One could read the rape of the concubine, not to mention the abduction of women at the festival, as confirming Pateman's thesis that violence and male sex-right subtend the fraternal social contract. One could read the woman's dismembered body as sign as confirming Kristeva's thesis that the sociosymbolic contract is a sacrificial contract. And one could confirm both with Rousseau's claim that, at the sight of a piece of the woman's corpse, the Israelites all began "crying in one voice," the "celestial voice" of the general will.

76. Rousseau, *Emile*, 323.

77. Rousseau, *The Government of Poland*, 15. One must see always and everywhere the image of the fatherland, beginning at birth: "The newly-born infant, upon first opening his eyes, must gaze upon the fatherland, and until his dying day should behold nothing else" (19). Needless to say, the very first gaze he beholds is that of the mother.

78. Rousseau, *Emile*, 322.

79. Ibid.

80. Rousseau, *The Government of Poland*, 14.

81. Ibid., 72.

82. Michel Foucault, "The Eye of Power," in *Power/Knowledge: Selected Interviews and Other Writings, 1972–1977*, ed. Collin Gordon (New York: Pantheon Books, 1980), 152.

83. Rousseau, *The Government of Poland*, 89.

84. Ibid., 15–16. For a thoughtful discussion of how Rousseau's critique of inherited property intersects with his attack on idleness, see Eisenstein, *The Radical Future of Liberal Feminism*, 68–71.

85. That spectacular display is constitutive of masculinity suggests that Rousseau does not depart from what Landes calls "the iconic spectacularity of the Old Regime." *Women and the Public Sphere*, 67. In fact, Rousseau is much closer to that mode of self-representation than Landes allows.

86. Rousseau, *The Government of Poland*, 18.

87. Ibid., 14. "One does not stamp out luxury with sumptuary laws. You must reach deep into men's hearts and uproot it by implanting there healthier and nobler tastes" (18).

88. Benjamin R. Barber, *Supermen and Common Men* (New York: Praeger, 1972), 61. As Thomas puts this point, "The articulation of the general will may depend upon an overcoming of distinctions among the (male) citizenry, but these distinctions have first to exist if they are to be overcome." "Jean-Jacques Rousseau, Sexist?" 202.

89. Compare my argument with Marshall Berman's thesis that the social contract is a "maternal state" in which child-citizens bask in the warmth of an unmediated "flow of nourishment, affection,

314   Feminist Interpretations of Jean-Jacques Rousseau

[and] love." *The Politics of Authenticity: Radical Individualism and the Emergence of Modern Society* (New York: Atheneum, 1970), 204. Berman draws largely on Rousseau's maternal images of the state in *Discourse on Political Economy*.

90. Rousseau, *The Government of Poland*, 69.
91. Derrida, *Of Grammatology*, 136.
92. Kristeva, *Powers of Horror*, 104
93. Rousseau, *Emile*, 372.
94. Felman, "Rereading Femininity," 28.

13

Republican Romance

Elizabeth Wingrove

On the death of Caesar I imagine one of our orators wishing to move the people; he exhausts all the commonplaces of his art to present a pathetic description of Caesar's wounds, his blood, his corpse. Antony, although eloquent, does not say all that. He has the body brought in. What rhetoric!

—*Emile*, 322–23[1]

Jean-Jacques Rousseau frankly acknowledged the sexual imperatives of his republicanism. Whether in *Emile*'s extended analyses or in fictional depictions like *La nouvelle Héloïse*, he regularly reiterates the close connection between his politics rightly instituted and masculinity and femininity rightly lived. Otherwise put, Rousseau's is a most intriguing sexism, a complex and even insightful account of the ways political agendas support, constrain, and construct sexual identities. And nowhere is that sexism and its intrigues more spectacular than in one erotic, perhaps pornographic, story that he composed, *Le Lévite d'Ephraïm*. It is a story of political fracture and (re)union, of retribution and justice, and of individual freedom and community loyalty, and it poses these problems and their solutions in terms of rape, murder, marriage, dismemberment, and homosexual desire. In this essay I take up the issue of coincident sexual and political experience in Rousseau's story with an eye on the rhetorical strategy suggested in the epigraph: one that "brings the body in." My aim is thus twofold: to offer a version of republicanism and gendered sexuality that takes seriously their mutual constitution and to offer an account of rhetoric made material. Bluntly put, my claim is that in Rousseau's republican romance sexual interaction is not *like* political interaction, nor are its identities preparatory in the sense of being prior or separate from politics; rather, the story of the Levite discloses how republican practices consist in the proper performance of masculinity and femininity.

With respect to my first aim, the approach I will use stands in sharp contrast with, on the one side, interpreters whose central concern is the fit, or lack thereof, between Rousseau's sexism and his democratic principles more generally. How does gender hierarchy survive his egalitarianism? Can his instrumental deployment of feminine wiles conform with his celebration of citizen probity? And what about that autocratic head of household who magically transforms in public into a democratic citizen? These are the sorts of puzzles that have presented themselves to democratic feminist critics, by which I mean those critically engaging a tradition of democratic political thought in which Rousseau occupies a pivotal, and problematic, location. On the other side are interpreters who find evidence that his gender scheme is the necessary counterpart to his political principles, rather than their simple contradiction. Precisely what Mary Wollstonecraft refers to as Rousseau's "unintelligible paradoxes" concerning women suggests that the (hetero)sexual relationship complements republican relations by offering a division of moral and social labor, and together the two realms sustain coherent, if unstable, structures of power and interdependence.[2]

These two approaches—emphasizing, alternatively, contradiction and complementarity in Rousseau's sexual politics—run the risk of obscuring important features of sex *and* politics, inasmuch as they both posit relatively discrete identities and locations proper to each dimension. This move tends to shore up the man/citizen dichotomy, while continuing the woman/mother/wife identity, and my worry is that this limits our analysis of the formative power of a politicized sexuality. Of course, an analytic distinction between sexual and political interaction remains unavoidable and even helpful; but in the lived experiences of Rousseau's republicans that difference collapses in the common practices of enacting one's sexuality. To be a citizen, in other words, is to be a man, and Rousseau's republican community is realized in the sexual interaction of properly gendered men and women.

But what does it mean "to be a man" in Rousseau's play of gender? Important here is the claim, persuasively argued by Penny Weiss and others, that appeals to nature as the source and substance of gender difference are insufficient: Rousseau clearly reveals, even if he then re-veils, the social and political expediency that drives his account of femininity and masculinity.[3] While the precise mechanisms and techniques through which these sexual categorizations are enforced have not been exhaustively explored, I assume it no longer satisfies anyone to take his rhapsodic evocations of nature for sociobiological commitments. And yet, in terms of the political work gender does in Rousseau's politics, there is an important difference between those who emphasize its symbolic dimensions. I want to address that difference here as one of levels of analysis. The first approach, inaugurated by Susan Okin's work, emphasizes the utility of the patriarchal family: women's privatization and domestication follow from the need for child rearers, for securing paternity, and for creating a public space emptied of potentially disorganizing sexual desire.[4] The second approach, influenced by psychoanalytic theory, emphasizes how and what women signify in Rousseau's work: with their engulfing powers, beguiling sexuality, and skillful dissimulations, women always signal the precariousness of a community of robust and guileless (male) citizens.[5] Here "woman" is an object of exchange in the symbolic economy, where, as Linda Zerilli puts it, she serves as a "scapegoat precipitated by the disorder in men: that feminine other within the citizen-subject who . . . 'will always be marked by the uncertainty of his borders.'"[6]

Setting aside obvious differences in theoretical and linguistic idiom, these two interpretive stances diverge in the manner in which each envisages the political stakes in Rousseau's gender scheme: while the functional approach works at the level of women's social labor and material contribution—what they, procreatively and sensually, *do* with, for, and to men, the semiotic approach emphasizes the meanings attached to maternal and sexual identity—how woman appears as symptom, an always overdetermined sign of male anxiety. Without diminishing the contributions of either approach, I suggest that moving between these levels of analysis is necessary to grasp the ongoing significance of Rousseau's sexual politics. I say "ongoing" because the stakes are not, to my mind, how best to salvage or savage Rousseau's political theory. Rather, they are whether his writing can inform current efforts to understand gender as a feature of politics, and politics as a feature of gender. I suggest that Rousseau has a contribution to make on this score, in his complex and rather hideous depictions of performative sexuality.

I introduce a notion of performative sexuality to advance my second aim, to sketch the logic and process of a bodily and embodied "eloquence." As I use it, performative sexuality is a category responsive to the need to move between the functional material and semiotic levels of (feminist) analysis; it thus constitutes a coherent and useful contribution to political analysis. In terms of coherence, there has been some slippage in the way Judith Butler's account of gender performance has been taken up.[7] On the one hand, her introduction of performativity to subvert any hint of an essential sexual identity led many readers to conclude that it denied the materiality of sexed subjects: a performative identity was seen as an unreal or perhaps surreal display neither rooted in nor limited by physical bodies. On the other hand, Butler's depiction of the drag show as exemplary led many readers to conclude that drag is paradigmatic, and thus to the woefully inadequate conclusion that gender identity could be fitted as readily as a string of pearls or a codpiece, and discarded just as easily. Similarly, in terms of usefulness, envisioning drag as the paradigm of gender performance left some wondering if parody was an adequate model for political agency. Butler's more recent explications of her position may or may not satisfy her critics.[8] I mention these issues here because they illustrate what I take to be primary concerns and confusions that the category of performance scares up.[9]

My use of the term does not correspond to any particular anxiousness about the status of the subject as unified and fixed. While I share the antifoundationalism that animates these concerns, I am more anxious about questions of governance, of modern political authority and rule, and here an antifoundationalist commitment urges one away from forays into the self and toward relations that structure the community. In this sense performance connotes behavior, the actions and reactions of individuals, over and against their inner states. Politically performance is an apt category inasmuch as what matters most within the context of the state is not what people think but what they do. But this suggests another potential pitfall, namely, the anticipation that a performing subject might be merely, *acting*, pretending to be what they might otherwise not *really* be. In this context I find detours into authenticity as problematic as those into decentered selves: intriguing but potentially depoliticizing. As I use it, performance responds to the need to figure how citizen-subjects enact need, desire, and fear, without being stymied by the inconstancy of their foundations. I thus want to emphasize action over self-understanding as authoritative or dispositive, but not in such a way that behavior is divorced from a social account of its meaning. This latter possibility—sexual-political performers as automatons—is utterly at odds with Rousseau's approach, and appears to me to be incomprehensible in its ineloquence.

On the other hand, performance, unlike behavior, connotes theatricality, which I have elsewhere argued is central to Rousseau's account of masculinity and femininity.[10] The model of the theater suggests that gestures, poses, and words exhaust an actor's meanings, and successful communication depends upon good depictions. While I want to hold on to these suggestions, it is important that they not be taken to mean that gender, for Rousseau or for us, is "nothing more than a way of speaking, a matter of words and clothes."[11] These contingent, improvisational, and wholly specular dimensions of gender should not obscure the less contingent material bases on which they work. I do not mean by this that bodies constitute either the origins of or limits to sexual identity: I mean that they are the sit of gender's construction. Thus the materialism I want to underscore has less to do with anatomies than with actions, and what matters politically in sexual performances is that males act like men and females act like women.[12] That they do not always do so is clear: effeminate courtiers, those intrepid Spartan mothers, and the gender inversions of the salon all attest to the precariousness and motility of gender. But what holds it in place, so to say, what on Rousseau's telling operates as a natural sign, is the physical body.[13] For this reason, how and what women and men signify for Rousseau is always a question of how and what their bodies do: sexuality is thus, like all other political issues, a question of controlling performance.

Why sexuality emerges as the central trope in Rousseau's republican discourse is a complex issue, one beyond the scope of this essay. But we must notice how his account of language, developed in both the *Essay on the Origin of Languages* and *Emile,* insistently underscores the force of natural signs: the first and still most compelling means of signification, he argues, is material. Blood, bodies, and physical gestures convey meaning more truly than words alone because they move the eyes as well as the ears.[14] He readily concedes that, given the current (read degenerate) state of human need, verbal articulations have become indispensable: to move the heart now requires these "accents of the passions," and voice must join with gesture to arouse interest and desire. But for Rousseau it is never a question of the one supplanting the other: the power of discourse remains dependent on its convergence with things material, and, in the end, it is the language of sensations that guarantees the proper moral effects.[15] His sexual rhetorical strategy, then, is certainly in keeping with Marc Antony's, whose eloquence consists in mastering a particular kind of performative: rather than merely doing things with words, he does things with bodies.[16]

I

Le Lévite d'Ephraïm was never published during Rousseau's lifetime, although it was his intention to do so in a volume that would include the *Essay on the Origin of Languages* and a short piece on theatrical imitation.[17] This suggests that he considered the *Lévite* pertinent to his theories of communication, theatricality, and the political significance of the two. The theme of representation runs through all three texts, and while the *Essay* and *Imitation théâtrale* address primarily symbolic and cultural practices, in the *Lévite* these issues are figured through a dilemma of political representation. It is a story of the shattering and then the recomposition of the twelve tribes of Israel during the time prior to Israel's unified rule. Rousseau's version is generally faithful to the plot line, if not the language, of the original story as it appears in Judges 19–21, although where it diverges is significant. In its barest particulars his version is as follows: A Levite from the town of Ephraïm has retired with his concubine to a bucolic retreat, where he hopes to live with her in mutual joy and sweet isolation.[18] But after a while she tires of him, and flees to her ancestral home. The Levite promptly goes to fetch her, and is on his way home with her when night falls and they are forced to stay the night in the town of Gibeah. They are given lodging there by an old man who is also originally from the town of Ephraïm. During the night the house is attacked by young men from the tribe of Benjamin who lust after the handsome Levite and demand that the old man send him out. Horrified that the laws of hospitality might be broken, the old man tried to offer them his daughter instead. But the Levite intervenes, refuses to let the young daughter go, and sends out his concubine instead.

The young Benjamites promptly brutalize and rape her. In the morning, after finding her in the last throes of death on the doorstep, the Levite cuts up the corpse and sends one piece to each of the leaders of the twelve tribes. After gathering to hear the Levite's story, the leaders take a collective oath never to allow their daughters to marry into the murderous tribe of Benjamin and further set out to destroy the Benjamites in battle. In the civil wars that follow, the unified tribes come very close to annihilating the Benjamites; but they stop short when only six hundred men remain. It dawns on them that annihilating this tribe would inevitably mean annihilating their brothers, who are still, regardless of their crime, of God's people.

So the victorious unified tribes resolve to save the Benjamites, which means finding wives for the survivors while still honoring the collective vow against intertribal marriage with them. Four hundred of the needed virgins are seized from the town of Jabés, which had refused to send soldiers to participate in the civil wars: we are told by Rousseau that their disobedience against the common cause justifies the destruction of the town. The Benjamites are advised to abduct the final two hundred virgins from the town of Shiloh, where an upcoming festival will find them isolated, dancing in a grove.

But no sooner is the abduction underway than the Shiloh maidens' cries attract the attention of their townsmen, who come running to their defense. At this point the tribal elders step in and try to persuade the Shiloh community that their women must be taken by the Benjamites in order that the tribe survive. Everyone is moved by the plight of the Benjamites, except the fathers of the maidens, who remain outraged by their daughters' plight. The crowd eventually agrees that the young women should decide their own fate. Here Rousseau introduces the characters of Axa, a Shiloh virgin and daughter of the man who orchestrated the plan to rescue the Benjamites, and Elmacin, her fiancé. When Axa chooses to forswear her own desire and give herself to a Benjamite, the spectacle moves first Elmacin to accept her decision and pledge himself to a spiritual (read celibate) life, and then the other Shiloh virgins to imitate her. The narrative concludes: "With this touching display, a cry of joy arose from the middle of the people; Virgins of Ephraïm, through you Benjamin shall be reborn! Blessed be the God of our Fathers! there is still virtue in Israel."[19]

It is an understatement to say that this tale of political and social crises is shot through with dilemmas of gender, sex, and desire. Indeed, the interpenetration of, on the one hand, questions of community identity and security and, on the other, questions of sexuality and sexual and eroticized violence makes it difficult to settle upon *the* subject of this story: is Rousseau depicting the perilous disruptions of homosexual desire, the multiform process of women's subjugation, or the concomitantly fragile and overpowering prerogatives of collective need? It hardly seems necessary to choose: surely the *Lévite* is "about" all of these things, not to mention a range of possible subjects in excess of authorial intention and historical situation. And yet, to the degree one focuses on the narratological thrust of the story there is a recurrent temptation to move toward an ordering foundationalism. Which desires motivate and which are compensatory, what eludes communal norms and what can be recuperated by or contained within them, what is authentic and what is perverse: attending to the process and the power of the story's unfolding entices the reader into thinking in terms of these relationships of priority, if not causality.

I want to resist making these moves inasmuch as *my* motivating desire is to explore how the story uses gendered sexuality to instantiate the complexity and paradox of republican political agency. From this perspective, what constitutes authenticity and what constitutes perversion—of identity, of desire—cannot be assessed at any distance from the politics to which they give form: sexuality is not the subject of political intervention or control but is itself a politics. From this perspective, how Rousseau organizes a libidinal economy *is* how he organizes sovereignty, and the tortured version of consent we find here is exemplary of a republican world in which agreement to be ruled means that "no" sometimes means "yes." This is a disorienting world of desires that blur into aversions, subjects that fade into objects, and will that bleeds into submission. And while recognizing and sustaining distinctions between these terms means, indeed, everything, we miss an opportunity to explore the political process and utility of their collapse if we read this story as one of corruption, usurpation, transgression, repression, or any other degenerative process through which something unaffected is made otherwise.

This means that one must read Rousseau against the grain of his own self-presentation: the story of a fall—from grace, innocence, security—appears throughout his political and literary writings. This recurrence figures prominently in Thomas Kavanagh's reading of the *Lévite*, where he identifies a "structure of denigration centering on victimage and violence which is the core of a macrotext including not only Rousseau's autobiographical works, but the major themes of his political writings."[20]

According to Kavanagh this metanarrative is further illuminated by the circumstances of the *Lévite*'s composition, which the *Confessions* reports was during Rousseau's flight to Switzerland precipitated by *Emile*'s condemnation and suppression. He insists that "Rousseau's obsession with this story justifies our approaching this text as a kind of overdetermined symptom."[21]

It is certainly true that Rousseau put great stock in his ability to produce such tender prose during such dire times; he writes in the first preface to the *Lévite*, "If ever any just man deigns to take my defense in compensation for such outrages and libels, I want only these words as praise: 'in the most cruel moments of his life he wrote *Le Lévite d'Ephraïm*.'"[22] And no one could deny the overdetermined quality of the story's imagery and language. But here a preoccupation with narrative and rhetorical continuity between texts obscures the particular themes of political fracture, political (re)union, and the centrality of women's bodies to those processes. Further, while Rousseau's perceived victimization and women's depicted evisceration might well be consonant, a biographically reductionist reading misses the isomorphism that emerges from these parallel presentations. In fact, Rousseau's own self-styling in the *Confessions* continues the structural correspondence between sexual and political practice that appears in the *Lévite*, as well as in the *Discourse on Inequality*, *Letter to D'Alembert*, *La nouvelle Héloïse*, and other texts. In all these accounts the possibility of securing a stable republican community turns on the interaction between men and women, and in all these accounts the proper organization of sexual desire turns on the establishment of a stable republican community.

Again, the story of the Levite comes from the final three chapters of the Book of Judges, which tells stories of the Israelites after their initial conquest of Canaan and before their unification under monarchical rule. The book's general themes are of recurrent crises, both social and natural, and of subsequent deliverance under the divinely inspired guidance of various judges.[23] Throughout Judges the Israelites are depicted as a disobedient but repentant people, prone to transgress Yahweh's law and then be returned to favor through one man or woman's temporary leadership, often military in nature. The concluding verse of the book, immediately following the story of the Levite, reads: "In those days there was no King in Israel; every man did that which was right in his own eyes."[24]

Rousseau's story begins, rather than ends, with this declaration. After two short introductory paragraphs in which he provides some highlights of the story to follow he begins: "In the days of liberty when no one ruled over the Lord's people, it was a time of license where each person, recognizing neither magistrate or judge, was his own master and did whatever seemed good to him." He continues: "Israel, still scattered over the fields, had few large towns and the simplicity of its *moeurs* made the empire of law superfluous; but all the hearts were not equally pure, and the vicious found the impunity of vice in the security of virtue" (1208–9). This vision of dispersed families, simple mores, and always threatening excesses of will and desire is also found in the *Discourse on Inequality*, during that "golden age" of human development described by Rousseau as "maintaining a middle position between the indolence of our primitive state and the petulant activity of our egotism."[25] Although it clearly represents a moment prior to the establishment of civil society and state, this middle position is an important step toward them. Both its loose kinship associations and its "duties of civility" characterize a nascent political community.[26] It remains importantly precontractual, and thus nonjuridical, but it is not without emergent norms and modes of justice. The description Rousseau provides in the *Discourse on Inequality* is strikingly reminiscent of that given in the *Lévite:* "With morality beginning to be introduced into human actions, and everyone, prior to the existence of laws, being sole judge and avenger of the offenses he had received, the goodness appropriate to the pure state of nature was no longer what was appropriate to an emerging society; . . . it was necessary for punishments to become more severe in proportion as the occasions for giving offense became more frequent; and . . . it . . . was for the fear of vengeance to take the place of the deterrent character of laws."[27]

The problems of justice and vengeance are of course central to the story of the *Lévite*, which Rousseau characterizes in an opening paragraph as a story of "civil wars" (1208). Lacking established government and thus positive law, Israel cannot be considered a fully realized political community. But the law of Yahweh (indeterminately combining moral and natural law) remains the touchstone of duty, and thus of disobedience and transgression. Through it the twelve tribes identify the need to avenge the Benjamites' trespass as well as their subsequent obligation to preserve the tribe as an indispensable part of their community. As an actual figure in the drama, Yahweh is typically obscure and paradoxical: he both promises the unified tribes' victory over the Benjamites and admonishes them for the "unjust vows" they have taken in this regard (1220). But it is not, finally, his will or his might that dictates the fate of the twelve tribes; it is their own fitful realization of who they are and how that shared identity overrides tribal particularity, both particular transgressions and particular retributions. The consolidation of community on which Rousseau ends his story—the cry of joy and blessing that arises "from the midst of the People"—begins when the tribes gather to learn of the Benjamites' crime. Brought together by the graphic advertisements of the concubine's body, the heretofore scattered tribes are now referred to as "the People of God," "the Lord's People," and then simply "the People" (1216–17).[28]

By the end of the story the reader is presented with "a moral and collective body composed of as many members as there are voices in the assembly."[29] While not, as in the *Social Contract*, instituted juridically, this community's devotion to a common cause is guaranteed by the same formula of shared *moeurs* and familial identity; and similar to the situation of citizens who resist the general will, the protorepublicans in the *Lévite* will find themselves "forced to be free." On occasion this entails the perverse logic of destroying in order to save, that is, the massacre of the townsfolk of Jabés; on other occasions the enforcement of freedom plays out through individual wills and (thus) on their living bodies, that is, the virgins of Shiloh. This last case offers a brutal embodiment of the paradox of republican freedom: that liberty requires submission. "What?" cry out the fathers who have rushed to the aid of their daughters, "Will the daughters of Israel be subjugated and treated like slaves under the eyes of God? . . . Where is the liberty of God's people?" (1222). Here women assume a starring role as exemplars of the tribes' status as a free people and as redeemers of the political community. And they make good on that freedom and that redemptive possibility by accepting their ravishers. In other words, they secure the community and its republican possibilities by consenting to be raped.

This final bodily manifestation of a general will, to which I will return shortly, is preceded by numerous examples of how women secure the social structure, and in each case the functional and symbolic aspects of women's bodies interpenetrate. At various points they appear as offering or shield (Levite's concubine to the men of Gibeah), as epistle (her dismembered corpse), as consolation and plunder (the Jabés virgins), and as oblation (the Shiloh virgins). But these objectifications do not adequately capture the importance of gender to this social and political drama, which is driven by sexual and procreative crises. The story itself unfolds around two dilemmas of desire: the first involving a failure to sustain mutual (heterosexual) attraction, the second involving nonmutual and (thus?) socially disorganizing (homosexual) desire.

The narrative begins with a depiction of the Levite's relationship with his concubine, whom Rousseau takes pains to paint as a wife *manquée:* in a speech made by the Levite and in the only footnote to the text, Rousseau conjectures that Mosaic law must have prohibited their marriage.[30] The Levite proposes that she come to live with him anyway: "We will be united and free; you will be my happiness and I will be yours" (1209). But the young woman tires of their mountain retreat, described in detail as a site of bucolic splendor and abundance, and she returns to her family. The biblical version says, "His concubine played the whore against him, and went away from him unto her father's house"; Rousseau writes, "The young woman became bored with the Levite, perhaps because he left her nothing to desire" (1210).[31] What was to be mutual fulfillment ends in boredom and deadened desire, and what was to be self-sufficiency ends in an unhappy isolation. The subsequent threat to and reconstitution of the sociopolitical order follow on this twofold failure of desire and interdependence.

The second dilemma arises in the town of Gibeah. Ready to bed down in a public square, the Levite and his concubine are offered lodging by an old man. Because he is also, like the Levite, from the tribe of Ephraïm, the old man insists it is his duty to provide for them. When the Levite is later besieged in the old man's home, the Benjamites' sexual passion is signaled as a problem of hospitality.[32] The Bible states that the townsmen cried out to the old man, "Bring forth the man that came into thine house, that we may know him." Rousseau's version is, "Give us this young stranger that you received into your home without [our] leave, so that his beauty might pay the price of this refuge and he might atone for your temerity" (1213). The text explains that their passion had been aroused earlier when they first saw the Levite, but because of a "lingering respect for the most sacred of all places, they did not want to lodge him in their homes in order to violate him." Their plan, rather, was to violate him later in the public square. The old man implores them to understand his duties as a host—"Do not violate sacred hospitality!"—and tries to give them his daughter as a substitute (1214). In the biblical version the men refuse the offer; in Rousseau's version the Levite prevents the daughter from leaving the house and wordlessly hands over his "beloved companion" instead.

It is noteworthy that Rousseau says little apropos the "unnaturalness" of homosexual desire. This is suggested directly only once, when the old man tells the Benjamites that their demands will "outrage nature" (1214). But the men themselves are described as "without yoke, without brake, without restraint" (1213) when they come after the Levite, and Rousseau's prose strips them of their masculinity only in describing the concubine's brutalization.[33] The tone recalls aspects of the *Confessions'* representation of homosexual desire. There, in a story of his stay at a Turin hospice, Rousseau describes his reaction to the sexual overtures of an older neophyte, a Moor, with equal parts amazement and disgust. Depicting an extraordinary naivete, he writes that he was neither angry nor indignant at the man's behavior, "for I did not have the least idea what it was all about."[34] His principal distress seems to have been aesthetic: "I could not understand what was the matter with the poor man . . . and truly I know of nothing more hideous for someone of cold blood to see than that obscene and foul demeanor and that terrifying face on fire with the most brutal lust; I have never seen another man in that state, but if we appear like that to women, they must indeed be fascinated not to find us horrifying [*en horreur*]."[35]

When Rousseau reports the incident publicly and in great detail the following morning, he is rebuked by a hospice administrator for making a fuss over nothing: the Moor's actions were "forbidden [like] fornication, but for the rest, the desire [*intention*] was not an offense to the person who was its object, and there was nothing to be bothered by in having been found attractive." Rousseau is so struck by this straightforward approach, as well as by the "natural manner" of an ecclesiastic listening in on the discussion, that he decides "this was no doubt an accepted practice [*usage admis*] in the world."[36] Thus his personal, intense dislike for the whole business, which he takes pains to underscore, is not expressed as moral outrage: despite an abundance of fitting tropes—desire, religion, age, race—the language of transgression is absent. Perhaps most striking are the lessons he takes from this experience—first, to be aware of the possibility of future pederastic overtures, and second, to esteem women more highly: "It seemed that I owed them, in sentiments of tenderness, in personal homage, the reparations of my sex, and the most ugly of she-monkeys [*guenons*] became in my eyes an adorable object through the memory of that false african."

Homosexual desire is treated less as a moral challenge to the natural order than as an opportunity to shore up an engendered social organization. So, too, in the *Lévite* the Benjamites' lust signals dilemmas of intertribal versus intratribal identities and public versus private space, and in both cases the affirmation of boundaries requires the affirmation of heterosexual desire, first, in the form of women's brutalization and, second, in the form of their dutiful compliance. But the concubine's sacrifice also marks a challenge to the community's unity and will, that "intrigue and partial association" Rousseau condemns in the Social Contract.[37] When messengers are sent to the Benjamites demanding that the culprits be turned over, the tribe refuses and rushes to defend Gibeah, "resolved to fight alone against the reunited people." What began as a challenge to hospitality becomes, through the concubine's rape and murder, a challenge to collective security.

The second half of the Lévite is driven by maternal crises as the realization that the Benjamites must be preserved quickly reduces to the imperative to find them mates. And while here the problem appears to be simple reproduction, the drama of missing mothers is signaled in the opening paragraph when Rousseau introduces the Benjamite tribe as the "sad child of pain who caused your mother's death" (1208). The mother in question is Rachel, who died giving birth to the tribe's namesake and founder, her second son Benjamin. The symbolic legacy of its origin foreshadows the tribe's later procreative crisis, both of which implicate women as critical sites of social continuity and order. This use of women and heterosexual desire to make and mark social organization is illustrative of Gayle Rubin's influential argument on gender as a function of kinship structure.[38] As her analysis makes clear, procreative strategies are always also questions of how cultural and social systems are imposed on the natural world. And, indeed, in the Lévite precisely an obstruction to the "traffic in women" threatens the security of intertribal relations: the tribes' oath never to allow marriage between their women and the Benjamites interrupts the normal patterns of exchange. The problem that then confronts them is how to honor their vow and still make the necessary transactions. Rousseau's resolution of this problem illustrates Rubin's claim that men are the "exchange partners" and thus the beneficiaries of the social organization that such exchanges secure.[39] But his account also underscores women's capacity for agency in a way that Rubin's does not. From a political perspective the issue is not how authentic their choices are, but how their capacity to want and to will figures in the constitution of a republican community.

Wives are secured for the Benjamites in two separate incidents. In the first, simultaneously keeping their oath and preserving their "brothers" prompts the unified tribes to massacre an entire town. The disobedience that authorizes the massacre is uncovered only as a consequence of the tribes' intention to get around their vow: "To elude such a cruel oath [and] contemplating new carnages, they took a census of the army to see if, despite the solemn obligation, any of them had failed to show up, and they found no one from Jabés" (1220). The tribes do not raid Jabés for women; rather, they exterminate the men who would otherwise exercise their right to determine how the women will marry. But Rousseau's description of the transaction leaves room to doubt its legitimacy. Explaining the position of the Jabés townsfolk with respect to the civil war, Rousseau writes: "Less concerned with punishing the crime than with spilling fraternal blood, [they] refused vengeances more atrocious than the transgression, without considering that the violation of an oath and desertion from the common cause are worse than cruelty" (1220). The subsequent executions are called "murders," which Rousseau describes with a ferocious detail found nowhere in Judges. And there is no pretense of justice in the actual delivery of the Jabés virgins, who are compared to "prey." The section describing their nuptial embrace "by hands dripping with the blood of their kin" ends with the following, astonishing lament: "Oh [female] sex, always a slave or a tyrant, whom man oppresses or adores, and yet whom he can only make happy or be happy [with] by allowing to be his equal" (1221).[40]

In the second incident and unlike the first, a raid is precisely what is required because the townsmen have done nothing to endanger their rights. Here honoring their collective oath *requires* that the Shiloh women be taken against their townsmen's will. The sociopolitical imperative repeats a formula familiar from the *Social Contract*: the sanctity of the "common cause" requires overcoming individual wills, and yet the autonomy of those willing subjects is confirmed precisely in its negation. Men's wills are here manifest in their right to exchange and withhold women, and it appears that respecting their sovereignty entails violating women's bodies. But Rousseau's narrative complicates this conclusion. When the people of Shiloh, gathered together for a public festival, realize what is happening, they rush to defend the women. They stop only after village elders "make their voices heard, and the people, moved by compassion for the Benjamites, become concerned on their behalf."[41] The text is explicit that only the fathers remain steadfast; they insist that their daughters be allowed to decide their fate in an appeal to the crowd that makes a direct connection between the women's situation and the liberty of all. The crowd's assent to their proposal hinges on the recognition that the demands of equity outweigh compassion for the Benjamites: "Divided between justice and pity, the assembly finally decides that the captives will be set free and decide for themselves what to do" (1222).

At this point Rousseau has strayed far from the biblical version, which covers the whole incident with this passage: "And the children of Benjamin took them wives, according to their number, of them that danced, whom they caught: and they went and returned unto their inheritance, and repaired the cities, and dwelt in them" (Judges 21:23). This terse denouement is followed by two brief verses, one of which recounts the subsequent dispersal of the Israelites, "every man to his tribe and to his family," and the second of which consists in the statement, quoted above, that this was a time lacking in political authority (Judges 21:24–25). Rousseau's elaborations, by contrast, provide both a closing scene of social unity and a familial and sexual *spectacle* in which the recognition of women's will confirms the beneficent coercion of the "common cause."

The scene begins when the Benjamites are forced to set the women free. Whereas earlier they had openly attacked (and "the chase animated [the women's] color and the ravishers' ardor"), they must now "try to replace force with means more powerful over [the women's] hearts" (1222). The savaging becomes courtship. Extending their arms in a gesture of escort, the Benjamites present their case: "Daughters of Shiloh, will you be happier with someone else? Are the last of the Benjamites unworthy of persuading you?" Axa, unlike some of the other maidens, remains unimpressed by this coy display, and she rushes to her mother's arms. Her father then steps forward and asks her to "Do your duty and save me from disgrace [*opprobre*] among my brothers" (1223). Never denying her right to choose, he suggests that he, too, loves Elmacin, who "was to be the consolation of my old age: but the welfare of your people and the honor of your father must outweigh him." His words by themselves do not affect her, "but lifting her eyes, she meets those of her venerable father; they say more than his mouth; she makes her choice." Elmacin, meanwhile, calms the agitated crowd by responding to Axa's choice with his own vow to remain celibate and enter a religious order. The virgins, the crowd sings out, have saved the people of Israel.

With this Byronic, if not bathetic, conclusion Rousseau has furnished the fundamentals of a republican romance. The community must express a general will both engendered and endangered by individual desire. Enforcing that will thus entails the coincidence of fulfillment and coercion.

In the *Social Contract*, this twofold relationship is mapped out on a citizen who is simultaneously sovereign and subject, and it finds its quintessential and paradoxical formulation in the dictum that he be "forced to be free." In the *Lévite* these paradoxical relations characterize sexual performances in which the simultaneous recognition and refusal of individual will structures the community. This is most evident and most brutal for the women, but it is also true for the men: the Levite, the old man of Gibeah, Axa's father, and her fiancé, and of course the lustful young men of Gibeah are all denied satisfaction. My point is not to equivocate on who suffers the most, but to underscore that the grammar of sexual interaction is also the grammar of political interaction, and when the Shiloh virgins consent to be raped, they hold in place a political community whose foundation is consent to the terms of one's domination.

But now the problem of authenticity—here, of will and choice—seems inescapable. After all, in the *Social Contract* men's bifurcated sovereign-subject identity is said to enable genuinely autonomous action; in what sense can women in the drama just sketched be anything more than what Rubin calls "semi-objects," in distinction to the "subject" position occupied by male exchange partners?[42] By insisting on the salience of women's agency I am perhaps as guilty in the eyes of Rubin as is Claude Lévi-Strauss, whose late acknowledgment that "even in a man's world, [a woman] is still a person" and thus a generator of signs rouses her disgust. When Lévi-Strauss writes that women's dual role as sign and as agent explains why "the relations between the sexes have preserved affective richness, ardour and mystery," Rubin is dumbfounded that he is "presenting one of the greatest rip-offs of all time as the root of romance."[43] But I think that Rousseau demonstrates how romance consummates the rip-off, or in other words, how women's status as generator of signs is crucial to a social system organized by sexuality and is paradigmatic of a political order that is always, in the final instance, coercive.

In some sense all of Rousseau's accounts of social power and control suggest that the capacity for autonomy is the consequence of a rip-off: a bad deal drives the plot of the *Discourse on Inequality*, and the same deal is "rendered legitimate" in the *Social Contract*. The transformation from slave to citizen cannot be a consequence of a contractual foundation or the existence of a general will because both are also present in the *Discourse on Inequality*.[44]

> By what conceivable art could one have found the means to place men to subjection in order to make them free? To use the goods,

> the manual labor, and even the very life of all its members in
> service to the state without forcing them and without consulting
> them? To bind their will by their own consent . . . How is it
> possible that they obey and no one commands, that they serve
> and have no master? . . . These wonders are the work of the law.[45]

And the *Social Contract* tells us that the "most important of all" laws is
"not engraved on marble or bronze, but in the hearts of the citizens."[46]
The legitimacy of the social contract, finally, depends on a similarity of
situation and a unity of interest that are every day manifest in ingrained
"habits." What matters in a republic is that men and women know "how
to act well," and to this end the essential political task is to engender the
proper needs, desires, and fears: "If it is good to know how to use men as
they are, it is even better still to turn them into what one needs them to
be. The most absolute authority is that which penetrates to the inner
part of a man and is exerted no less on his will than on his actions. It is
certain that in the long run people are what the government makes
them."[47] What the government "needs them to be" is masculine and
feminine, a project that guarantees right action precisely by "penetrating
to their inner parts" and shaping their very experience of wanting. And
in Rousseau's sexual politics, that experience of wanting unites desire
and submission as inseparable elements of (hetero)sexuality. This "true
constitution" engraved on republican hearts remains legible in the sexual
performances through which political community is organized in the
Lévite. Of course women's expressions of will in that story are wholly
gendered: that they will play their roles properly is guaranteed by a femininity that finds permeable the line between coercing and courting and
values devotion to fathers and others over self. And this is paradigmatic
of republican citizenship; Rousseau would much prefer that his republicans freely choose to be forced, rather than force them to be free.

The troubling indiscernibility in the *Lévite* between consent and force
and pleasure and pain does not vitiate individual autonomy; on the contrary, in Rousseau's account the confusion is definitive of it. This remains
suspiciously paradoxical as a logical proposition, but Rousseau does not
intend his citizens to reason it out. Rather, he intends them to feel it; or,
like the Legislator of the *Social Contract*, he intends to "persuade without
convincing."[48] This distinction, which is discussed at length in both the
Essay on Languages and *Emile*, differentiates between what can be rationally demonstrated and what can be sensually confirmed.[49] For Rousseau

the confirmation of a political relationship (always in need of a basis "more solid than reason alone") consists in the experience and the expression of desire.[50] "The ecstasies of tender hearts appear utterly fanciful to anyone who has not felt them. And the love of country, a hundred times more ardent and delightful than that of a mistress, likewise cannot be conceived except by being felt. *But it is easy to observe, in the hearts it inflames and in all the actions it inspires,* that fiery and sublime ardor which the purest virtue is lacking when it is separated from the love of country."[51]

II

The possibilities of a political *éducation sensible* are signaled in Rousseau's own life story, in the *Confessions'* account of his self-described "brutal sensuality." It is difficult to read the descriptions of his personal blend of sexuality and domination and not agree with Jean Starobinski that "it took Freud to 'think' Rousseau's feelings."[52] But Starobinski also observes that the speculative if fertile ground of psychoanalytic causality remains less important than does Rousseau's own interpretation of his life's events, and the interpretation he provides of his sexual desires makes them inseparable from his desire for justice. Both originated in early experiences of domination, the first a beating administered by the young Mlle Lambercier in response to a childish transgression, and the second a beating administered by his uncle for a crime that Rousseau insists he did not commit. The first beating produces "an admixture of sensuality" in the "pain and shame of punishment," whereas the second produces only "diabolical obstinacy" and despair.[53] The first solidifies his lifelong "perversity," the second solidifies his lifelong horror of injustice. "Who would imagine that I owe one of the most vigorous elements in my character to the same origins as the weakness and sensuality that flows in my veins?"[54]

If this were a unique depiction of a heady conflation between pleasure and domination, we might do best to smile or cringe at Rousseau's personal revelations and move on. So, too, if this were an isolated account of coinciding erotic and moral arousal. But these themes abound in Rousseau's sexual politics. In *Emile*, for example, the pupil's introduction to morality and society hinges on his sexual initiation: only Sophie can guarantee a proper political disposition for Emile, and she does so through sexual interaction that alternately casts him as the sovereign husband and the submissive lover. She, likewise, is presented alternately as a virtuous wife whose modesty "asks to be conquered" and an imperious mistress whose "least favors [are] acts of grace."[55] And while these roles are always circumscribed by paternal authority, the tutor repeatedly reminds both of them that "you are free, and the question here is not one of marital duties"; it is instead a question of "mutual desire."[56] In their individual interaction *Emile*'s "everyman" and "everywoman" enact a dialectic of (sexual) control that reappears in the *Lévite* at the level of social organization.

Similarly, in *La nouvelle Héloïse* the relationship between Julie and St. Preux is characterized by dominant/submissive role-playing rooted in mutual desire. There the protagonist's social and moral maturation parallels an alternatively gratified and refused passion, which Julie controls through her dual roles as wife and lover. In the first capacity she remains physically unobtainable, providing instead an "idea of perfection" that St. Preux suggests is always necessary to inspire and sustain love.[57] In the second capacity her control of St. Preux's sexual satisfaction, and thus of his will, produces a submission indistinguishable from pleasure: "obeying you [gives me] the same charm one would find in self-gratification."[58] And at the end of the novel St. Preux demonstrates his successful political socialization by intervening to prevent his mentor from making an unsuitable marriage: willingly assuming the role Julie's father had played earlier in his own life, St. Preux signals his commitment to the social order by upholding its rules of sexual organization. Like Elmacin's, St. Preux's devotion to the "common cause" is generated through his romantic devotion.

Rousseau's appeal to gender relations as the fulcrum for political sensibilities extends to his depictions of citizen-state interactions. There, in a public realm emptied of women, republican postures retain the form and the meaning of masculinity rightly performed. This is most evident in *Political Economy*, whose didactic tone draws heavily on gender metaphors to signal the sensibilities necessary for patriotism and republican statecraft. The problem of political rule is fundamentally a problem of desire: because "the authority the populace accords to those it loves and by whom it is loved is a hundred times more absolute than all the tyranny of usurpers," politicians must realize that "the greatest support for public authority lies in the hearts of the citizens."[59] But this desire must be inseparable from the experience of submission: "The government would

have a difficult time making itself obeyed if it limits itself to obedience.
. . . If you want the laws obeyed, make them beloved so that to get men
to do what they should, it is enough that they think that they must do
it."[60] And they will "think that they must do it" so long as political life
continues sexual and maternal attachments. The republican state must
"show itself as the common mother of all citizens," which is accomplished if "children are raised in common and in the bosom of equality,
if they are imbued with laws of the state and maxims of the general will,
instructed to respect them above all things, if they are surrounded by
examples and objects that constantly speak to them of the tender mother
who nourishes them, of the love she bears for them, of the inestimable
benefits they receive from her, and in turn of the debt they owe her."[61]

This maternalizing of the general will offers another lens on Rousseau's
well-noted preoccupation with mothering. In *Emile* he writes, "Do you
want to bring everyone back to his first duties? Begin with mothers."[62]
Political Economy echoes this exhortation with "Do we want people to be
virtuous? Let us begin by making them love their country."[63] At stake in
both cases is the citizen-child's attachment to the source of his protection
and nurturing, and, through her, his identification with other citizen-
siblings. Where maternal love wanes, the tutor insists, family members
"hardly know one another."[64] Where patriotism fades, Rousseau advises
the statesman, "country means no more to [the citizens] than it does to
foreigners."[65] The duties between mother and child, *Emile* continues, "are
reciprocal, and if they are ill-fulfilled on one side, they will be neglected
on the other."[66] The commitments of society, *Political Economy* repeats,
"are reciprocal in nature, [and thus] no one owes anything to someone
who claims to owe nothing to anybody."[67] And as Rousseau's obsession
with the moral travesty of wet-nursing makes clear, maternal devotion
must be *felt*: the mother's body provides the sensuous confirmation of
maternal solicitude, and "where I find a mother's care do not I owe a
son's attachment?"[68]

In *Political Economy* maternal solicitude is explicitly presented as a
political expedient to citizen-brothers, "who will never substitute for the
actions of men and citizens the sterile and vain babblings of sophists, and
[who will] one day become the defenders and the fathers of the country
whose children they have been for so long."[69] But these citizens are never
only sons and fathers; they are also lovers, and their political performances require "the ecstasies of tender hearts." Rousseau's prose in *Political
Economy* is replete with images of seduction: the "inflamed hearts," the

"fiery ardor," and the passion produced by "immortal actions whose radiance dazzles our feeble eyes" all suggest erotic postures. And of course a man's passion—without which he would "certainly be a very bad citizen"—follows the logic worked out on the characters of Emile and St.-Preux: love of country, Rousseau writes, is the best means by which to guarantee citizens' good behavior because "every man is virtuous when his private will is in conformity with the general will in all things, and we willingly want what is wanted by the people we love." Rousseau's advice to politicians repeats the observations he makes about women: "Respect [the citizens'] liberty and your power will increase daily; never go beyond your rights, and eventually they will be limitless." Thus it was, Rousseau effuses, that Rome "became mistress of the world."[70]

III

Many feminist interpreters have pointed to the importance of romantic and familial experience in Rousseau's republican project. While some emphasize its noninstrumental and particular attachments, others emphasize how it contains chaos coded as feminine sexuality. In either case, the relationship between femininity and republicanism is a negative one: the maintenance of public space means that women must be privatized. But the republican romance I have teased out of Rousseau's writings suggests we move carefully on this score. On the one hand, it's clear that Rousseau disapproved of the public women of the ancien régime; the saloniéres and actresses, to say nothing of bourgeois Parisiennes, disrupted the boundaries of private and public. And certainly the absence of women in the Social Contract, even in its discussion of families, is striking.[71] On the other hand, Rousseau's evocations of maternal and erotic identities in his account of citizen-subjects and their state blurs the opposition between femininity and republicanism. Or perhaps, it undermines any easy move from this opposition to a related one between sexuality and publicity. Not only does Rousseau depict republican practice as continuous with sexual practice but, additionally, his account of the republic's incorporation and its expression of a general will are simultaneously depictions of a sex/gender system in motion.

If women are above all a source of sexual and procreative labor, then perhaps Rousseau's public/private divide serves to manage and control these functions while marking off a space where men can live as citizens. But this risks underestimating the salience of women's wills and overestimating the extent of citizens' "denaturing." On the first score Rousseau's sexual politics depends upon a dynamic and ambivalent exchange that a wholly teleological definition of women can obscure. The limited possible outcomes to these exchanges do not necessarily put them in opposition to some other, muscular version of political autonomy; they are instead exemplars of citizenly decision making in the context of an unalterable, constant, and supremely sovereign general will, where even or especially the citizens' lives must be available for sacrifice. On the second score, a denatured public realm doesn't readily fit with the habits of masculinity that constitute republican action: the citizen needs a man's erotic, familial, and material attachments, to say nothing of the bodily signs of a manly carriage.[72]

If woman is above all a sign, then the public/private motility of gender might well reduce to literary play: the mother/mistress-state is a powerful trope, one used regularly in nationalist cant. But Rousseau's rhetorical strategy demands material authentication, and for him tropes are meaningful only "when passion holds our eyes spellbound."[73] This was evident to the ancients, who "acted much more by persuasion and by affections of the soul because they did not neglect the language of signs. . . . In regard to government, the august display of royal power impressed the subjects. . . . [a] throne, a scepter, a purple robe, a crown, a diadem were sacred things to them." But now that "we make an affectation of abolishing these signs," the result is an effacement of "royal majesty" from the subjects' hearts.[74] Political authority depends upon a patriotic passion that itself depends upon the "language of signs." The modern state is an abstraction (and a bloodless one at that) hard pressed to rouse the needed ardor.[75] But if togas, sagums, and fasces are no longer viable, there are always the citizens themselves.[76]

To the degree that masculinity is a *habitual* practice, public space can safely be turned over to warriors, athletes, and voters "perfectly independent" of others and prone to avoid complexifying discussions at all costs.[77] But if, as I've suggested, the notion of performance includes a specular and sensuous dimension, then one should anticipate the recurrent public appearance of women's bodies, those "examples and objects" of tender mothers and beloved mistresses. This is certainly the case in Rousseau's depictions of that republican exemplar Sparta. Of course, these illustrations are often inaccurate; but they do provide an (imagined) historical corrective to the homosexuality that in fact characterized public sexuality in that city-state.[78] In his own republican fantasies—in *Letter to D'Alembert, La nouvelle Héloïse, Considerations on the Government of Poland*, and *Lévite*—Rousseau relies upon festivals, the *cercles*, village dances, and other carnivalesque gatherings to depict the sexual and familial *moeurs* that constitute "true constitutions." Some are sexually segregated, for example, the Genevan *cercles*, while others have the express purpose of publicly organizing seduction, for example, the marital balls described in *Letter to D'Alembert*. But in every case, women's presence as witnesses, revelers, and/or subjects to be seduced is critical: as both agents and objects, they partake of the language of signs.

The suggestion that women be seen as political actors in Rousseau's republican drama remains a peculiar proposal, but especially so if one takes the periodic gestures of isolated and silent voters to be definitive of the action. I have pointed instead to the more numerous and detailed textual accounts of citizenship as public gathering and (self-)display. In so doing I have introduced the notion of performance to underscore both the theatrical and material aspects of women's participation. I have further suggested that this is not in opposition to, but conforms with, men's political agency, which on Rousseau's account is precisely the expression of properly masculine desire, need, and fear. To the degree that this interpretation situates political agency within the context of specular and sensuous experience, it is consistent with the developmental trajectory outlined in *Emile*, as well as with Starobinski's analysis of the allure of unmediated or transparent communication, where seeing is believing.[79] At the level of the individual, what is experienced as the immediacy of passion in fact mediates, for men and women, the paradoxical political imperatives of submission and control. At the level of community the effect is a gender *spectacle* that negotiates intrasocial organization and national identity through fantasies of bloodline, maternal solicitude, and "natural" desires. Citizenship, on this interpretation, is a somatic experience.

And yet Rousseau's dream of transparency is just that, the apex of *Emile*'s developmental trajectory is the capacity to reason, and perhaps what I have parsed is less a grammar of political action than of ideology (in the good old-fashioned Marxian sense of the word). Here the notion of performance tends to erase the possibility of political agency, suggesting instead what Butler describes as "the reiterative and citational practice by which discourse produces the effects that it names."[80] A skeptical

reader might concede that this is plausible as an account of gender identity, where "reiterative practices" are words, gestures, styles, and bodily
displays and the "effect" they produce is a sexual identity heralded as
prediscursive ("natural"). But she might question its applicability to a
democratic political identity, where the conclusion seems to be that consent is never a meaningful opportunity, but merely an effect produced
by the "reiterative practice" of, on my account, gendered sexuality. Her
suspicions would presumably be acute with regard to Rousseau's political
theory, which is singularly preoccupied with the problems and promises
of individual freedom.

Two remarks are in order. First, Rousseau's commitment to individual
liberty and his (somewhat begrudging) awareness of the deliberative capacity on which it depends does not lead him to shy away from the paradox of origins. On the contrary, he fully appreciates the problematic
relationship of cause and effect. This is evident in his characterization of
the Legislator's task, which is likened to "chang[ing] human nature": "for
an emerging people to be capable of appreciating the sound maxims of
politics and to follow the fundamental rules of statecraft, the effect would
have to be the cause. . . . And men would be, prior to the advent of laws,
what they ought to become by means of the law."[81] Similarly, the *Social
Contract*'s credit/debit sheet lists moral liberty as an acquisition that
comes *only with* the making of the contract, but that act is itself incomprehensible without the moral capacity for consent.[82] The logical tension
in these accounts eases when we consider that Rousseau is situating the
capacity for autonomy and its concomitant dispositions precisely within
the framework of the performative: there is no ground for consent prior
to its enactment, and in a very concrete way we create the possibility of
moral opportunities through our practices. This is reminiscent of another
old-fashioned Marxian category, namely, praxis: "We set out from real,
active men, and on the basis of their real life-process we demonstrate
the development of ideological reflexes. . . . Life is not determined by
consciousness, but consciousness by life."[83] The materialism prescribed
here parallels to some extent the notion of performance as I have used it
to unpack Rousseau: not as an effort to get behind or under or before
political and sexual awareness, but as a way to approach that awareness
where it is realized, in the bodily, "real life-processes" of existing as masculine and feminine beings. Where my use of performance differs from
Marxian praxis is in the latter's confident appeal to "real men" as a starting point: on my account, the experiential and empirical "reality" of

sexed bodies is always a site at which politics occurs, rather than the self-evident origin or cause of politics. In addition, the priority relationship between mind and body—or consciousness and life—on which Marx's appeal appears to depend cannot be sustained within the model of the performative, which, as I use it, insists that intentions are always embodied, and bodies are always intentional.[84]

This brings me to my second remark, which concerns the problematic nature of consent for both men and women in Rousseau's republic. I have been at some pains to underscore that it is differently problematic: not only are the differences as significant as bodily integrity and political opportunity, but the observation that the agency Rousseau accords to men is not so very different from the agency he accords to women, *by itself* contributes little to ongoing issues of (legitimate) governance. But if we consider how these asymmetrical and yet both compromised capacities for political action are sustained, we have a better understanding of Rousseau's solution to the modern dilemma of governance. This is the dilemma of conventional authority, which finds its quintessential expression in Thomas Hobbes: sovereignty must in the final instance be based on consent, but governmental authority that is not absolute is no authority at all (and it's usually not much of a government). Hobbes's solution, of course, is to insist that the contractors choose freely to alienate completely their powers, and in the process he guts the notion of consent: "Fear is the passion to be reckoned on," and whether I agree with a knife to my throat or as a result of prudential reasoning, in either case I have consented.[85] For interpreters with a wide range of political commitments, Rousseau represents a substantial improvement: however deeply flawed his republican solution, they argue, at least he's working the problem of sustaining individual *political* freedom. But what I mean to suggest in identifying masculine performance as the crux of Rousseauian citizenship is that he is merely resituating the Hobbesian dilemma. For Rousseau, erotic desire is the "passion to be reckoned on," and if we perform as his ideally gendered men and women, then perhaps no ruler will ever need to put a knife to our throats.

Ultimately, then, Rousseau's republican romance is a prod to thinking about the instability of consent in sexual and political relationships. That it remains unintelligible when divorced from worldly and bodily conditions seems to be a point in need of regular repetition. Likewise, the "reiterative and citational practice" through which effects—sexual identity, the capacity for consent—become real never occur only or primarily in discursive acts: they require materiality, a "language of signs" in which bodies are essential, and they often rely upon violence, the everyday fears of women and sexual minorities in addition to state-orchestrated varieties. The conclusion to draw from an analysis of sexuality as performative thus is not and cannot be that consent is a chimerical effect of those practices, but rather that sexuality is a critical, even necessary, location for re-imagining and reenacting consent.

Notes

Earlier versions of this paper were presented at the Annual Meetings of the American Political Science Association in August 1996, where it was awarded a prize by the Foundations in Political Thought section, and at the Comparative Studies in Social Transformation Faculty Seminar at the University of Michigan in October 1996, whose participants I thank for their thoughtful criticisms. I have benefited enormously from comments by Don Herzog, Yopi Prins, Kali Israel, Catherine Brown, Jackie Stevens, Arlene Saxonhouse, Steve Engelmann, Susan Okin, and members of *Representations'* editorial board.

1. Jean-Jacques Rousseau, *Emile*, trans. Allan Bloom (New York, 1979). After a first full citation for each, works by Rousseau will hereafter be designated in the notes by short title followed by page reference.

2. Mary Wollstonecraft, *A Vindication of the Rights of Women* (Buffalo, N.Y., 1989), 98.

3. Penny Weiss, "Anatomy and Destiny: Rousseau, Antifeminism, and Woman's Nature," in *Gendered Community: Rousseau, Sex, and Politics* (New York, 1993).

4. Susan Okin, *Women in Western Political Thought* (Princeton, N.J., 1979), part 3. See also Lynda Lange, "Rousseau: Women and the General Will," in *The Sexism of Social and Political Theory*, ed. Lorenne Clark and Lynda Lange (Toronto, 1979), 41–52; and Carol Pateman, "'The Disorder of Women': Women, Love, and the Sense of Justice," *Ethics* 91, no. 1 (1980): 20–34, and Carol Pateman, *The Sexual Contract* (Stanford, Calif., 1988), 96–102.

5. See Sarah Kofman, "Rousseau's Phallocratic Ends," in *Revaluing French Feminism*, ed. Nancy Fraser and Sandra Bartky (Bloomington, Ind., 1992), 46–49; and Linda Zerilli, *Signifying Woman: Culture and Chaos in Rousseau, Burke, and Mill* (Ithaca, N.Y., 1994).

6. Zerilli, *Signifying Woman*, 19. Zerilli is quoting Julia Kristeva, *Powers of Horror: An Essay on Abjection*, trans. Leon Roudiez (New York, 1982), 63.

7. See Judith Butler, *Gender Trouble: Feminism and the Subversion of Identity* (New York, 1991).

8. Judith Butler, *Bodies That Matter* (New York, 1993) and Judith Butler, *Excitable Speech: A Politics of the Performative* (New York, 1997).

9. For a different but related take on the problems and possibilities opened up by Butler's work, see Eve Kosofsky Sedgwick, "Queer Performativity," in *GLQ: A Journal of Lesbian and Gay Studies* 1, no. 1 (1993): 1–16.

10. Elizabeth Wingrove, "Sexual Performance as Political Performance in the *Lettre à M. d'Alembert sur les spectacles*," in *Political Theory* 23 (Nov. 1995): 585–616.

11. Zerilli, *Signifying Woman*, 164 n.

12. The use of "male" and "female" here might suggest to some that I am still relying on an unproblematically natural difference anterior to politics; I can only repeat that these terms refer to

bodily sites, and concerns about their status as origin is exactly the sort of materialism I am uninterested in pursuing.

13. Rousseau's position owes much to what Thomas Laqueur has argued are new natural scientific accounts of sexual difference emerging in the eighteenth century. See Thomas Laqueur, *Making Sex: Body and Gender from the Greeks to Freud* (Cambridge, Mass., 1990).

14. See Jean-Jacques Rousseau, *Essay on the Origin of Languages*, in *The First and Second Discourses and Essay on the Origin of Languages*, ed. and trans. Victor Gourevitch (New York, 1986), 240–43, and Rousseau, *Emile*, 322–23.

15. Rousseau, *Essay on Languages*, 278: "We do not realize that often [sensations] affect us not only as sensations but as signs or images, and that their moral effects also have moral causes."

16. I play, of course, on J. L. Austin's formative account of performative speech acts, *How to Do Things with Words* (Cambridge, Mass., 1975).

17. Jean-Jacques Rousseau, *Le Lévite d'Ephraïm*, in *Oeuvres complètes*, 4 vols., Bibliothèque de la pléïade (Paris, 1959–69), 2:1920. All translations from this edition are mine.

18. A Levite is a member of the tribe of Levi, entrusted to oversee the temple and its sacred vessels.

19. *Oeuvres complètes*, 2:1223. All subsequent page references to *Lévite* will be given in the text.

20. Thomas Kavanagh, "Rousseau's *Lévite of Ephraïm*: Dream, Text, and Synthesis," in *Eighteenth-Century Studies*, 16, no. 2 (Winter 1983): 148.

21. Kavanagh, "Rousseau's *Lévite*," 151.

22. *Oeuvres complètes*, 2:1206.

23. The Hebrew is *shofet* and has a range of political and administrative connotations. See *The Anchor Bible: Judges*, trans. and commentary Robert Boling (Garden City, N.Y., 1975), 6a:5–7.

24. Judges 21:25, in *The Holy Bible*, King James Version (New York, 1910). Subsequent biblical citations are to this edition unless otherwise noted.

25. Jean-Jacques Rousseau, *Discourse on the Origin and Foundation of Inequality Among Men*, in *Rousseau: The Basic Political Writings*, ed. and trans. Donald Cress (Indianapolis, Ind., 1987), 65.

26. *Discourse on Inequality*, 64.

27. Ibid., 65.

28. For a discussion of "the people" as a political category, see Jean-Jacques Rousseau, *On the Social Contract*, in *Political Writings*, 147.

29. *Social Contract*, 148. The imagery of state as body reappears again on 150.

30. *Lévite*, 1209. See also Rousseau's more extended discussion of this issue in a first draft of the footnote at 1922.

31. The English and French translations of the relevant verse (Judges 19:2) vary with respect to how the concubine's behavior is characterized, that is, as adulterous versus as irritated or angry. In the face of conflicting textual sources, Robert Boling suggests that irritation or anger is the more likely referent because "it is odd that a woman would become a prostitute and then run home." He concludes with the more compelling observation that "as Israelite law did not allow for divorce by the wife, she became an adultress by walking out on him"; *Anchor Bible*, 6a:273–74. We do not know which translation Rousseau used, but in my perusal of eighteenth-century French Bibles, the most frequently used verb is *paillarder*, roughly translated, "to act licentiously."

32. The *Anchor Bible* commentary on this passage suggests something similar: "The initial and determinative offense is a violation of the law of hospitality"; 6a:276.

33. *Lévite*, 1215: "Alas! She is already dead! Barbarians, unworthy of the name of men [*le nom d'hommes*]; your howling resembles the cries of the horrible Hyena, and like it, you devour cadavers!"

34. *Oeuvres complètes*, 1:67.

35. Ibid. I am following J. M. Cohen's translation of Jean-Jacques Rousseau, *Confessions* (London, 1953), 71.

36. *Oeuvres complètes*, 1:68.

37. *Social Contract*, 156.

38. Gayle Rubin, "Traffic in Women: Notes on the 'Political Economy' of Sex," in *Toward an Anthropology of Women*, ed. Rayna Reiter (Rapp) (New York, 1975), 157–210.

39. Rubin, "Traffic in Women," 174.

40. The original reads: *"Sexe toujours esclave ou tiran, que l'homme opprime ou qu'il adore, et qu'il ne peut pourtant rendre heureux ni l'être, qu'en le laissant égal à lui."* My thanks to Bill Paulson for helping me navigate the syntax of this sentence.

41. From this point on Rousseau writes in the present tense.

42. Rubin, "Traffic in Women," 176.

43. Ibid., 201. Rubin quotes Claude Lévi-Strauss from *The Elementary Structures of Kinship* (Boston, 1969), 496.

44. See *Discourse on Inequality*, 69, 75.

45. Jean-Jacques Rousseau, *Discourse on Political Economy*, in *Political Writings*, 116–17.

46. *Social Contract*, 172.

47. *Discourse on Political Economy*, 119.

48. *Social Contract*, 164.

49. *Essay on Languages*, 240–42, 248; and *Emile*, 321–23.

50. *Discourse on Inequality*, 75–76.

51. *Discourse on Political Economy*, 120, emphasis mine.

52. Jean Starobinski, *Jean-Jacques Rousseau: Transparency and Obstruction*, trans. Arthur Goldhammer (Chicago, 1988), 115. Starobinski is here borrowing from Eric Weil, who remarked that "it took Kant to think Rousseau's thoughts"; Eric Weil, "Jean-Jacques Rousseau et sa politique," *Critique* 56 (January 1952): 11.

53. *Confessions*, 25, 30.

54. Ibid., 28.

55. *Emile*, 477.

56. Ibid., 476–77.

57. See Rousseau, *La nouvelle Héloïse*, part 1, letter 24, and part 3, letter 18, on the "ideas of perfection" that love requires, in *Oeuvres complètes*, vol. 2.

58. *Oeuvres complètes*, 2:122. I have rendered the French *se contenter soi-même* as "self-gratification" and, perhaps in the process, lost the sexual connotations of the original.

59. *Discourse on Political Economy*, 121.

60. Ibid., 119. I have altered Cress's translation. The original reads: *"Si vous voulez qu'on obéisse aux lois, faites qu'on les aime, et que pour faire ce qu'on doit, il suffise de songer qu'on le doit faire"*; *Oeuvres complètes*, 3:252.

61. *Political Writings*, 125–26.

62. *Emile*, 46.

63. *Discourse on Political Economy*, 122.

64. *Emile*, 46.

65. *Discourse on Political Economy*, 122.

66. *Emile*, 46.

67. *Discourse on Political Economy*, 117.

68. *Emile*, 45.

69. *Discourse on Political Economy*, 126. I have changed what seems to me to be a mistake in Cress's translation. The original reads: *"substituer des actions d'hommes et de citoyens au stérile et vain babil des sophistes"*; *Oeuvres complètes*, 3:261.

70. *Discourse on Political Economy*, 123. See *Emile*, 392–93.

71. In addition to the discussion of population growth as a sign of good government, women appear obliquely in a final footnote, which addresses civil versus religious control of marriage: "Is it not clear that the clergy—if master of whether to marry or not marry people . . . —[w]ill dispose of

inheritance, offices, the citizens, the state itself, which could not subsist if composed solely of bastards?" *Social Contract*, 227.

72. Of course, the problems of bodily representation multiply when one recognizes, as Rousseau does, that sociopolitical experience shapes demeanor and form. "An insolent air belongs only to slaves," he writes in a discussion of Emile's comportment, "Independence has nothing affected about it"; *Emile*, 337. He illustrates the point with a story taken from Claude-Adrien Helvétius, where a man's timid glances, uncertain bearing, and hanging head announce his political subjugation. What Rousseau deduces, however, is a refreshing absence of courtier affectation, and thus the manly exterior of a true citizen. The hunched comportment of a German Elector or the social ungainliness of a free republican? Rousseau's appeal in the *Discourse on the Arts and Sciences* suggests a simpler sign: "A good man is an athlete who enjoys competing in the nude; he is contemptuous of all those vile ornaments which would impair the use of his strength, most of which were invented merely to conceal some deformity"; *Political Writings*, 4.

73. *Discourse on Political Economy*, 247.

74. *Emile*, 321–22. Rousseau's footnote to this discussion includes the following: "Thus the Venetian government, in spite of the collapse of the state, still enjoys all the affection and adoration of the people thanks to the pomp of its antique majesty. . . . the ceremony of the bucentaur, which makes so many fools laugh, would cause the population of·Venice to shed all its blood for the maintenance of its tyrannical government." The translator's note explains that the ceremony Rousseau refers to was a yearly public ritual during which the Doge stood on the state's galley (named the Bucentaur) and was wed to the Adriatic; ibid., 491 n. 66.

75. See *Emile*, 40: "Public instruction no longer exists and can no longer exist, because where there is no longer fatherland, there can no longer be citizens. These two words, *fatherland* and *citizen* should be effaced from modern languages."

76. "But what will be the objects of [Geneva's republican] entertainments? What will be shown in them? Nothing if you please . . . [l]et the spectators become an entertainment to themselves; make them actors themselves; do it so that each sees and loves himself in the others so that all will be better united"; Jean-Jacques Rousseau, *Letter to D'Alembert*, in *Politics and the Arts: Letter to M. D'Alembert on the Theatre*, trans. Allan Bloom (Ithaca, N.Y., 1960), 126. Rousseau lists the objects of ancient republican display in *Emile*, 322. See Allan Bloom's note, ibid., 491 n. 71: "'Toga: the outer garment of a citizen. Sagum: the military cloak.' (*Oxford English Dictionary*)." A fasces is "a bundle of rods bound up with an axe in the middle and its blade projecting; these rods were carried by lictors before the superior magistrates at Rome as an emblem of their power"; *Oxford English Dictionary*, s.v. "fasces."

77. See *Social Contract*, 156, 172, 206. Paeans to the virtuous citizen as warrior and athlete also appear in *Letter to D'Alembert*, *Discourse on the Arts and Sciences*, *Emile*, and *Considerations on the Government of Poland*.

78. Rousseau's source was apparently Plutarch. The extent of his borrowing from Plutarch's account is almost as striking as the degree to which he recasts that account, eliminating any mention of homosexuality and pedophilia, as well as any mention of the Spartan women's cross-dressing and sequestration (both presented as strategies to contain and nurture heterosexual desire); see Plutarch, "Lysurgus," in *Plutarch's Lives*, ed. Arthur Clough (London, 1929), 1:59–90.

79. *Emile*, 323: "Clothe reason in a body if you want to make youth able to grasp it. Make the language of the mind pass through the heart, so that it may make itself understood. I repeat, cold arguments can determine our opinions, but never our actions. They make us believe and not act. . . . [I]f this is true for all men it is *a fortiori* true for young people, who are still enveloped in their senses, and think only insofar as they imagine."

80. Butler, *Bodies That Matter*, 2.

81. *Social Contract*, 164.

82. Ibid., 151.

83. Karl Marx, *The German Ideology*, in *The Marx-Engels Reader*, ed. Robert Tucker (New York, 1972), 154–55.

84. I say that Marx's appeal "appears" to rest on this priority relationship, but I am not convinced that this follows necessarily from his account. For an interesting discussion of these issues see Andrew Parker, "Praxis and Performativity," *Women and Performance* 16 (1996): 265–75.

85. Thomas Hobbes, *Leviathan*, ed. Michael Oakeshott (New York, 1962), 111.

14

The Coupling of Human Souls

Rousseau and the Problem of Gender Relations[1]

Rebecca Kukla

Rousseau believed that freedom was humankind's "noblest faculty." Freedom, for Rousseau, consisted in the ability to satisfy one's desires without being dependent on alien persons. At the same time, he believed that by joining forces with others, we could greatly increase our ability to satisfy our desires and lead fulfilling human lives. But joining forces with others seems on the face of it to make us dependent on those others. Hence he saw the fundamental task of social theory as finding "a form of association that defends and protects the person and goals of each associate with all the common force, and by means of which each one, uniting with all, nevertheless obeys only himself and remains as free as before."[2] The solution to this problem, for Rousseau, will depend on our ability to *reconstruct* human nature. Since dependence on an alien will rob us of our freedom, mutually dependent humans must be reconstructed so that they are not alien to one another. In the case of the mutual dependence of citizens within a state, the reconstruction takes the form of creating beings who identify with—or derive their sense of self from—the social whole, and who are similar enough in tastes and values to maintain such an identification. Thus the legislator must be "capable of changing human nature, so to speak; of transforming each individual, who is by himself a perfect whole, into a part of a larger whole from which the individual receives . . . his life and being; . . . of substituting a partial and moral existence for the physical and independent existence we have all received from nature."[3] In becoming social beings we are recreated according to the needs of the social whole with which we are to identify. The man who 'imbibed the love of the fatherland with his mother's milk'[4] has a nature that is specially designed to harmonize with and suit the needs of the state. While it is sexist of Rousseau to insist that Sophie ought to be brought up as a relative being made to suit man's needs, we must remember that Rousseau believes that properly socialized men are also such relative beings, though they are raised not for their wives but for the state.

As this comment reminds us, civic life is not the only realm in which humans become so deeply involved in one another's lives as to risk dependence on each other—partnerships between men and women[5] are at least as central to human life as are commitments to a political body. Rousseau talks about gender relations in terms similar to his discussions of civic relations. Members of a couple are transformed by their relationship, giving up their original nature and receiving a new one, and between them forming a single being. As I will be arguing, many of the same concerns arise in the case of this unification—both man and woman risk losing their freedom by uniting with each other. However, a man and a woman face a special problem that the citizens participating in the general will do not. Citizens all are basically the same sort of being as one another, and hence it is a manageable task for the legislator to make them similar enough to each other that they can unite and identify with a common entity in which they all partake.[6] Furthermore, they all share a common understanding of the nature of human relating, mutuality, and exchange. However, Rousseau believes that men and women have drastically different natures. Hence it is a nontrivial problem to bring them to identify with a single being. As I will explain in detail, men and women are embedded in social relations in very different ways. What it means for another person to become non-alien to them is different in each case. Briefly, women make another non-alien by becoming involved with that other *as other*, while men make another non-alien by eliminating any difference between them. Also, men and women cannot join forces by *contract*, because their understanding of exchange and mutuality is different; they operate within different economies. For these reasons, the question of how a man and a woman can unite and remain free is a more complex one for Rousseau than his more famous civic dilemma. Commentators such as Jones[7] interpret Clarens, the utopian homestead of Rousseau's novel *Julie, ou La nouvelle Héloïse*,[8] as a small-scale exemplification of the ideal state as presented in the *Social Contract*. But there is a crucial difference: Clarens, an example of unity in the private domain, must negotiate gender differences and gender relations, and this is in fact central to its organization, whereas the *Social Contract* describes the creation of an ideal state not articulated by gender differences, because women are supposed to be restricted to the private domain and kept out of its affairs altogether. This difference between the household and the state—that, in preserving the freedom of their members, the former but not the latter must negotiate gender differences—could be unimportant only given the liberal view that gender differences are only skin-deep, so to speak, and don't affect the core of human nature and the possibilities for human relating. But Rousseau, as a great deal of interpretive scholarship has emphasized, held just the opposite view.

In the remainder of this paper, I will explore Rousseau's account of how a man and a woman could unite without restricting each other's freedom, or how they could cease to be alien to one another, despite their fundamental differences. I believe that many commentators who have discussed Rousseau's views on women and gender relations have become confused or twisted Rousseau's words in the process of trying to find a *single* Rousseauian story about how gender relations are supposed to work.[9] I will argue, on the other hand, that Rousseau presents us with not one but three models of how such a unification can occur. Hence my argument will show that the problem of social association is approached in not one but many ways in Rousseau, and also that the gender of a subject is deeply relevant to the nature of the dilemmas of social association that he or she faces. At the end of this paper, I will suggest that these conclusions ought to have led Rousseau to recast the terms of the problem or *civic* association, and to have seen this problem as inextricably bound up with the face of patriarchy. In particular, I will claim that his assumptions about the nature of the *citizen* depend upon his failure to problematize the patriarchal family. But to start with, I must spend some time describing Rousseau's understanding of the nature of the genders and their differences.

The Nature of the Genders

A word is necessary on Rousseau's very concept of 'nature', before we can make sense of his understanding of man's and woman's nature. I will treat this topic, which deserves a study of its own, only very perfunctorily here. Rousseau is commonly described as an unmitigated enthusiast of 'the natural', who is happy to infer how things should be from how they 'naturally' are. While it is true that, for example, he insists in *Emile*[10] that humans are best educated by 'following nature', it is hard to reconcile this naive view with his central thesis that freedom depends on the manipulation and reconstruction of nature. Certainly, since the legislator can and should *change* human nature, Rousseau cannot be read as taking our nature to be essential and immutable. In fact, he cautions that "One must not confound what is natural in the savage state with what is natural in the civic state."[11] And while Emile's tutor is not in the business of directly changing *human* nature, he reconstructs and alters Emile's natural environment a great deal, and thereby shapes his pupil as he sees fit.

Thus when Rousseau valorizes following nature, we must remember that this is a nature which changes and which can be manipulated by humans. The 'nature' that Emile's education follows is one created by human hands. When Rousseau claims that men and women are different *by nature*, we cannot presuppose, as Okin[12] does, that he is attributing an essential character outside of human control to either gender. Equally unfair is Weiss'[13] argument that because Rousseau's remarks on women are stated in a normative voice, and because he suggests methods for turning girls into beings who fit his model of the ideal woman, we can conclude that Rousseau was a social constructionist with regard to gender, who believed gender differences were created rather than natural. This is a faulty argument because the natural and the created do not exclude each other for Rousseau. Human nature, far from being immutable, is characterized first and foremost by what Rousseau calls its *perfectibility*—it is always changing and progressing, undergoing further sophistication and further allowing us to fulfill our potential over time. Furthermore, *we* are the agents of that development; we can and do reconstruct our nature, and it is only determined that we will change. Rousseau's human nature is closer to Hegel's than to a blind, unchanging, deterministic force beyond human control. Hence when Rousseau insists that the natural is good, he is not making a naive inference from 'is' to 'ought'. Something may be natural and not yet existent, and the very concept of the natural contains within it the idea of progress toward human good.

Humans in the savage state do not recognize themselves or other humans as distinct subjects. They live solitary, self-sufficient lives. The need for copulation exists, but it is purely physical; although this need can be filled only by other people, it does not take them as other subjects but merely as objects capable of being used to satiate a desire. Sexual desires are not particularized—"In the former state, all women are suitable for all men [and presumably *vice versa*], because both still have the primitive and common form."[14] Hence these desires do not compromise freedom, because they do not recognize alien others as their object.

Although we begin as self-centered and self-contained individuals, Rousseau identifies two impulses that make us reach out to others.[15] These are expressed by the first two phrases that Rousseau thinks require linguistic expression: *aimez-moi* (love me) and *aidez-moi* (help me).[16] Humans originally feel no need for either the love or the help of others, but through the course of civilization, we all come to rely on others to satisfy both types of needs.

"Aidez-moi" gives voice to our reliance on others for material sustenance, our dependence on others for meeting our material desires. This need for others develops when we become unable to satisfy such needs and desires on our own, due to a scarcity of resources, an increase in our desires, or increased difficulty of satisfying these desires. In these cases, we reach out to others as tools for helping satisfy these needs, and as far as possible, we use others just as we would use our hands, or inanimate instruments, as extensions of our own wills. But other people bear an essential difference from our old tools, they have wills of their own, and hence cannot automatically be used as extensions of our own wills. There is no longer an immediate relationship between what we will our 'tools' to do and what they do. Instead of individuals directly exploiting each other, they thus set up a *reciprocal economy*: I help you so that you will help me.[17] Rousseau considers this a crucial element in our transformation into social beings. What is manipulated in this economy is the ability to obtain material goods. The value of someone or some material object to us is, within this economy, directly measured by our ability to use him/her/it to satisfy our material needs. It is an important feature of this economy that goods within it are interchangeable according to their value. As long as I receive help for a 'fair price', it doesn't matter who helps me, and as long as my possessions are worth enough to allow me to meet my desires, it doesn't matter what I possess. The objects of exchange are not particular things or people, but units of value contingently instantiated by concrete equivalents.

"Aimez-moi" expresses a need incommensurable with the need for objects, namely the need to be cared for by another person. We want others to desire things for us in virtue of the fact that we desire them, independent of any material need we might have for their help—we need someone who desires that our ends be fulfilled, even if that desire is ineffectual within the economy of exchange. This need by its nature cannot be filled by objects, but only by other people with desires and interests in their own right. Care cannot be bartered within the economy of object exchange, since we want others to care for our well-being as an end in itself. I cannot trade some of my love for an equal amount of yours. Love has an economy—I inspire your love by loving you. But it cannot be assigned an exchange value. I do not automatically cease to deliver purchased goods or labour if payment is not forthcoming. Furthermore, the economy of love is *particularizing* instead of universalizing. Love singles out a particular person and makes that person uninterchangeable, intimately connecting the ends of the lover and the loved. By the very nature of the bond, the love object cannot be simply exchanged for another, even if another would reciprocate with more love. Neither are we indifferent to who loves us.

Hence, the economy of love cannot be mapped onto or subsumed by the economy of object exchange, for they have different structures, and our need for love cannot be analyzed as just another material need. Although we give objects in order to receive objects, it is part of the economy of object exchange that we would rather receive the goods for free, and the best exchange for an individual is one where what he receives most outweighs what he gives. On the other hand, the most fulfilling love relationship is mutual—we all prefer to receive the love of those whom we love, and a totally one way exchange loses its interest for us. "Love implies mutuality, which precludes a crudely instrumental view of the loved as object . . . the object of one's love must be a subject as well."[18] Love, unlike material exchange, does not objectify the other by making her value commensurable with that of material objects.

The need for love and the need for help are both equally 'natural', though both require specific social circumstances to emerge. How is the need for others' love born? Our perfectibility demands that if we can adopt tools, practices, or ways of thinking that increase our freedom and our ability to fulfill our potential, we will. Men and women eventually discover that they are better off working together than alone, for as Julie says, "Human souls need to be coupled to be worth their full price."[19] Close proximity awakens the human desire for care and companionship, leading people to discover that "Our sweetest existence is relative and collective."[20]

When men and women join forces, they discover that they can accomplish more by introducing a division of labour along gender lines. As a result of this division of labour, which requires men and women to engage in different activities and develop different skills (and here, Rousseau's account gets murky—the reader receives no details as to why tasks and skills break up in the specific way that they do), men and women become social beings in different ways. Women interact with others and derive their self conception within the economy of care, while men do so within the economy of object exchange. Both genders, in interacting with others in a social world of interdependencies, must try to avoid dependency on alien others. The *masculine principle* of acting in the social world, as I will call it, is to try to eliminate dependence on others by increasing one's material advantage, and by having enough power over others that their distinct will cannot restrict one's freedom. The *feminine principle* is to involve one's self with others, to develop caring bonds which make one's interests intimately connected to the interests of these others, so that those others cease to be alien.[21] Neither the masculine nor the feminine principle operates in the state of nature, where distinct persons are not recognized or confronted at all.

With these two approaches to others go two different self-conceptions, or senses of one's own identity and nature. Men remain self-contained beings for whom anything which is not a direct extension of their will is alien and threatening to freedom. The human world, for men, divides into self and alien other, so that anything which cannot be appropriated and made to become part of the self remains alien. Men have, once out of the state of nature, ceased to be totally self-contained, but their aim is to be able to deny this as much as possible. Women, on the other hand, have a 'relational' self, in a sense very close to that which has been made popular by recent feminist theorists such as Carol Gilligan and Nancy Chodorow.[22] They are selves whose interests and identity can only be understood in relation to the particular others with whom they have formed bonds of care. They are not necessarily *extended* selves, who have made others a part of the self—something which men can do, as we will see—but selves whose identity makes necessary reference to distinct others.

Masculine and feminine power are different as well: Man controls by appropriating other subjects and reducing them to objects who can be exploited as direct extensions of his will. Woman controls by loving and earning love, so that others act in her interest. She leaves the will of others unappropriated, and influences these wills *as* distinct from her own. Man extends himself by extending his material possessions and his buying power, woman by forming bonds with others. These two forms of power are illustrated by Julie and her father, who form the centers of two overlapping and often conflicting circles of control. Julie's control of those around her is formidable: "The empire that Julie exercises over all those around her is frequently emphasized in the book."[23] She controls not through force, but through her love for those around her and theirs for her. Her father creates an equally thorough domain of control based on fear. He has proven his power and is master of those around him. These empires of control are both so powerful, despite their different forms, that Julie's mother is killed by the strain of being torn between them when they place conflicting demands on her. Julie governs those around her, influencing the wills of others while those remain other. Her father, in contrast, *commands* and others obey. Those he has mastered are not, relative to him, autonomous wills at all. It makes no sense to speak of him governing, because only that which can act autonomously can be governed. Man has no interest in governing, for we govern only that which is other, and man seeks to *eliminate* otherness. Woman governs and obeys, while man commands and is governed.[24]

The masculine approach to others is abstracting—it analyzes human situations in terms of the rules of exchange, and takes individuals as interchangeable except in so far as they have specific properties relevant to their use-value. The feminine approach is particularizing, forging bonds with particular others, and becoming involved in the concrete details of their interests, needs, etc. In this, also, Rousseau's account bears a striking resemblance to the accounts of writers like Gilligan and Chodorow. Rousseau somewhat arbitrarily extends this feature of men's and women's interactions with others to their styles of thought in general: Women are supposed to be more suited to analyzing the particular and the concrete, while men are more adept at manipulating abstract principles. Julie and Claire scorn politics, despite their intelligence, and despite their dexterity at grasping and illuminating the complexities of *particular* moral and social situations. Julie explains that the realm of politics is 'too far' from her to 'touch' her very much.[25] The feminine relation to the world has, as Irigaray[26] would say, the immediacy of touch—women confront the world and others neither by appropriating it nor by considering it from an 'objective' distance, but by concretely involving themselves with it. Politics requires thinking about all citizens, abstracted from which concrete individuals they happen to be: "The subject of laws is always general. . . . The law considers the subjects as bodies and actions in the abstract, never a man as an individual or a particular action."[27] Women cannot care about such a class. On the other hand, man can approach the world only indirectly, by categorizing it, so that he can subsume a situation under general rules. But the concrete is too complex to be fully captured by these categorizations. Rousseau, echoing much of our intellectual tradition, insists that man creates systems and principles, and woman applied them: "The quest for abstract and speculative truths, principles and axioms in the sciences, for everything that tends to generalize ideas, is not within the competence of women . . . all their studies ought to be related to practice. It is for them to apply the principles man has found, and to make the observations which may lead to the establishment of principles."[28] Because men learn better through being taught general theories, and women through concrete examples, Rousseau wrote speculative, philosophical works for his male audience, while *Emile* and *Julie*, which make their points through concrete narrative illustration, were intended for good mothers and young women, respectively.

A woman exists in her relations to particular others, and derives identity through them, because her ends are irreducibly tied up with theirs. Julie makes it clear that she exists in her relations to others in her speech to her loved ones on her death bed: "No, my friends, no, my children, I am not leaving you, I am staying with you, so to speak; in leaving you united, my mind, my heart stay with you. You will see me without cease between you."[29] I think that this notion of the woman as existing *between* others, rather than, for example, in the eyes of others or as an extension of others, is an important key to Rousseau's conception of women's nature. A woman cares what others think of her, because she cares about her affect on them *as others*, and not just as indirect routes to determining what she thinks of herself. The socialized man cares about his appearance, but only insofar as he assimilates others' perceptions of him into his own self-conception. When men care about others' opinions, they have submitted to *amour propre*, the trap of using others to construct a self-image, which is different from being genuinely concerned with their reactions. *Amour propre* makes men dependent on alien wills, in a way that women are not.

Women's concern for others' opinions is hard to distinguish from *amour propre* from a masculine perspective. In *Emile*, a fundamentally masculine work about the education of an independent man by another man, Rousseau writes that "what is thought of [a woman] is no less important to her than what she actually is" (364). But in *Julie*, a work revolving around women, it is clear that this whole phrasing of the situation is masculine, since this distinction between the real self and the self for others does not exist for women, who exist *between* their loved ones. Julie's identity is constructed within the network of social relations that form her world; she has no 'private' self which can be understood independent from this network. *Emile* shows how women look from *within* a masculine world view, which is appropriate since Sophie shows up in *Emile* only as a relative being designed and understood in terms of Emile's needs. Other works of Rousseau's show that he is not limited to this perspective, but rather is committed to the deeply different and incommensurable perspectives of the genders.

Now that I have portrayed Rousseau's vision of the genders and their differences, I am in a better position to ask the question, how is it possible for such different beings to combine their forces and become mutually dependent without restricting each other's freedom? Or, in Rousseauian terms, how can such different beings cease to be *alien* to one another? A man, with his atomic self-conception, cannot take a woman as non-alien unless she ceases to be distinct from his will. But this appropriation enslaves the woman. She is robbed of her power unless she can remain other to the man, since her power lies in forming relationships. On the other hand, a man will be non alien to a woman if they become involved in each other's interests, but this involves a reduction in power and freedom on the man's terms, since she will still be alien to *him*. Although freedom and non-alienation are crucial for both genders, they take different forms in each case. For a man, freedom involves independence from everything which is not-self, whether his self is his own individual existence, or whether he has come to identify with a larger whole such as the general will, and to take this social whole as his true self (as he does if he is a citizen). Woman does not find freedom in this way, since freedom involves satisfying needs, and for her this includes deep involvements with others with whom she does not directly identify. Hence a fully developed free woman is neither a man nor a citizen. When a man bonds with another, he must become *one* with this other so as to remain self-contained. Julie and Claire, however, are 'inseparable', and incomplete without each other, but they are not *one*. Irigaray would claim that they are neither one nor two; their lives and identities *touch*, in a form of non-separation foreign to men.[30]

Men can take as non-alien only that with which they identify. Hence if both partners in a relationship are to remain free, there must be some form of identification between them. There are a limited number of possibilities for how this could occur. Either one partner's nature must be reconstructed so as to correspond with the other's, or both must be remade so as to form one new harmonious unit, with which both come to identify.

The simplicity of the first option makes it attractive. The seductiveness of domination and submission stems from the straightforward ease of simply subsuming the will of one under the will of the other. The completeness and simplicity of relations of domination and submission give them a seductive advantage over the project of trying to construct a unity out of two fundamentally different beings. It is tempting to totally subjugate the other, gaining the desired object without compromise, and also, once the subjugation is complete, without resistance. At the same time, especially when we consider our partner worthy of our desire, it is tempting to submit completely, thereby relating ourselves to the desired partner and regaining our freedom by living *through* the other. The seductiveness of domination and submission emerges out of all Rousseau's discussions of sexual dynamics. It seems, for him, to be a crucial element of sexuality. The difficult balancing of the needs of both partners has none of the seduction of the total abandon involved in the domination of one partner and subjugation of the other. Yet we will see that relationships in which the identity of one partner subsumes the other are self-undermining.

The tension between the attractiveness of relationships of domination and submission, and their ultimate instability, is a theme of *Julie*, which presents itself as a work about the rightness and desirability of balanced relationships, best exemplified by conjugal affection, but which is as much about the seduction of relationships of domination and submission. Both the *Confessions*[31] and *Julie* portray the seductive side of being punished. When we are punished by one whom we love, this is evidence of our inability to vary our will from the beloved, and hence of our success at identifying with her. Rousseau's own sexual awakening takes place while he is being punished by a woman who is a mother figure to him: "I had discovered in the shame and pain of the punishment an admixture of sexuality which had left me rather eager than otherwise for a repetition by the same hand."[32] Rousseau has received proof that he *cannot* vary his will from that of his subjugator, and this proof is not undesirable. This formative experience led Rousseau, in his own analysis, to seek out maternal women, such as Mme. de Warens, who could dominate him, and with whom the subjugation of his will to theirs was certain. Partial subjugation involves a loss of freedom, but total subjugation allows the rebirth of freedom through a full adoption of the will of the dominator.

There will be two kinds of relationships of domination and submission, depending on whether the man or the woman dominates, since masculine power and feminine power have such different forms. We can better understand Rousseau's often seemingly contradictory views on women if we see that he does not have a single account of the relation between the genders, but presents several possibilities. His alternating contempt for women's weakness and his fear of their purported enormous power also makes more sense once we understand that in some relationships, the feminine principle is dominant, and in others it is subjugated. For instance, he claims in *Emile* that "[Men] ought to be active and strong, [women] passive and weak. One must necessarily will and be able; it suffices that the other put up little resistance."[33] But at the same time, this would serve as a poor description of many relationships he describes as admirable, such as that between himself and Mme. de Warens, or between Julie and her lover, St.-Preux. With this in mind, I turn to an exploration of the possibilities Rousseau presents for how human souls can be 'coupled' so as to be worth their full price.

Feminine Domination: Romantic Love

The feminine relation between two people is love. Loving another requires involving oneself with the will and interests of the other, while still recognizing that person as other. Since love requires an other, neither lover can cease to be a subject with a personal will and private interests—neither can be objectified or appropriated by the other. Rousseau councils Emile and Sophie on how to remain in love in the following passage: "Let each of you always remain masters of his own person and his caresses, and have the right to dispose of them to the other only at his own will . . . pleasure is legitimate only when desire is shared."[34] However, a partnership between a man and a woman will generally not be a pure love relationship, for such a relationship is not suited to man's nature, nor will it satisfy his needs and desires under normal circumstances. A pure love relationship is based entirely on the feminine principle, and it includes no possession. Since Rousseau, like most writers, considers sex to involve conquest and possession, love can involve desire, but not sex. I will call a pure love relationship between a man and a woman romantic love, for reasons that will emerge. As long as the relationship is one of romantic love, the woman's will dominates; these relationships are "extolled . . . by women in order to establish their ascendancy and make dominant the sex that ought to obey."[35] Romantic love contains special properties and tensions in virtue of the fact that it is fundamentally foreign to the masculine partner.

Rousseau sometimes suggests, for instance in *Emile*, that optimally a couple should begin in a romantic relationship, during a courting stage in which (optimally) no sex occurs. Within the romance, the woman has set the terms—it is she who both attracts and resists, bonding the man to her while holding herself apart and not letting him possess her. But because the man has power too, he normally eventually succeeds in at least partially possessing the woman (bodily and spiritually), at which time their love ceases to be pure, and the couple moves from romance to conjugal 'affection'. It is desirable, according to Rousseau, that the intoxicating, subsuming romantic love into which the woman seduces the man is thus transformed into the conjugal bond. But occasionally, the woman's strength is so great relative to the man's that their relationship remains defined entirely by her terms, becoming a permanent romance incompatible with possession. If the man wishes to stay in this relationship and yet remain free, he must relinquish his will to possess her, and indeed his entire original nature, and regain his freedom by making his will and interests match hers, so that she can never place alien demands on him which he is constrained by his love to meet. His interests must become purely her interests, and he must allow her to take responsibility for his existence, while he begins to live *through* her. As masculine and non-relational, he cannot involve his will with hers while keeping them distinct—he only knows how to be free as a self-contained, independent being. Hence, to remain in a love relationship with a woman he cannot possess, he submerges his original, individual being and takes on that of the state instead. He allows her will and interests to guide and give shape to his existence. In the early stages of Emile and Sophie's relationship, when it consists of love without possession, Emile is Sophie's 'slave,'[36] and "It is Sophie's soul which appears to animate him."[37] But Sophie, despite her original intoxicating influence, is not strong enough to keep this hold over Emile when the tutor removes him forcefully from her presence, allowing the relationship to progress to a more balanced stage. Emile's loss of identity and his remaking in Sophie's image is only superficial and incomplete.

Not so in the case of two relationships involving women strong enough to totally dominate their loved ones: Julie and St.-Preux, and Mme. de Warens and Rousseau. The many narrative parallels between Rousseau's created heroine Julie and his real life protector Mme. de Warens suggest that he intended them to play similar exemplary roles in his writings. Both were seduced early in life by their tutors, leading them away from what Rousseau considered the virtuous chastity appropriate for them. And the 'ideal' relationship between Julie, her husband, and her ex lover St.-Preux closely mirrors that between Mme. de Warens, her partner Claude Anet, and Rousseau, while the character descriptions of Anet and Julie's Wolmar are similar.[38] My claim is that Rousseau uses his relationship with Mme. de Warens and Julie's relationship with St.-Preux to exemplify relations of feminine domination—permanent romantic love relationships which exclude the possibility of possession, in which the men happily allow their identities to be entirely remade in the image of their beloved. St.-Preux allows Julie to govern him completely—he goes where she wishes and acts as she suggests, even after she marries someone else.[39] (One can hardly imagine Sophie being so bold in her directions.) Rousseau makes it clear that their relationship is utterly centered around and defined by her, as is emphasized by the fact that their letters are addressed *to* Julie and *from* Julie, while her lover is never referred to in the addresses at all. In fact, he has no name independent of her; when he is 'named' at all, it is by the pseudonym St.-Preux (or 'gallant saint'), which is actually a description rather than a name, and moreover a description which seems to make reference to his relationship with Julie.

But although St.-Preux has remade himself into a being defined by Julie, his nature is still deeply masculine. He derives the entire content of his self-conception from her and her alone: "Let the rest of the world think of me what it likes, all my price is in your esteem."[40] This is a masculine approach to identity formation, in that it takes a single, isolated individual as definitive of that identity. Julie never submerges herself in her lover in this way, nor does any woman in Rousseau's romantic relationships. When her friend Eduoard Bomston offers her and St.-Preux a private retreat where they could be together in peace, Julie turns it down, citing her concerns for and obligations towards others in the social world in which she travels, particularly her family. We can assume that St.-Preux would not have had the same reservations about the offer. Julie constantly reminds St.-Preux of the importance, in general and to her, of taking into account the needs and opinions of many people. As a being defined by her bonds to others, she need not lose these multiple bonds in uniting with a partner, and in fact to do so would be to lose herself to him. On the other hand, identity is self-contained for the man, and hence he can only involve himself with her and make her non-alien (and hence his bond to her non-constraining) by identifying with her *completely*. He remains self-contained and self-centered, and his masculine sense of self has merely transferred itself to a new object. Rousseau says of his relation with Mme. de Warens, "I did not think, feel or breath except through her."[41] Rousseau's identity is so subsumed by hers that he is incapable of taking on a distinct, masculine role in her life after Anet's death.[42]

Why are Julie and Mme. de Warens capable of dominating their partners? Rousseau stresses that both have that specifically feminine power, an enormous capacity to love. More prosaically, both are above their lovers in social rank, and Mme. de Warens has the advantage in age as well, making it socially awkward for their lovers to assert their will against them. Both, interestingly, are portrayed as being self-sufficient and worldly to the point of being somewhat masculinized, even while retaining their very feminine approaches to the world. Rousseau describes Mme. de Warens as having a 'male mind'—"She was born for affairs of state . . . she always planned on a large and theoretical scale."[43] This description of a woman is supposed to be impossible, not to mention unseemly, according to most of Rousseau's statements on women. Julie is highly intelligent and educated; she can write and philosophize, two skills that Rousseau elsewhere insists are beyond the capabilities of women.[44]

Julie's cousin Claire, who, as I will discuss later, is even more masculine, claims that she and Julie 'know too much'.[45] Julie has no real material need for men, and hence she (and her lover) can survive with only her will directing. Sophie could never maintain a dominant position because she is too feminine and hence too unbalanced. She can't stand dirt and doesn't understand abstract ideas—two partners acting under the guidance of her will alone would perish. (Appropriately, she is also of a slightly lower rank than Emile. Rousseau needs Sophie to be as shallow and uninformed as she is in order to avoid the possibility that she will dominate Emile.) This difference is important, if we remember that for Rousseau, the only reason we change our nature to harmonize with others is that it is somehow necessary or advantageous for us to be dependent on those others. Since we want to avoid dependence on an alien will, we remake our nature so that the will of the other with whom we have joined forces is no longer alien. Julie and Mme. de Warens have no need to be dependent on others, and hence it is not they but their partners who alter their nature and identity.

Both women are powerful enough to eliminate the possibility of being possessed by their lovers. St.-Preux is shaped entirely by Julie and does not take her as alien, and hence he does not try to possess her. Once she marries another man, she and St.-Preux remain in love, but any possibility of possession is removed; this state of perpetual love without ownership, and hence without the battle of wills involved in a struggle for ownership, is the perfect romantic relationship. What is important to the man within such a relationship is not possessing the woman—if he tried it, he would meet with resistance, and his freedom would be compromised—but rather coming to be directed by her so that he can identify fully with her. Rousseau writes of a journey, "Since it was under Mme. de Warens' command that I departed, I regarded myself as still living under her direction, which was more important to me than living beside her."[46] Masculine possession would destroy love, since it compromises the subsumption of the man's will under the woman's, and with it his ability to take himself as living through her. Claire explains this to St.-Preux in explaining to him why he must physically leave Julie: "You will tell yourself, 'I know how to love', with a more durable and more delicate pleasure than you would taste in saying 'I possess that which I love', for the latter wears itself out even as it delights; but the other lasts forever and you will delight in it even when you would not have loved anymore."[47]

Schwartz observes that the perfect object of Rousseau's love is one he 'cannot hope to possess', for "the imagination's infatuation cannot long survive contact with the reality of the imagined object."[48] This introduces another aspect of the interplay between love and possession. The love of a man for a woman to whom he has submitted himself, and whose existence he has taken on, must posit the woman as *ideal*, so as to make her worthy of his complete submission. He uses her as the sole guide and measure of his actions, and hence he must take her as an unerring standard of *correct* action, worthy of replacing all other forms of justification. Thus romantic love involves illusion and self-deception—any prolonged contact with the loved woman will force the conclusion that the lover's idealized image of her is just that. The realization that she is capable of imperfection would make her use as an absolute standard impossible, destroying the complete relation of female domination. On the other hand, as masculine, the man cannot love without desiring to possess, and hence his position contains a tension, for he desires something which the very act of possessing would destroy. He desires the woman as a perfect love object, but possessing her would reveal her not to be this object. Romantic love is sustained by a perpetual state of unfulfilled desire, maintained through the impossibility of this fulfillment together with an upholding of an idealized, illusory image of the woman.[49]

Romantic love is thus based on imagination—what is loved by the man is an image rather than a concrete person. He desires something that does not exist in the form he desires it. While the concrete woman cannot be in his presence long without destroying the illusion, the image of his beloved must be present to him at all times, to serve as a constant guide of his actions—if it leaves him, he would have to act on the basis of his own, separate will, thus reaffirming his distinctness from her, and eliminating his ability to find freedom by living through her. St.-Preux is directed by and in love with an ever-present image of Julie. This image is concrete—it is only after Julie sends St.-Preux a portrait of herself that he can make moral decisions in her absence. He often repeats that it is her 'image' that keeps him virtuous. Later, Wolmar suggests that St.-Preux is in love with the Julie of the past (the one in the portrait) rather than with the actual person before him. Mme. de Warens, too, can be better loved when she is not present, so that reality does not impinge upon the perfection of her image: "Sometimes I left her, to give myself over to her there and to think of her with greater pleasure . . . [in] my refuge . . . I had her as I wanted her."[50] During the early, romantic, female-dominated stages of their relationship, Emile is described as being guided by the image of Sophie; "he is chaste because of the image of his beloved."[51] No such story applies to the dominant woman, who as the controlling will needs no image of the beloved to guide her. She needs no illusions, for this relationship of involvement without possession is natural to her. While she loves and desires to be loved, she need not subsume herself in the other. She confronts the full concrete reality of her lover, rather than creating a selective image of him as he does of her.

Purely feminine love, including no desire for possession, is non-sexual. Actually, both Julie and Mme. de Warens are possessed sexually—once each—by their lovers, but these encounters merely display the *discordance* of sexual activity within these feminine relationships. Rousseau describes sex with Mme. de Warens as unerotic, upsetting, and mildly repugnant. Julie feels that this is the one time she has lost control, and she sees the event as destroying the purity and perfection of her relationship with St.-Preux. After the event, which involves masculine mastery incompatible with the domination of her will, the tables are temporarily turned between them, and she apparently begins to live through her lover instead of *vice-versa*: "Since I no longer dare to gaze upon myself, I will cast my gaze with more pleasure upon he whom I love. I give you all that you remove of my self-esteem, and you become only more dear to me in forcing me to hate myself."[52] For Julie, living through her lover is clearly an act of defeat. Despite this lapse in her control and her lifelong regret of it, she never lets it happen again, and soon ensures that the possibility is eliminated by sending her lover away so that she may love him on her own terms.

These relationships of feminine domination are unstable. Even if the woman is as ideal as Julie, the feminine principle allows the expression of only half our humanity, while perfectibility demands that we live up to our full capacity. Pure romantic love relationships, which demand that both partners live by the principles of one gender, could not befit us. Julie remarks on St.-Preux's inability to be complete in his subjugated role: "I had always seen him timid and fearful, the fear of displeasing me, and perhaps the secret shame of a role so little worthy of an honest man, giving him before me I don't know what servile and base countenance."[53] On its own this is not conclusive, since devotion to a powerful woman might persuade a man to stay in this unfortunate position. What truly undermines these relationships is the fact that the woman's very power ends up defeating its own purposes.

We have seen that the man submerges himself into the woman's identity in the purely romantic relationship. He lives through her, letting her define his existence. The result is that they become in effect one person. They are no longer two people involved with each other as other, but a single being, as St. Preux explains: "Do two lovers love one another? No, *you* and *me* are forbidden words in their language; they are no longer two, they are one."[54] But look what has happened! The woman wanted to love and be loved by *another*, and this was essential to the completion of her own identity. In her power she has succeeded so completely in involving herself with another that she has erased his otherness, and she now loves only herself. Her strength, which resisted the will of the man to dominate her, has also eliminated his separateness. The man has not become her possession; he has not been objectified. Rather, he has become *her*, or a partial mirror of her, in which she can find no more than was already in her before he came along. She has so completely shaped her lover that he can no longer satisfy her needs. He loves and idealizes her to such an extent that he believes that only she herself is perfect enough to be worthy of her love; he concludes that to earn her love he must become her. In a crucial letter, St.-Preux writes to Julie, "Take of what is mine everything that remains to me, and put what is yours completely in its place. No, angelic beauty, celestial soul, it is only sentiments like yours that can honour your attractions: You alone are worthy of inspiring a perfect love, you alone are suited to feel it. Ah! Give me your heart, my Julie, to love you as you deserve to be."[55] This is the classic Rousseauian remaking of human nature—just as the legislator replaces the private will and individual identity with the general will and *amour de la patrie*, remaking the citizen in the image of the state, the man in love replaces his nature with his beloved's. But such submission and remaking leaves the woman incomplete, with her needs unfulfilled. Sophie, for instance does "not want a lover who kn[ows] no other law than hers. She wants to reign over a man she has not disfigured."[56] Because she is so much more powerful than he, St.-Preux cannot fulfill this need for Julie. Her power disfigures him; their relationship demands that he be remade in her image. Hence their relationship is ultimately unsatisfying, for her, in her dominant position, more so than for him. She feels she needs to marry Wolmar, despite (or because of) their lack of romantic love for each other. She could not marry the submissive St.-Preux, who cannot provide her with the *other* she needs. Despite her power, her identity is relationally defined, and she needs to be involved with an other in order to be complete and satisfied. Even as a child, she has Claire as her 'inseparable', without whom she is incapable of judging and controlling her actions. A woman can never be self-contained, and hence she needs a partner who is distinct from her and not just an image of her that in no way extends her existence. Thus extreme feminine power, in its complete ability to obtain what it desires, destroys and disfigures this object in the process of obtaining it, leaving those very desires unsatisfied.

Masculine Domination: Mastery and Slavery

When the masculine partner dominates a relationship, the relationship is not one of romantic love but of the use and objectification of one partner by the other. When the man is powerful enough relative to the woman that her influence over him is nil, he becomes her master and she becomes his slave. She becomes, that is, a direct extension of his will, a possession which he can manipulate directly, an *instrument*. She is not his double but his appendage. Just as Rousseau, in the *Reveries of a Solitary Walker*,[57] finds freedom and independence from other men by perceiving them as 'automata', a man with enough power can avoid dependence on an alien being by managing to perceive his woman as an object rather than as a subject with a distinct will. This relationship is seductive to the woman, just as romantic love was for the man. The woman loves the man and cares about his interests, and hence she has a desire to satisfy *his* desire to own her. By submitting to him, she hopes to earn his love and prove hers. While the submissive male remained self-contained by taking on another's identity, the submissive female analogously defines herself in terms of a man, but retains her feminine perspective, insistently seeing their relation as a love relation. Like the submissive man, the submissive woman is sustained by an illusion, for the dominant man has no interest in loving her or recognizing her love—this would require taking her as another, distinct subject, and this is just what he wants to deny. When masculine domination is complete, the woman loses her identity and will altogether, and is not governed so much as appropriated. One cannot govern an object with no independent will, for there is nothing with principles to direct; one can only command and be obeyed, as one gives a computer commands, where the very act of commanding causally determines that the command will be obeyed.

Finding and interpreting relationships of masculine domination in Rousseau's writings is tricky, because his perversely exaggerated perception of women's power led him to believe that true male domination was rare if not impossible. Women, he claims, are so dexterous at manipulating men's wills that even when they seem to obey, they are actually obeying an order that they have influenced men into giving them. In *Emile*, he asserts that women's control is so perfect that rape and sexual exploitation are impossible, because any sexual act can only result form the woman intentionally letting down her resistance (we have seen that he does not go so far in *Julie*). However, there are several excellent examples of relations of masculine domination in Rousseau's writings, whether or not he recognizes them as such. The most self-conscious of these is that between Julie and her father, Baron de'Etange.[58] The Baron counts Julie among his possessions—he feels free to give her to Wolmar as payment of a debt, thereby taking her as an object with a certain (very high) value within the masculine economy. He does this without considering her interests or welfare, or her particular suitability to the man he has chosen. He has no bond to her as a particular individual—she is valuable to him not for who she is, but for her place in the economy of exchange. She is his daughter, and hence plays a certain role in his life *qua* instantiator of that description. His rights over her are not based on any particular bond between them, but are simply the rights of paternity. This is all characteristic of the thoroughly masculine, abstracting and objectifying approach to others.

The Baron's absolute paternal authority over Julie is seductive, though not explicitly erotic. After he has beaten her, they are reconciled in what is hard to distinguish from a love scene. Julie gets a sensual satisfaction from being punished at his hand, which resembles Rousseau's enjoyment of his early punishment at the hands of a beloved authority figure. "I told him, and I believe it, that I would be only too happy to be beaten every day for the same price, and that there is no treatment so harsh that a single of his caresses doesn't erase down to the bottom of my heart."[59] Julie considers her father worthy of possessing her, and so she happily submits to his exercises of power over her, which demonstrate this possession. Of course, Julie's objectification is far from complete. He has subjugated her only within a restricted domain—we have seen her to have immense power in her own right. This is as much male domination as Rousseau will recognize as possible.

Although Rousseau claims that there can be no male domination in sexual partnerships, he in fact portrays liaisons in which the domination of the man is almost total. His claim is that women are so powerful that they must be almost entirely subjugated in order for the relationship to be equal. For instance, men should marry below their rank, for superior rank will solidify the natural tendency for women to dominate.[60] One relationship Rousseau portrays involves such complete male domination that it takes the acuity of paranoid and misogynist eyes to discern the influence of the woman's hidden hand within it—this is his own relationship with his wife, Thérèse. Thérèse's complete absence of distinct personhood for Rousseau is made clear by his consideration of himself as *solitary* when he is only with her. Throughout the *Reveries of a Solitary Walker* and the last part of the *Confessions*, Rousseau engages in detailed analyses of his condition of utter solitude, and it comes as a shock in this context to be reminded that he had his wife by his side throughout this period. When Rousseau speaks of himself and Mme. de Warens as 'one being', it is clear that the being is *her*, whereas when he speaks of his solitude in later life, he manifestly considers himself to be alone with *himself*. Thérèse is so totally subsumed by Rousseau that she has completely ceased to exist for him; he takes her to be a useful object in his natural environment.

If a man's ideal love object is an unpossessable woman—one who is intelligent and self-sufficient enough to free him from the responsibility to act autonomously, who is a man's ideal woman to possess and master? The main thing is that she present as little an obstacle to his will as possible, while still being useful; in other words, she must have a low cost/benefit ratio in the economy of exchange. It must be worth his while to keep her. Rousseau writes of Thérèse, "With all her limitations—her stupidity if you like—this creature is a most excellent advisor in difficult situations."[61] She is a totally dehumanized 'creature', a tool serving a purpose for him that other objects cannot serve. Rousseau describes her stupidity in gleeful detail.[62] This stupidity makes her helplessly unable to act autonomously, and it prevents her from having any ideas of her own, which would remind Rousseau of her existence as an other with an alien stance on whom he depends. Rousseau's attachment to Thérèse's stupidity, as well as his cruel failure to recognize her as a subject with emotional needs, is revealed in a passing anecdote: "Once I made a dictionary of her sayings to amuse Mme. de Luxembourg, and her blunders have become famous in the circles in which I have lived."[63] Sophie, who is more intelligent, must be actively prevented from forming ideas which differ from Emile's. Of Sophie, Rousseau writes, "far from wanting to subject [her husband] to her tastes, she will adopt his."[64] She is prevented from acquiring knowledge before marriage, so that Emile can teach her, creating a mind for her that will harmonize with his own. This is necessary to legitimize Emile's dependence on her, his only 'chain', because it prevents her being alien to him.

Can such a master/slave relationship fulfill either partner? Our familiarity with Hegel's analysis should make us *prima facie* suspicious of such a possibility. The mastered woman can be happy if she upholds the illusion that her devotion to the man has created a love bond between them. Her happiness is self-deceptive, for her love is not in fact being returned, and hence she is not complete. But if Rousseau were to follow out the implications for the man in such a relationship, he would conclude that his needs are also not satisfied through mastery of his woman. His dependence on her as a tool is legitimized by her lack of otherness, but this objectification is ultimately an illusion that cannot be maintained. The ways in which the woman is useful to him are ways that require her to exercise her capacities as a thinking, active being, which of course she actually is. Advisor and household manager are not functions that can be carried out by any objects, and hence the woman is not in fact interchangeable with material goods. She may appear objectified, but no objects could fill the needs she fills, and hence the man must ultimately recognize his dependence on another.

Furthermore, this dependence is particularly damaging, because he has approached her in a purely masculine fashion, and thus has in no way involved himself with her *as other*. Hence her will, on which he depends, remains entirely alien to him. If his power had been less, the relationship would not have been so purely masculine, and hence she would not have been so alien.

For her part, the woman cannot in fact become an object for the man no matter how much she wants to. The most she can do is to *allow* herself to be taken as one, but in the last analysis she obeys him of her own choice. So long as this is the case, her slavery and her status as a possession are not complete. If she were to truly lose her autonomy and become a pure object, the man could only direct her by force. This would reveal her as a costly possession, because he would spend as much energy forcing her actions as she would save by acting for him, especially because the ways in which she was particularly useful to him required her to be able to judge and act autonomously. In this case his mastery will be empty, for it will not extend his power. The man ends up in the paradoxical situation of needing both to objectify the woman, and to keep her as another, distinct subject, for he is dependent on her to do things she can only do by virtue of her status as a person. Hence the master cannot succeed in his project of objectifying the other and ridding himself of dependence on alien wills.

The master faces a further problem—one which makes more of an appearance in Rousseau's writings. Although the masculine subject lacks the skills needed to operate within the feminine economy of care, and places more emphasis on material power than on human bonds, all humans require both care and help from others in the social state. Normally, the man counts on receiving this care from the woman in return for providing for her, and hence he need not concern himself with his lack of skills in forming caring relationships. But the man who has fully objectified and eliminated the otherness of his woman can no longer receive care and companionship from her. This is, of course, the tragedy of Rousseau's own situation. He finishes his life deeply miserable about his own solitude, and laments that his inability to identify and harmonize his will with the social whole have deprived him of the companionship he desperately desires.[65] But as I have remarked, he has Thérèse with him the whole time. She cannot satisfy this need, which it is usually the woman's specific job to satisfy, just because he has so thoroughly dominated and dehumanized her.

Thus both purely feminine and purely masculine relationships, in which one partner dominates and the other submits, ultimately undermine their own aims, leaving the dominant partner unsatisfied and unfree. What alternatives are there? Can men and women avoid these totalizing relationships of domination and submission and find a more fulfilling means of relating, which allows them to be fully human and free, and to maximize their power? Exploring these questions will constitute the final stage of my analysis.

Conjugal Affection

If members of a couple are to unite and become non-alien to each other, but without one dominating the other, then somehow they must harmonize two wills and sets of interests, and they must operate on both the feminine and the masculine principles. The man, who is free only when self-contained, can only become deeply involved with and dependent on another, if he and that other somehow become *one being*, while his identity and sense of self lie in this larger, unified being, rather than with his original, private self. This is how he manages to bind himself without losing his freedom to the social whole: The social contract and the general will unify the citizens into a single being, and each citizen gives up his (sic) private identity and adopts a 'partial and moral existence' in which he identifies with the whole. As Gauthier[66] explains, according to Rousseau, once a man has become dependent on others, he can be redeemed only through his sense of self coming to rest in the whole unit on which he is dependent. If he is to unite with a woman, the same thing must happen. This is what is required for them to unite by the *masculine principle*, which demands that persons are self-contained units, while all others are alien to them. If they were to unite by the *feminine principle*, each would take on the interests of the other as other, while remaining distinct and autonomous beings. But such a unification would be impossible for the man. (Although Rousseau doesn't point this out, the woman is more flexible; there is nothing in her nature which precludes her joining with another in a masculine fashion.) Hence they must unify by identification rather than by relation.

But there is not automatically a single, coherent whole for each partner to identify with—such a whole must be *constructed*, and it cannot be constructed simply by combining their interests, since there is no *a priori* way of creating a whole which expresses its constituent parts; according to the *Social Contract*, even the law of majority rule only expresses the interests of *all* those involved only if everyone freely agrees to abide by it. Hence the partners' nature must be *altered* so that they form one being. If they unite by the masculine principle, then they can become one person either by becoming identical, or by each forming a different part of a whole being, from which they each derive their sense of identity. The first is impossible, since men and women have such different natures, and hence the last option is the only viable one. Each partner must become only a partial person, who does not act for his or her private self, but for the whole, as a hand does not act *for* itself but for the person to which it belongs.

The marriage relationship is the paradigmatic case of an attempt by a man and a woman to unify in this way. The advantage of such a unification is that, while both partners become only partial people living in the name of the greater whole they form together, each can act according to the principle which suits him or her best, while still enjoying the fruits of the combined forces of the masculine and the feminine principles. The partners can each act within the domain in which they are most skilled, while identifying with a being who achieves true human completeness by being adept within both the masculine and the feminine domain. Hence perfectibility demands that we attempt such a union. It is only in the context of this sort of relationship that Rousseau introduces other members of the domestic sphere, such as children and servants, into the picture. A household or family requires both masculine and feminine guidance in order to function, and is thus not a possibility within relationships of domination and submission. However, at least according to Julie, running a household is the point of marriage. This means that the picture will now be even more complicated, for it is not only a man and a woman who must harmonize, but a whole household.

Rousseau's most thoroughly explored example of such a union is the marriage of Julie and M. Wolmar. In the first half of *Julie*, Julie is torn between her commitments to two relationships in which she is involved—her feminine romance with her lover, in which she dominates, and her masculine relationship with her father, in which she is submissive. These relationships are both seductive and incompatible with one another, and since both are ultimately inadequate, no correct choice between them is possible. She frees herself of the totalizing commitments of each through her passionless marriage, through which she hopes to begin a balanced relationship and form a complete being with a 'single soul'.[67] This relationship allows for effective action, for neither partner is forced to operate in an inappropriate domain, nor excluded from a proper domain of action. As a unit, the Wolmars are capable of functioning both economically and personally in a healthy and productive way that partners in relationships of domination and submission cannot. Rousseau stresses that Julie and Wolmar are incomplete as individuals, and that their union completes them. Wolmar needs people—they are 'necessary' to him—but he lacks the emotions and skills that would bond them to him. More mundanely, his marriage to Julie makes him much wealthier, hence bettering his position in the masculine economy of exchange. Julie, it goes without saying, is portrayed as being 'incomplete' without a husband, and a household and children to govern and care for, which we have seen that St.-Preux (and her father, of course) could never provide for her.

Once married, both are transformed into parts of a single being, yet both contribute to that being by doing what they do best. Julie takes over the role of the moral judge and manager of particular personal relationships. She *governs* those around her by involving her existence with theirs. Rousseau describes her influence over the servants and neighboring peasants, which she gains by caring about their welfare, and knowing them well enough as concrete individuals to relate to them in all of their particularity, down to guiding their choice of mates. Wolmar, on the other hand, takes care of the economic affairs of the household; he also sets down its general rules, which it is up to Julie to interpret in particular cases. He creates the order that keeps things productive and efficient, and she motivates others to uphold that order by dispensing with her affections in proportion to their success along these lines. By acting in harmony with one another the successful married couple can function well within a world constituted by relations of both care and exchange, whose negotiation requires both general understanding and concrete judgment.

Julie and Wolmar, in forming a single being, do not *collaborate* in their actions at each point, for their approaches and skills are different, and deciding on each action together would compromise both. Rather, each partner has control within her or his proper domain, and since each identifies with the same whole, and has the interests of the whole at stake, their independent actions harmonize. Wills cannot be combined without compromising the freedom of the parts, so instead they are harmonized, and complement one another. Julie emphasizes the spouses' separate functions, writing that "wife and husband are certainly destined to live together, but not in the same manner; they must act in concert without doing the same things."[68]

In order for the Wolmar household, the famous Clarens, to function harmoniously, without any alien restriction of wills, the environment must be carefully constructed so that each person's role (not just Julie's and her husband's, but their children's and servant's)[69] fits with the whole. Furthermore, each person's will and desires must correspond with that role, while their identity and self conception must be defined by the whole. Thus, Clarens is a 'controlled despotism',[70] where nothing takes place which is not rigidly governed and constrained. If anyone's actions transgress the carefully designed structure, then the household ceases to form a unified single being. If anyone *wishes* to act other than how they are supposed to act; then they immediately lose their freedom, and become constrained by the now-alien whole to which they belong. Hence not only must everyone act as they are supposed to, but they must be made, without feeling coerced, to want to act this way. Clarens is successful because "One always recognizes there the hand of the master, and one never feels it; he [Wolmar] has so well ordered things from the start that at present everything works all on its own, and one enjoys liberty and order at the same time."[71] Hence both the characters and the actions of the members of the household, including Wolmar and Julie themselves, must be very carefully controlled. Jones writes, "The economic [and, as Jones points out later in this paragraph, personal] success of Wolmar's system depends totally on the maintenance of balance, on the maintenance of things as they are, and the only manner that he has of accomplishing this feat is by imposing the most rigorous restrictions on every facet of life."[72]

The identification with a larger whole, and the corresponding split between the acting individual and the subject of that individual's self-deception, do not come naturally, but must be carefully maintained. Once individuals give up their original identity and become partial persons dependent on the whole, failure of identification with the whole, or any failure of the whole to meet their needs, will leave them dependent half-persons. The freedom of the balanced marriage relationship, as exemplified by Clarens, is thus a freedom produced by rigorous control.

It is important to remember that this vision of what is required in human interactions is only one possibility that Rousseau presents. Commentators (such as Jones and Gauthier) often take Clarens as representing Rousseau's *single* vision of ideal human relationships. But as I have presented Rousseau's works, and *Julie* in particular, such carefully harmonized uniting of distinct wills is presented as an option only after feminine domination and masculine domination have also been presented as possibilities. All these possibilities involve the reconstruction of the nature of at least one partner, but only the balanced relationship requires the careful harmonizing of distinct wills which in turn requires the strict adherence to order of a household like Wolmar's. When Jones notices[73] that Julie's conceptualization of ideal human relationships in terms of 'love and innocence' has given way in Clarens to the priority of 'order and rule', he offers no explanation for this switch, because he assumes that human relations for Rousseau follow a single ideal. But when Julie equates paradise with the reign of 'love and innocence', she is discussing her relation of feminine domination, whereas the 'order and rule' of Clarens make it an ideal example of a harmonized conjugal household.

However, even this carefully harmonized relationship is ultimately unstable and unsatisfactory—Clarens contains 'the seeds of its own destruction'.[74] The problem arises from the fact that maintaining the harmony between people, preserving at the same time, their unity, distinct roles, mutual dependence and freedom, is such a delicate affair that the lives of those involved must be preserved in a *static* arrangement. Any change in the arrangement is likely to cause disorder, and the system is too fragile to absorb developments in the personalities of the participants.[75] However, the *Discourse on Inequality* teaches us that human history is *dynamic*; human perfectibility drives us toward evolution and change. For Clarens to be a success, the Wolmars must not only create a static harmony, but ensure that the stasis continues. But to do this is to violate the one firm law of human nature, which demands that people and their institutions change and progress. Perkins writes, "[Wolmar's] science, no matter how moral, has taken for its standard the static perfection of the state of nature, has tried to chain history. History is dynamic, changing, striving."[76] Rousseau's romantic vision of humans as essentially striving to perfect themselves rules out the permanence of a static order ensuring harmony. To enforce this stasis is stifling—the equivalent of death. When Julie's social universe becomes perfectly co-ordinated, and her relations to others become fully harmonious, she feels ready to die, and soon does so. At this moment of perfect balance she feels '*too happy*', and needs to escape (through death), since any change could only detract from the perfect harmony of her world.[77] Gauthier points out that for Rousseau, too much harmony leads to 'boredom, stultification and ignorance', and our perfectibility demands our escape.[78] Humans are meant to strive for total social identification and harmony, but they are not meant to live in an artificially constructed state of it.

The reason the constructed harmony of a Clarens is imperfect is that it always has the potential to be disrupted. It is not a guaranteed harmony, but one that is at the mercy of contingencies. In *Julie*, St.-Preux seems to embody this threatening contingency, this ever present possibility of disruption and chaos. Julie and St.-Preux's illegitimate sex is the product of the unexpected and uncontrolled desire he causes in her, which violates her otherwise impeccable self control. Later, the accidental discovery of St.-Preux's letters causes strife in Julie's otherwise harmonious family. His unpredictable temper causes conflict among her well ordered circle of friends. He refuses to marry Claire, contrary to Julie's plans. His very presence at Clarens destroys Wolmar's well-laid plans, for he is the only one there who cannot play his proper role (he cannot cease to be in love with Julie), and his presence leads to Julie's admission on her death-bed that her adulterous love for him could not be erased by her harmonious home-life. St.-Preux is a romantic figure, not only through his relationship to Julie, but also through his disruption of any attempt to settle for a prearranged static human order.

Emile and Sophie, Rousseau's other famous married couple, face a similar problem. They too enjoy harmony and freedom because they are living a carefully constructed existence. Their environment has been specially designed to ensure that their relationship will work, and that together they will be free. But the contingency of this freedom and harmony is displayed in *Emile and Sophie*,[79] the sequel to *Emile*, in which Emile and Sophie move to Paris. As soon as they leave their controlled environment and enter the chaotic city, their unity and freedom fall to pieces. Sophie ends up pregnant by another man; Emile abandons her and ends up enslaved. Here, Paris plays the disruptive role that St.-Preux plays in *Julie*. The disruption can have its source in individual character or in the general environment, but either way, it is an ever-present threat. Perfectibility makes the eventual dissolution of conjugal harmony inevitable.

Hence the problem of gender relations remains unsolved. We cannot find freedom through a union with a member of the opposite sex, whether one partner or the other's will dominates, or whether both together form a new, joint being. Rousseau's writings on gender leave the reader in a state of *aporia*.

Regendering the Social Subject: Beyond Man and Woman

I want to end by taking up two final issues. The first arises as follows: No relation between the genders seems satisfactory, and yet for Rousseau, our perfectibility demands some form of coupling. This is because humans cannot accomplish as much by acting on the feminine or the masculine principle alone as they can by combining forces. In the state of nature, when humans as yet had no self conscious personhood, and felt neither the need nor the inclination to reach out to others, neither gender's current specific skills were needed. However, in the thoroughly social world, neither gender's skills are dispensable. These facts do seem to suggest one final way out of the dilemma. Since human nature is always changing and being constructed to suit specific purposes anyhow, why couldn't an individual in this articulated social world learn to act on both the feminine and the masculine principle, all on his or her own? This would avoid the problem of maintaining a contingent harmony between distinct wills. Such an individual would have to *bisexualize* him- or herself, relating to others as others and becoming involved with them, but not involved enough to become a relational self dependent on others for complete existence. Could there exist a bisexual person, self-sufficient enough to be a subject in her own right, and yet also possessing the competence needed to interact with others in this social world?

This possibility is very attractive to Rousseau. He takes it as a real option, and potential examples of it show up in his writings. For instance, Julie's cousin Claire chooses to remain free and self-contained rather than to remarry. She is incapable of romantic love, but deeply capable of friendship, able to involve herself with others while remaining independent of them. Her bisexuality is evident in her relationship with Julie, which comes close to a love affair. Her feelings towards Julie are driven by both a masculine need to find a single ideal role model, and by a feminine desire for mutual commitment and care. She relates bisexually to her own child as well: she paternalistically chooses a spouse for her daughter, but chooses him based on the feminine basis of particularized care and attachment, rather than on general social rules. St.-Preux also seems to choose this route for himself, as the next best thing after having Julie. He chooses to feminize himself and remain independent rather than uniting with another women. Finally, Rousseau himself, in the guise of Jean-Jacques in *Rousseau, Juge de Jean-Jacques*,[80] chooses the solitary path rather than risk persecution and constraint.

Despite the presence of this option in his writing, it is important to see that, far from taking the romantic individualist line often associated with him, Rousseau clearly portrays all these individuals as partial failures, who have compromised themselves in order to remain safe. There is only so much we can accomplish if our existence remains self-contained, once we live in a social world where those around us are joining forces with each other. We can remain free and capable of meeting our goals only if we strictly curtail those goals, as the hermit Jean-Jacques does. Despite his choices, St.-Preux still insists, "I am convinced that it is not good that man be alone. Human souls need to be coupled to be worth their full price, and the united force of friends . . . is incomparably larger than the sum of their individual forces."[81] Self-sufficiency is good in that it insures our freedom while maintaining our personhood, but it lessens us in limiting our use of our full human capacities.

It is part of Rousseau's romanticism that he thinks no human relationships are satisfactory as they are—rather, each type of relation leads to a demand that we continue to strive for more freedom and to further fulfill our potential. While it is true that for Rousseau, "the problem of women remained an insoluble dilemma,"[82] this doesn't necessarily show that women throw a monkey wrench into an otherwise unproblematic account of social relations, as some feminist commentators suggest. Rather, the aporetic nature of human relations of all sorts lies at the very heart of Rousseau's thought. Rousseau can be read as spending his life developing the claim that the constructed nature which we must have in a social world is intrinsically problematic, though our necessary fate. Although Rousseau himself ended his life submerged in pessimism about the human condition, earlier works such as *Julie* and *Emile*, which leave us with unresolvable dilemmas and unsatisfactory solutions, need not be read as pessimistic, but rather as displaying Rousseau's belief that human progress and change is an unending process, and that to find a 'perfect' situation and stay there is to die. After all, if the only permanent and essential feature of human nature is our perfectibility, then if we actually reached some final utopian state and had no more tensions to resolve, we would cease to be human. Rousseau's account of gender relations is an excellent case of this principle.

Finally, I want to show a limitation in Rousseau's imagination on these issues. Throughout this paper, I have been focusing on Rousseau's views on freedom within relationships in the private domain, where gender is a central issue, but I have also drawn on Rousseau's discussions of social structure and freedom in the public domain, allowing them to illuminate my account. In both cases, Rousseau believes that individuals must completely identify with the larger unit, and have their nature reconstructed so as to harmonize with that unit, in order to be free. I have argued that Rousseau describes not one but several possibilities for how this could occur at the private level.

But this raises a question: Why are the citizens of the state, who come to identify with the public whole, clearly portrayed as *masculine* subjects? Men not only identify with the state; they identify with their families or their partners as well, as we have seen. It is not actually individual men who are citizens, but family units composed of members who identify with these units, spearheaded and represented by the patriarch. The masculine nature of the family units is clear from the fact that in his political writings that do not directly address gender, he simply refers to the citizens of the state and the participants in the general will as men. It is only from his accounts elsewhere of the construction of the private domain, and from some passages in the *Discourse on Inequality* in which he describes the transition from the era where the family is the primary social unit to the era of the primacy of the state, that we can tell that they are actually men as identified with the family unit. However, given that a family unit is by nature the joining of a man and a woman into a new being, it is not clear at all what the gender of this new being should be, or why it should relate to other units according to the masculine rather than the feminine principle. Rousseau is at pains to describe a proper marriage relationship as drawing on the skills and natures of both sexes, criticizing relations based on one gender only. But when he turns to public life these claims about the public domain seem to be forgotten, and relations are entirely masculine, based not on the involvement of different units with each other as *other*, but on their involvement insofar they all identify with a single being, the state as guided by the general will.

Rousseau often claims that it is men's job within the family to deal with affairs of state, and woman's to tend to domestic affairs. Thus one might argue that this is why public affairs are conducted by masculine principles, and why as far as politics is concerned, family units can be considered purely in terms of their male representatives. However, this seems to reverse the issue: The *reason* that men are better at dealing with public affairs is because these affairs are masculine in structure. For instance, as Lynda Lange points out, "citizenship requires the ability on the part of the individual to transcend personal, particular interests."[83] This, we have seen, is a distinctly masculine ability, for Rousseau, and so, Lange argues, women by nature cannot be included in the general will. A couple in a relationship of female domination, guided by the woman's will alone, could never function in the public domain. The question, therefore, is *why* public affairs are conducted according to masculine principles, especially since women are supposedly the ones who are better at managing human interactions.

The answer is that the problems the social contract and the formation of the general will were designed to solve were themselves masculine problems—the whole setup is meant to address the problem of how men can join forces and increase their power by becoming dependent upon one another while remaining free. This is a specifically masculine problem, since women can be involved with others without compromising their freedom, and the solution is also specifically masculine—the creation of a single general will with which all citizens identify, thereby eliminating involvement with *otherness*. But of course, the problem of how family units relate to one another while retaining their freedom need not be a *masculine* problem, unless their character is masculine already. So we have come full circle: we are still stuck with the question of why, when we create a new being out of two genders, is that new being gendered masculine?

Rousseau sets up our transformation from natural beings into social beings as a transition from our harmony with Mother Nature to our (fraught) harmony with the Fatherland.[84] By the time the public domain emerges in human history, it is a domain constituted by masculine entities facing masculine dilemmas of identity, dependence, and freedom. But a piece in the story of male domination seems missing from Rousseau's writing, allowing us to ask what political possibilities he might have been able to envisage if he had not taken this domination for granted. What if social subjects were not gendered male? If the gender of the family unit had been either feminine or bisexual, the problems of constituting the public domain would have been very different, because the unit trying to join with others would have had a different nature. Presumably in such a case, women would have been responsible for affairs of state, or else women and men would have been responsible for different aspects of these affairs. The result, according to Rousseau's own account of gender and gender relations, would have been a very different picture of the possibilities, needs, and troubles of social association—perhaps it would be one which avoided some of the deep problems that eventually led Rousseau to despair of the possibility of finding true freedom within civic life.

Notes

1. Many people have helped me give shape to my thoughts on Rousseau. In particular, I owe thanks to David Gauthier, Philip Heyland, and the members of the University of Pittsburgh feminist philosophy reading group.

2. J. J. Rousseau, *On the Social Contract*, ed. R. D. Masters, trans. I. K. Masters (New York: St. Martin's Press, 1978), 53.

3. *Ibid.*, 68.

4. J. J. Rousseau, *On the Government of Poland*, trans. W. Kendal (Indianapolis: Hacket, 1985), 19.

5. Throughout this paper I will discuss only heterosexual relationships when considering exclusive, long-term partnerships (whether sexual or not) between two individuals. Not surprisingly, Rousseau never explicitly considers how homosexual relationships complicate the picture, and my restriction seems sensible given the era and milieu of the author I am interpreting.

6. I discuss the issue of how the citizen is gendered in the last section of this paper.

7. James F. Jones, *La nouvelle Heloïse: Rousseau and Utopia* (Geneva: Droz, 1977).

8. J. J. Rousseau, *Julie ou La nouvelle Heloïse* (Paris: Editions Garnier Fréves, 1960).

9. For example, see Z. E. Eisenstein, *The Radical Future of Liberal Feminism* (Boston: Northeastern University Press, 1981); S. M. Okin, *Women in Western Political Thought* (Princeton: Princeton University Press, 1979); P. Weiss, "Rousseau, Antifeminism, and Women's Nature," *Political Theory* 15 (1987).

10. J. J. Rousseau, *Emile, or on Education*, trans. A. Bloom (New York: Basic Books, 1979).

11. *Ibid.*, 406.

12. Okin, *Women in Western Political Thought*, *op. cit.*

13. Weiss, "Rousseau, Antifeminism, . . .," *op cit.*

14. Rousseau, *Emile, op. cit.*, 406.

15. This sentence could be read as an ontogenetic or a phylogenetic claim. From the first sentence of the *Discourse on the Origins of Inequality*, which begins "L'homme est neé . . .," Rousseau carefully maintains this ambiguity.

16. See the *Discourse on the Origin of Inequality* in J. J. Rousseau, *First and Second Discourses and Essay on Origin of Language* (New York: Harper and Row, 1986), hereafter cites as *2nd Disc*. Rousseau sometimes considers pity another equally fundamental drive. I will ignore pity here, because its role in his account is unclear, and since pity does not seem to work differently for men and women in Rousseau's account, it is not directly relevant for my purposes.

17. *Ibid.*, 172.

18. Joel Schwartz, *The Sexual Politics of Jean-Jacques Rousseau* (Chicago: University of Chicago Press, 1984), 81.

19. Rousseau, *Julie, op. cit.*, 204. All translations of passages from this text are my own.

20. J. J. Rousseau, "Rousseau, Juge de Jean-Jacques" in *Oeuvres Complétes de Jean-Jacques Rousseau* (Paris: Gallimard, 1959), 813.

21. Rousseau, of course, does not think that men are totally and without exception restricted to the masculine principle, and women to the feminine principle. All humans reach out to others for both care and material sustenance, and hence these are descriptions of tendencies, not absolutes.

22. See, for example, C. Gilligan, *In a Different Voice* (Cambridge, Ma.: Harvard University Press, 1982).

23. Schwartz, *The Sexual Politics . . . , op. cit.*, 121.

24. Rousseau, *Emile . . . , op. cit.*, 408.

25. Rousseau, *Julie . . . , op. cit.*, 284.

26. Luce Irigaray, *This Sex Which Is Not One*, trans. C. Porter (Ithaca: Cornell University Press, 1985).

27. Rousseau, *On the Social Contract, op. cit.*, 66.

28. Rousseau, *Emile . . . , op. cit.*, 368.

29. Rousseau, *Julie . . . , op. cit.*, 714.

30. Okin comments that Rousseau allows a man to be either an individual or a citizen, but doesn't allow a woman to be either (Okin, *Women in Western, op. cit.*, 194). This is true, but misleading in its negative tone. Both individuals and citizens, as Rousseau understands them, are subjects who conceive of themselves as self-contained, and who take everything which is not-self as alien. Hence women, who are not atomic beings of this sort, fit into neither category.

31. J. J. Rousseau, *The Confessions* (Harmondsworth: Penguin, 1977).

32. *Ibid.*, 25.

33. Rousseau, *Emile* . . . , *op. cit.*, 358.

34. *Ibid.*, 447.

35. Rousseau, *First and Second Discourses, op. cit.*, 135.

36. Since this is a love relationship, Emile is not in fact Sophie's slave, for she does not own him. But as I have remarked, *Emile* is told from a masculine perspective, and interprets women in masculine terms.

37. Rousseau, *Emile* . . . , *op. cit.*, 415.

38. Rousseau describes relations between himself and Anet, his competitor for Mme. de Warens' love, in glowing utopian terms (Rousseau, *Confessions, op. cit.*, 172–3). One's suspicions as to the sincerity of this description may be aroused by the fact that a character named Claude Anet turns up in *Julie:* the ungrateful husband of a servant who appeared virtuous, but turns out to be base and unworthy, abandoning his wife and child, and returning at the end of the novel degraded, humiliated, destroyed, and groveling on all fours for forgiveness. It is hard to avoid concluding that Rousseau harbored some hostilities towards his rival.

39. Rousseau, *Julie* . . . , *op. cit.*, 674.

40. *Ibid.*, 81.

41. Rousseau, *Confessions, op. cit.*, 193–4.

42. *Ibid.*, 198. Of course, if the man were truly to take on the identity of the woman, it would not be an isolated but a feminine, relational identity. But while the characters in Rousseau's writings seem able to alter the *content* of their nature—their interests, goals, etc.—they do not seem capable of changing the structure of this nature. It isn't clear whether this is supposed to be an absolute limit to the malleability of human nature, whether these characters are just too short sighted and don't see the changes they would need to make, or whether such radical change is possible but very difficult. In any case, St.-Preux at least is persistently unable to see the limitations of his attempt to 'become' his beloved.

43. *Ibid.*, 137.

44. The existence of these notable exceptions to Rousseau's general remarks about women should suffice to call into question the claim that Rousseau is a strict gender essentialist, allowing no variation at all from the gender roles assigned by society into his metaphysics or his ethics.

45. Rousseau, *Julie* . . . , *op. cit.*, 19.

46. Rousseau, *Confessions* . . . , *op. cit.*, 60.

47. Rousseau, *Julie* . . . , *op. cit.*, 299.

48. Rousseau, *The Sexual Politics* . . . , *op. cit.*, 110.

49. At this point, the appropriateness of my calling these relationships 'romantic' should be clear.

50. Rousseau, *Confessions* . . . , *op. cit.*, 176.

51. Schwartz, *The Sexual Politics* . . . , *op. cit.*, 102.

52. Rousseau, *Julie* . . . , *op. cit.*, 77.

53. *Ibid.*, 409.

54. *Ibid.*, 125.

55. *Ibid.*, 125.

56. Rousseau, *Emile* . . . , *op. cit.*, 339.

57. J. J. Rousseau, *Reveries of a Solitary Walker*, trans. P. France (Harmondsworth: Penguin, 1979).

58. The fact that this is not a literally sexual relationship does not detract from its pertinence in the context of this paper. It is clearly an intimate heterosexual relationship which helps constitute and define Julie's identity. In fact, a relationship of pure masculine domination could not be erotic, since the erotic, for Rousseau and his generation, essentially involves conquest *and* resistance.

59. Rousseau, *Julie* . . . , *op. cit.*, 151.

60. It is peculiar that Rousseau can claim that unless checked, women will naturally subjugate men, and that women are at the same time the sex that 'ought to obey'. This tension reaffirms that Rousseau's conception of the natural is complex, and that there is no direct association between what is natural and what is right, as Okin argues there is.

61. Rousseau, *The Confessions* . . . , *op. cit.*, 311.

62. *Ibid.*, 311–32.

63. *Ibid.*, 311.

64. Rousseau, *Emile* . . . , *op. cit.*, 407.

65. See especially the *Reveries*, 117–18.

66. D. Gauthier, "The Politics of Redemption," *University of Ottawa Quarterly* 49 (1979), 329–56.

67. Rousseau, *Julie* . . . , *op. cit.*, 374.

68. *Ibid.*, 42.

69. One might wonder, given this detailed discussion of the possibilities for human relationships, what the precise relationship between the children and domestics, amongst themselves and to Julie and Wolmar, is supposed to be. Rousseau gives no attention to this question, beyond emphasizing that they too are part of the whole person constituted by the family unit, that they must identify with it while performing their harmonious function within it. He does not draw an explicit distinction between the 'single soul' formed by the married couple and the 'single soul' formed by the whole household. We can presume that while the married couple have escaped domination and submission, they are in a dominant position relative to the other members of the household, whose identities are thus not parts of but subsumed by the whole, which gets its character from the couple.

70. Schwartz, *The Sexual Politics* . . . , *op. cit.*, 125.

71. Rousseau, *Julie* . . . , *op. cit.*, 274. This is, of course, also how Emile manages to be free. It is only because his tutor has so carefully tailored his environment, to both suit his abilities and shape his desires, that Emile can function 'on his own' and experience freedom.

72. Jones, *La nouvelle Heloïse* . . . , *op. cit.*, 60.

73. *Ibid.*, 60.

74. *Ibid.*, 96.

75. See D. Gauthier, "Le Promeneur Solitaire: Rousseau and the Emergence of the Post-Social Self," *Social Philosophy and Policy* 8, 35–58; M. L. Perkins, *Jean-Jacques on the Individual and Society* (Lexington: University Press of Kentucky).

76. Perkins, *Jean-Jacques Rousseau* . . . , *op. cit.*, 140.

77. Rousseau, *Julie* . . . , *op. cit.*, 677.

78. Gauthier, "The Politics of Redemption," *op. cit.*, 332.

79. In Rousseau, *Oeuvres* . . . , *op. cit.*

80. Rousseau, *Oeuvres* . . . , *op. cit.*

81. Rousseau, *Julie* . . . , *op. cit.*, 204.

82. Okin, *Women in Western Political* . . . , *op. cit.*, 166.

83. L. Lange, "Women and 'The General Will'," *University of Ottawa Quarterly* 49 (1979), 401–11.

84. See Linda Zerilli's discussion of Rousseau's gendered metaphors for the state of nature and for civil society in chapter 2 of her *Signifying Woman: Culture and Chaos in Rousseau, Burke, and Mill* (Ithaca: Cornell University Press).

15

On the Social Contract

Monique Wittig

I have undertaken a difficult task, which is to measure and reevaluate the notion of the social contract, taken as a notion of political philosophy. A notion born with the seventeenth and eighteenth centuries, it is also the title of a book by J.-J. Rousseau.[1] Marx and Engels criticized it because it was not relevant in terms of class struggle and therefore did not concern the proletariat. In *The German Ideology* they explain that the proletarian class, due to its relation to production and labor, can only confront the social order as an ensemble, as a whole, and that it has no choice but to destroy the state. In their opinion the term "social contract," which implies a notion of individual choice and of voluntary association, could possibly be applied to the serfs. For in the course of several centuries they liberated themselves one by one, running away from the land to which they belonged. And it is also one by one that the serfs associated to form cities, hence their name, *bourgeois* (people who have formed a bourg).[2] (It seems that as soon as Rousseau developed the idea of the social contract as far as it has ever been developed, history outdated it—but not before some of his propositions were adopted without amendment by the French Revolutionary Assembly.)

I have always thought that women are a class structured very much as was the class of serfs. I see now that they can tear themselves away from the heterosexual order only by running away one by one. This explains my concern for a preindustrial notion such as the social contract. For the structure of our class in terms of the whole world is feudal in essence, maintaining side by side and in the same persons forms of production and of exploitation that are at the same time capitalist and precapitalist.[3]

In broad terms that is one aspect of my task. Another aspect has to do with language. For to a writer language offers a very concrete matter to grasp hold of. It seems to me that the first, the permanent, and the final social contract is language. The basic agreement between human beings, indeed what makes them human and makes them social, is language. The story of the Tower of Babel is a perfect illustration of what happens when the agreement breaks down.

Since I have used the term "heterosexual contract"[4] several times in my past writings, as well as referring to the "social contract as heterosexual," it has become my task to reflect on the notion of the social contract. Why is this notion so compelling even though it has supposedly been given up by modern science and history? Why does it reverberate here and now far from its initial momentum in the Enlightenment of the eighteenth century? Why at the same time did I urge vehemently that we should break off the heterosexual social contract? The general question of the social contract insofar as it encompasses all human activity, thought, and relations is a philosophical question always present as long as "humankind [that] was born free . . . is everywhere in chains," to quote Rousseau. Its promise of being achieved for the good of all and of everyone can still be the object of a philosophical examination, and, since it has not been fulfilled by history, it retains its utopian dimension. Thus formulated in its general aspect, the question extends to all humankind. Now when I say let us break off the heterosexual contract per se, I designate the group "women." But I did not mean that we must break off the social contract per se, because that would be absurd. For we must break it off as heterosexual. Leaning upon a philosophical examination of what a well-established social contract could do for us, I want to confront the historical conditions and conflicts that can lead us to end the obligations that bind us without our consent while we are not enjoying a reciprocal commitment that would be the necessary condition for our freedom, to paraphrase Rousseau.

The question of the social contract in the very terms of Jean-Jacques Rousseau is far from being obsolete, for, in what concerns its philosophical dimension, it was never developed further. The question of the sexes, which itself delineated very narrowly the general design of society, if approached from a philosophical point of view, encompasses and embodies the general idea of social contract. There are historical reasons as well to resuscitate the notion of social contract that have to do with the structures of the groups of sex and their particular situation among the relations of production and social intercourse.

The main approach to the notion of social contract must be a philosophical one, in the sense that a philosophical point of view allows the possibility of synthesis, in contrast to the divided point of view of the social sciences.[5] And indeed "social contract" is a notion of political philosophy, the abstract idea that there is a pact, a compact, an agreement between individuals and the social order. The idea came into existence with the English philosophers of the seventeenth century, Thomas Hobbes (*Leviathan*) and John Locke (*Treatise of Government*), and the French philosophers of the Enlightenment, chiefly Rousseau. The appearance of the idea according to the historians of ideas was a result of the questioning of the old medieval theories concerning the state. According to these theories the state could only be a theocracy, since all authority emanates from God, and kings rule to achieve a divine order, as they are kings by divine right.

Philosophers long before the "social contract" came into existence had their attention fixed on the composition of society. The philosophers were apprentice legislators and rulers. They thought about the best government and the ideal city. Political questions were then asked, taught, and discussed as philosophical questions, politics being a branch of philosophy. There was a narrow margin between their elaborations and utopia, since many of them had been confronted with practical problems: Plato was called to the court of Sicily by Denys the tyrant. Then later on he taught and educated his nephew who was to become a king. Aristotle was the preceptor of Alexander. Plotinus was given the means by another

tyrant to construct and create the ideal city, a long-time object of speculation and hope. Being caught in such a close connection between speculation and ruling, the philosophers must have known that there was a
utopian limit to their creations. I imagine it thus, because of the trials
they had to go through in reality when they approached too closely to
the throne. In the ninth book of *The Republic* Socrates and Glaucon
discuss the perfect city and its ideal form:

> GLAUCON: "But the city whose foundation we have been describ-
> ing has its being only in words; there is no spot on earth where it
> exists."
> SOCRATES: "No; but it is laid up in heaven as a pattern for him
> who wills to see, and seeing, to found that city in himself.
> Whether it exists anywhere, or ever will exist, is no matter."

No wonder then that Rousseau in the opening of *The Social Contract*
addresses the reader thus: "I may be asked whether I am a prince or a
legislator that I should be writing about politics." And Rousseau, who
wanted to distance himself from those he called with contempt the
philosophers, says; "I answer no." But several of his propositions were
adopted directly, without transformation by the Revolutionary Assembly.
These direct connections of the philosophers to tyrants, kings, and political assemblies may seem to us to belong to the domain of the marvelous.
However, we can remember how recently President Kennedy asked the
members of his staff to prepare a report on the situation of women. And
the initiative of these women gave birth to one of the first detachments
of the women's liberation movement, instigated by persons all very near
to the "throne."

But if, at the start of politics, a philosopher like Aristotle was aware
that society was a "combination," an "association," a "coming together,"
it was not a voluntary association. For Aristotle, society could never be
established with the agreement of its members and for their best good,
but as the result of a *"coup de force,"* an imposition of the clever ones
upon the bodily strong, but feeble-minded ones. Indeed for Aristotle the
strong, the powerful, are those with intelligence, while those possessing
bodily strength fall into the category of the weak. In his words: "Essential
is the combination of ruler and ruled, the purpose of their coming together being their common safety. For he that can by his intelligence
foresee things needed is by nature ruler and master; while he whose

bodily strength enables him to perform them is by nature a slave, one of those who are ruled. Thus there is a common interest uniting master and slave."[6] Hobbes and Locke use the terms *covenant, compact, agreement,* and after them so does Rousseau, while he emphasizes a term much more politically rigorous: *the social contract.*

Covenant, compact, agreement refer to an initial covenant establishing once and for all the binding of people together. According to Rousseau the social contract is the sum of fundamental conventions which "even though they might never have been formally enunciated are nevertheless implied by living in society." Clearly, in what Rousseau says, it is the real present existence of the social contract that is particularly stimulating for me—whatever its origin, it exists here and now, and as such it is apt to be understood and acted upon. Each contractor has to reaffirm the contract in new terms for the contract to be in existence.

Only then does it become an instrumental notion in the sense that the contractors are reminded by the term itself that they should reexamine their conditions. Society was not made once and for all. The social contract will yield to our action, to our words. Even if we say no more than Rousseau: "I was born the citizen of a free state and the very right to vote imposes on me the duty to instruct myself in public affairs, however little influence my voice may have in them."

Rousseau is the first philosopher who does not take it for granted that, if there is such a thing as a social contract, its nerve is "might is right" (and under other phraseology belonging to the conscious or the unconscious order, modern historians and anthropologists seem to yield to the inevitability of this principle in society in the name of science). Nothing is more enjoyable than his sarcasm about the "right of the strongest," which he shows to be a contradiction in terms. In *The Social Contract* he says:

> The strongest man is never strong enough to be master all the time. . . . The "right of the strongest"—a "right" that sounds like something intended ironically, but is actually laid down as a principle. . . . To yield to force is an act of necessity not of will; it is at best an act of prudence. In what sense can it be a moral duty? . . . Once might is made to be right, cause and effect are reversed. . . . But, what can be the validity of a right which perishes with the force on which it rests? If force compels obedience, there is no need to invoke a duty to obey, and if force ceases to compel

obedience, there is no longer any obligation. Thus the word "right" adds nothing to what is said by "force," it is meaningless.

I come back to the historical situation women are in, and which makes it at least appropriate for them to reflect upon what has affected their existence without their agreement. I am not a prince, I am not a legislator, but an active member of society. I consider it my duty to examine the set of rules, obligations, and constraints this society has placed upon me, if rules and obligations provide me with the freedom I would not find in nature, or if it is not the case to say with Rousseau that society has taken us in, in these terms: "I make a covenant with you which is wholly at your expense and wholly to my advantage; I will respect it so long as I please and you should respect it as long as I wish." (The term is used here rhetorically, since everybody knows that there is no way out of society.) But whether we want it or not, we are living in society here and now, and proof is given that we say yes to the social bond when we conform to the conventions and rules that were never formally enunciated but that nevertheless everybody knows and applies like magic. Proof is given that we say yes to the social bond when we talk a common language as we do now. Most people would not use the term "social contract" to describe their situation within the social order. However, they would agree that there are a certain number of acts and things one "must do." *Outlaw* and *mad* are the names for those who refuse to go by the rules and conventions, as well as for those who refuse to or cannot speak the common language. And this is what interests me when I talk of the social contract: precisely the rules and conventions that have never been formally enunciated, the rules and conventions that go without saying for the scientific mind as well as for the common people, that which for them obviously makes life possible, exactly as one must have two legs and two arms, or one must breathe to live. Being tied together by a social link, we can consider that each and every one of us stands within the social contract—the social contract being then the fact of having come together, of being together, of living as social beings. This notion is relevant for the philosophical mind, even if it is not instrumental anymore for the scientific mind, through the established fact that we live, function, talk, work, marry together. Indeed the conventions and the language show on a dotted line the bulk of the social contract—which consists in living in heterosexuality. For to live in society is to live in heterosexuality. In fact, in my mind social contract and heterosexuality are two superimposable notions.

The social contract I am talking about is heterosexuality.

The problem I am facing in trying to define the social contract is the same kind of problem I have when I try to define what heterosexuality is. I confront a nonexistent object, a fetish, an ideological form which cannot be grasped in reality, except through its effects, whose existence lies in the mind of people, but in a way that affects their whole life, the way they act, the way they move, the way they think. So we are dealing with an object both imaginary and real. If I try to look at the dotted line that delineates the bulk of the social contract, it moves, it shifts, and sometimes it produces something visible, and sometimes it disappears altogether. It looks like the Möbius strip is fake, because only one aspect of the optical effect appears distinctly and massively, and that is heterosexuality. Homosexuality appears like a ghost only dimly and sometimes not at all.

What then is heterosexuality? As a term it was created as a counterpart of homosexuality at the beginning of this century. So much for the extent of its "it-goes-without-saying." Jurists would not call it an institution, or, in other words, heterosexuality as an institution has no juridic existence (marriage's jurisdiction in French legislation does not even mention that the partners of the contract must be of different sexes). Anthropologists, ethnologists, sociologists would come to take it for an institution, but as an unwritten, unspoken one. For they assume a quality of already-there, due to something exterior to a social order, of two groups: men and women. For them, men are social beings, women are natural beings. I compare it to the approach of psychoanalysts when they assume there is a preoedipal relation of the child to the mother, a presocial relation which in spite of its importance for humankind does not emerge from history. This view has for them the advantage in terms of the social contract of doing away with the problem of origins. They believe that they are dealing with a diachrony instead of a synchrony. So does Lèvi-Strauss with his famous notion of the exchange of women. He believes that he deals with invariants. He and all the social scientists who do not see the problem I am trying to underline would of course never talk in terms of "social contract." It is indeed much simpler to take what I call "social contract" in terms of status quo, that is, in terms of something that *has* not changed, *will* not change. Thus we have in their literature these words: *fathers, mothers, brothers, sisters,* etc., whose relations can be studied as though they had to go on as such for ever.

Aristotle was much more cynical when he stated in *The Politics* that things *must be:* "The first point is that those which are ineffective without each other *must be* united in a pair. For example, the union of male and female" (emphasis added). Notice that this point of the necessity of heterosexuality is the first point of *The Politics*. And notice also that the second example of "those . . . which *must be* united as a pair" is found in "the combination of ruler and ruled." From that time on, male and female, the heterosexual relationship, has been the parameter of all hierarchial relations. It is almost useless to underline that it is only the dominated members of the pair that are "ineffective" by themselves. For "ruler" and "male" go very well without their counterpart.

Now I return to Lèvi-Strauss, for I am not going to pass by the idea of the exchange of women, which until now has been so favored by feminist theoreticians. And not by chance, since with this theory we have revealed the whole plot, the whole conspiracy, of fathers, brothers, husbands against half of humankind. For the masters, slaves are certainly more transient than women in the use one can have of them. Women, "the slaves of the poor" as Aristotle called them, are always there at hand; they are the valuables that make life worthwhile according to Lèvi-Strauss (Aristotle would have said it not very differently: they make for the "good life"). When Lèvi-Strauss described what the exchange of women is and how it works, he was obviously drawing for us the broad lines of the social contract, but a social contract from which women are excluded, a social contract between men. Each time the exchange takes place it confirms between men a contract of appropriation of all women. For Lèvi-Strauss, society cannot function or exist without this exchange. By showing it he exposes heterosexuality as not only an institution but as *the* social contract, as a political regime. (You have noticed that sexual pleasure and sexual modes are not the question here.) Lèvi-Strauss answers the charges of antifeminism which such a theory rewarded him with. And, although he conceded that women could not be completely superimposable with the signs of language with which he compared them in terms of exchange, he had no reason to worry about the shocking effect such a theory can have upon women, any more than Aristotle had when he defined the necessity of the slaves in the social order, because a scientific mind must not be embarrassed and shy when dealing with crude reality. And this is crude reality indeed. There cannot be any fear of a rebellion in the case of women. Even better, they have been convinced that they want what they are forced to do and that they are part of the contract of society that excludes them. Because even if they, if we, do not consent, we cannot think outside of the mental categories of hetero-sexuality. Heterosexuality is always already there within all mental cate-gories. It has sneaked into dialectical thought (or thought of differences) as its main category. For even abstract philosophical categories act upon the real as social. Language casts sheaves of reality upon the social body, stamping it and violently shaping it. For example, the bodies of social actors are fashioned by abstract language (as well as by nonabstract lan-guages). For there is a plasticity of the real to language.

Thus heterosexuality, whose characteristics appear and then disappear when the mind tries to grasp it, is visible and obvious in the categories of the heterosexual contract. One of them which I tried to deconstruct is the category of sex. And it is clear that with it we deal with a political category. A category which when put flatly makes us understand the terms of the social contract for women. I quote from "The Category of Sex" (with slightly revised wording):

> The perenniality of the sexes and the perenniality of slaves and masters proceed from the same belief. And as there are no slaves without masters, there are no women without men. . . .
>
> The category of sex is the political category that founds society as heterosexual. As such it does not concern being but relation-ships (for women and men are the result of relationships), al-though the two aspects are always confused when they are discussed. The category of sex is the one that rules as "natural" the relation that is at the base of (heterosexual) society and through which half of the population, women, are "hetero-sexualized." . . .
>
> Its main category, the category of *sex, works specifically, as "black" does, through an operation of reduction, by taking the part for the whole, a part (color, sex) through which the whole human being has to pass as through a screen.* (Emphasis added)

When Adrienne Rich said "heterosexuality is compulsory," it was a step forward in the comprehension of the kind of social contract we are dealing with. Nicole-Claude Mathieu, a French anthropologist, in a remarkable essay on consciousness, made it clear that it is not because we remain silent that we consent.[7] And how can we consent to a social contract that reduces us, by obligation, to sexual beings meaningful only through their reproductive activities or, to quote the French writer Jean Paulhan, to beings in whom everything, even their minds, is sex?[8]

In conclusion I will say that only by running away from their class can women achieve the social contract (that is, a new one), even if they have to do it like the fugitive serfs, one by one. We are doing it. Lesbians are runaways, fugitive slaves; runaway wives are the same case, and they exist in all countries, because the political regime of heterosexuality represents all cultures. So that breaking off the heterosexual social contract is a necessity for those who do not consent to it. For if there is something real in the ideas of Rousseau, it is that we can form "voluntary associations" here and now, and here and now reformulate the social contract as a new one, although we are not princes or legislators. Is this mere utopia? Then I will stay with Socrates's view and also Glaucon's: If ultimately we are denied a new social order, which therefore can exist only in words, I will find it in myself.

Notes

1. *The Social Contract, or Principles of Political Right* (1762), by J. J. Rousseau, citizen of Geneva.

2. Colette Guillaumin, "Pratique du pouvoir et idée de Nature: 1. L'appropriation des femmes; 2. Le discours de la Nature," *Questions féministes* n°2 et n°3 (1978). Translated as "The Practice of Power and Belief in Nature: 1. The Appropriation of Women; 2. The Naturalist Discourse," *Feminist Issues* 1, nos. 2 and 3 (Winter and Summer 1981).

3. See Colette Capitan Peter, "A Historical Precedent for Patriarchal Oppression: 'The Old Regime' and the French Revolution," *Feminist Issues*, 4, no. 1 (Spring 1984): 83–89.

4. See my "The Straight Mind" and "One Is Not Born a Woman," in *The Straight Mind and other Essays* (Boston: Beacon Press, 1992).

5. This statement by Marx and Engels is particularly relevant to the modern situation.

6. See Aristotle, *The Politics*.

7. Nicole-Claude Mathieu, "Quand céder n'est pas consentir. Des déterminants matériels et psychiques de la conscience dominée des femmes, et de quelques-unes de leurs interprétations en ethnologie," in *L'Arraisonnement des femmes, Essais en anthropologie des sexes* (Paris: Editions de l'Ecole des Hautes Etudes en Sciences Sociales, 1985). Translated as "When Yielding Is Not Consenting. Material and Psychic Determinants of Women's Dominated Consciousness and Some of Their Interpretation in Ethnology," *Feminist Issues* 9, no. 2 (1989), part I.

8. Jean Paulhan, "Happiness in Slavery," preface to *The Story of O*, by Pauline de Réage.

Select Bibliography

Bloch, M., and J. H. Bloch, "Women and the Dialectics of Nature in Eighteenth-Century French Thought." In *Nature, Culture, and Gender*, edited by Carol P. MacCormack and Marilyn Strathern. New York: Cambridge University Press, 1980.

Bloom, Allan. "Rousseau on the Equality of the Sexes." In *Justice and Equality Here and Now*, edited by Frank S. Lucash. Ithaca: Cornell University Press, 1986.

Blum, Carol. *Rousseau and the Politics of Virtue*. Ithaca: Cornell University Press, 1986.

Brown, Wendy. *Manhood and Politics: A Feminist Reading in Political Theory*. Totawa, N.J.: Rowman and Littlefield, 1988.

Butler, Melissa. "Early Liberal Roots of Feminism." *American Political Science Review* 72, no. 1:135–50.

Canovan, Margaret. "Rousseau's Two Concepts of Citizenship." In *Women in Western Political Philosophy*, edited by Ellen Kennedy and Susan Mendus. New York: St. Martin's Press, 1987.

Colmo, Ann Charney. "What Sophie Knew: Rousseau's *Emile et Sophie, ou Les Solitaires*." In *Finding a New Feminism: Rethinking the Woman Question for Liberal Democracy*, edited by Pamela Grande Jensen. Lanham, Md.: Rowman and Littlefield, 1996.

Coole, Diana. *Women in Political Theory*. Sussex, Eng.: Wheatsheaf Books, 1988.

Disch, Lisa. "Claire Loves Julie": Reading the Story of Women's Friendship in *La Nouvelle Heloise*." *Hypatia* 9, no. 3 (1994): 19–45.

Eisenstein, Zillah. *The Radical Future of Liberal Feminism*. Boston: Northeastern University Press, 1981.

Elshtain, Jean. *Public Man, Private Woman*. Princeton: Princeton University Press, 1981.

Emberley, Peter. "Rousseau and the Domestication of Virtue." *Canadian Journal of Political Science* 17, no. 4 (1984).

Falco, Maria, ed. *Feminist Interpretations of Mary Wollstonecraft*. University Park: Pennsylvania State University Press, 1996.

Fauré, Christine. *Democracy Without Women: Feminism and the Rise of Liberal Individualism in France*. Translated by Claudia Gorbman and John Berks. Bloomington: Indiana University Press, 1991.

Fermon, Nicole. *Domesticating Passions: Rousseau, Women, and Nation*. Hanover: University Press of New England, 1997.

———. "The Female Fulcrum: Rousseau and the Birth of Nationalism." *Philosophical Forum* 28, nos. 1–2 (1997): 21–41.

Gatens, Moira. *Feminism and Philosophy*. Bloomington: Indiana University Press, 1991.

———. "Rousseau and Wollstonecraft: Nature vs. Reason." In *Women and Philosophy*, edited by Janna L. Thompson. Bundoora, Aus.: Australian Association of Philosophy, 1986.

Graham, Ruth. "Rousseau's Sexism Revolutionized." In *Woman in the Eighteenth Century and Other Essays*, edited by Paul Fritz and Richard Morton. Toronto: Hakkert, 1976.

Keohane, Nannerl O. "But For Her Sex": The Domestication of Sophie." *University of Ottawa Review* 49 (1979): 390–400.

Kofman, Sarah. *Le respect des femmes: (Kant et Rousseau)*. Paris: Editions Galilee, 1982.

Kukla, Rebecca. "Making and Masking Human Nature: Rousseau's Aesthetics of Education." *Journal of the British Society for Phenomenology* 29, no. 3 (1998): 228–51.

———. "Performing Nature in the Letter to M. D'Alembert." In *Rousseau on Arts and Politics: Autour de la Letter d'Alembert*, edited by M. Butler. Ottawa: Pensées Libres, 1998.

Landes, Joan. *Feminism, the Public, and the Private*. Oxford: Oxford University Press, 1998.

———. *Women and the Public Sphere in the Age of the French Revolution*. Ithaca: Cornell University Press, 1988.

Lange, Lynda. "A Feminist Reads Rousseau: Thoughts on Justice, Love, and the Patriarchal Family." *APA Newsletter on Feminism and Philosophy*, June 1989.

———. "Rousseau and Modern Feminism." *Social Theory and Practice* 7, no. 3 (1981): 245–77. Also in *Feminist Interpretations and Political Theory*, edited by Carole Pateman and Mary Lyndon Shanley. University Park: Pennsylvania State University Press, 1991.

———. "Women and the General Will." In *The Sexism of Social and Political Theory: Women and Reproduction from Plato to Nietzsche*, edited by Lorenne Clark and Lynda Lange. Toronto: University of Toronto Press, 1979.

———. "Women and Rousseau's Democratic Theory: Philosopher Monsters and Authoritarian Equality." In *Modern Engendering*, edited by Bat-Ami Bar On. Albany: State University of New York Press, 1994.

Le Doeuff, Michèle. "Women, Reason, Etc." *Differences: A Journal of Feminist Cultural Studies* 2, no. 3 (1990).

Lloyd, Genevieve. *The Man of Reason: "Male" and "Female" in Western Philosophy*. 2d ed. Minneapolis: University of Minnesota Press, 1993.

———. "Rousseau on Reason, Nature, and Women." *Metaphilosophy* 14 (1983): 308–26.

McMillan, Carole. *Women, Reason, and Nature*. Princeton: Princeton University Press, 1982.

Makus, Ingrid. *Women, Politics, and Reproduction: The Liberal Legacy*. Toronto: University of Toronto Press, 1996.

Marso, Lori. *(Un)Manly Citizens: J.-J. Rousseau's and Germaine de Stael's Subversive Women*. Baltimore: Johns Hopkins University Press, 1999.

Martin, Jane Roland. *Reclaiming a Conversation: The Ideal of the Educated Woman*. New Haven: Yale University Press, 1985.

———. "Sophie and Emile: A Case Study of Sex Bias in the History of Educational Thought." *Harvard Educational Review* 51 (1981): 357–72.

Matthes, Melissa M. *The Rape of Lucretia and the Founding of Republics: Readings in Livy, Machiavelli, and Rousseau*. University Park: Pennsylvania State University Press, 2000.

May, Gita. "Rousseau's Anti-Feminism Reconsidered." In *French Women in the Age of*

Enlightenment, edited by Samia Spencer. Bloomington: Indian University Press, 1984.

Misenheimer, Helen Evans. *Rousseau on the Education of Women*. Washington, D.C.: University Press of America, 1981.

Morgenstern, Mira. *Rousseau and the Politics of Ambiguity: Self, Culture, and Society*. University Park: Pennsylvania State University Press, 1996.

Ogrodnick, Margaret. *Instinct and Intimacy: Political Philosophy and Autobiography in Rousseau*. Toronto: University of Toronto Press, 1999.

Okin, Susan Moller. "Women and the Making of the Sentimental Family." *Philosophy and Public Affairs* 11, no. 1 (1982).

———. *Women in Western Political Thought*. Princeton: Princeton University Press, 1979. (2d ed., 1992).

Pateman, Carole. "'The Disorder of Women': Women, Love, and the Sense of Justice." *Ethics* 91 (1980): 20–34.

———. *The Sexual Contract*. Stanford: Stanford University Press, 1988.

Pope, Barbara Corrado. "The Influence of Rousseau's Ideology of Domesticity." In *Connecting Spheres: Women in the Western World, 1500–the Present*, edited by Marilyn Boxer and Jean Quataert. New York: Oxford University Press, 1987.

Rapaport, Elizabeth. "On the Future of Love: Rousseau and the Radical Feminists." *Philosophical Forum* 5 (1973): 185–205.

Rorty, Amelie Oksenberg. "Rousseau's Therapeutic Experiments." *Philosophy* 66 (1991): 413–34.

Schwartz, Joel. *The Sexual Politics of Jean-Jacques Rousseau*. Chicago: University of Chicago Press, 1984.

Shanley, Mary Lyndon, and Carole Pateman, eds. *Feminist Interpretations of Political Theory*. University Park: Pennsylvania State University Press, 1991.

Shklar, Judith. *Men and Citizens: A Study of Rousseau's Political Theory*. Cambridge: Cambridge University Press, 1969.

Simon-Ingram, Julia. "Expanding the Social Contract: Rousseau, Gender, and the Problem of Judgment." *Comparative Literature* 43 (Spring 1991).

Still, Judith. *Justice and Difference in the Works of Rousseau: Bienfaisance and Pudear*. Cambridge: Cambridge University Press, 1993.

Tuana, Nancy. *Women and the History of Philosophy*. New York: Paragon House, 1992.

Weiss, Penny A. *Gendered Community: Rousseau, Sex, and Politics*. New York: New York University Press, 1993.

———. "Rousseau, Antifeminism, and Women's Nature." *Political Theory* 15, no. 1 (1987): 81–98.

———. "Wollstonecraft and Rousseau: The Gendered Fate of Political Theorists." In *Feminist Interpretations of Mary Wollstonecraft*, edited by Maria Falco. University Park: Pennsylvania State University Press, 1996.

Weiss, Penny A., and Gina Shapiro. "Jean-Jacques Rousseau and Mary Wollstonecraft: A (Live) Conversation." In Penny A. Weiss, *Conversations with Feminism: Political Theory and Practice*. Rowman and Littlefield, 1998.

Wexler, Victor. "Made for Man's Delight: Rousseau as Antifeminist." *American Historical Review* 81 (1976): 266–91.

Wingrove, Elizabeth. *Rousseau's Republican Romance*. Princeton: Princeton University Press, 2000.

———. "Sexual Performance as Political Performance in *Lettre a M. D'Alembert*." *Political Theory* 23 (1995): 585–616.

Wollstonecraft, Mary. *A Vindication of the Rights of Woman*. Edited by Carol H. Poston. New York: W. W. Norton, 1988.

Zerilli, Linda. *Signifying Woman: Culture and Chaos in Rousseau, Burke, and Mill*. Ithaca: Cornell University Press, 1994.

Contributors

LEAH BRADSHAW is associate professor and chair in the Department of Political Science at Brock University, St. Catherines, Ontario, where she has been known to teach an entire course on Rousseau's *Emile*. She is the author of *Acting and Thinking: The Political Thought of Hannah Arendt* and has published articles and review essays in *Interpretation*, *Canadian Journal of Political Science*, *Review of Politics*, and *Queen's Quarterly*. Current research interests are tyranny in Western political thought, and emotivism as the basis of judgment.

MELISSA BUTLER is professor of political science and chair of the Division of Social Science at Wabash College in Crawfordsville, Indiana. She is the editor of *Politics and the Arts: Autour de la Lettre à d'Alembert* and of numerous articles on modern political theory and feminist thought.

SARAH KOFMAN is agrégée de philosophie et assistante at the Sorbonne in Paris. She is the author of numerous books in feminist thought and cultural and literary studies. Her books translated and published in English include *The Enigma of Woman: Woman in Freud's Writings; Nietzsche and Metaphor;* and *Smothered Words*.

REBECCA KUKLA is associate professor of philosophy and political science at Carleton University, Ottawa, Canada. She has published on Rousseau, Hegel, feminist theory, aesthetics, media studies, epistemology, and philosophy of mind, in journals such as *Journal of Aesthetics and Art Criticism*, *Philosophical Studies*, *Journal of the British Society for Phenomenology*, and *British Journal of the Philosophy of Science*. She is currently working on two monographs: one on Rousseau's aesthetics and one on the role of myth, memory, and misrecognition in enabling the possibility of objective judgment.

LYNDA LANGE is in the Department of Philosophy at the University of Toronto. She is a co-editor of *The Sexism of Social and Political Thought* (1979), and numerous essays on Jean-Jacques Rousseau and feminist philosophy. Besides feminist political philosophy, her current work includes postcolonial studies in philosophy. An essay in this area appeared in *Thinking from the Underside of History*, edited by Eduardo Mendieta and Linda Alcoff.

INGRID MAKUS is associate professor in the Department of Politics at Brock University in St. Catherines, Ontario. She is the author of *Women, Politics, and Reproduction: The Liberal Legacy*. Her most recent article is "Community, Birth, and Citizenship," in *Cana-*

dian Political Philosophy, edited by Ronald Beiner and Wayne Norman. Current interests include debates over identity politics and rights discourse, as well as questions about political continuity through the education of citizens and the establishment of justice between generations.

LORI JO MARSO is the author of *(Un)Manly Citizens: J. J. Rousseau's and Germaine de Staël's Subversive Women* (Johns Hopkins University Press, 1999). She teaches feminist theory and political philosophy at Union College in Schenectady, New York, and is currently at work on a book titled *Dilemmas of Difference: Feminist Thinkers and the Demands of Feminine Desire*.

MIRA MORGENSTERN received her Ph.D. in political theory from Princeton University. She is author of *Jean-Jacques Rousseau and the Politics of Ambiguity*. Her recent writings have included a consideration of Rousseau and postmodernism in *Historical Reflections/Reflexions historiques*, as well as a consideration of Rousseau's theories of the self in *Essays on the Modern Identity*. She is currently working on a study highlighting the creation of political discourse in the Bible.

SUSAN MOLLER OKIN is professor in the Department of Political Science at Stanford University. She is the author of *Women in Western Political Thought and Justice; Gender and the Family;* and *Is Multiculturalism Bad for Women?* as well as many articles in political theory and feminist thought.

ALICE ORMISTON has her Ph.D. in political theory from the University of Toronto. Her dissertation was written on Hegel. She is currently teaching at Brandon University, Manitoba, Canada.

PENNY WEISS is associate professor of political science at Purdue University. She is author of *Gendered Community: Rousseau, Sex, and Politics;* and *Conversations with Feminism: Political Theory and Practice;* and is co-editor with Marilyn Friedman of *Feminism and Community*. She is a "master gardener" and soccer coach, and her specialty is the history of feminist theory.

ELSE WIESTAD is a member of the Department of Philosophy at the University of Oslo, Norway. She is the author of *The Great Hundred Year Waves: Gender Debate in the Last 300 Years* (Oslo: Emilia Press, 1994 [published in Norwegian]). Her specialty is gender theory in early and late modernity.

ELIZABETH WINGROVE is associate professor of political science and women's studies at the University of Michigan, Ann Arbor. She is the author of *Rousseau's Republican Romance* and of articles in *Political Theory, Signs, Representations* and elsewhere. She is currently at work on a project concerning eighteenth-century epistolary culture.

MONIQUE WITTIG is a novelist and the author of several books of theory, including *The Lesbian Body* and *The Straight Mind and Other Essays*. She is winner of the Prix Medicis and a professor in the Department of French and Italian at the University of Arizona.

LINDA ZERILLI is associate professor of political science and associate director of the Walt Whitman Center for the Culture and Politics of Democracy at Rutgers University. She is the author of *Signifying Woman: Culture and Chaos in Rousseau, Burke, and Mill.*

Index